MW00575498

BETWEEN MUTINY AND OBEDIENCE

BETWEEN MUTINY AND OBEDIENCE

THE CASE OF THE FRENCH
FIFTH INFANTRY DIVISION
DURING WORLD WAR I

Leonard V. Smith

PRINCETON UNIVERSITY PRESS   PRINCETON, NEW JERSEY

Library of Congress Cataloging-in-Publication Data

Smith, Leonard V., 1957–
Between mutiny and obedience : the case of the French Fifth
Infantry Division during World War I / Leonard V. Smith.
p.   cm.
Based on the author's thesis (doctoral—Columbia University).
Includes bibliographical references and index.
ISBN 0-691-03304-8
1. World War, 1914–1918—Regimental histories—
France.   2. France. Armée. Division d'infanterie, 5—
History.   3. Military discipline—France—History—20th
century.   4. Mutiny—France—History—20th century.   I. Title.
D548.3.S63   1994
940.4′1244—dc20   93-26816   CIP

This book has been composed in Linotron Sabon

Princeton University Press books are printed
on acid-free paper and meet the guidelines
for permanence and durability of the Committee
on Production Guidelines for Book Longevity
of the Council on Library Resources

Printed in the United States of America

1   3   5   7   9   10   8   6   4   2

To Ann Woodson Ramsey

An order is an active reality only in garrison life. In battle it is annulled by the enemy, who issues a contrary order. In addition, an order is an order only if it is obeyed. This is the case in the barracks, though very rarely during war, at least absolutely. Too much happens to change the situation between the issuing of the order and its reception. Besides, war has a good way of teaching us how to disobey. If the orders had always been obeyed, to the letter, the entire French army would have been massacred before August 1915.
—*Jean Norton Cru, Témoins (1929)*

At the very heart of the power relationship, and constantly provoking it, are the recalcitrance of the will and the intransigence of freedom.
—*Michel Foucault, "The Subect and Power" (1982)*

Contents

Contents

List of Illustrations

* Figures IV-1 through V-4 come from a collection taken during Gen. Charles Mangin's command of the 5ᵉ DI and given to the Bibliothèque Nationale by the Mangin family.

List of Tables

Preface

AT THE EARLIEST STAGES of my career, I fretted endlessly about being tagged a "military historian." For years, I stubbornly insisted that although I wrote about soldiers and even a few generals, I did not write military history. Mostly, I felt at that time a need to bow to prevailing academic prejudices. But I also persisted in this denial because I refused to make any sort of scholarly comment on military efficiency, on why France won or at least failed to lose World War I. I declined and still decline to make any sort of judgment on whether even the small piece of the French army studied here fought effectively or ineffectively, judgments I have always considered myself unqualified to make by training and even inclination.

But time and gainful employment have enabled me to outgrow my earlier prejudices against the term "military history." I continue to believe that whatever its other properties, war remains an intensely social activity. Consequently, soldiers and even generals remain part of society, and have their own social history. But I have become much more aware that social history and military history are complementary rather than mutually exclusive. Readers should categorize what follows as they think best.

The particular topic explored here concerns the balance of power within the French army, which I argue shifted away from the formal command structure and toward a group I define as "soldiers." Here, the term refers to someone receiving an order at the time he receives it. In this way, it becomes possible to examine the pivotal role of intermediary figures between generals and privates, especially junior officers, who both exercised formal command authority and shared the physical risks and hardships of the men in the lower ranks. Essentially, this study argues that over the course of World War I, battlefield soldiers determined how they would and would not fight the war, and hence altered the parameters of command authority in accordance with their own perceived interests. The French army mutinies of 1917 thus become an explicit manifestation of an internal struggle within the French army that continued for the duration of the war.

Methodologically, this book approximates a French-style local study, though it has a far more narrative structure. It tells the story of one French regular-army infantry division (the 5e Division d'Infanterie, or 5e DI) from 1914 to 1918. It thus partakes of the virtues and vices of the French social history method of examining an elaborate *problèmatique* through a relatively tiny but closely examined empirical base. Well aware of the limitations of such a study, I make no claim to having the last word on the questions explored here. I have tried to be provocative, and to invite comparison and disputation.

This book had its original incarnation as a doctoral dissertation at Columbia University. My advisor there, Professor Robert O. Paxton, deserves first and foremost thanks. In numberless and often unspoken ways, he has served as an exemplary scholar and teacher. His gift for guiding without dictating provided the best counsel I could have hoped for. Two other Columbia professors provided invaluable input as well. During my first year of graduate school, Professor Isser Woloch began the daunting task of turning me into a serious historian, while Professor István Deák introduced me to armies as suitable terrain for social history. Professors Allan Silver and Jack Snyder gave excellent interdisciplinary perspectives as readers on the dissertation committee. Professor Sir Michael Howard of Yale University provided both constant intellectual challenge and friendship during my year there.

Ever since we first met at the archives in 1986, Professor Douglas Porch of The Citadel has been an enthusiastic supporter of my work, most recently as the author of a thoughtful and challenging reader's report for Princeton University Press. I thank him for his interest and time. The other reader did an equally fine job, and some day I hope to learn her or his identity. Persuading a publisher to accept one's first book is supposed to be a laborious and generally dreadful experience. I am pleased to say that I would not know, because of the exquisite professionalism of the history editor at Princeton, Lauren Osborne. Bill Laznovsky did a superb job of copyediting the manuscript.

I have a special debt to the staff of the Archives de l'Armée de Terre at the Château de Vincennes. Over the years, their knowledge and unceasingly warm welcome have done much to belie the stereotype of the French *fonctionnaire*. In their way, they have done much to convince me that there is something to my thesis about the nature of military authority.

Over a time of at least perceived penury in academia, this study has been supported generously, not to say lavishly. Research grants included a Predissertation Travelling Fellowship from the Council for European Studies, a Bourse Châteaubriand from the French government, a Haskell Graduate Fellowship from Oberlin College, and two research fellowships from Reid Hall (Columbia University). The writing of the dissertation was supported by a Whiting Fellowship at Columbia. A John M. Olin Postdoctoral Fellowship at Yale University and a summer research stipend for new faculty from Oberlin College supported the reworking of the manuscript into its present form. Oberlin also provided a subvention for the illustrations. I am happy to acknowledge my deep gratitude to all these sources.

My greatest debt is to my friends, without whose support this effort would long ago have seemed pointless. Over the past eight years, Ann

Woodson Ramsey has listened to explanations of this project without number and with wildly fluctuating degrees of coherence. More than any other individual, she saw me through the personal and professional dramas behind this book. I am proud to dedicate it to her. Barbara Prisco, Pamela Radcliff, Mark Shulman, Christopher Rankin, and the graduate students' Social History Group at Columbia also helped see me through this project in a variety of ways.

It has been my honor and privilege to begin my teaching career at my *alma mater*, Oberlin College. My colleagues there have welcomed me with the greatest possible warmth, and have helped give me a sense of place such as I have rarely known. Marcia Colish and Clayton Koppes deserve special mention. Ray Smith provided invaluable assistance with the mysteries of word-processing software and with the preparation of the bibliography and the maps. As time goes on, Oberlin students remind me more and more of French soldiers in the ways they relate to authority. I look forward to continuing the task of learning and labor there.

Oberlin, Ohio
May 1993

BETWEEN MUTINY AND OBEDIENCE

CHAPTER I

Introduction

THE THEORY OF WAR, OBEDIENCE,
AND MILITARY AUTHORITY

WAR has generally been conceived as an intensely hierarchical activity, thought out and organized from above, and executed (however imperfectly) from below. Religious and secular formulations of the theory of war have maintained that calculation—such as a prudential assessment of the good versus the evil brought about by war or in modern utilitarian parlance the cost versus the benefit—separate war from asocial or animalistic violence. Since people will make different calculations about war and all calculations cannot be treated equally lest chaos ensue, obedience to hierarchy has been taken as a given, concerning both how wars are carried out and how they are understood historically.

This book interrogates the notion of obedience, first at a broad theoretical level and then at a very specific empirical level. This introductory chapter provides the conceptual framework and argument. The first two sections will briefly illustrate some of the ways in which military authority has come to be understood in the theory of war as a unilateral exercise of power from above. The norm of obedience to authority, I will suggest, did not change substantially with secularization. Absolute divine authority in the medieval period was replaced by absolute "natural" authority in the early modern period, which was in turn replaced by absolute "political" authority in the nineteenth century. In the final two sections of the chapter, I will propose an alternative model of military command authority and explain how that model will function in the remainder of the book.

OBEDIENCE TO GOD AND NATURE:
THE MEDIEVAL AND EARLY MODERN PERIODS

The religious formulation of the theory of war is most commonly known as Just War theory (in Latin *ius belli*). Directly in the medieval period and indirectly in the early modern period, the *ius belli* were considered to have come from a divine and hence absolute source—God. Killing, of course, had been a sin ever since Cain slew Abel. Yet God Himself had authorized killing in a host of other biblical episodes, such as the conquest of Canaan under Joshua. But even in the Bible, God's absolute authority always reached the soldier through human and hence imperfect temporal leaders. The biblical record amply demonstrated to Jews and Christians that not all kings of Israel fought just wars.

Just War theory as currently understood has two main components, the *ius ad bellum* (the right to go to war) and the *ius in bello* (lawful behavior in the conduct of a war).[1] The *ius in bello* comprises two concepts, discrimination and proportionality. Both respond to the moral stipulation that the good brought about by war must outweigh the evil or harm. Discrimination prescribes immunity from violence for noncombatants, such as civilians, prisoners of war, or wounded combatants. Proportionality limits the types of weapons that may be used in war and specifies the conditions under which the allowed weapons may be used. Both discrimination and proportionality are supposed to limit the use of violence to the minimum level necessary to achieve the objectives of the war. A secularized and utilitarian formulation of proportionality will be proposed later as a basic principle in the argument of this book.

Alongside its aversion to killing, Judeo-Christian tradition has stressed obedience to temporal authority. The key question for soldiers in Just War theory thus has been the nature of their moral duty if their superiors ordered a use of violence soldiers considered unjust, in either a *ius ad bellum* or a *ius in bello* sense. How could the soldier judge correctly between the good of obedience and the evil of unjust killing?

Augustine of Hippo (354–430 C.E.) believed war to be the inevitable consequence of humanity's inherently sinful nature in the fallen state in the earthly city.[2] Certain wrongs could indeed be righted by violence, though a war could be just only if it were waged to bring peace. The evil of destruction must not exceed its just proportion to the good it promotes or makes possible. In *City of God*, Augustine had a simple but drastic solution to the problem of obedience.[3] Sadly but inevitably, all human judgment remains

[1] The history of the *ius belli* is considerably more complicated than this summary account suggests. James Turner Johnson, one of the foremost contemporary authorities on the development of the laws of war, has argued that a consensus has emerged on what constitutes what he calls the "classic doctrine" of the *ius belli* only since the 1950s. See his *Ideology, Reason, and the Limitation of War* (Princeton: Princeton University Press, 1975), p. 26. The contemporary terminology is employed here for purposes of clarity.

[2] See Frederick H. Russell, *The Just War in the Middle Ages* (Cambridge: Cambridge University Press, 1975), p. 16.

[3] See the example of the judge obliged by the nature of his profession to inflict judicial torture on the innocent in *City of God*, book XIX, chap. 6. This example was cited in R. A. Markus, "Saint Augustine's Views on the 'Just War,'" in W. J. Shiels, ed., *The Church and War: Papers Read at the Twenty-First Summer Meeting and Twenty-Second Winter Meeting of the Ecclesiastical History Society* (London: Basil Blackwell, 1983), p. 10.

clouded by sin in the earthly city. Christians must fulfill their social obliga-tions, even if they unintentionally commit unjust acts along the way. Tem-poral leaders are accountable to God for discharging these obligations; soldiers are accountable to their commanders. This meant unquestioning obedience to commands, whether the commands themselves were just or not: "For when a soldier kills a man in obedience to the legitimate author-ity under which he has served, he is not chargeable with murder by the laws of his country; in fact, he is chargeable with insubordination and mutiny if he refuses."[4] According to the Augustinian solution, obedience takes pre-cedence over individual conscience in a temporal world full of corruption and error.

As the decaying Roman Empire of Augustine's day came to an end, authority came to be administered through complicated and flexible oaths of fealty to individuals rather than to an abstract state. Throughout the Middle Ages, Augustine's formula of the primacy of the Christian soldier's duty to obey was weakened, but never really abandoned. Most medieval theorists agreed with canonist Gratian, who wrote in the middle of the twelfth century that the Christian was obliged to obey except when obe-dience unambiguously put that soldier's soul in jeopardy.[5]

The secularization of Just War theory began with the reintroduction of Aristotelian political theory, particularly in the work of Thomas Aquinas (1225–1274). In a radical departure from Augustine, Aquinas concluded that earthly affairs were governed according to natural law, which was consistent with God's eternal and divine law, but unlike them was compre-hensible on the basis of human reason alone. "Every act of reason," he wrote, "is based on principles that are known naturally. . . ."[6] Temporal authority, then, exists to serve "rational" or "natural" ends, specifically the Aristotelian end of the common good.[7] To Aquinas, the "natural" was both morally good and realizable, despite human frailties in calculation and judgment. Humanity, or at least temporal leaders, could become prin-

---

[4] *City of God*, book I, chap. 23. Henry Bettenson, trans. (New York: Penguin Books, 1972), p. 37. This example was cited in Russell, *The Just War*, p. 22.

[5] See Russell, *The Just War*, pp. 68–71. This apparently straightforward principle could lead to some complex particulars. Robert of Courson, for example, advised knights who considered their souls imperiled neither to obey nor disobey (and hence possibly lose their lands and/or their lives), but to wash their hands of the situation entirely by embarking on a crusade in the Holy Land. Stephen Langton, perhaps more problematically, suggested that knights follow their lords to the dubiously just war in question, but then withdraw or somehow exempt themselves before a battle actually began.

[6] *Summa Theologica*, I^{a}I^{ae}, q.91, a.3, ad.2, cited in Dino Bigongiari, ed., *The Political Ideas of St. Thomas Aquinas: Representative Selections* (New York: Hafner Press, 1952), p. 14.

[7] See Russell, *The Just War*, pp. 261–63, and the rather less accessible Joan D. Tooke, *The Just War in Aquinas and Grotius* (London: S.P.C.K., 1965).

cipally and directly responsible for all human activities, including war.[8]

In the early modern period, an expansive notion—the "natural" right of self-defense—became the principal justification for fighting a war. Most theorists stopped short of Niccolò Machiavelli's sweeping and completely secular assertion in *The Prince* (1514) that war was just whenever and however the prince deemed it essential to the security of the state.[9] The Spanish Dominican Francisco de Vitoria (1492–1546) concluded that indigenous peoples in the Americas who "attacked" Christians in the New World attempting peacefully to spread their religion could justly be punished by war according to natural law.[10] Another Spaniard, the Jesuit Francisco Suàrez (1548–1617) approved of internal coercion of religious practice to ensure the "natural" unity of the state.[11]

At first glance, regulating war by natural law could not be more straightforward. Natural law, sovereign in worldly affairs and fully knowable by human reason, was nevertheless perfect because it emanated directly from God. Accordingly, all calculations about war were theoretically subject to the same ostensibly objective criteria. Yet given the diversity of human reasoning, the question thus persisted of the subject's duty in the event of an incorrect (and hence unjust) calculation on the part of the sovereign.[12] Both Vitoria and Suàrez advised the sovereign to take the well-reasoned counsel of notables, though the ultimate responsibility for the war remained with the sovereign. Notables as well as commoners were obliged to obey unless their souls were manifestly imperiled, much as had been the case with medieval theory.[13]

But there existed within natural law the basis for rethinking this solution. Basing political society on natural law increased human responsibility for temporal affairs, and more specifically human responsibility for determining the common good. Not surprisingly, this posed the question of with whom and under what circumstances this responsibility lay. This,

[8] It bears noting here that the *ius belli* had never been entirely religious. Elaborate secular procedures for truces, ransom, and the like developed, particularly by the fourteenth century. See M. H. Keen, *The Laws of War in the Late Middle Ages* (London: Routledge and Keegan Paul, 1965).

[9] Paradoxically, Machiavelli based this assertion on a most Augustinian view of human nature: "for how we live is so far removed from how we ought to live, that he who abandons what is done for what ought to be done, will rather learn to bring about his own ruin than his preservation." *The Prince*, chap. 15, Luigi Ricci, trans. (New York: Random House, 1950), p. 56.

[10] Francisco de Vitoria, *De Indis et De Jure Belli Reflectiones*, cited in Johnson, *Ideology, Reason*, pp. 154–58.

[11] Francisco Suàrez, *On Faith*, cited in ibid., pp. 163–64.

[12] Despite their extensive use throughout this period, mercenaries, who killed for cash alone, found general disapproval under natural law theory of the just war, much as they had in medieval theory. See Russell, *The Just War*, pp. 242–44.

[13] See Johnson, *Ideology, Reason*, pp. 178–85.

in turn, raised the question of the natural relationship between the "natural" sovereign authority and those over whom it ruled.

The Dutch jurist Hugo Grotius (1583–1645) posited that sovereigns ought to make public their reasons for going to war, and thus subject to the reflection and judgment of all subjects. If those subjects concluded that the war was unjust, they were obliged to abstain on *natural* (as opposed to theological) grounds.[14] John Locke (1632–1704) carried the notion of just disobedience on secular grounds even further. For Locke, temporal authority existed as a contract, in which individuals in political society surrendered their natural right of self-defense to the sovereign. A sovereign who misused this authority through an internal or external unjust war broke the contract. Accordingly, the subject in such a situation could not only justly refuse to take part in the war, but could overthrow the sovereign.[15]

But Locke and other early modern theorists concerned themselves only with *political* society. The right to participate remained strictly circumscribed by rank and property. Political society pointedly excluded most soldiers in the field, who certainly lacked the right of resistance to officers, who served as the extension of the sovereign's authority. The social role of the soldier in an ancien régime army corresponded to that of the politically excluded urban and rural poor, the classes from which most soldiers originated. Secular authority expected absolute obedience on the battlefield, with serious infractions punishable by instant death.[16] But with the beginning of the French Revolution in 1789, a situation emerged in which the borders of the political community began to expand, with dramatic consequences for both the practice and the theory of war.

CLAUSEWITZ: OBEDIENCE TO "POLITICS"

The Declaration of the Rights of Man of 1789 sought to put into practice in France a new definition of the "natural" relationship between rulers and the ruled. This definition involved popular sovereignty, which argued that legitimate political authority existed in the collectivity of freeborn citizens rather than in the monarch. As Jean-Jacques Rousseau had posited in *The Social Contract* (1762), popular sovereignty sought to reconcile obedience

[14] Hugo Grotius, *Rights of War and Peace*, cited in ibid., p. 220.

[15] John Locke, *Two Treatises of Civil Government*, cited in ibid., pp. 232–33. See also Richard H. Cox, *Locke on War and Peace* (Oxford: Clarendon Press, 1960).

[16] This did not mean, to be sure, that ancien régime warfare proceeded without restraints. On the contrary, professional weapons and professional manpower proved so expensive, and the chances of seriously upsetting the geopolitical balance in Europe so remote, that war remained limited both in objectives and in execution. Geoffrey Best, *Humanity in Warfare* (New York: Columbia University Press, 1980), especially chap. 1, "The Late Enlightenment Consensus."

and freedom by making each citizen the author as well as the subject of political power: "Each one, while uniting with all, nevertheless obeys only himself and remains as free as before."[17]

When France went to war to defend popular sovereignty in 1792, the new theory of political authority made possible a new practice of warfare. Defending the *patrie* became every male citizen's first and foremost duty to the collectivity. This made possible a higher degree of national mobilization than had ever been the case in European history. Citizen-soldiers were still expected to obey their commanders. But they were now told that obeying authority was in a sense obeying themselves, since they and their compatriots made up the collective body in which sovereignty lay. As Jean-Paul Bertaud, John Lynn, and others have convincingly argued, Revolutionary ideology remained critical in the conscription, training, and fighting of the French army, even as it reprofessionalized in the years after the *levée en masse* of 1793.[18]

After the final defeat of the French by a coalition of dynastic forces in 1815, a Prussian staff officer, Karl von Clausewitz (1780–1831) set about rethinking the theory of war in light of the altered practice of war.[19] Clausewitz's masterpiece, *On War*, was published one year after his death.[20] Like many in the German elite of his day, Clausewitz had divided sentiments about the French Revolution and its terrible genius, Napoleon Bonaparte. As Peter Paret put it, "Clausewitz's sarcastic comments on the self-proclaimed saviour of humanity in Paris went hand in hand with admiration for the energies they generated."[21]

Ancien régime armies epitomized the underlying weakness of the dynastic states before 1789. Clausewitz maintained that in the pre-Revolutionary dynastic state, the army had been allowed to exist as an end in itself, "to form a state within a state, in which violence gradually disappeared."[22] The Revolution and Bonaparte had "purified" war by erasing

[17] *The Social Contract*, chap. 6, Donald A. Cress, trans. (Indianapolis: Hackett Publishing Company, 1983), p. 24.

[18] See Jean-Paul Bertaud, *The Army of the French Revolution*, R. R. Palmer, trans. (Princeton: Princeton University Press, 1988, originally published in French in 1979); and John A. Lynn, *The Bayonets of the Republic: Motivation and Tactics in the Army of Revolutionary France, 1791–94* (Urbana: University of Illinois Press, 1984). A more recent synthesis of the rapidly expanding social history of the French army of the Revolution is Alan Forest, *The Soldiers of the French Revolution* (Durham: Duke University Press, 1990).

[19] The standard work on Clausewitz in English remains Peter Paret, *Clausewitz and the State: The Man, His Theories, and His Times* (Princeton: Princeton University Press, 1976).

[20] The edition used here is Karl von Clausewitz, *On War*, Michael Howard and Peter Paret, trans. (Princeton: Princeton University Press, 1976).

[21] Paret, *Clausewitz and the State*, p. 20.

[22] Clausewitz, *On War*, p. 591. This was, for Clausewitz, a particular case of the general phenomenon of the decadence of the European aristocracies and their resulting abdication of their "natural" responsibilities under the society of orders. This decline, Clausewitz believed,

the artificial barriers between military and civilian society, thus making possible a truly "national" war. As he observed:

> Since Bonaparte, then, war, first among the French and subsequently among their enemies, again became the concern of the people as a whole, war took on an entirely different character, or rather closely approached its true character, its absolute perfection. There seemed no end to the resources mobilized; all limits disappeared in the vigor and enthusiasm shown by governments and their subjects.[23]

The dynastic powers defeated Napoleon, Clausewitz concluded, only when they learned to copy the French secret of national war—first in Spain in 1807, then in Austria in 1809, in 1812 in Russia, and finally in 1813 in Germany.[24] In *On War*, Clausewitz sought to establish a new theory of war that the dynastic powers could use to prevail against any latter-day versions of Napoleon that revolutions might produce in the future.

Clausewitz's divided sentiments on the French Revolution are reflected in his rethinking of the theory of war in ways whose historical significance can scarcely be exaggerated. On the one hand, Clausewitz eagerly embraced the rationalism of the Revolution. This meant nothing less than a radical completion of the secularization of the theory of war. Since the writing of the biblical texts, calculations behind war had been accountable to some fixed and absolute source of authority—first to God and then to "nature" under natural law, which had been given by God.

Clausewitz eliminated the problem of human calculations falling short of ideals provided by God or nature by changing the entire equation. He maintained that war was in itself a conceptual constant, defined simply as "an act of force to compel our enemy to do our will."[25] As a result, there was no reason intrinsic to war for limiting it in any way. Proportionality, the limiting of war for any moral reason, whether based in divine or natural law, represented for Clausewitz nothing more than a kind-hearted fantasy.[26]

The control of war by some fixed and absolute morality, however imperfectly interpreted by the human beings implementing it, was replaced by a variable—politics. From this comes Clausewitz's most famous statement, that war is "a true political instrument, the continuation of political activity by other means."[27] Military figures of whatever rank serve simply as

---

had brought on the Revolution in the first place. See *Umtriebe* (1821), translated as *Turbulences* in Carl von Clausewitz, *De la Révolution à la restauration: écrits et lettres*, Marie-Louise Steinhauser, ed. and trans. (Paris: Gallimard, 1976), pp. 385–428.

[23] Clausewitz, *On War*, pp. 592–93.

[24] See ibid., p. 592.

[25] Ibid., p. 75.

[26] See ibid., book 1, chap. 1, sec. 3.

[27] Ibid., p. 87.

state instruments bearing arms. The soldier became a total professional analogous to a civil bureaucrat, responsible only for executing orders but relieved from autonomous moral judgment regarding them. War differs from administration only by its use of physical violence: "What remains peculiar to war is simply the peculiar nature of its means. War in general, and the commander in any specific instance, is entitled to require that the trend and designs of policy shall not be inconsistent with these means."[28]

War itself thus becomes a policy tool totally predictable in its function and results. From the interaction of the constant (war) and the variable (politics) comes Clausewitz's often cited but misunderstood distinction between total and limited war. Any correctly calculated war has a predetermined end (*Zweck*) that can be achieved using the available means (*Mittel*), through a series of intermediary stages (*Ziele*).[29] At any given stage, be it the taking of a bridge, a cavalry assault, or a siege, there is no logical reason to constrain violence in any way. Violence in war is always total; only the political *Zweck* can properly be limited.

But on the other hand, even as Clausewitz embraced the rationalism and secularism of the French Revolution, he adamantly refused to concede that revolutionary ideology had played a significant role in creating the French war machine. For him, the Revolution had swept away the decadent and feeble royal army but Napoleon had succeeded as a new monarch rather than as the heir to the Revolution.[30] According to Clausewitz's ideal, armed forces, as pure instruments of state, could not have political identities of their own—certainly not identities having anything to do with popular sovereignty.

Clausewitz considered obedience on the part of soldiers as much a given as any preceding theorist of war. In an ideally functioning apolitical military machine, authority would run unimpeded from the sovereign to the lowest common soldier in the field. The common soldier, either as citizen-soldier or even as subject-soldier, actually received very little attention throughout *On War*. Disobedience became a technical problem, part of general "friction"—that array of natural and human impediments ranging from the weather to mechanical failure that may obstruct the perfect operation of any military machine: "A battalion is made up of individuals, the least important of whom may chance to delay things or somehow make them go wrong. The dangers inseparable from war and the physical exertions war demands can aggravate the problem to such an extent that they must be ranked among its [friction's] principal causes."[31]

---

[28] Ibid.

[29] See Michael Howard, *Clausewitz* (Oxford: Oxford University Press, 1983), p. 35.

[30] In addition to *On War*, see Carl von Clausewitz, *Historical and Political Writings*, Peter Paret and Daniel Moran, eds. and trans. (Princeton: Princeton University Press, 1992).

[31] Clausewitz, *On War*, p. 119.

As for the sort of large-scale popular uprising that had taken place in Spain following Napoleon's 1807 invasion, Clausewitz considered "the people in arms" an undeniably powerful but unreliable weapon, "an outgrowth of the way in which the conventional barriers have been swept away in our lifetime by the elemental violence of war."[32] He revealingly avoided commenting on whether this development was beneficial or not, and limited his analysis to determining when popular resistance was likely to prove militarily effective. War, including even social movements brought into existence by war, must not be allowed to influence politics. "Politics" remained the "high politics" of sovereign and court.

By avoiding the possible military implications of popular sovereignty, Clausewitz arrived at a mechanistic solution to the relationship between war and politics. This solution proved remarkably durable in nineteenth-century Europe, not least because no war between 1815 and 1914 required national mobilization on the scale of the wars of the French Revolution.[33] But particularly in France, "politics" proved variable in ways that Clausewitz had refused to concede, as the country at least theoretically embraced popular sovereignty by becoming a republic in 1871. As I will argue in chapter 2, it proved unrealistic to expect that a mass conscript army of citizen-soldiers under the French Third Republic *could* serve as a purely administrative apparatus—even before August 1914. The concept of an "apolitical" army, this study will argue, is fundamentally inconsistent with an army of citizen-soldiers. By definition, the citizen-soldier will not entirely relinquish the rights of the citizen. Authority and obedience will be thus constantly subject to questioning and negotiation from below.

OBEDIENCE, POWER RELATIONS, AND PROPORTIONALITY IN THE FRENCH ARMY DURING WORLD WAR I

Clausewitz's ideal of an army as an unreflective institutional machine has pervaded our historical understanding of what happened on the World War I battlefield. Conventional military historians have accepted obedience as a given and any form of nonobedience as "friction," an anomaly distorting how war ought to have operated historically.[34] This has led to a

---

[32] Ibid., p. 479.

[33] For a fine broad and comparative overview of the transition from the nineteenth century to the time of the world wars, see David Kaiser, *Politics and War: European Conflict from Phillip II to Hitler* (Cambridge: Harvard University Press, 1990), chap. 4.

[34] Conventional military historians have, it must be stressed, produced a sophisticated if professionally oriented literature exploring "why men fight." A fine synthesis of this literature is Richard Holmes, *Acts of War: The Behavior of Men in Battle* (New York: The Free Press, 1985).

remarkably consistent system of narratives portraying World War I soldiers as tragic victims, lambs led over the top and into the slaughter under circumstances far beyond their control.

This image of the totally victimized soldier draws upon the undeniably hideous relationship among the means of destruction employed, the stalemated nature of most of the fighting, and the questionable war aims of most of the protagonists. In the language of conventional military history, the tactical stalemate on the Western Front and the ensuing strategic consequences can be explained quite simply. Once the failure of the German invasion of August 1914 thoroughly exhausted the immediately available resources of the French, German, and British armies without producing a decisive outcome, a consistent pattern of warfare developed that persisted until 1918. Both sides found protection in complicated systems of trenches guarded by barbed wire and machine-gun placements. Further reinforced by second, third, and sometimes fourth lines of trenches and by artillery to the rear, these defensive positions could not be pierced at all except through extraordinary concentrations of men and artillery. Even then, as Hew Strachan put it in succinct professional language: "The difficulty of amassing sufficient strength—not only in men but also in artillery—for an attack meant that offensives were mounted on too narrow a front. They could thus be enfiladed by defending artillery. The reserves to support the push were often too far in the rear to exploit any success in time."[35] Moreover, the attacking artillery proved highly ineffective at its assigned task of destroying enemy barbed wire and forward positions. More often, the offensive barrage simply churned No Man's Land into all but impassable mud and alerted the defenders of the impending infantry assault.

The technological parameters of World War I combat remained essentially fixed from the fall of 1914 to the spring of 1918. Accordingly, the strategic politics remained fixed for much of this period as well. The Germans, holding hostage much of northeastern France, could bide their time and hope for greater success on the more malleable Eastern Front. The French, on the other hand, either had to continue attacking within the existing technological parameters or negotiate. Given the strength of the German position, negotiating meant accepting some sort of military defeat. As a result, French generals sought victory through an unrepentant attachment to the military doctrine of all-out offensive doctrine (*offensive à outrance*) with which they had begun the war. Lacking any other doctrine that promised military success, they persisted in a strategy of hurling masses of men against invariably superior defensive firepower—with results often of hundreds of casualties for every yard gained, and some one

---

[35] Hew Strachan, *European Armies and the Conduct of War* (London: George Allen & Unwin, 1983), p. 138.

million French soldiers dead even before the siege of Verdun.[36] In Clausewitzian terms, war and politics (or at least "high politics") had reached an impasse. The result for soldiers, we have come to understand, was complete helplessness in the face of unlimited terror.

This view even pervades what could be called the "new military history" of World War I, which has endeavored to go beyond the didactic function of conventional military history. Richard Baynes's study of the Second Scottish Rifles at the Battle of Neuve Chapelle in 1915 emphasized small-group loyalty as a motivating factor, but one that functioned through the bond of class deference linking the rank and file to the officer/gentleman.[37] Eric Leed's immensely thoughtful study of combat and identity in World War I posited mass alienation, which occurred because soldiers were coerced by the authority structure into giving up their own identities in order to face the unequal struggle between artillery and infantry, between "implacable machines and diggers."[38] Even Tony Ashworth's groundbreaking study of tacit truces across No Man's Land, which has greatly influenced this work, concluded that the policy of constant aggression mandated by the command structure prevailed in the end.[39]

That the influence of an authority-generated model for understanding soldierly behavior persists even in the most innovative works on World War I is not surprising.[40] The thoughts and deeds expected of soldiers by their commanders at least appear to exert overwhelming dominance over the archival record. Orders of various kinds represent the most complete series of records in military archives. Corresponding behavior from below has too often been seen only in terms of this preexisting picture.

It must be stressed early and forcefully that no effort is made throughout this study ever to deny or in any way to minimize the horrors of the World

---

[36] Col. Pierre Guinard, Jean-Claude Devos, and Jean Nicot, *Inventaire sommaire des archives de la guerre: Série N, 1872–1919*, vol. 1 (Troyes: Imprimerie La Renaissance, 1975), p. 213.

[37] Richard Baynes, *Morale, A Study of Men and Courage: The Second Scottish Rifles at the Battle of Neuve Chapelle, 1915* (London: Cassels, 1967).

[38] Eric Leed, *No Man's Land: Combat and Identity in World War I* (New York: Cambridge University Press, 1979), p. 100.

[39] Tony Ashworth, *Trench Warfare, 1914–1918: The Live and Let Live System* (New York: Holmes & Meier, 1980).

[40] Contemporary literature on Just War theory has also assumed that soldiers' behavior primarily reflects that of their commanders. This literature has been particularly haunted by the United States experience in Vietnam, and has explored why laws of war imposed from above have been disregarded from below in the form of war crimes. Indeed, contemporary Just War theory literature and the literature on "why men fight" seem to show two sides of the same coin. If morale serves the purpose of calling forth soldierly aggression, the laws of war serve the purpose of containing and controlling that aggression. See, for example, Peter Karsten, *Law, Soldiers, and Combat* (Westport, Conn.: Greenwood Press, 1978) and Johnson, *Just War Tradition*, p. 174.

War I battlefield. My intention rather is to demonstrate that the standard narrative of the massacre of the innocent, even if steeped in justified moral outrage, does not tell us all we need to know about what happened to soldiers during the war. In the French army, orders to attack often included particular objectives to be taken by particular times, *coûte que coûte* (at whatever cost). Since casualties, however high, were always less than 100 percent (unless the unit concerned simply surrendered), we must infer that at some point attacks were broken off in defiance at least of the letter, if not ultimately the spirit, of written orders. As Jean Norton Cru observed in one of the quotations used as an epigraph, if French soldiers had followed all their orders to the letter, the entire French army would have been exterminated by August 1915. This book is based on the premise that from the first days of the war, a gray area existed between command expectations and what soldiers in the trenches determined was possible. Like No Man's Land itself, that gray area was contested for the duration.

What follows is a story of forms of resistance to authority that have hitherto generally been ignored, seen as distorting anomaly, or misunderstood as very sad but very hopeless. The intent here is simply to bring soldiers into the mainstream of social history. Certainly, other social groups have been found to be far less helpless then their formal status would suggest. Political scientist James Scott, to cite but one example, explored forms of subtle peasant resistance in a Malaysian village.[41] Obfuscation, petty deceit, and shortchanging on dues, he found, constituted a sort of war of attrition on authority far more significant in the end than open peasant revolts, which tended to rise and fall spectacularly. More recently, Scott has posited a more widely conceived dialogical interpretation of authority. He has explored a dichotomy in rural resistance between a "public transcript" comprising not only written words, but also a wide array of customary behavioral patterns "describing the open interaction between subordinates and those who dominate" and a "hidden transcript," a "discourse [of resistance] that takes place 'offstage,' beyond direct observation by powerholders."[42]

At a general theoretical level, this study is informed by the work of someone far more associated with domination than resistance—the *adulte terrible* of post-structural epistomology, Michel Foucault. Foucault is best known for theoretical/historical works arguing that institutions such as the school, the asylum, the clinic, and the prison all serve essentially the

---

[41] James C. Scott, *Weapons of the Weak: Everyday Forms of Peasant Resistance* (New Haven: Yale University Press, 1985).

[42] James C. Scott, *Domination and the Arts of Resistance: Hidden Transcripts* (New Haven: Yale University Press, 1990), pp. 2, 4.

same function of surveillance and control of the human body and soul.[43] In the 1980s, historians turned to Foucault probably more than any other single theorist to fill in the void left by the decline and fall of Marxism. At the same time, though, others have found themselves frustrated and sometimes enraged by Foucault's reluctance to provide solutions or even much hope for the human condition.[44]

But much less well known is Foucault's interest in the last years before his death in 1984 in the role of freedom in the power relationship.[45] This late interest is captured in the quotation from "The Subject and Power" (1982) used as an epigraph to this book.[46] In the essay, Foucault drew a distinction between power relations and physical domination. In the latter, he observed, "where determining factors saturate the whole, there is no relationship of power; slavery is not a power relationship when man is in chains."[47] "Power," on the other hand, "is exercised only over free subjects, and only insofar as they are free."[48] Foucault observed in a January 1984 interview that "if there are relations of power throughout every social field it is because there is freedom everywhere."[49]

Resistance and struggle rather than outright domination, it turns out, characterize power relations. Foucault coined a neologism drawn from a word of Greek origin, agonism, to describe ongoing confrontation and strategizing: "a relationship which is at the same time reciprocal incitation and struggle; less of a face-to-face confrontation which paralyzes both sides than a permanent struggle."[50] In the ever-changing relationship between power and the subject, the possibility always exists of reversal, based on "a certain essential obstinacy on the part of the principles of freedom. . . ."[51] Rarely do confrontations result in total domination. Rather,

[43] See, for example, *Folie et déraison: histoire de la folie à l'age classique* (Paris: Plon, 1961), and *Surveillir et punir: naissance de la prison* (Paris: Gallimard, 1975). The influence of this *pur et dur* Foucault is also present in this study, particularly chaps. 6 and 7.

[44] An articulate example by a self-confessed liberal is Michael Walzer, "The Lonely Politics of Michel Foucault," *The Company of Critics: Social Criticism and Political Commitment in the Twentieth Century* (New York: Basic Books, 1988), pp. 191–209.

[45] Some of Foucault's intellectual heirs have much emphasized this trend. See particularly Graham Burchell, Colin Gordon, and Peter Miller, eds., *The Foucault Effect: Studies in Governmentality* (Chicago: University of Chicago Press, 1991).

[46] The essay is included as an Afterword in Herbert L. Dreyfus and Paul Rabinow, *Michel Foucault: Beyond Structuralism and Hermeneutics*, 2d ed. (Chicago: University of Chicago Press, 1983), pp. 208–26.

[47] Ibid., p. 221.

[48] Ibid.

[49] "The Ethic of Care for the Self as a Practice of Freedom: An Interview with Michel Foucault on January 20, 1984," translated by J. D. Gauthier, S.J., in James Bernauer and David Rasmussen, eds., *The Final Foucault* (Cambridge: MIT Press, 1988), p. 12.

[50] Foucault, "The Subject and Power," p. 222.

[51] Ibid., p. 225.

confrontations eradicate the rules of the old power relationship and put in place new ones. A confrontation ends "when stable mechanisms replace the free play of antagonistic reactions." New limits of the power relationship are thus constituted, and the strategic struggle resumes on the new basis.

The analytical approach used here uses this model of a power relationship rather than an authority-generated view of soldiers' experience. Soldiers' behavior was not a function of the wishes of those commanding them—at least not entirely. Neither formal command authority nor obedience is taken here as a given. Rather, command authority as explored here reflected a negotiated balance-of-power equation linking the protagonists. This settlement then set the parameters of command authority. As the components of the balance-of-power equation changed, these parameters were in turn renegotiated. The story to be told here explores how this process took place between a particular group of French soldiers and their commanders. Throughout this study, the term "soldier" will signify someone receiving an order at the time he receives it, independent of rank.

To phrase this approach in Clausewitzian terms, the variable of politics came to determine the constant of war in the French army during World War I, but hardly "politics" as Clausewitz envisioned it. What Clausewitz's system would consider the technical problem of "friction" in fact concealed a complex power relationship between French citizen-soldiers and their commanders. Both sets of protagonists in this power relationship operated within parameters set by a paradox implicit in the official French ideology of popular sovereignty, of soldiers' being expected to obey a source of authority originating, ultimately, in themselves and their compatriots. "Politics" not only issued variable commands; politics itself proved variable in ways Clausewitz failed to appreciate.

"War," on the other hand, in the sense of a fixed "total" use of force toward some determined political end, did indeed operate much as Clausewitz believed it should. But before 1918, making war "total" did not render it decisive, despite national mobilization far beyond anything foreseen by Clausewitz. The stalemated combat that resulted from the existing technological parameters brought to the fore the key issue negotiated between soldiers and their commander—the perceived relationship between ends and means on the battlefield.

This perceived relationship will be analyzed according to a principle of proportionality, different from but analagous to the principle as it operated in Just War theory. Proportionality in Just War theory seeks to limit violence in war for moral reasons, so that the good of the aims to be achieved by war outweighs the evil of the destruction wrought. The resulting calculus is accountable to a fixed and absolute source of moral authority, most often religious. Here, however, the calculus joining ends and means remains utilitarian and thus flexible. Proportionality is analyzed more as an issue between French soldiers and their commanders than between soldiers and their nominal German enemies. For French soldiers, the issue revolved around whether and under what circumstances they considered the levels of offensive violence expected of them relevant to the goal they shared with their commanders of winning the war.

In essence, this study explores how command authority within the French army changed as calculations of proportionality changed and diverged among soldiers and their commanders. These differing calculations resulted in confrontations that altered the parameters of formal command authority and thus of the power relationship within the French army. Over the course of World War I, these confrontations actually shifted the balance of power within the French army in favor of battlefield soldiers. Through a long and costly process beginning in August 1914, French soldiers learned to place their own limits on the violence ordered by their commanders.

THE CASE OF THE 5ᵉ DIVISION D'INFANTERIE

Historians, to paraphrase E. M. Forster in *Howard's End*, must constantly reconcile two unattainable goals, seeing things clearly and seeing them whole. Particularly in French social history, a favored vehicle for striking a balance has been the local study. The historian chooses a unit of investigation large enough to make possible meaningful generalizations, but small enough to study intensively. The unit of investigation selected here is one regular-army infantry division, which would comprise some twelve to fifteen thousand men at any given time. The particular division selected was the Fifth Infantry Division, hereafter referred to by its French name, the 5ᵉ Division d'Infanterie (5ᵉ DI).

Studying a division offers the possibility of examining the argument outlined here in some detail for a unit of still-manageable size. The division was the basic building block of the French army in World War I, that is, the smallest unit comprising infantry, artillery, engineering, and medical sub-units. It was also the smallest unit whose État-Major or general staff contained the three standard bureaus that characterized larger units—*Effectifs* (troop strength and logistics); *Renseignements* (intelligence); and *Opérations* (battlefield operations). The number of documents generated by a division was thus much greater than for any of its constituent parts. To be sure, a regiment generally had a greater permanence and historical identity (real or fictitious) than a division. But the composition of a division did not change often, and never without a compelling reason, such as the mutinies of 1917. Especially with a charismatic commander as a unifying force, a divisional sense of identity was certainly possible.

The 5e DI was chosen for a variety of practical and methodological reasons. First, the documentary record for this division proved among the most extensive and comprehensive in the entire French army, not least because of the professional ambitions of its commanding general. To be sure, the 5e DI does not in many respects represent a "typical" French division, though it would be hard to say which division would. Indeed, it is the very atypicality of the 5e DI that makes it especially interesting. For if World War I represents an extreme case of apparent soldierly helplessness in the face of military authority, the 5e DI represents an extreme case within the French army. My point is to show that even here, a "hidden transcript" of resistance and confrontation existed behind the "official transcript" of obedience and massacre.

At first consideration, the combat record of the 5e DI invites puzzlement, if not confusion. The 5e DI was rushed to Belgium in August 1914 as part of Gen. Charles Lanrezac's Fifth Army. The division suffered extremely heavy casualties in the Battle of the Frontiers (as much as one-third to one-half of most units within a week), only to counterattack on September 6 to the acclaim of a rescued nation at the Battle of the Marne. During this battle and the purge of generals that accompanied it, Gen. Charles Mangin assumed command of the division, which he led until June 1916. Mangin, one of the most thoughtful, articulate, and persistent adherents of *offensive à outrance* led the 5e DI in its highly praised (if not conspicuously successful) engagements in 1915 at Neuville–St. Vaast in the Artois. Mangin and the 5e DI achieved an international reputation in May 1916, when the division spearheaded the attack to retake the fort at Douaumont at a critical stage during the siege of Verdun. According to a divisional history, a German communiqué of 24 May 1916 referred to the 5e DI as "*die beste französische Division* [the best French division]."[52]

Then, after nearly a year without a pitched battle, the 5e DI was scheduled to resume the attack in the Chemin des Dames offensive in April 1917. The division was supposed to have been used in exploiting the rupture of the German line so extravagantly promised by Gen. Robert Nivelle. But in the wake of the costly failure of these initial attacks, the 5e DI—praised as elite since the Marne—experienced by Guy Pedroncini's reckoning the highest incidence of mutinies of any division in the French army.[53] The mutinies occurred *without* the division's having participated in a single attack in the offensive. In May and June 1917, units of all four regiments refused at one time or another to take up positions in the trenches.

[52] Louis Lecoc, *Pages héroiques de la 5e Division d'Infanterie* (Paris: S.T.D.I.5, 1918), p. 77.

[53] Guy Pedroncini, *Les Mutineries de 1917* (Paris: Presses Universitaires de France, 1967), p. 62.

Scarcely less surprising was the recapturing of the 5ᵉ DI's reputation the following year, when the division played an important role in the Allied counteroffensives in the summer and fall of 1918 that finally ended the war—at a level of casualties not seen since Verdun. The all-too tempting conclusion is that the repression of the mutinies through courts-martial and reorganizing the division effectively removed resistance to command authority, that is, that the "high politics" of commanders triumphed over the "low politics" of soldiers. It is the purpose of this study to demonstrate that a much more complicated—and less dismal—process was at work.

CHAPTER II

The Army and the Republic in Provincial France

MILITARY LIFE IN ROUEN BEFORE AUGUST 1914

THE HISTORIOGRAPHICAL LITERATURE on the French army before World War I has adopted whole-heartedly Clausewitz's dictum that politics determines war, essentially as Clausewitz understood it. That is to say, historians have focused their attention on how national politics has influenced the military efficiency of the French army of August 1914. The pivotal event was that most famous of modern French *affaires*, following the Dreyfus case.[1] In 1894, a court-martial convicted Capt. Alfred Dreyfus, an Alsatian Jew assigned to the general staff, of espionage for passing secret documents to the Germans. The case became an *affaire* as more and more public figures became convinced of Dreyfus's innocence, notably after Emile Zola's "J'accuse" article of 1896. The stubborn refusal of the army to admit judicial error despite the feebleness, not to say nonexistence, of the evidence against Dreyfus brought to the surface a variety of deep conflicts within Third Republic political culture. In addition to the perennial Left-Right fracture, old animosities were rekindled between the army and civilian society and among Catholics, Protestants, and Jews.

Two intertwined issues have remained central in assessing the impact of this turmoil: the role of the army both as protagonist in and a victim of political conflict; and the resulting effect on military preparedness and efficiency in August 1914. At least until recently, most historians wrote from a position of sympathy with one faction or another and concluded that because of the triumph of that side or another one, the French army proved either effective or ineffective. Historians have remained convinced that national politics profoundly influenced military efficacy, but agreement even among authors with similar political views has ended there.

For example, Joseph Montheilhet, in the tradition of the Socialist Jean Jaurès, criticized the career army establishment as an unimprovable reactionary element, unable to learn the virtues of republican government even after the chastening experience of the Dreyfus Affair.[2] The victory at the

---

[1] See the recent comprehensive overview by Michael Burns, *Dreyfus: A Family Affair, 1789–1945* (New York: Harper Collins, 1991).

[2] Joseph Montheilhet, *Les Institutions militaires de la France, 1914–1932: de la paix armée à la paix désarmee* (Paris: Librairie Felix Alcan, 1932). For Jaurès, see his own *L'Armée nouvelle: l'organisation socialiste de la France* (Paris: L. Rouff, 1911).

Marne in 1914 came about through a Jacobin-Republican *furia francese* that persisted despite the best efforts of the reactionary professional army. In contrast, other republican sympathizers such as Paul-Marie de la Gorce, Richard Challener, and David Ralston, have argued that the strength of the French army in 1914 drew directly from republican reforms, which effectively mobilized the "nation at arms" and diluted aristocratic reactionary elements.[3] On the political Right, Raoul Girardet connected French military inefficiency with the passing of aristocratic military society over the course of the nineteenth century and the emergence of a new class of military functionaries.[4]

More recent historiography has tended not to take Left/Right sides, but rather to shift blame for military inefficiency to national political muddle. Douglas Porch, for example, avoided Girardet's right-wing political views but presented an even harsher view of republican military reforms.[5] Porch castigated the Radical Party for all but fatally emasculating the army in the years between the Dreyfus Affair and 1914 in its vengeful crusade to rise to the top of the parliamentary heap. Allan Mitchell concluded that fear of Germany weighed more heavily on the minds of all military reformers, Left and Right, than their hatred of each other.[6] The problem for the French, according to Mitchell, was that because of the national political muddle, they imitated the Germans incompetently.

But the focus on military efficiency in the historiographical literature on armies has tended to direct attention more toward how armies *ought to* have functioned than how they actually did. This chapter explores additional meanings of Clausewitz's dictum that politics determines war. Certainly, there is much to be said for the view that the French army was "unprepared" to fight a major war in August 1914 as traditional military historians define the term. But particularly in peacetime, all armies serve a variety of social and political roles, some of which have very little to do with military preparedness.[7] From this perspective, the "inefficiency" or even "incoherence" of the French army before August 1914 takes on a very different appearance.

[3] Paul-Marie de la Gorce, *La République et son armée* (Paris: Fayard, 1963); Richard Challener, *The French Theory of the Nation in Arms, 1866–1939* (New York: Columbia University Press, 1952); David Ralston, *The Army of the Republic: The Role of the Military in the Political Evolution of France* (Cambridge: Harvard University Press, 1967).

[4] Raoul Girardet, *La Société militaire dans la France contemporaine: 1815–1939* (Paris: Plon, 1953).

[5] Douglas Porch, *The March to the Marne: The French Army, 1871–1914* (Cambridge: Cambridge University Press, 1981).

[6] Allan Mitchell, *Victors and Vanquished: The German Influence on Army and Church after 1870* (Chapel Hill: University of North Carolina Press, 1984), p. 246.

[7] See, for example, István Deák's examination of the role of Habsburg officers in keeping ethnic peace in *Beyond Nationalism: A Social and Political History of the Habsburg Officer Corps, 1848–1914* (New York: Oxford University Press, 1990).

The portrait sketched here of the army in general and the 5e DI in particular before August 1914 emphasizes institutional and doctrinal peculiarities resulting from the parameters set by national politics. These peculiarities played an important role in shaping the power dynamic between soldiers and commanders once the war began. The first section of the chapter will explore the role of the army in provincial political life as a regional reflection of the modus vivendi worked out between the army and the Third Republic in the years between the Dreyfus Affair and August 1914. The second section examines the contrast between the highly centralized nature of command authority at the strategic level (according to Plan XVII), and the highly decentralized nature of command authority at the tactical level (according to the April 1914 infantry regulations). This contrast was highlighted by the limited degree to which the doctrine of the offensive permeated actual army life in the provinces. I will argue in chapter 3 that this doctrinal "incoherence" inadvertently contributed to the flexibility of the French army on the battlefield in August 1914. The third section of the present chapter will describe the particular collection of citizen-soldiers in the 5e DI that left Normandy at the mobilization.

MILITARY PROVINCIAL NOTABLES AND THE CIVIL FUNCTIONS OF MILITARY DISPLAY

In peacetime as throughout the war, the 5e DI formed part of the 3e Corps d'Armée (3e CA). Before the war, both units were headquartered in Rouen in Upper Normandy. The recruitment area was the 3e Région Militaire, which comprised the departments of the Seine-Inférieure, the Calvados, the Eure, as well as the arrondissements of Mantes and Versailles from the Seine-et-Oise. It drew additional recruits from eight arrondissements in Paris. While a precise prewar figure does not exist, it seems that the majority of the men of the 5e DI were from Normandy or the Seine Basin.[8] Since the other infantry division in the 3e CA, the 6e DI, was based in Paris, prewar military life in Rouen for the 3e CA and the 5e DI were almost interchangeable. Of the two brigades that the 5e DI comprised, the 9e Brigade (comprising the 39e and 74e Régiments d'Infanterie) was based in

---

[8] As late as March 1917, by which time the regional character of units in the French army had been diluted considerably, about two-thirds of the men in the division still came from the prewar recruitment areas. In the 74e RI, for example, about 50 percent of the men came from Normandy, about 20 percent from Paris and its environs, and the remaining 30 percent from elsewhere in France. Gen. Henri de Roig-Bourdeville, "Notice sur la 5e Division d'Infanterie," 22 March 1917, 5e DI, 1e Bureau, 24 N 76. Service Historique de l'Armée de Terre, Archives de Guerre, Château de Vincennes, Vincennes, France. Série N (1879–1919). Throughout this study, all archival references are from this collection unless otherwise noted.

Rouen, while the 10ᵉ Brigade was based in Caen along with one of its regiments (the 36ᵉ RI). The other regiment, the 129ᵉ RI, was based in Le Havre.[9]

Upper Normandy was mostly agrarian before World War I, with the noteworthy exceptions of the textile center of Rouen and the harbor city of Le Havre.[10] Its working class was visible and politically active, but profoundly outnumbered.[11] Politically, the area was well suited to peaceful cohabitation between the professional army and the Republic, though it must be kept in mind that explicit political activities by officers on active duty remained strictly forbidden. Like women, soldiers were not even allowed to vote until after World War II.[12] As exemplified by Normandy's favorite sons of the prewar period, Richard Waddington and Félix Faure, the region was a bastion of conservative republicanism, the northern tip of the conservative, Catholic crescent running northeast from the Vendée.[13] It was an area in which, as Jean-Jacques Becker put it, "respect for the army and the established order was a constant."[14]

One of the French army's most important functions in Normandy and elsewhere involved publicly displaying the agreement between the army and the Republic to coexist in the aftermath of the Dreyfus Affair. The key figures in displaying this modus vivendi were the senior commanders, who fulfilled the functions of military notables, analogous to those of a prefect, a senator, or a local marquis.[15] These eight senior officers (the corps commander, the division commander, the two brigade commanders, and the four regimental commanders) shared a number of qualities, none of which

[9] The local archival sources for this period are disappointingly meager. The archives of the Department of the Seine Maritime in Rouen have no documents on civil-military relations before August 1914, and only one carton covering the subject for the whole period 1914–1920. The other major source for the whole World War I period, Sous-série J (Fonds Lafond) contains miscellaneous papers of a local newspaper publisher and has little that is unavailable elsewhere.

[10] A readable general history of the region appears in the "Univers de la France" series. Michel de Bouard, director, *Histoire de la Normandie* (Toulouse: Edouard Privat, 1970).

[11] There had been a socialist conference in Le Havre as far back as 1880, and the 1912 conference of the Confedération Générale du Travail held there reaffirmed the vows of workers' representatives to resist the outbreak of any European war. See Robert Brecy, *Le Mouvement syndical en France, 1871–1921: essai bibliographique* (Paris: Mouton & Cie., 1963).

[12] William Serman, *Les Officiers français dans la nation* (Paris: Aubier Montaigne, 1982), p. 41.

[13] See André Siegfried's classic, *Tableau politique de la France de l'ouest sous la troisième république* (Paris: A. Colin, 1913).

[14] Jean-Jacques Becker, *1914: Comment les français sont entrés à la guerre* (Paris: Presse de la Fondation national des Sciences publiques, 1977), pp. 51–52. All translations are my own unless otherwise noted.

[15] Military notables are examined at greater length in Leonard V. Smith, "Command Authority in the French Army: 1914–1918: The Case of the 5ᵉ Division d'Infanterie," (Ph.D. diss., Columbia University, 1990), pp. 41–57.

would prove necessarily consistent with the skills that would be required of them once the war broke out.

All of these officers came of age professionally during the late 1890s, that is to say, during the height of the Dreyfus Affair. This necessitated a high degree of political skill, or at least a developed capacity to stay out of trouble.[16] Although explicit references to national political preferences are nonexistent in officers' personal dossiers, the scandal over *l'affaire des fiches* demonstrated that Radical politicians were not above eliciting information on officers' political and religious preferences through dubious means.[17] Nonetheless, a wide range of political and personal sympathies existed in the highest reaches of the French officer corps.[18]

Military notables also needed to be perceived as professionally capable, though "objective" information along these lines cannot easily be obtained. Between 1905 and 1912 officers were allowed to see their own evaluations, which Douglas Porch concluded made them hopelessly vague and complimentary.[19] It should be noted, however, that the same problem existed in wartime evaluations. In any event, "accurate" prewar assessments of officers' wartime abilities would have required a prescience of World War I warfare denied to all high military officials everywhere.

One can state far more categorically that military notables needed financial backing considerably in excess of their salaries.[20] A major source of funds to cover such deficits was officers' wives, who played a crucial but as yet quite unexplored role in financing the French officer corps.[21] It does not

[16] See Walter Barge, "The Generals of the Republic: The Corporate Personality of High Military Rank in France: 1899–1914" (Ph.D. diss., University of North Carolina–Chapel Hill, 1982). According to French law, personal dossiers are closed for 120 years after the officer's birth, though at the discretion of archives personnel, a shorter summary (the *état des services*) can be made available.

[17] The affair concerned allegations that surfaced in November 1904 that General André had used information gathered by the Grand Orient to ensure the political rectitude of officers.

[18] The monarchist views of Hubert Lyautey, not to mention his promiscuous homosexuality, did not prevent him from making enough friends in Republican circles to be granted a key command in Morocco under the André war ministry. See Douglas Porch, *The Conquest of Morocco* (New York: Alfred A. Knopf, 1982), chap. 6. Likewise, Charles Mangin was for a time a protégé of the monarchist Lyautey, yet married the daughter of one-time War Minister Godfroy Cavaignac, scion of a conservative republican dynasty.

[19] Porch, *March to the Marne*, p. 179.

[20] For example, according to one 1913 estimate appearing in the periodical *Armée et Democratie*, a lieutenant with a wife and one child living in relatively inexpensive Verdun needed over 4,800 francs per year to meet his living and professional expenses. His salary provided only a bit less than 3,400 francs. See William Serman, *Les Officiers dans la nation: 1848–1914* (Paris: Aubier Montaigne, 1982).

[21] Officers of ambition without family money still had to marry well. Although the long-standing requirement of a dowry capable of generating 1,300 francs per year had been abolished as far back as 1900, this simply rendered a *de jure* requirement a *de facto* one. See Porch, *March to the Marne*, p. 29.

seem unreasonable, in short, to suggest that the military notables of the 3ᵉ Région attained their positions for three sets of reasons. First, they had no political enemies or stronger political friends. Second, they were believed simply to be "good" officers according to professional standards of the prewar army. Finally, they could secure the funds necessary to pay for their social role. None of these factors ensured continued success in August 1914.

The most public displays of the modus vivendi between the army and the Republic in the garrisons of France took place on the *fête nationale* of Bastille Day, July 14.[22] The army, for its part, could recover from its post-Dreyfus battering through basking in the affection of a forgiving Republic, while at the same time reliving the French tradition of military panache. Republicans, for their part, could simultaneously assert their devotion to a strong national defense and to the effective reassertion of civilian rule.

As one local newspaper put it: "In Rouen, as in all cities that have a garrison, the review of the troops is without question the high point of the *fête nationale*."[23] These spectacles would consist of a parade led by civil and military notables that would include all local regular-army infantry, cavalry, and artillery detachments. The festivities concluded with displays of military prowess at the local race track and speeches by the notables. After 1907, changes in the order of precedence at such functions required generals to march behind prefects and colonels behind subprefects, a reversal of the practice that had been in place since the time of Napoleon.[24] But little evidence of the animosities engendered by these changes appears in accounts of the celebrations, as newspapers of varying political shades competed with each other in their praise of the army. As the center-left *La Dépêche de Rouen et de Normandie* put it in July 1913: "The greatest progress that the army has made has been to become the image of the Republic, while at the same time becoming, as certain reactionary generals themselves recognize, 'the greatest army in the world.'"[25]

Though a relative dearth of material exists for junior officers, noncommissioned officers (NCOs) and common soldiers, the public compromise between the army and the Republic certainly proved less glamorous for

---

The original documents available to study this question are practically overwhelming. Since each officer needed approval from his commanding officer before he could marry, a dossier was prepared on the proposed marriage that included a police report on the wife and a marriage contract of frequently twenty-five pages or more detailing the future spouse's property and expectations. Particularly revealing would be a comparison of the wife's property and the husband's rate of promotion.

[22] On the history of Bastille Day celebrations, see R. Sanson, *Les 14 juillet, Fêtes et consciences nationales: 1789–1975* (Paris: Flammarion, 1976).

[23] *Journal de Rouen*, 15 July 1914.

[24] Porch, *March to the Marne*, p. 87. On the origins of the Napoleonic practices, see Jean-Paul Bertaud, "Napoleon's Officers," *Past and Present* (no. 112, August 1986), pp. 96–97.

[25] *La Dépêche de Rouen et de Normandie*, 15 July 1913.

them than for the military notables. For common soldiers, conscription remained what Napoleon had made it, in Isser Woloch's words, "the touchstone of the relationship between the state and civil society."[26] In the life cycles of young Frenchmen, obligatory military service was at best an interruption, at worst a serious strain on family economies. But in politically conservative Normandy, signs of antimilitarism were almost trivial.[27] No doubt partly because of a lack of material, antimilitarism in northern France has not received the attention it has in the south.[28]

The subdued reaction in Rouen to the passage of the Three-year Law in August 1913 perhaps best illustrated the character of the compromise between the army and the Republic there. The law sought to increase the number of trained active soldiers by adding a third year of compulsory military service. In the long run, this would have diminished the need to rely on less-indoctrinated reservists. Historians have portrayed the law as everything from a much-belated stopgap measure to counteract German military superiority to the last step in the triumph of bloody minded nationalists like President Raymond Poincaré. As debate over the law came to a climax in May 1913, protests broke out in several areas of France, mostly among young men about to be conscripted or currently serving conscripts who found their release from the army delayed by a year. The most serious incidents took place in the south, but nationally reported incidents also occurred in Paris, Mâcon, Nancy, and Châlons-sur-Marne.

In sharp contrast, the editor of the *Journal de Rouen* commented with pride that "never has the least indiscipline been reported among the troops stationed in our city."[29] The only incident of any sort reported in the local press was listed in the local news section of the *Journal de Rouen* on 22 May 1913, below an article reporting on a meeting of the local modern painting society. The incident involved suspicions that the usual meeting of retired soldiers at the Hôtel de Ville would be disrupted by an antimilitarist demonstration. The authorities canceled the meeting and, perhaps

---

[26] Isser Woloch, "Napoleonic Conscription: State Power and Civil Society," *Past and Present* (no. 111, May 1986), p. 101. See also Michel Bozon, *Les Conscrits: arts et traditions populaires* (Paris: Bibliothèque Berger-Levrault, 1981).

[27] Jean-Jacques Becker's survey of antimilitarism in the Calvados uncovered nothing more subversive for the entire period 1907–1913 than a handful of "seditious cries" and antimilitary posters. *Le Carnet B: les pouvoirs publics et l'anti-militarisme avant la guerre de 1914* (Paris: Éditions Klinksieck, 1973), pp. 93–102.

[28] The foremost student of antimilitarism in the south is Roland Andréani. See his "Armée et nation en Languedoc méditerranéen" (Thèse d'état, Université de Montpellier, 1975); and "Anti-militarisme en Languedoc avant 1914," *Revue d'histoire moderne et contemporaine* 20 (1973). See also J. Masse. "L'Anti-militarisme dans le Var avant 1914," *Cahiers d'histoire* 8 (1968); and Jules Maurin, *Armée, guerre, société: soldats languedociens, 1889–1919* (Paris: Publications de la Sorbonne, 1982), pp. 167–87.

[29] *Journal de Rouen et de Normandie*, 22 May 1913.

through force of habit, ordered the arrest of the secretary-treasurer of a construction workers' union in Rouen on the charge of inciting soldiers to desert.[30]

No convictions directly traceable to protests over the Three-year Law were handed down at the 24 May and 30 May meetings of the 3e Corps d'Armée court-martial, though there was the normal handful of convictions for draft evasion in peacetime.[31] The center-left but virulently anti-socialist *Dépêche de Rouen*, delighted at the rescuing of the Republic from the specter of socialist chaos, shouted its triumph on 8 July: "Now is not the time to let up. The Confédération général du Travail, which has been party to these atrocious excitations, must pay the penalty for its culpable wildness."[32] In conservative Normandy, the newspaper preached to the converted.

"*OFFENSIVE À OUTRANCE*" IN THE PROVINCES

Among those who have found the French army militarily wanting in August 1914, the doctrine of the offensive (also known as *offensive à outrance*) has been described in particularly scathing terms.[33] At the strategic level, the doctrine resulted in a quixotic assault on the "lost provinces" of Alsace and Lorraine, a hilly region ideally suited to the defense. At the tactical level, as will be shown, soldiers past a certain point were expected to pursue their objectives without regard whatsoever to casualties—hardly a doctrinal approach well suited to demographically inferior France. Moreover, the training of French soldiers in the new doctrine has been widely portrayed as gravely inadequate.

But it would seem that a logical problem exists in this conclusion. For surely if *offensive à outrance* was as misconceived as its critics maintain, poor indoctrination did not necessarily disserve French soldiers. Also, if other questions are posed besides military efficiency, the doctrine and its application have a variety of interesting implications. In fact, I would argue, the doctrine of the offensive existed mostly as a Parisian fad crudely

[30] *Dépêche de Rouen*, 2 July 1913.

[31] *Journal de Rouen*, 25, 31 May 1913.

[32] *Dépêche de Rouen*, 8 July 1913.

[33] See, for example, Douglas Porch, "Clausewitz and the French: 1871–1914," in *Clausewitz and Modern Strategy*, Michael I. Handel, ed. (London: Frank Cass, 1986), p. 287. In addition to the works cited earlier on the preparedness of the French army, see also Eugène Carrias, *La Pensée militaire française* (Paris: Presses Universitaires de France, 1960); Henri Contamine, *La Revanche, 1871–1914* (Paris: Berger Levrault, 1957); and Steven E. Miller, ed. *Military Strategy and the Origins of the First World War* (Princeton: Princeton University Press, 1985).

aped in the provinces.[34] The result proved a large discrepancy between the theory of the offensive and what was likely to happen once the theory was put into practice. In the events of August 1914, soldiers had to cope with this discrepancy largely on their own.

One of the most significant peculiarities in French prewar planning involved the contrast between the highly centralized nature of authority at the top of the command structure in wartime and its highly diffused nature at the bottom. Contrary to its historical reputation, the notorious Plan XVII was in fact a plan only for the *mobilization* of the French armies.[35] The plan did not necessarily mandate the disastrous offensive into Alsace and Lorraine. But operational authority in Plan XVII was far more centralized in the hands of the commander-in-chief (Gen. Joseph Joffre) than had been the case with previous French war plans.[36] Joffre had complete discretion to determine where the German threat lay and how best to deal with it, as well as complete authority in wartime to name and remove his subordinates.[37]

Even army commanders, in charge of hundreds of thousands of men, had limited operational discretion. Individual armies according to Plan XVII were to be directed according to a famous document drawn up by Col. Loyzeau de Grandmaison, "Instruction sur la conduite des grandes unités": "In an army, the importance of the manpower placed in action over the considerable extent of the front does not permit him [the army commander] to stop the battle formations or modify them considerably over the course of the action."[38] Any operational alterations could take place only under the close supervision of Joffre's liaison officers, who in the event essentially determined which commanders would be removed. As will be shown in chapter 3, the discretion of the army commander proved an especially thorny issue between Joffre and the commander of the Vᵉ Armée, which comprised the 5ᵉ DI.

---

[34] That shades of opinion existed within the military elite right up to 1914 has been suggested in Contamine, *La Revanche*, and in Michael Howard, "Men against Fire: The Doctrine of the Offensive in 1914," in Peter Paret, ed., *Makers of Modern Strategy: From Machiavelli to the Nuclear Age*, 2d ed. (Princeton: Princeton University Press, 1986), pp. 510–26.

[35] Jules Isaac, *Joffre et Lanrezac: étude critique des témoignages sur le rôle de la Vᵉ Armée (août 1914)* (Paris: Etienne Chiron, Editeur, 1922), pp. 15–22.

[36] See E. Desbrière, "La Genèse du Plan XVII," *Revue d'histoire de la guerre mondiale* 1 (1923), p. 108.

[37] See Ministère de la Guerre, *Les Armées françaises pendant la grande guerre* (Paris: Imprimerie Nationale, 1922–1939), tome 1, caps. 1 and 2. Hereafter in this study referred to as AFGG. See also (Anonymous) *Le Plan XVII: étude stratégique* (Paris: Payot & Cie., 1920), chap. 4.

[38] Etat-Major de l'Armée, 3ᵉ Bureau, Plans-Mobilization, 1874–1914, 7 N 1788. (The document is undated, but was probably written late in 1913.)

Corps commanders found themselves even more restricted than army commanders, since the general staff considered an army corps "no more than an organ of tactical execution." Infantry divisions, "by definition the weakest units comprising troops of all arms," were barely mentioned at all in the document, since they received "only short-term missions that maintain close dependence on superior authority."

This concentration of authority at the top of the French command structure contrasted sharply with the highly decentralized nature of authority at the bottom, where it reached the people at physical risk in battle. In a real sense, the infantry regulations in place in August 1914 gave junior officers, NCOs, and common soldiers more latitude over their behavior than Plan XVII gave army commanders. To some degree, this result responded to the problem inherent in any tactical doctrine. Tacticians must choose between dense formations, which maximize command control but which can expose troops to heavy losses from concentrated fire, and dispersed formations, which provide much more flexibility but much less direct control.[39] But the regulations in place in August 1914 were also a response to the acknowledged superiority of defensive firepower.

The last set of tactical regulations for the infantry issued before the war appeared in April 1914.[40] Although the impact of these rules on the training of the 5e DI before the war was limited, it may be assumed that all officers were familiar with them and that they constituted the closest thing to a theoretical foundation for the first battles of the war. Included are all the sins of omission and commission associated with *offensive à outrance*—the primacy of moral forces and the use of the bayonet in the final assault. Although the regulations do not belabor the point, they provide no delusions about the price to be paid by the infantry, whose task "cannot be fulfilled except through prolonged and constantly renewed efforts, with an enormous expenditure of physical and moral energy and with bloody sacrifices."[41]

Enemy positions were to be overcome in three stages: the approach, the attack, and the assault.[42] The overall objective involved minimizing the advantage of defensive firepower by minimizing the distance between the attackers and the defenders by bringing the defenders to within rifle range (about 500–600 yards) before provoking a major engagement. The first stage involved getting the attacking troops as close to the target as possible without drawing enemy fire, since at this stage "all maneuvers

[39] For a concise summary, see Joseph C. Arnold, "French Tactical Doctrine: 1870–1914," *Military Affairs* 42 (1978), pp. 61–67.

[40] Ministère de la Guerre, *Réglement de manoeuvre d'infanterie du 20 avril 1914* (Paris: Henri Charles Lavauzelle, 1914).

[41] Ibid., p. 126.

[42] See ibid., pp. 115–27.

under enemy fire [would] expose the infantry to useless losses."[43] At this stage, regimental colonels would command the operation in constant communication with battalion commanders, who would in turn have constant communication with company commanders.

The attack proper would begin when the battalion commanders communicated the particular objectives to the company commanders: "The companies of the first line must be able to fight as soon as they are on the point of penetrating the zone of fire of the enemy infantry. In consequence, the companies set up a line of sharp-shooters, sheltered as much as possible from sight and from fire, that progresses rapidly toward the enemy until the objective of the attack is visible."[44] Once the captains ordered fire to commence, authority would devolve to the section commanders. It was assumed that the different elements of the attacking infantry would be advancing unevenly, with the faster advancing units covering the slower ones.

Only at the last stage of an attack, the assault, would aggression without calculation of risk be given full reign. All firepower, offensive and defensive, was to be subordinated to moral force: "At this moment, the combatants have as one man the will to engage the enemy with the bayonet."[45] At the cry from officers and NCOs of "*En avant à la baïonnette*! [Forward with the bayonet!]" the hitherto dispersed formations would descend on the demoralized enemy in hand-to-hand combat. Given the near-absence of formal command authority at this stage, the expected unanimity of action could occur only with corresponding unity in the collective mind of the attackers.

Any doctrine so dependent on the state of mind of its soldiers had to require considerable indoctrination quite lacking in the French army of August 1914. The 1914 regulations represented a wishful prognosis of the state of the army after the reforms of the Three-year Law had been fully implemented. The regulations anticipated that soldiers would spend their first year becoming "soldiers of the ranks," learning only the "mechanics of movement" under the constant supervision of their immediate commanders.[46] Only in their second year would they become acquainted with the "special functions that might fall to a soldier on the field of battle."[47] In the third year, the more capable conscripts would become noncommissioned officers. It was hoped that in this manner, the long-standing and desperate shortage of sergeants and corporals could eventually be remedied.

[43] Ibid., p. 115.
[44] Ibid., p. 123.
[45] Ibid., p. 125.
[46] Ibid., pp. 14–15.
[47] Ibid.

In short, one may doubt that the Three-year Law, which was supposed to extend the doctrine of the offensive beyond the École Supérieur de Guerre and the Paris military *salons* into the countryside, actually made much difference in August 1914. The parsimonious Republic, which in any event drained its military budgets to fund the conquest of vast tracts of African deserts and Indochinese jungles, had long failed to fund the training its espoused doctrine required. As late as 1912, only one-third of active troops and one-quarter of the reservists would visit a training camp in any given year.[48]

Moreover, the first new conscripts under the Three-year Law, who comprised approximately one-third of the regular soldiers of August 1914 arrived with their units only after the fall of 1913. These soldiers had thus served only about ten months learning the "mechanics of movement" when they had to face the Germans in Belgium. The 3ᵉ CA commander in August 1914, Gen. Henry Sauret, complained in October 1914 that he had been given command of an army corps that "had not during this year undergone either instruction in shooting or a sojourn in the instruction camp. Their whole preparation in the application of the new infantry regulations thus had to be inevitably incomplete."[49]

The most prominent intrusion of tactical or even military indoctrination into what literary accounts described as the sleepy and even boring life of soldiers in the 3ᵉ Région was the yearly fall maneuvers.[50] Maneuvers have long provided fodder for critics of the "preparedness" of the French army before 1914, whatever their ideological or intellectual persuasions.[51] To be sure, prewar maneuvers partook more of Bastille Day military display (and the compromise between the army and the Republic that display exemplified) than of wartime offensives or trench warfare. But for exactly this reason, maneuvers demonstrated that French soldiers before the war were empty vessels, to be left to their own devices to learn how to conduct a war no one had meaningfully anticipated before August 1914.

Maneuvers took place in four-year cycles. During the first two years of the cycle, maneuvers were carried out at the divisional level, with the largest scale of simulated combat pitting brigade against brigade. In the third year, maneuvers took place at the army corps level, with the largest

[48] *France Militaire*, 9 and 15 February 1912, quoted in Porch, *March to the Marne*, p. 201.

[49] Personal dossier, Henry-Sebastien Sauret, Gx/3, G.D., 550.

[50] Literary sources for the prewar period include Lucien Descaves (129ᵉ RI in Le Havre), *Sous-Offs: roman militaire* (Paris: Éditions Stock, 1889); André Maurois (74ᵉ RI in Rouen, around 1903), *Mémoires* (Paris: Flammarion, 1970), chap. 5, "École de Compagnie"; and Henri Dutheil (general staff secretary, 5ᵉ DI), *De Sauret la honte à Mangin le boucher: roman comique d'un état-major* (Paris: Nouvelle Librairie Nationale, 1923).

[51] See, for example, Monteilhet, *Les Institutions militaires de la France*, p. 313; and Porch, *March to the Marne*, pp. 178–79.

scale of combat division versus division. Every fourth year, the celebrated *grandes manoeuvres* took place in which whole armies took part. The last *grandes manoeuvres* involving the 5ᵉ DI took place in Picardy in 1910. In other words, only some of the reservists in 1914 had any direct experience in maneuvers at the army level. The last simulated battle, in which approximately two-thirds of the regular 5ᵉ DI soldiers of August 1914 took part, were the army corps maneuvers of September 1913.

The maneuvers were divided into three parts, with competitive exercises at the regimental, divisional, and army corps levels. The attention paid to the physical frailty of the troops seems ironic in light of the physical demands that were to be made on them one year later: "The first day must not lead to very great fatigue on the part of the troops, and the theme of the operations must not be too complicated."[52] The first exercise of the 39ᵉ RI, for example, began at 0630, and had the losing team in headlong retreat by 0800. By 0900, the exercise was over, and "an absolute silence succeeded the rapid 'tac-tac-tac' of the machine guns, the crackling of the rifles, and the great voice of the canons."[53] Another, simpler maneuver was executed by 1030, and by 1330, the 39ᵉ RI was back in its bivouac. At the camp, "the excellent regimental band, always directed with talent by its kindly leader, M. Levêque, gave a concert very much appreciated in the countryside."[54]

Celebrations of martial ardor could not be marred even by a clearly bungled maneuver. In a night attack executed at 0200 on 7 September, a company of the 36ᵉ RI (from Caen) had managed to get itself entirely surrounded by the opposing team, which promptly charged *à la baïonnette*. In keeping with the spirit of the affair, the outnumbered company of the 36ᵉ RI responded in kind. Although the referee counted the entire company as casualties, the correspondent from the *Journal de Rouen* noted, "he did not reproach the foot soldiers of Caen for hurling themselves *à la baïonnette* on their adversaries. 'When one is in a bad situation, the best way out of it is to attack.' This is a concept that might have something to it; it is in any case that of a radical partisan of the offensive, which corresponds best to the French temperament."[55]

The most elaborate display was reserved for the last phase of the maneuvers, which pitted the 5ᵉ DI against the 6ᵉ DI for three uninterrupted days, 9–11 September. During the first two days, the maneuvers were observed by Vᵉ Armée commander Gen. Joseph Gallieni in the course of his yearly inspection. Initially, the 6ᵉ DI had very much the best of the exercise, with the 5ᵉ DI almost constantly in retreat or preparing defensive positions. By

---

[52] *Journal de Rouen*, 3 September 1913. The 1913 maneuvers may be followed here almost hour by hour, as well as in *La France militaire*.

[53] Ibid.

[54] Ibid.

[55] Ibid., 8 September 1913.

the last day, the white team (the 6^e DI) looked as though it would drive the opposing red team (the 5^e DI) from its position until a counterattack by the latter restored the balance, as if by *deus ex machina*. The ensuing spectacle, orchestrated to stop at exactly the appropriate moment, enabled all to return to their garrisons with their martial self-respect intact:

> An immense clamor arises from the field of battle, the musicians play, the flags wave. The charge accelerates and, marching double time, the masses fall one upon the other. It is only when they are upon each other that the officers intervene to stop them.
>
> All the generals are present at this supreme encounter. It is however, the *Marseillaise* whose tones rise up, followed by the *Chant du Depart* played by the band of the 39e Regiment. At other places on the battlefield, other bands play their favorite airs during which the formations of the encounter reconstitute themselves. . . . Finally, at 1:30 PM, the assembly called to order by General Valabrègue announces the end of the maneuvers, and this call is received by new clamors of joy.[56]

This rosy picture of the martial vigor of the local forces did not long endure. The *Journal de Rouen*, which had provided such glowing reports of the maneuvers themselves, ran a series of very different articles just one month later. It noted that the 3e Région militaire held the dubious honor of having the highest proportion of men in any region in France in its Class of 1913 fit only for auxiliary service (11.6 percent). Citing demon liquor as the culprit, the *Journal de Rouen* lamented the bygone days, "when Normandy furnished Napoleon with his most beautiful grenadiers."[57] In an article on the national shortage of active and reserve officers, the newspaper commented that "the latest maneuvers made more cruelly apparent the disquieting gaps that continue to render hollow the officer corps."[58] Even with the call-up of existing reserve officers, it was noted that in some units "in which a captain was indispensable, one saw certain groups reduced to a single officer, sometimes even a second-lieutenant."[59] Little had changed one year later.

General Gallieni wrote a scathing inspection report.[60] Although the report covered two other army corps in addition to the 3e CA, the opinions expressed in the report may help explain why Gallieni resigned command of the Ve Armée before the war broke out.[61] In his comments on the

[56] Ibid.
[57] Ibid., 15 October 1915.
[58] Ibid., 18 October 1913.
[59] Ibid.
[60] Fonds Gallieni: Documents divers, 1913–14, "1913: Rapports d'Inspection," 6 N 44.
[61] The ostensible reason for Gallieni's resignation was Joffre's refusal to expand the size of the northernmost French army, but Gallieni's opinion of the units under his command could

conduct of divisions, commanders of defensive positions were taken to task for being sufficiently cognizant of "neither the initial tactical position, nor the terrain, nor of the received defensive mission." His criticisms of attacks contained chilling premonitions of the disasters of the Battle of the Frontiers: "Although the attackers were informed of the presence of an enemy in defensive positions, and that they ran the risk of being surprised within range of the enemy batteries already in position, the attackers proceeded as though in a chance skirmish." Specifically, he complained that the attackers were supported only by a handful of advance guns rather than by the entirety of the artillery at the division's disposal.

On the deployment of the infantry itself, Gallieni added the remarkable criticism that "some units executed flank movements under the fire of enemy artillery and infantry." Moreover, "certain counter-attacks have been pronounced without a definite objective. Also, though launched quite correctly, they would have been predestined to fail disastrously, because they would have degenerated almost immediately into a disordered and undirected movement." Finally, he labeled the expertise of infantry rifle fire in the simulated combat of maneuvers "barely sketchy." Citing the perennial problem of insufficient instruction in the training camps, he concluded: "In fact, the battalion, the tactical unit of the infantry, whose instruction must be pushed to the highest degree and maintained with the greatest care, is never completely instructed. It is for this reason that the battalion continually falls into the same errors." Plainly, the practical implications of the compromise between the army and the Republic were not lost on Gallieni.

THE SOLDIERS AND OFFICERS OF THE 5e DIVISION D'INFANTERIE ON 4 AUGUST 1914

The drama of the mobilization unfolded in Rouen much as elsewhere in France. In the local press, a wave of apprehension following the assassination of Archduke Franz Ferdinand on 28 June shortly gave way to a fascination with the seamy but engrossing saga of Mme. Henriette Caillaux, whose trial began on 20 July.[62] Following the general mobilization ordered by President Poincaré on 1 August, the local press conveyed an image

---

scarcely have made his decision more difficult. See Jack Snyder, *The Ideology of the Offensive: Military Decision Making and the Disasters of 1914* (Ithaca: Cornell University Press, 1984).

[62] Mme. Caillaux, the wife of Interior Minister Joseph Caillaux, shot the editor of *Le Figaro* in response to that newspaper's publication of some love letters from Mr. Caillaux to his mistress, who later became his first wife. See Edward Berenson, *The Trial of Madame Caillaux* (Berkeley: University of California Press, 1992).

almost of bafflement followed by a firm but remarkably restrained resolution to prevail in the coming trial. The stridently nationalist *Journal de Rouen* wrote that the news of the mobilization "was received by our fellow citizens with emotion certainly, but with an equal degree of sangfroid and patriotic resignation."[63] Protest against the coming war was as muted as resistance to the Three-year Law had been.[64]

To be sure, a few unseemly displays of nationalist hysteria disrupted the otherwise dignified and well-ordered transition to war in Normandy, such as the crowd of some one thousand people in Rouen that destroyed the gardens in front of a local hotel when it sought an alleged traitor who uttered the cry "Down with the army!"[65] In Caen, a purveyor of candies had to convince hostile locals that he sold no German wares.[66] But overall, solemnity rather than crazed nationalism characterized local accounts. France, not having started the war, was nonetheless determined to finish it, and to settle the old score of Alsace and Lorraine at the same time. But for the time being, war aims as stated in an editorial in the *Dépêche de Rouen* went no further:

> Our firm belief is that Germany will lose even on the battlefield and that our boys who depart so gallantly will return bringing, not the Victory of Berlin, which is a pretentious horror, but the piece of territory that was torn from France forty-five years ago, from which the scar is not yet healed.[67]

In the flurry of haste that accompanied the mobilization, only the number of bodies under the colors was recorded without further specification. In most cases, common soldiers and noncommissioned officers were counted as one category.[68] Thus, most of what is known of the common soldiers of August 1914 consists of a few informative generalizations. The fifteen hundred or so soldiers from each regiment already on active duty when the war broke out may be presumed to be divided about equally

[63] *Journal de Rouen*, 2 August 1914.

[64] On 29 July, somewhere between four hundred and two thousand people (the estimates provided by the prefect and *L'Humanité*, respectively) led by railroad workers from the Rouen suburb of Sotteville turned out to protest the anticipated outbreak of war. This led officials to forbid demonstrations planned for 30 July in Rouen and Le Havre. Antiwar activities in the Calvados were limited to a demonstration involving some one hundred unionists and the seizure of a handful of antiwar pamphlets by the police. Becker, *1914*, pp. 152–55.

[65] *Journal de Rouen*, 3 August 1914.

[66] *Journal de Caen*, 6 August 1914.

[67] *Dépêche de Rouen*, 4 August 1914.

[68] According to one estimate, two-thirds of the NCOs were professionals in 1913. Over the course of the war, however, some 80 percent of the NCOs had been civilians or reservists before the war. Col. Pierre Carles, *Un Historique des sous-officiers français* (Vincennes: SIRPA-Terre, 1988), pp. 143, 163.

among the Classes of 1911, 1912, and 1913. Since the call-up of the class occurred at age twenty, this made them twenty-one to twenty-three years old. All were trained at a time of desperate shortage of noncommissioned officers, a shortage that was actually made worse by the increase in soldiers on active duty because of the Three-year Law.[69] As already suggested, much of the training they did receive had little to do with what would shortly be expected of them. Only the first two classes would have bene-fitted from the dubiously useful maneuvers of 1913. At best, they would have had only a passing familiarity with the infantry regulations of April 1914.

Perhaps the most striking observation that can be made concerning all the regular soldiers of August 1914 is the generally ignored fact that ap-proximately one-half of them were actually reservists.[70] Reservists from the four most recently retired classes, in this case, the classes of 1907–1910 (men aged 24–27) were mobilized in frontline active army units. The decades of controversy over "reserves" in fact involved the classes of 1903–1906 (ages 28 to 31), which were assigned to special reserve units, and were indeed kept from the front lines until dire necessity drew them into battle.[71] For the reservists mobilized with the active units, their military experience would have been a fading memory only sparsely refurbished by refresher training courses. In 1908, the biannual training period for reser-vists had been cut from sixty-nine to forty-nine days, for the reason that the shortage of training camps meant that too much time was simply frittered away in the barracks.[72] It is difficult to see how much of the particulars of the fad of the offensive could have trickled down to them.

More is known of the officers of the mobilization because of a list, the *état nominatif des officiers*, compiled on the first page of the regimental diary, the *Journal de Marche et des Opérations* (*JMO*). These lists provided the names of battalion, company, and section commanders on the day the regiments left Normandy.[73] These names may then be looked up in the

[69] See Porch, *March to the Marne*, p. 197. Low pay for NCOs and the meritocratic Napoleonic tradition of relatively open access to the officer corps were considered to be the most important explanations.

[70] See Jules Isaac, "L'Utilisation des réserves dans l'armée française et dans l'armée alle-mande en 1914," *Revue d'histoire de la guerre mondiale* 2 (1924), p. 328. The percentage of reservists in regular units was approximately the same as in the German army. The figure even in the relatively professional British army that landed in France was about 40 percent.

[71] On how varying attitudes over reserves affect the predecessors of Plan XVII, see E. Desbrière, "La Genèse du Plan XVII"; and Snyder, *The Ideology of the Offensive*, pp. 57–106.

[72] See Porch, *March to the Marne*, p. 204.

[73] See 26 N 618 (39e RI), 26 N 612 (36e RI), 26 N 686 (129e RI). No *état nominatif* exists for the fourth regiment, the 74e RI, but an approximation has been made based on the regimental register of officers.

regimental registers, which provide a two-page resumé (the *état des services*) for each officer.[74] Information has been gathered on 148 active and reserve officers directly exercising command authority over infantry troops at the mobilization. It must be stressed that this parting snapshot proved quite ephemeral. As will be shown in the next chapter, officers suffered comparable casualty rates to those of the men who served under them.

Considered as a group, several interesting characteristics of the officers of the mobilization stand out.[75] The career officers of the 5ᵉ DI comprised a composite of graduates of the military academy of Saint-Cyr and of men who had risen through the ranks through a one-year course for infantry NCOs at Saint-Maixent. Nearly 60 percent of the lieutenants had been promoted from the ranks. Approximately one-third of the captains had had experience in the colonies, though virtually no one below that rank had. The average age of about fifty for majors and about forty for captains suggests that the 3ᵉ Région was something of a backwater, an area that attracted career officers who could complete their careers in peace and security, but who did not entertain much hope of achieving great things.

Perhaps the most striking characteristic of the junior officers of the 5ᵉ DI is that there were not nearly enough of them.[76] A fully mobilized active regiment should have had fifteen lieutenants (one for each company, plus one commanding each of three machine-gun companies). In each addition, each regiment was supposed to have had twelve regular army second-lieutenants, plus twelve reserve lieutenants, and twelve reserve second-lieutenants. The deficits are shown in table II-1. These figures indicate that throughout the 5ᵉ DI, second-lieutenants were performing the duties of lieutenants, reserve officers the duties of active ones, and NCOs the duties of officers.[77] Although precise figures are not available, it is certain given the deficit in the army as a whole that at least a comparable deficit existed in the NCO ranks.

Even among those junior officers present, of the forty-three lieutenants on active duty, no less than thirty-one had held that rank for over five years, nineteen for over eight years. This reinforces the image of the 3ᵉ Région as a backwater, since the vast majority of the lieutenants in the 5ᵉ DI plainly were not headed for brilliant military careers. The shortage of fully trained

---

[74] These registers do not have carton numbers and are identified simply as *contrôle des officiers* for the regiment in question.

[75] See Smith, "Command Authority," pp. 82–84.

[76] For each regiment, there are many officers listed in the *Annuaire des officiers* as being on active duty who do not appear in the *état nominatifs*. While the reasons for the discrepancies are not entirely clear, the explanation is probably that most of the missing officers were placed in reserve units or were considered unfit to go on campaign.

[77] The shortage of junior officers in the French army had deep roots. Applications to Saint-Cyr fell from 1,870 in 1900 to 880 in 1912, and to Saint-Maixent from 810 to 380 in the same period. *France militaire*, 12 June 1912.

TABLE II-1
Deficits in Junior Officers, 5ᵉ DI, August 1914

Rank	39ᵉ RI	74ᵉ RI	36ᵉ RI	129ᵉ RI	Total 5ᵉ DI
Lt.	3	2	6	5	16 (of 60)
2d Lt.	10	7	5	4	26 (of 40)
Lt. (res.)	11	n.a.	7	10	28 (of 36)
2d Lt. (res.)	3	n.a.	0	3	6 (of 36)

active second-lieutenants is actually much worse than these figures indicate, since Saint-Cyr and Saint-Maixent were emptied at the mobilization
to help fill the army's deficit in junior officers. No less than twenty of the
twenty-two second-lieutenants for whom information on education is
available were actually cadets, thirteen of them at Saint-Cyr and seven at
Saint-Maixent. Although reserve second-lieutenants were relatively plenti-
ful, all of the officers for whom information is available had received their
reserve commissions through the debatably successful program to create
élèves officiers de réserve.[78] When this already inadequate encadrement
was severely depleted in the first days of fighting, the stage was set for a
thorough transformation of the lower-level leadership.

In short, the politics of ideological conflict and practical compromise did
much to shape the character of military institutions and experience in
France before August 1914. The Republic kept the army poor, politically
constrained, and on the parade ground. The army remained suspicious and
wanting self-esteem, which it sought through a perilous new doctrine of
the offensive. The Republic and the army met in ritual, which displayed
their working relationship but which proved quite irrelevant to real wartime experience. In military ritual, whether on the Bastille Day parade
ground or on the simulated battlefield of army maneuvers, commanders
and soldiers performed more or less according to the Clausewitzian ideal.
Military notables led, while more and less ambitious officers, along with
NCOs and conscripts, followed. But, perhaps inevitably, the rituals of parade and maneuver disguised a potential for Clausewitz's "friction" that
few foresaw before the shooting started. The wartime dynamic of authority
relations emerged from this potential friction, as the most trained and the
least trained commanders and soldiers in the French army ended up learning the art of real war together.

[78] This program was created in 1905 to overcome the dire shortage in the junior officer
ranks and to sweeten the pill of conscription for the abler draftees. After one year of service in
the ranks, a soldier passing the required exams could spend his second year in a reserve officer
training program, the first half with the rank of *aspirant* and the second with the rank of
second-lieutenant in the reserve. See Col. Pierre Guinard, Jean-Claude Devos, and Jean Nicot,
Inventaire sommaire des archives de la guerre: Série N (1872–1919) (Troyes: Imprimerie La
Renaissance, 1975), p. 27.

CHAPTER III

The Battles of August–September 1914

THE PIECES OF DEFEAT, VICTORY, AND PROPORTIONALITY

"THE HISTORY of a battle," the Duke of Wellington once observed, "is not unlike the history of a ball!"[1] Certainly, if a ball comprises hundreds of conflicting or contradictory individual and collective narratives, a battle comprises thousands. Traditional military history, in John Keegan's memorable analogy to Anglo-Saxon jurisprudence, has tended to generate a particular kind of narrative, designed to ascertain a particular point. The story ends when a "verdict" has been reached as to whether a battle or war has been won or lost.[2] But examining how the parameters of command authority in the French army changed over the course of World War I calls for a different type of battle narrative, an "inquisitory" approach, drawing on Keegan's analogy to Roman jurisprudence. This chapter thus begins with an explanation of the alternative narrative approach used here. The concepts of "defeat" and "victory" by no means disappear from the analysis. But my objective is to develop an alternative narrative technique explaining how confrontations and negotiations took place within the power relationship linking French soldiers and commanders.

Certainly, the first month of the war lends itself to intense narration. For the 5ᵉ DI, more days of pitched battle and maneuver took place in the first month of the war than in the next seventeen months put together. Many of the possible outcomes occurred in one form or another in an amazingly compressed time—not only unambiguous defeat and victory, but also complete obedience and disobedience, as well as much in between. Collectively, these experiences involved a phenomenon analyzed by Eric Leed and others as "liminality," in which preexisting conceptions about war were suddenly and brutally stripped away as soldiers experienced actual battle for the first time.[3] So much happened so fast that it is useful to think of the

---

[1] Quoted in John Keegan, *The Face of Battle: A Study of Agincourt, Waterloo and the Somme* (New York: The Viking Press, 1976), p. 117.

[2] See the brilliant discussion of the traditional battle narrative and its limitations in ibid., chap. 1.

[3] See Eric Leed, *No Man's Land: Combat and Identity in World War I* (Cambridge: Cambridge University Press, 1979), especially pp. 12–33. See also Richard Holmes, *Acts of War: The Behavior of Men in Battle* (New York: The Free Press, 1985), chap. 2.

experiences of this period almost as a collection of pieces, which would be
sorted out by soldiers and their commanders over the rest of the war.

THE "DOCUMENTARY" AND THE "WORKLIKE"
IN THE BATTLE PIECE

To its protagonists at all levels, a battle exists at first only in fragments,
whether through scraps of delayed and often misleading information trick-
ling back to the command centers during the battle, or through the isolated
world of all but indescribable chaos experienced by actual combatants.
The documentary record, whether orders, reports, or memoirs, comprises
efforts to impose a cognative order on the battle, situated at various points
in relation to it in time. A battle is constructed historically through continuing this rendering of textual information.

According to military history tradition, the basis for the imposed cognative order on battle has been distinguishing who "won" from who "lost,"
and why. As the work of Hayden White suggests, the requirements of the
"win/lose" narrative have done much to determine which questions military historians ask and where they look to find answers.[4] Military history
has been what White called "ironic" history *par excellence*. The detachment and "objectivity" of time and distance have afforded the professional
historian an inherently superior position from which to pass judgment.
Military historians, like military commanders, have tended to believe that
in the end, the outcome of battles is determined largely by the quality of
leadership. Accordingly, documents generated by the uppermost reaches of
the authority structure—such as orders, official histories, and memoirs of
great personnages—have received a highly privileged status. Other forms
of documentation, even when brought to bear by the most thoughtful and
talented military historians, have generally been used in a strictly supporting role, to demonstrate the constructed effectiveness or ineffectiveness of
the authority structure.

But different questions can be addresssed only with different sorts of
narratives. In order to structure battle narratives in this study, I have bor-
rowed an idea from the intellectual historian Dominick LaCapra (who in
turn drew from Martin Heidigger).[5] LaCapra made a distinction in any

[4] See Hayden White, *Metahistory: The Historical Imagination in Nineteenth-Century
Europe* (Baltimore: Johns Hopkins University Press, 1973); and *The Content of the Form:
Narrative Discourse and Historical Representation* (Baltimore: Johns Hopkins University
Press, 1987).

[5] Dominick LaCapra, "Rethinking Intellectual History and Reading Texts," in *Rethinking
Intellectual History: Texts, Contexts, Language* (Ithaca: Cornell University Press, 1983), pp.
23–71. The most relevant text from Heidigger is "The Origin of the Work of Art," in *Poetry,*

primary or secondary text between the "documentary," which records empirical reality, and the "worklike" (the rest of a text's meaning). He maintained that by focusing on the documentary, historians (intellectual and otherwise) unnecessarily foreshorten the limits of historical imagination. Intellectual historians, for example, concentrate on those writers whose lives and works most lend themselves to paraphrase and thus to the construction of what in the end are empirically derived narratives. To apply this observation to conventional military history, the empirical reality dominating the documentary approach has involved explaining how particular pieces of territory came to be occupied by definable quantities of men and materiel—the end result being a battle won or a battle lost.

In contrast to the documentary, the "worklike," according to LaCapra, can be drawn out only through imagination, speculation, and interpretation. Not surprisingly, the concept is highly malleable and transitory. Indeed, it is virtually open-ended:

> The "worklike" supplements empirical reality by adding to it and subtracting from it. It thereby involves dimensions of the text not reducible to the documentary, prominently including the roles of commitment, interpretation, and imagination. The worklike is critical and transformative, for it deconstructs and reconstructs the given, in a sense repeating it but also bringing into the world something that did not exist before it in that significant variation, alternation, or transformation.[6]

The distinction between the "documentary" and the "worklike" is itself somewhat arbitrary in any historical document, depending largely on whether one believes in the existence of an objective historical "reality" apart from the texts that identify it. In any event, the problem with a concept as expansive as "worklike" is that it can be deconstructed and reconstructed into incoherence. My intention is to expand the possibilities of the battle narrative by exploring tensions and ambiguities in a wide variety of historical texts, without becoming totally absorbed in the intricacies of contemporary literary theory.

To bridge the gap between the familiar and the experimental, I will provide here two accounts of each battle. A "documentary" or "win/lose" narrative will provide a severely simplified paraphrase of the empirical outcome of the battle in the conventional sense. In a parallel "worklike"

Language, Thought, Alfred Hofstadter, trans. (New York: Harper & Row, 1975). A fine short survey of the work of both White and LaCapra appears in Lloyd S. Kramer, "Literature, Criticism, and Historical Imagination: The Literary Challenge of Hayden White and Dominick LaCapra," in Lynn Hunt, ed. *The New Cultural History* (Berkeley: University of California Press, 1989), pp. 97–128.

6 LaCapra, "Rethinking Intellectual History," p. 130.

narrative, I will construct a body of experience through interpreting the documentary record in which soldiers and their commanders negotiated the parameters of each others' authority. It bears repeating here that "soldier" refers to someone receiving an order at the time he receives it, independent of military rank. For reasons of clarity and euphony, I will refer to the narratives simply as "win/lose" and "experiential."

SOLDIERS WITHOUT COMMANDERS: THE PIECES OF DEFEAT AT CHARLEROI

The win/lose narrative of the 5ᵉ DI's role in the Battle of Charleroi can be easily established.[7] Charleroi was a clear-cut German victory that could have ended the war had the Vᵉ Armée and the British forces not escaped envelopment by retreating.[8] In conventional military history parlance, the battle was more lost by the French than won by the Germans, at both the strategic and operational levels. The German numerical superiority in men and artillery was real, but not in itself decisive.[9]

The heart of the strategic problem for the French was the position of the Vᵉ Armée, assigned to protect the French left flank along the Belgian frontier. Gen. Joseph Joffre, the supreme French commander, did not want the Vᵉ Armée to advance beyond the Sambre River so that it could support an attack on the German center by the IIIᵉ and IVᵉ Armées.[10] Vᵉ Armée commander Gen. Charles Lanrezac, in contrast, believed that the principal threat to the French forces lay in a German invasion through Belgium, the magnitude of which he considered clear as soon as the Germans violated Belgian neutrality on August 4.[11] It will be recalled from chapter 2 that the French war plan highly circumscribed the operational discretion even of army commanders. As a result, Lanrezac argued, Joffre had left the Vᵉ Armée in a sort of limbo, forbidden to advance far enough into Belgium to link up with the Belgian army, but still committed to some sort of offensive

---

[7] The 5ᵉ DI's sector was actually some four kilometers to the east of Charleroi, but for purposes of clarity, the generally known name of the battle will be used here.

[8] Throughout this study, French terms such as *armée, régiment, bataillon*, and *compagnie* will be used after an identifying number and capitalized to indicate proper names.

[9] Henri Contamine has estimated that in the Vᵉ Armée sector, 235 French and British infantry battalions faced 264 German ones. The French and British had 227 batteries of light artillery and 21 batteries of heavy artillery, while the Germans had 252 light batteries and 36 heavy batteries. "Réflexions sur les forces en présence à la bataille des frontièrs," *Revue d'histoire de la guerre mondiale* 16 (1938), p. 38.

[10] Joseph Joffre, *Mémoires: 1910–1917*, 2 vols. (Paris: Plon, 1932), vol. 1, pt. 2, chaps. 2–3.

[11] See Gen. Charles Lanrezac, *Le Plan de campagne français et le premier mois de la guerre (2 août–3 septembre 1914)* (Paris: Payot & Cie., 1921), chap. 2.

posture. His army had thus been prevented from setting up proper defensive positions.[12]

The positioning of the 5e DI along the Sambre epitomized the ambiguous position of the Ve Armée (see map III-1).[13] As of 20 August, the forward guard of the division (only one battalion, from the 39e Régiment d'Infanterie) was responsible for securing access across the Sambre from Montagnies-sur-Sambre to Pont-de-Loup. This meant protecting one bridge in Montagnies-sur-Sambre, three bridges in Châtelet, and one bridge in Pont-de-Loup. The rest of the division was posted well behind the forward positions, too far back to be able to quickly engage the Germans on the other side of the river or even to set up a strong defensive position to protect the passages themselves. There is no evidence that Lanrezac, the 3e CA or the 5e DI commanders had any idea that the Germans were as close to the Sambre on 20 August as proved the case.

Once the Germans took the crossings at Farcines and Roselies by nightfall on 21 August, the 3e CA and 5e DI commands made a problematic situation much worse. At 2100, 5e DI commander Gen. Elie-Joseph Verrier ordered a counterattack on Roselies to be executed at 0030 on 22 August by two battalions of the 74e RI. The attack, his orders stated, would "affirm our moral superiority,"[14] and was undertaken upon "the advice of the general commanding the 3e Corps."[15] Neither division nor the corps commanders appeared to have had reliable intelligence concerning German strength at the crossings, or even to have ordered artillery support. The entire division artillery regiment (a total of 36 of the 75mm pieces) was posted well behind the front lines, with the mission of protecting the main body of the divisional infantry and the relief of the frontline units.[16]

[12] The weight of historical opinion has come to rest with Lanrezac's interpretation. Jules Isaac nicely summarized both sides of the story and, in the best French academic tradition, split the difference. *Joffre et Lanrezac: Étude critique des témoinages sur le rôle de la Ve Armée (août 1914)* (Paris: E. Chiron, 1922).

[13] This narrative derives principally from the regimental diaries (*Journal des Marches et des Opérations* [JMOs] from the 5e DI and its constituent units. The archival references are as follows: 5e DI (26 N 268); 9e Brigade d'Infanterie (26 N 497); 10e Brigade d'Infanterie (26 N 498); 36e Régiment d'Infanterie (26 N 612); 129e Régiment d'Infanterie (26 N 686); 39e Régiment d'Infanterie (26 N 618); 74e Régiment d'Infanterie (26 N 660); 274e Régiment d'Infanterie (26 N 735); 43e Régiment d'Artillerie (26 N 980). Hereafter, these documents will be identified in the text simply as the JMO for the unit in question. The JMO for the 3e CA for August–September 1914 is currently missing from the Vincennes archives.

[14] Ordre Général No.22 (for 22 August 1914), 5e DI, 3e Bureau, "Ordres d'Opérations," 24 N 78.

[15] 5e DI JMO, 21 August 1914.

[16] Given the lack of attention in French doctrine to the coordination of artillery and infantry even during attacks, Verrier's deployment is not in itself surprising. See Lt. Col. M. Aublet, "L'Artillerie française de 1914 à 1918," *Revue militaire française* 33 (1929), sec. 3, pp. 350–53.

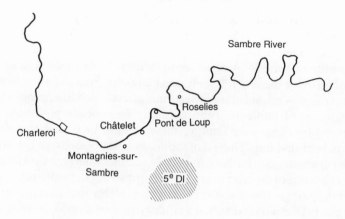

MAP III-1. The Sambre Valley, 20 August 1914

At around 0300 on 22 August, Verrier received word that the attack on Roselies had failed with heavy casualties. Undaunted, he ordered a new attack on Roselies at daybreak by two battalions from the 129e RI and one from the 36e RI. This attack met with similar results, as did two more attacks ordered for 1015. In the wake of these disasters, Verrier attempted around 1055 to order a general offensive by the 5e DI. But by noon, he recognized the inevitable and ordered a retreat that had already begun in the field without his intervention. In all, the 5e DI had retreated over ten kilometers since first making contact with the Germans. Similar or worse situations prevailed elsewhere in the Ve Armée, and by the evening of August 23, General Lanrezac communicated to General Joffre his intention to order the retreat of the entire Ve Armée.[17] This withdrawal had also begun in advance of the orders authorizing it.

At 0430 on 24 August the German pursuit in the sector of the 5e DI began with artillery attack with "efficacious fire that, it seemed, had a terrible effect on morale."[18] At this point, serious signs of disintegration emerged in both the 3e CA and the 5e DI commands. Half of the division (the 10e Brigade, comprising the 36e RI and the 129e RI) did not receive an itinerary of the retreat until 0530, by which time it was daylight. As a

[17] Ve Armée, Télégramme a G.Q.G., no. 241, 21h30, 23 August 1914, in AFGG, tome 1 (Annexe), no. 1120.
[18] 5e DI JMO, 24 August 1914.

result, a retreat under cover of darkness was impossible, and the "disengagement was painful."[19] The 39e RI received no itinerary at all, and retreated completely on its own.[20] As the day progressed, however, the retreat of the division became more organized and continued with relatively few casualties until the stand near Guise on 29 August.

The Battle of Charleroi was the second costliest battle fought by the 5e DI during the entire war, exceeded only by the attack at Douaumont near Verdun in 1916. As gleaned from the *JMO*s, total casualties were 49 officers and 3,891 NCOs and common soldiers. In other words, some 20 percent of the infantry officers and some 32 percent of the infantry NCOs and common soldiers were killed, wounded, or missing.[21] Of course, these figures must be used with some caution, since some of the wounded would eventually have been able to return to the fight. Also, over 1,000 of the NCOs and common soldiers were reported missing; a number probably turned up later during the retreat. But in all, only the fact that the 5e DI avoided annihilation or encirclement by departing mitigated the calamity that was the Battle of Charleroi.

The experiential narrative will argue that the win/lose outcome the Battle of Charleroi inadvertently provided a formative lesson in self-reliance for the soldiers of the 5e DI.[22] This lesson was based in the results of an extreme divergence of views as to the utility of aggression on the battlefield. The command structure more or less ordered the combat soldiers into a trap, then itself collapsed as the French position deteriorated. For the people at physical risk, the command structure first provided inappropriate direction, and then none at all. Consequently, battlefield soldiers ended up disregarding command intentions (such as they were) and imposing their own solution on the situation.

Of course, this study is hardly the first to observe that, professional myth aside, soldiers do not normally allow themselves to be massacred if they have any say in the matter. The point here may seem obvious, but it remains significant. From the first days of the war, battlefield soldiers made their own calculation of the military utility of their efforts and imposed their own version of proportionality on the command structure. At Charleroi, soldiers of the 5e DI drew their own conclusions from the pieces of defeat.

General Verrier's Ordre Général No. 22 provided the key to the division command's understanding of the situation: "The general commanding the

---

[19] Ibid.

[20] 39e RI *JMO*, 24 August 1914.

[21] These percentages are based on round figures of 280 infantry officers (including the DI staff) and 12,000 NCOs and common soldiers (four regiments at 3,000 men per regiment).

[22] It bears repeating here that throughout this study, the term "soldier" refers to someone receiving an order at the time he receives it, independent of rank.

5ᵉ DI has insisted on affirming our moral superiority to the enemy in ordering a counterattack on Roselies."[23] The result was the ill-fated plan to retake the lost crossings of the Sambre without artillery support or even reliable intelligence as to German strength. Henri Dutheil, a staff secretary with the 5ᵉ DI, described the reactions of the division command to the fall of Roselies on 21 August.[24] According to Dutheil, the senior divisional staff resolutely refused to comprehend the gravity of the situation, and seized upon the most optimistic scenario:

> As night fell, the most menacing rumors circulated. When the reports arrived, they no longer corresponded to the situations they claimed to elucidate. Orders are contradictory, inexecutable. With the phone ringing the entire evening Lucien [a lieutenant on the division staff] never left the receiver. *Roselies has fallen into the hands of the enemy. What is to be done?* Retake the village at any cost. Two hours later a reconnaissance patrol reported that Roselies seemed unoccupied. So then, we have to install ourselves there in order to prevent an eventual return of the adversary.[25]

The need to reverse the setback appears to have served as a sort of informational filter that predisposed the divisional command to accept without confirmation the report that Roselies was unoccupied, for reasons that do not seem difficult to decipher. The loss of the bridges across the Sambre would mean the end of French offensive hopes in Belgium. If Roselies were conceded as lost, the war would have come to the French, precisely the situation the doctrine of the offensive and Plan XVII were supposed to avoid. Verrier's order suggests that for him the critical issue remained a moral one, to which physical circumstance had to be subordinated.

The 5ᵉ DI command slid from misdirection to providing no direction at all, as the division and army corps commands collapsed before the German artillery assault on 24 August. An inquest conducted in the fall of 1914 by Lanrezac's replacement as Vᵉ Armée commander, Gen. Louis Franchet d'Esperey, thoroughly documented the ensuing vacuum in command authority.[26] Just to cite a few of many possible examples, in his summary report to Joffre, Franchet d'Esperey repeated Sauret's claim that Verrier "absolutely lost his head, acted contrary to my orders, and left his troops without direction in an incoherent manner."[27] Captain Bourgine of the 3ᵉ

---

[23] 5ᵉ DI, 3ᵉ Bureau, Ordres d'opérations, 4 August 1914–17 May 1917, 24 N 78.

[24] Henri Dutheil, *De Sauret la honte à Mangin le boucher* (Paris: Nouvelle Librairie Nationale, 1923). Dutheil was a Parisian *literato* who dedicated his book to the pornographer and Action Française notable Leon Daudet.

[25] Ibid., p. 50. Emphasis in original.

[26] The resulting documents from the inquest are divided among the Sauret and Verrier personal dossiers (Gx/3, G.D. 500 and Gx/3 G.D. 500, respectively).

[27] Franchet d'Esperey to Joffre, 6 November 1914, in Sauret personal dossier.

CA staff commented that by 23 August, Verrier "seemed no longer to be able to keep his attention on anything but details far removed from the operations."[28] Captain Dhé, another staff officer from the 3ᵉ CA, maintained that a lieutenant on the division staff exercised effective command during these days.[29]

Sauret, for his part, fared no better in the inquest. Colonel Belle, commander of the 3ᵉ CA engineers, arrived at 3ᵉ CA headquarters in Chastres at about 1600 on 23 August to deliver a reconnaissance report requested by Sauret.[30] He was surprised to hear from a common soldier that "they've all gone." Belle put himself at the disposition of Gen. Gabriel Roquerol, commander of the 3ᵉ CA artillery, who by coincidence had arrived at Chastres at about the same time. Roquerol himself reported that Sauret could not be located until after 2100 on 23 August, when he was finally briefed on events on his own army corps.[31] When Roquerol tried to find the 3ᵉ CA headquarters the next day, it had disappeared again. At this point, Roquerol apparently assumed de facto command of the 3ᵉ CA.[32] When Sauret and Roquerol finally met again early on 25 August, an ugly scene ensued over the conduct of the corps command structure.

It is difficult to gauge the immediate effect of this vacuum in command authority on the battlefield soldiers of the 5ᵉ DI. It will be shown shortly that junior commanders could encounter great difficulties finding their immediate superiors for hours at a time; they were probably then not much concerned with events at the 3ᵉ CA or 5ᵉ DI general staffs. But it seems clearer that the episode became clearly etched into the memory of the division's combat experience. A bicycle messenger from the 74ᵉ RI, Charles Toussaint, recalled how an officer from another division, Col. Jean Estienne of the 22ᵉ Régiment d'Artillerie, informed the colonels commanding the 74ᵉ, 39ᵉ, and 36ᵉ RI that they were basically on their own.[33]

---

[28] "Compte rendu du Capitaine Bourgine de l'E.M. de 3ᵉ Corps d'Armée au sujet de certains faits se rapportant au debut de la campagne et concernant MM. les Généraux Verrier et Bloch," 2 November 1914, Sauret personal dossier. It is worth noting that staff officers proved remarkably adept at avoiding removal themselves.

[29] "Compte-rendu de Capitaine Dhé de l'État-Major du 3ᵉ Corps d'Armée au sujet de faits reprochés au généraux Verrier et Bloch," in ibid. For Sauret's communications with Lanrezac, see 3ᵉ CA, 3ᵉ Bureau, Correspondance expédiée, 6 August–31 December 1914, 22 N 99.

[30] "Rapport de Colonel Belle, Cdt. le Génie de la 3ᵉ Corps d'Armée, au sujet de certains faits dont il a été témoin dans les journées du 23 et 25 août, 1914," 2 November 1914, in Sauret personal dossier.

[31] Untitled report by Roquerol, 2 November 1914, in ibid.

[32] Joffre commented of Roquerol in his memoirs: "In the 3ᵉ CA, during the whole part of the Battle of Charleroi, orders could only be given by General Roquerol, commander of the corps artillery, who had to take command during the most critical part of the day, when the corps commander could not be located." *Mémoires*, vol. 2, p. 302.

[33] This same Estienne was the father of the French army's first tank units.

I can still see Colonel Estienne, standing solidly with his feet apart, his képi disheveled, organizing some sort of park for his cannons. Energetically, and without mincing words, he addressed the three colonels, saying in substance: "S[auret] and V[errier] have taken off. We now have to shift for ourselves, and to assign roles and positions to occupy."[34]

Clearly the formal channels of command authority no longer existed in the same form. As a bicycle messenger, Toussaint was in an ideal position to disseminate this information among his comrades.

Our understanding of World War I combat has provided graphic images of what actually happened on the battlefield in the kind of situation in which the 5e DI found itself at Charleroi. Dutheil described the first infantry attacks according to standard literary conventions well established by the time his account was published in 1923. Dutheil described a massacre of the innocents and ended his story there. Soldiers were led to the slaughter through the willful blindness of their commanders; these soldiers acquiesced, tragically, but unquestioningly:

> The tactic was the following: as soon as they supposed that they recognized the line held by the enemy and determined the distance between us and them, it was *"En avant, à la baïonnette!"* The Germans, well hidden, had to do nothing more than fire on the pile of them.
>
> I saw the division crumble away. . . . In thirty minutes it was finished. France had broken the point of her sword.[35]

It must be stressed that Dutheil could not have witnessed the attack firsthand unless he had abandoned his duties as staff secretary. But the sort of image he evokes has come to be accepted as the unvarnished truth, despite the fact that if this were so, every last soldier should have ended up a casualty. Attention, my argument suggests, must be directed not just toward how World War I attacks began, but how they ended and by whose authority.

Even such apparently unpromising documents as the regimental diaries (*JMO*s) permit such an analysis. The spare account in the *JMO* of the 74e RI suggests that the soldiers assigned the task of carrying out the initial counterattack on Roselies reacted differently to the discrepancy between expectations and physical reality than did Verrier and Sauret. At about 0030, the 1e and 3e Bataillons left Aiseau for Roselies, a march of about three

---

[34] Charles Toussaint, *Petites Histoires d'un glorieux régiment: vecues par Charles Toussaint, soldat de 1ere classe au 74e Régiment d'Infanterie en guerre* (Montvillieres [Seine-Maritime]: Binesse, 1973), p. 7.

[35] Dutheil, *De Sauret la honte*, p. 52.

kilometers. The 1ᵉ Bataillon approached from the east, the 3ᵉ from the west:

> The battalions were able to penetrate the village, whose issues were not guarded. Some groups were even able to get as far as the outskirts of the other side of the village. Toward 0300, a violent fusillade broke out from the houses inside the village, which were organized defensively with machine guns.
>
> Violent fighting in the streets ensued, and the 74ᵉ suffered very heavy casualties. The units could not even figure out a way to retreat.

Though this is fundamentally a straightforward story of an ambush, there had to have been more going on here than first meets the eye. An attack by two battalions in August 1914 would have involved about 2,000 men (including the officers). Casualty reports, though inevitably somewhat suspect for this chaotic first phase of the war, by no means indicate total annihilation. The casualties for the whole regiment reported in the 5ᵉ DI *JMO* (all ranks) comprised 42 killed, 258 wounded, and 841 missing. Even if every single casualty came from the two battalions attacking Roselies and every single man reported missing was permanently *hors de combat* (disabled), some 50 percent of the attackers survived, despite the allegation that the units found themselves so heavily engaged that they were not even able to determine a line of retreat.

The *JMO* accounts of the attack on Roselies at dawn on 22 August by two battalions from the 129ᵉ RI reveal a similar tale. They also show how the gap between the theory and the practice of the doctrine of the offensive was filled in by battlefield soldiers themselves. The attack by the 129ᵉ RI had the intentions both of rescuing the soldiers from the 74ᵉ RI and of fulfilling the original goal of throwing the Germans back across the Sambre. In principle, the divisional command structure had learned its lesson, and had ordered artillery support from one group (comprising twelve 75s) from the divisional artillery, though the evidence strongly suggests that artillery support did not appreciably reduce the risk incurred by the attackers.[36]

The *JMO* of the 129ᵉ RI recounted an attack that actually followed the April 1914 infantry regulations fairly closely. The attackers endeavored to get as close to the enemy lines as possible without provoking a response.

---

[36] It is hard to know just what the artillery would have been firing at, since presumably troops from the 74ᵉ RI were still trapped in the village. A twenty-one-year-old conscript in the 43ᵉ RA, Jacques Brunel de Pérard, did not smell powder at all on either 21 or 22 August, although he was not assigned to the group supporting the Roselies attack. As late as 1600 on 23 August, he was able to report that "my battery has not yet fired, and the other two in the group have fired but very little. . . ." *Carnet de route, 4 août–25 septembre 1914* (Paris: Georges Crès & Cie., Editeurs, 1915), p. 50.

But at the moment of truth, when there remained nothing more to be done about the physical risks, troops were sent forward without further regard to defensive firepower:

> The two battalions were deployed in extended order some 800 meters from the village and came forward to the attack via the southern outskirts of the village. . . . The outskirts of the village were taken, and the two battalions penetrated the village itself to regain the northern outskirts, and from there to reach the bridges over the Sambre. But in the interior of the village, the two battalions ran into retrenchments, barricades, crenelated houses, etc., that did not permit them to progress. At the same time, they were threatened on their right flank by a line of enemy riflers and by machine guns set up on a slag heap. After having struggled for about one hour in the village, they were forced to fall back as far as ridge 175, where they reconstituted their units. From there, they returned to Binche, where they were placed in reserve.

In the 129e RI account, soldiers eventually took matters into their own hands, as did the soldiers of the 74e RI. Having entered the zone of maximum danger, the battalions of the 129e RI fought the good fight under horrific circumstances for about one hour, at which point it became clear that the intentions of the attack were not going to be fulfilled. They then disengaged and retired. Like the 74e RI attackers, many soldiers from the 129e RI lived to tell the tale.[37]

The April 1914 infantry regulations were certainly vague and perhaps even insincere on what soldiers should do if an attack failed. A battalion commander, for example, was told that "whatever happens, he has the obligation to commit his troops to the last man and even to intervene personally in the struggle to attain the objective fixed by the superior authority."[38] Such zeal could hardly have been in the French army's best interests in all circumstances, if the result proved complete annihilation and a battalion-size hole in the French position. Moreover, few battlefield soldiers who believed otherwise could expect to live long. The gray area thus implicit in French combat theory became subject to soldierly discretion in practice.

One account described the growing irrelevance of the command struc-

---

[37] According to calculations of officer casualties from the *état nominatif* and the *états des services*, 9 officers were killed and 2 were captured. The losses among common soldiers and NCOs were 58 killed, 567 wounded, and 50 missing. Even if all of these casualties came from the 1e and 3e Bataillons, at most only 58 soldiers were killed out of some 2,000 participating in the Roselies operation. The figure of 567 wounded is indeed enormous. But the fact that they were counted as wounded and not missing indicates that they made it back to the French lines.

[38] Ministère de la Guerre, *Réglement de manoeuvre d'infanterie du 20 avril 1914* (Paris: Henri Charles Lavauzelle, 1914), chap. 3, art. 2, p. 143.

ture even in a unit not involved in the ill-starred counterattacks.[39] J. La Chausée, an adjutant commanding a section in the 39e RI, recounted the events of the morning of 22 August, when the 39e RI was attacked in the town of Châtelet on the left of the 5e DI position. La Chausée noted only one formal order received all day, via a messenger from the company commander bearing a verbal order to retreat without engaging the enemy. He recalled with pride that "the case being grave, I responded that I would not execute the retreat without a written order."[40] When the messenger returned with the necessary document (itself probably no mean undertaking under the circumstances), La Chausée began the retreat. He did so with uncertain geographic bearings, however, since his only map was torn from an atlas and lacked even village names. Although he reported that his men retained perfect discipline and retreated "as one man . . . I did not know where to go, and decided to march in a southerly direction."[41]

Disorder increased over the course of the day in the units surrounding La Chausée's. At one point, the echelons of La Chausée's section found the road "strewn with men lying down all over the place."[42] When he asked who commanded these troops, no one answered. La Chausée's own efforts to organize these men completely failed. When his own section resumed the retreat, La Chausée remarked, "The others did not follow. And there were more than one hundred men there who were going to be taken prisoner."[43]

La Chausée soon lost contact with any unit larger than his own. When he found time to tally the men under his command, 125 were counted "from three companies, and included almost an entire section that was abandoned by its officer, a reserve second-lieutenant known to me."[44] For his part, he continued the retreat on his own initiative; by nightfall, his cartographic resources had failed him entirely, and he regained his bearings only by using the North Star. The disintegration of formal command authority is especially intriguing here given that actual Germans are curiously absent in much of La Chausée's account. Mention of contact between the enemy and his section remained rare, and almost invariably favored the French. No mention was ever made of casualties, and he maintained a deafening silence on the doctrine of the offensive.

---

[39] Capitaine J. La Chausée, *De Charleroi à Verdun dans l'infanterie* (Paris: Éditions Eugene Figuière, no date, depôt légal, 1934). La Chausée is the pen name of Julien Cauchy, of the 2e Bataillon, 7e Compagnie. He was an adjutant in the regular army when the war broke out.
[40] Ibid., p. 22.
[41] Ibid., pp. 23–24.
[42] Ibid., p. 27.
[43] Ibid.
[44] Ibid., p. 28.

During the retreat after Charleroi, 3ᵉ CA artillery commander General Roquerol recalled a conversation with an officer just promoted from colonel to brigadeer general, and brought in as the new commander of the 6ᵉ DI (the other infantry division of the 3ᵉ CA). This officer happened to be one Philippe Pétain. When Roquerol complained generally about not receiving more precise orders, Pétain responded prophetically: "What do you want? Everything we've learned has become false. We have to relearn our calling from top to bottom."[45] Common soldiers were not the only ones to experience liminality.

THE PIECES OF VICTORY: THE BATTLE OF GUISE

As constructed by conventional military history, the Battle of Guise on 29–30 August altered the course of the opening phase of the war. The Vᵉ Armée showed that it could still fight after the Charleroi disaster by delivering a riposte that changed the whole direction of the German invasion.[46] After the battle, the Germans decided to redirect their forces south to pursue the still-intact French and British forces instead of proceeding southwest toward Paris. In so doing, they effectively abandoned the Schlieffen Plan, which was based on the encirclement of the allied forces. With Paris now beyond their grasp and with the enemy retreating too fast to be encircled, the German armies in the coming days succumbed to overextension and exhaustion. The Vᵉ Armée thus laid the groundwork for the Battle of the Marne.[47]

In "win/lose" terms, the fighting in the 5ᵉ DI sector turned out to be of secondary importance to the battle as a whole. The fighting in the 5ᵉ DI's sector, the area around the Bois de Bertaignemont and the Ferme de Bertaignemont, nicely fits John Keegan's definition of the "soldier's" battle: "one in which the two sides, having blundered unawares into each other, fight it out undirected by higher command until one or the other breaks."[48] Even the official French army history, whose interest in high-

[45] Gen. Gabriel Roquerol, *1914: Le 3ᵉ Corps d'armée de Charleroi à la Marne, essai de psychologie militaire, les combatants et le commandement* (Paris: Éditions Berger-Levrault, 1934), p. xviii.

[46] The Battle of Guise, like the Battle of Charleroi, gave rise to a major dispute between Joffre and Lanrezac, this time over the timing and location of the riposte. See Joffre, *Mémoires*, vol. 1, pp. 316–53; and Lanrezac, *Plan de campagne*, chap. 8.

[47] See Col. Charles Menu, "Les Journées des 29 et 30 août 1914," *Revue militaire française* 55 (1935), pp. 145–92, 281–321.

[48] John Keegan, *Opening Moves: August 1914* (New York: Ballentine Publishers, 1971), p. 108.

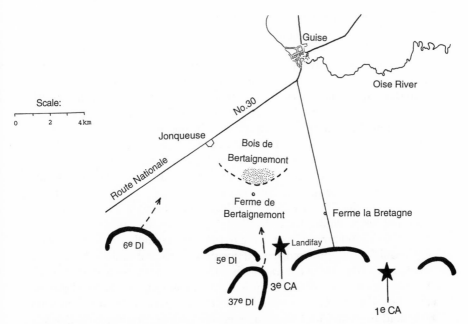

Map III-2. The Battle of Guise, 29 August 1914

lighting French audacity scarcely needs explanation, does not indicate who attacked whom.[49]

Around 0400 on 29 August, the 36ᵉ RI was sent to occupy the hills north and west of Jonqueuse, with the mission of securing positions for the 3ᵉ CA artillery, which would in turn support an infantry assault on St. Quentin later in the day.[50] When the regiment reached the Ferme de Bertaignemont, a cavalry officer assured the 36ᵉ RI commander that there would be no difficulty occupying the assigned positions. Consequently, the components of the regiment dispersed in the relevant directions, only to fall into a storm of fire from German artillery, machine guns, and infantry. An attempt to secure the farm by the 274ᵉ RI (the reserve regiment of the 74ᵉ RI and used in combat for the first time) also failed. The 74ᵉ RI was then sent in to secure the farm, but "was unable to progress because of the lack of artillery support."[51] Another attack further to the west, by the 129ᵉ RI facing the Bois de Bertaignemont, also failed. Its efforts were not assisted by the fact

[49] See AFGG, tome 1, vol. 2, p. 70.

[50] This narrative is based on the JMOs for the 5ᵉ DI and its constituent units.

[51] 5ᵉ DI JMO, 29 August 1914. Roquerol and Verrier blamed each other for this situation. For one side of the story, see Gen. Gabriel Roquerol, *La Bataille de Guise, 29 août 1914* (Paris: Berger-Levrault, 1932), p. 20.

that the division artillery, belatedly arriving in the zone of the fighting, fired by mistake on the attacking French troops.

Rather to its own surprise, the 39ᵉ RI finally secured the farm in collaboration with units from the 1ᵉ CA. At an undisclosed time (probably sometime late in the morning) elements of the 39ᵉ RI moved northwest from Landifay, where they encountered the retreating units of the 36ᵉ RI. An assault on the farm from the northeast made irregular progress, until the regimental colonel ordered a pause in the assault for the divisional artillery finally to be used to some beneficial effect. At long last, "well-regulated fire" on the German positions to the south and west of Bertaigne-mont enabled the advance of the 39ᵉ RI to continue.[52] Despite strong German resistance around the Ferme la Bretagne, sections from the 2ᵉ Bataillon of the 39ᵉ RI entered the Ferme de Bertaignemont, assisted to their left by battalions from the 38ᵉ DI.[53] Finally, at 1900, the soldiers of the 39ᵉ RI found themselves treated to that rarest of sights in World War I, a ceremonial entry into an occupied position—war as it had worked during maneuvers. The 39ᵉ RI *JMO* noted: "The fire having ceased, we entered Bertaignemont, the colonel in the lead, flag deployed, and the band playing the *Marseillaise*." Casualties in the 5ᵉ DI, though only about half of what they had been at Charleroi, remained very heavy: 26 officers and 1,865 NCOs and common soldiers killed, wounded, or missing.[54]

Despite some residual fire from the German artillery, the 5ᵉ DI remained firmly in command in the area around the Ferme de Bertaignemont as 30 August dawned. Its mission for the day was "first of all to fortify the positions reached at the end of the previous day and to throw back across the Oise any enemy that tried a crossing, without moving beyond the river."[55] The division was supported around the farm by a brigade from the 1ᵉ CA. But at 1030, the 5ᵉ DI received orders to retreat in the direction of Laon, for reasons of overall strategy that did not directly concern the

[52] Oddly, this artillery success, the first by the division artillery since the war began, in not mentioned in either the 5ᵉ DI or the 43ᵉ RA *JMOs*, only in that for the 39ᵉ RI.

[53] Menu suggests that the Germans departed so as not to create a salient in the 5ᵉ DI sector, and not because of the French efforts there. See "Les Journées," pp. 320–21.

[54] 5ᵉ DI *JMO*, 29 August 1914. The regimental breakdown is as follows (*K* = killed; *W* = wounded; *M* = missing):

	Officers			NCOs and Men		
	K	W	M	K	W	M
39ᵉ RI	—	2	—	8	139	138
74ᵉ RI	1	1	1	—	35	142
36ᵉ RI	2	7	—	(681, not broken down)		
129ᵉ RI	—	7	—	66	490	150
274ᵉ RI	—	2	—	2	14	—

[55] 5ᵉ DI *JMO*, 30 August 1914.

division's sector. Thus began the main part of the retreat, which continued for six days and nights, with marches sometimes exceeding thirty kilometers per day.

The experience of the Battle of Guise proved highly ambiguous and subject to considerable reconstruction, even as battles go. Indeed, for most of the soldiers of the 5e DI, little distinguished the "victory" at Guise from the "defeat" at Charleroi. Certainly, the French had won a piece of contested terrain for the first time since the shooting started. But casualties had been heavy, and the gains were given up the next day without a fight. The protagonists could scarcely have known that they were involved in a maneuver that would make possible the Battle of the Marne, much less that that maneuver would be successful. The pieces of victory had to be put together after the fact.

To be sure, the command structure functioned much more coherently than it had at Charleroi.[56] But the command structure hardly "managed" the victory at the Ferme de Bertaignemont. Indeed, this immediate victory could scarcely be said to have been managed at all, and was in any event directly experienced only by three companies from the 39e RI. For many of the other soldiers, 29 August held something close to a repetition of the "escape or die" experience of Charleroi. They partook of the victory of the 39e RI only vicariously.

An unpublished memoir by a common soldier from the 36e RI, Jules Champin's *Mes Souvenirs*, demonstrated how the Battle of Guise proved a victory mostly in retrospect.[57] On 29 August, around dawn, Champin's section was in a position below a small knoll. Suddenly, the chasseurs from the 7e Régiment de Chasseurs à Cheval were "descended upon by Germans, which this time were not far away." Suddenly, the whole knoll was engulfed in German rifle fire. As the section dashed for cover, Champin hid behind a sheaf of wheat. The Germans by this time seemed everywhere:

In front of me, there is a whole *Boche*[58] company that is also firing ceaselessly, but they are well camouflaged. . . . I can hardly see them. I am careful to spot

---

[56] General Sauret was removed on 28 August, and his replacement, Gen. Emile Hache, drew nothing but praise for his conduct. See the evaluations by Franchet d'Esperey in the Hache personal dossier. Gx/3, G.D. 520. Even General Verrier received a favorable notice from one of his staff lieutenants for his "very calm attitude during a violent artillery attack" on 29 August. Report by Lieutenant Lucien, Verrier personal dossier.

[57] The full reference as cited on the title page is "Jules Champin, 36e Régiment d'Infanterie, 1e Bataillon, 1e Cie, 2e Section, 5e Escouade, Classe 1913, Soldat de 1ère classe, Tireur d'élite, *Mes Souvenirs*." This is a photocopy of a written manuscript, and was deposited with the library of the army archives at Vincennes in 1969 (côte D.227). The quotes here appear on pp. 13–14B.

[58] *Boche* is a derogatory French term for a German, meaning essentially "wooden head."

where the fire is coming from, and I think I am often the bull's eye. German bullets whiz around my ears without stopping and shells fall on all sides, a bullet hits the ground just in front of me but doesn't touch me. At the end of a moment that seemed to me to be very long, in fact interminable hours, I noticed that I didn't have any more cartridges. When I asked my comrades who were 4–5 meters away, they didn't answer my calls. They were all dead.

When the fighting died down a bit, Champin hid alongside an adjutant from the 3e Section, "my head between my legs and my haversack on my head; it seemed to me that I was better protected that way." In Champin's sector of the front, the French forces walked into a trap, just as they had at Charleroi.

As the lull in the fighting continued, Champin walked south to rejoin another unit from the 36e RI, since his own section had been "nearly annihilated." He succeeded in doing so toward the end of the day, as the regiment was regrouping. But no sooner had he relocated his regiment than he found that "we were parting again from our positions, and they are having us fix bayonets! Is something wrong here? [*Ça sent mauvais?*] We are all ready to charge when we learn that the Boches have withdrawn." One might view with some skepticism the notion that the 36e RI, which had suffered casualties of over two thousand men since the fighting started on 21 August, were willing to charge *à la baïonnette* the very Germans who had mauled them earlier in the day. But the point remained that the victory at Guise came as quite a surprise to Champin and his comrades, for whom 29 August held much pain and little glory.

The victory at Guise came as scarcely less of a surprise to one of the immediate victors. La Chausée's 7e Compagnie of the 39e RI was among those finally occupying the Ferme de Bertaignemont. For the morning of 29 August, his section was assigned to protecting an artillery piece from the division artillery. For the first time in his account, he admitted a situation in his concern for physical danger threatened to overwhelm his devotion to duty: "I asked to be assigned another position and not to remain so close to the point of artillery fire, which would shortly become a target for the enemy. But the lieutenant did not go along, and declared that in the interest of the artillery that were protecting the cavalry, I had to remain where I was."[59] He alluded to widespread consternation with the situation among his troops, who hitherto had exhibited nothing but perfect deference. Conventional bonds linking officers and soldiers were stretched to the breaking point: "We stayed there until the afternoon; and I had much difficulty making the men remain in place. It's hard to be pinned like that to the ground, waiting for death which is buzzing about every moment. You really need control to make people accept this situation."[60]

[59] La Chausée, *De Charleroi à Verdun*, p. 46.
[60] Ibid.

In the afternoon, when the French artillery had moved forward, La Chausée's company participated in what to his surprise turned out to be the final assault. When he received the order to move on the farm, he deployed his men with the utmost caution, in order to maximize covering fire from the individual squads. But shortly, German artillery fire rendered his efforts useless and the situation in his section again near to panic: "It was not long before we received in our turn an avalanche of shells. Since they were falling everywhere, we found ourselves in a critical situation, not knowing what to do to remedy it. At each moment, we saw the prospect of being blown to bits."[61]

As La Chausée described it, nightfall and the arrival of reinforcements from the 1ᵉ CA rescued his unit *deus ex machina*. With the sun setting, the German artillery barrage suddenly lifted, thus allowing the French to occupy the farm undisturbed except for a few rear-guard actions. With the 7ᵉ Compagnie now saved from what La Chausée saw as certain death, he recalled that, "in our ranks, enthusiasm was now everywhere. And even though I recommended to my men to keep an eye on the enemy's positions, everyone stood up to better contemplate this spectacle."[62] As the ceremonial entry of the 39ᵉ RI commander began, "we heard behind us the band playing, as though it were giving a concert. Everywhere people sang, and cried out."[63] Through no particular effort of its own, the 7ᵉ Compagnie had helped carry the day.

On 3 September, in the middle of the retreat, Champin participated in a successful rear-guard ambush of a German patrol. He remarked that "it was a bit like Guise." The disparity between this remark and his personal experience indicates how thoroughly the Battle of Guise had been reconstructed after the fact as a victory. Several sources recorded quite different views at the time, however, particularly after the pieces of victory were taken away upon the order to retreat on 30 August. The 5ᵉ DI *JMO*, for example, editorialized that the forced marches of 31 August and 1 September "wore out and demoralized the troops. There are many stragglers and pillagers, against whom draconian measures must be taken."[64] Champin himself affirmed that during the retreat "morale is not good, and not up to much." Even La Chausée, who had witnessed not twenty hours previously the ambiguous nature of the French success around the Ferme de Bertaignemont, recalled that the retreat seemed to him "inconceivable."[65] In his

[61] Ibid.

[62] Ibid., p. 48.

[63] Ibid., p. 49.

[64] These measures had to have been taken entirely outside the military justice system. There were no prosecutions at all pertaining to the first month of the fighting in the normal *conseils de guerre*. Unless all trace of the records has been lost or destroyed, even the special courts-martial or *cours martiales* set up by Joffre on September 6 did not exist in the 5ᵉ DI.

[65] La Chausée, *De Charleroi à Verdun*, p. 53.

opinion, "after having seen the enemy flee, we deplored being reduced to turning our backs on him again."[66] Guise proved a victory mostly in retrospect.

THE PIECES OF PROPORTIONALITY: THE MARNE AND THE ATTACK ON BRIMONT

The astonishing reversal of French fortunes at the Battle of the Marne, following the defeat along the frontiers, the ambiguous success at Guise, and the retreat deep into France, has come to be understood as one of the great victories of French military history.[67] The Ve Armée played a crucial operational role. It marched farther (first south and then north) and, despite its grievous losses, regained more territory after than any other army. The Ve Armée, alongside the battered remains of the British Expeditionary Force, played the key role in exploiting the gap between German I and II Armies.[68]

The "miracle of the Marne," moreover, became construed as the personal victory of Joffre.[69] The battle created huge expectations for the future, and lent credibility to Joffre's promises repeated through 1915 and 1916 that victory was just around the corner. The French high command drew the conclusion that if the Germans were just attacked head-on enough times, they sooner or later would collapse, just as they appeared to have collapsed along the Marne. Never in the twentieth century would confidence in senior command prognoses in France be higher than in the aftermath of the Battle of the Marne. The durability of this confidence proved astonishing. In a broad sense, the faith in the French army to effect a miracle with the country in mortal danger endured until June 1940.

But if the Battle of Guise proved more of a victory in retrospect than it seemed at the outset, the Battle of the Marne proved less. Since the Germans retreated so far so fast after 6 September, they could choose their own ground to make a stand. The positions they chose along the Chemin des Dames and the hills just north of Reims would not seriously be threatened until 1918. Even after the "Race to the Sea" of the fall of 1914, the Germans still held so much of northeastern France hostage that there was no question of the Germans and the Western Allies negotiating as equals. Thus, there was no question of their negotiating at all.

---

[66] Ibid., p. 52.

[67] The term "Battle of the Marne" will be used in a narrow sense here, meaning the beginning of the French counterattack near the Marne River on 6–8 September.

[68] See the description in AFGG, tome 1, vol. 3, chap. 1, pp. 1–69.

[69] The official history summarized this point of view: "The supreme commander carried the responsibility for these operations; to him before all returns the glory." Ibid., tome 1, vol. 3, p. 1317.

The "win/lose" record of the 5ᵉ DI illustrates nicely the situation confronting the French army as a whole. The division's own situation, however, was made much worse than it need have been through the overly ambitious efforts of its new commander. On 1 September, General Verrier was *limogé* and replaced by Gen. Charles Mangin.[70] Because Mangin's reach badly exceeded his grasp in the aftermath of the Battle of the Marne, he ended up losing both large numbers of men and a substantial amount of ground.

The retreat of the 5ᵉ DI after the Battle of Guise is shown in map III-3. The dated points indicate the daily positions of the division from the night of 30 August to the night of 13 September. In all, the soldiers of the division retreated some 132 kilometers between 30 August and the counterattack on 6 September, an average of over 22 kilometers per day. By Toussaint's reckoning, the 74ᵉ RI by the time of the counterattack had marched a total of 487 kilometers since the mobilization.[71] But despite the physical demands it made on the soldiers, the retreat provided something of an organizational respite. Reinforcements could be moved up, units reorganized, and surviving officers and NCOs redistributed to maximum effect. Mangin could also get to know his new unit in relative security.

The Battle of the Marne in the sector of the 5ᵉ DI progressed throughout the morning of 6 September without serious incident. Well-managed French artillery fire by the soon-to-be-legendary 75mm gun disrupted the German positions, and for the first time since the fighting began provided effective support for the infantry.[72] At around 1600, the German forces made their first stand, in attacking the 74ᵉ RI at Courgivaux, which changed hands no less than five times over the next twenty-four hours.[73]

[70] Mangin's career and character will be examined in greater detail in chap. 5. The verb *limoger* originated in the fall of 1914, when some one hundred generals or colonels commanding brigades were relieved of their commands by Joffre and sent to the distant 12ᵉ Région Militaire, whose main garrison city was Limoges. The term remains the colloquial French word for getting fired. See Lt. Col. André Cousine, "Essai historique du Terme 'Limoger': La 12ᵉ Région en 1914, Cinq departments" (unpublished paper, Service Historique de l'Armée de Terre, 1984).

[71] Toussaint, *Petites histoires*, pp. 30–31.

[72] See 5ᵉ DI, *JMO*, 6 September 1914. The "win/lose" narrative of the Marne and Brimont draws principally from this source.

[73] Total 5ᵉ DI infantry casualties, 6–7 September:

	Officers			NCOs *and Soldiers*		
	K	W	M	K	W	M
39ᵉ RI	3	8	—	55	253	162
74ᵉ RI	2	4	1	37	244	289
36ᵉ RI	(1, not categorized)			(160, not categorized)		
129ᵉ RI	2	1	—	45	295	50

Source: JMOs, 5ᵉ DI, 36ᵉ RI.
Note: The 274ᵉ RI was not engaged during these two days.

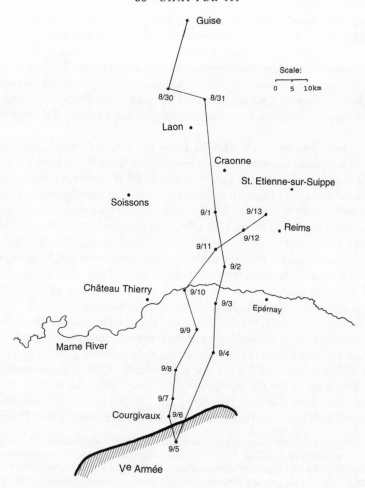

MAP III-3. The Retreat and Advance of the 5ᵉ DI, 30 August–13
September 1914

After Courgivaux was finally secured, no serious engagement with the
Germans took place for five days, during which time the division advanced
some 67 kilometers, a rate of progress unequaled by it during the rest of the
war. For this brief period, gains of over 10 kilometers per day came to be
expected.

On 12 September, the 5ᵉ DI began to encounter serious resistance in the
area just west of Reims (see map III-4). But given the success of the 5ᵉ DI
since 6 September, the optimistic itinerary for 13 September was not
surprising—Courcy, Brimont, and finally St. Étienne-sur-Suippe (some 10

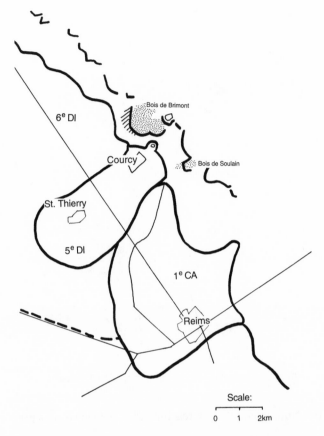

MAP III-4. Brimont/Courcy Sector, Evening of 16 September 1914

km beyond Courcy).[74] However, as shown on map III-5, the intervening terrain presented serious difficulties. The key to the position was the Bois de Brimont, with its fort at the top and its chateau to the French right. For the next four days, Mangin endeavored to take the hill by attacking on the right, via the chateau. But with the German artillery occupying the heights around Brimont and the Bois de Soulain, French infantry advancing from Courcy to the Bois de Soulain and the chateau remained heavily exposed. Given the dearth of heavy artillery and the flat trajectory and limited range of 75mm fire, the French artillery stood little chance of disrupting the

[74] See 5e DI *JMO*, 13 September 1914.

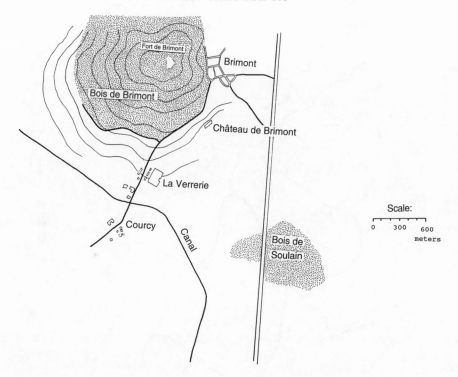

MAP III-5. Brimont–Courcy Sector, 17 September 1914 (detail)

German position. Even infantry reaching the chateau stood a great risk of being cut off.

This essentially occurred, as Mangin failed to grasp in time the gravity of the situation. At first, the French advance on 13 September proceeded more or less according to plan. Courcy was occupied by 1130 by the 129e RI. Over the course of the afternoon, the regiment occupied a glass factory (La Verrerie) just beyond the canal north of the village. The 36e RI, in the meantime, had crossed the canal east of Courcy, and occupied the western section of the Bois de Soulain, as far as an area within five hundred meters of the Château de Brimont.[75]

But by 14 September, German artillery from the Bois de Brimont had completely halted the French advance in the sector of the 5e DI. After the expenditure of some forty thousand shells by the 5e and 6e DI artilleries resulted in no additional ground gained, Mangin ordered a night attack on the Château de Brimont by the 36e RI. The 2e Bataillon attacked at 0230,

---

[75] The 39e RI was held in reserve at this point. The 74e RI and the 274e RI were supporting an attack by the 6e DI throughout this period, and their experience is not examined here.

and by 0630 occupied the chateau. It was joined in the early hours of 16 September by the 1e Bataillon of the 129e RI.

This advance, of course, actually made worse the exposure of the French infantry as long as the Germans held the hills around Brimont. Mangin's objective for the next two days was to extend the movement of the 129e RI from La Verrerie and the other two battalions from the 36e RI in the Bois de Soulain toward the chateau. Once this was accomplished, it was hoped, the massif of Brimont could be taken from behind by a joint effort of the 5e DI and the 1e DI to its right. But this effort never materialized, and in the meantime, the other battalions of the 129e RI and the 36e RI not stranded in the chateau remained pinned down in La Verrerie and the Bois de Soulin, respectively. Communications with the two battalions in the chateau became tenuous at best.

The initiative shifted completely to the Germans on 16–17 September, as they regained control of most of the Bois de Soulain. The 5e DI *JMO* commented that a counterattack *à la baïonnette* by the 36e RI on 16 September inflicted "heavy casualties," the sort of language that generally signified a conspicuous lack of success.[76] By the next day, communications with the chateau were cut off completely. A German infantry and artillery attack on La Verrerie and Courcy starting at 1400 was held off by the 129e and 39e RI, the latter now brought forward to help shore up the steadily weakening position of the division. Finally, sometime during the night of 17–18 September, the Germans attacked La Verrerie at the very moment that the 129e RI was being relieved by the 39e RI. Suddenly surrounded by the enemy, the troops from both regiments panicked and fell back moblike toward Saint-Thierry. Two additional companies from the 129e RI were lost in the rout.[77]

Mangin ordered a counterattack on Courcy at 0430 on 18 September. But no sooner did the (no doubt still disoriented) infantry from the 39e RI and 129e RI begin to move forward when according to the division *JMO* "enemy artillery opened violent fire. This settled the retreat of these units, which were very tired from four days of bombardment and fighting." The two battalions marooned in the chateau surrendered. Moreover, the 5e DI had been thrown back behind its positions on 13 September. Mangin ordered his troops to dig in at Saint-Thierry and regroup. Not for the last time during his command of the 5e DI, he had a good deal of explaining to do.[78]

[76] 5e DI *JMO*, 16 September 1914. The 36e RI *JMO* for the same date recorded that the attack actually came from the Germans, but was repulsed with the bayonet charge.

[77] The 129e RI *JMO* for the night of 17–18 September does not elaborate on just what became of these two companies. It noted simply that some reinforcements were "divided among the six companies remaining [of the original twelve]."

[78] For reasons that are not entirely clear, complete casualty figures are not available for the

Soldiers' experiences at the Battle of the Marne and of the attack on Brimont differed significantly from those of the first two battles of the war. Not only did the combat last for a considerably more protracted period, but the possibility emerged for the first time of stalemate, a gray area between winning and losing. Calculations as to the utility of aggression thus became possible on a different basis. The pieces of proportionality began to emerge, and consequently the rudiments of the broader pattern of the negotiation of command authority between soldiers and their commanders.

The utilitarian formulation of proportionality used here has two components—a willingness to fight aggressively if there exists some perceived utility; and ceasing aggression in the absence of that perceived utility. This formulation implies a highly "rational" conceptualization of battlefield experience, exactly where life and death must appear most irrational. Aggression seems especially irrational, since it implies seeking rather than avoiding physical danger. But the idea of "calculation" used throughout this study speaks more to processes occurring over the days, weeks, and years of the war rather than to the minutes or even hours of particular battlefield situations. In this sense, I would argue, aggression could indeed appear "rational" given the basic circumstances of the counterattack at the Marne.

It would be a mistake to underestimate soldiers' awareness of the overall military situation, and of their prospects for striking back at the invader. After all, even Joffre eventually figured out what the Germans were attempting in the Schlieffen Plan; it is hardly unreasonable to believe that the soldiers he commanded could not have done the same.[79] Captain Dhé, liaison officer between the 3e CA and the 5e DI, made precisely this argument: "Everyone was saying [during the retreat]: 'We will make an about-face.' The idea of the Marne surged up from the army itself. We were waiting for an order to turn around. We had faith in this, and this was the basis for the great victory of 6–9 September 1914."[80] For the soldiers in this situation, the order to return to the attack on 6 September could be

---

Brimont/Courcy operation. One of the few bits of information comes from the *JMO* of the 36e RI, reported that as of September 18 it had been reduced to 18 officers and 1,320 NCOs and common soldiers.

[79] French soldiers had good reason to believe that the Germans were probably even more exhausted than themselves, since they had been marching in summer heat since they crossed the Belgian frontier on 4 August. Even a casual glance at a map would also have suggested that in pursuing the Ve Armée south after Guise the Germans had left themselves vulnerable to an attack on their flank by the Paris garrison, which came in the form of General Gallieni's "taxis of the Marne."

[80] Quoted in Gen. Charles Mangin, *Comment finit la guerre* (Paris: Plon, 1920), p. 62.

interpreted as a sort of release, like letting go a stretched rubber band. Mangin would try to recapture this *fuite en avant* or "escape forward" when the 5e DI next took the offensive in 1915.

Paradoxically, the documentary record for the 5e DI during the Battle of the Marne is singularly sparse. Partly, this is because none of the soldiers who left memoirs participated. But throughout the war, the extent of documentation for an engagement by the 5e DI proved inversely proportional to that operation's success. Particularly in this early stage of the war, it was easy for all concerned to attribute the success to French moral superiority or to the genius of Joffre. The victory of the Marne needed less explanation than the calamity of Brimont/Courcy.

An intriguing exception, though, is a report on the fighting around Courgivaux by Captain Plessis of the 3e Compagnie of the 74e RI.[81] At around 1600 on 6 September, Plessis's battalion had just received the order to bivouac around the village of Courgivaux. As Courgivaux actually changed hands several times between 6 and 7 September, this report represented only a small snapshot of a much more complicated set of events. No sooner had the order to bivouac been received by Plessis's company when troops from the 1e Bataillon of the 39e RI to their right were seen retreating in great disorder under heavy German fire. The German attack intensified as Plessis's 1e Battalion of the 74e RI prepared to assist, and the French forces continued to fall back.

A "rational" calculation of likely utility combined with simple good luck to explain the born-again *furia francese*[82] in the 3e Compagnie. At about 1800, Plessis noted that "despite the intensity of the fire, the Germans seemed few in number," though he did not further explain this perception. Plessis gave the order: "Forward! There's no one in front of us." Despite his own courageous example, "a certain hesitation persisted, owing to the retreat of numerous men separated from their units." After a call to the "most courageous, first forty, then fifty, then sixty men from the 3e Compagnie led by a sergeant-major descended on the German positions crying "En avant!" Suddenly, the attack looked like one called for in the 1914 infantry regulations: "The general retreat toward the ravine was halted. The slackers gathered around us. The tide turned in an impressive manner. The enemy took flight without firing a shot."

[81] "Rapport du Capne. Plessis de la 3e Cie. du 74e Infie. sur un épisode du combat de Courgivaux (6–7 Sept.)," 5e DI, 3e Bureau, 24 N 97. The report is undated but "Reproduit, Thil, 8 novembre 1914" is noted at the end. Exactly why the report was written and why there are not more like it remains unclear. This company had participated in the ill-fated attack on Roselies on 22 August.

[82] *Furia francese* (Italian, meaning literally "French fury") is a term used to describe legendary Gallic bellicosity. Its origin is related to the fifteenth-century French invasion of Italy.

Some fifteen unfortunate Germans participating in the pursuit of the 39ᵉ RI found themselves surprised by the French host, now comprising men from at least three regiments. As they gunned down the hapless Germans in front of them, "the enthusiasm of the men in seeing them fall broke all bounds and it was impossible to hold them back. A bugler, without orders, sounded the charge."[83] The remaining Germans "disappeared into a nearby wood, leaving behind their rifles and their wounded." Although Plessis was not exactly shy about his own role, he attributed the success of this improvised French success to "the enthusiasm and the élan of the men who took part. They were guided by NCOs who knew how to maintain order in what was basically a crowd, with little homogeneity and much dispersion."[84]

No evidence exists raising doubt that this engagement took place much as Plessis described it. But the basic similarity to events at Guise bears emphasis. The German and French forces ran into each other, fought for a while, and the Germans retreated. Plessis offered no explanation of why at the moment he began his assault there were so few Germans in front of him. Indeed, he did not seem interested in the origin of his good fortune at all. Nothing could have been easier than believing that the Germans had fled because of French moral superiority. The consensus between soldiers and commanders at Courgivaux did not translate into unconditional obedience in all circumstances. When their good fortune changed in front of Brimont and Courcy, soldiers in the 5ᵉ DI came to estimate the utility of aggression quite differently.

This indeed occurred when German resistance began to stiffen on 12 September . Probably as early as 14 September, good reasons existed for believing that the Germans could not be dislodged from the Brimont sector—notably the terrain and the limitations of the 75mm cannon. But the more the Germans behaved like an immovable object, the more Mangin behaved as though he commanded an irresistible force. As a result, judgments of the utility of aggression by soldiers and their commanders began to diverge.

Frontline soldiers communicated their own assessment of their situation to the command structure through two dramatic gestures—the surrender of the two battalions in the Château de Brimont and the disorganized flight of the troops defending Courcy on the night of 17–18 September. By the morning of 18 September, even Mangin had to recognize that further offensive effort was so unfeasible he should not even attempt it. Although

---

[83] The 39ᵉ RI *JMO* credited Plessis with parrying the German attack, though it neglected to mention the disordered state of the regiment's retreating battalion during the day.

[84] The casualty figures cited earlier for the 74ᵉ RI were not broken down by battalion, so it is not possible to determine just how costly this engagement was.

neither soldiers nor commanders recognized the implications of what had happened at the time, a coherent command structure had seen its wishes countermanded from below.

An austere but poignant account of the surrender in the Château de Brimont survives from Maj. Léopold Duchemin, commander of the 1e Bataillon of the 129e RI.[85] Written in the form of a *JMO* from a German prisoner-of-war camp in November 1914, Duchemin defended the surrender of his unit according to a rudimentary principal of proportionality.[86] He and his men were willing to continue fighting as long as they perceived their efforts as potentially contributing in some way to the greater French cause. When these hopes were extinguished, they saw no point in dying for its own sake.

Duchemin moved his battalion from La Verrerie to the chateau in the early hours of 16 September to reinforce the 2e Bataillon of the 36e RI. But once inside the chateau, Duchemin quickly realized that "the position is bad." Moreover, the soldiers inside the chateau could see just how precarious their position was at any given time, since the chateau remained high enough to provide a clear view of French forces south of them, specifically their weakening and soon broken hold over the Bois de Soulain.

At 1600 on 16 September, Duchemin was informed by his counterpart from the 36e RI of "important enemy movements" north of the woods. Over the next four hours, the soldiers in the chateau watched the Germans descend on the woods, "dispersed and in swarms. They advanced in a continuous movement, without firing, and without being fired upon by our artillery." Shortly thereafter, they witnessed a "flood of runaways" (*flot de fuyards*) followed by a "huge column" retreating in the direction of Reims. The Bois de Soulain was evacuated. Duchemin summarized his plight:

> The position in the Château de Brimont, very much in question while we held the Bois de Soulain, now found itself isolated in the middle of enemy lines and without communications with the rear. No provision had arrived at the battalion for 46 hours; it had been in the firing line for 86 hours. The ammunition of the companies facing the northwest and the northeast was beginning to run out.

[85] Chef de Bataillon Léopold Duchemin, "129ème Régiment d'infanterie, 1er bataillon, journal de marches et d'opérations, du 12 août au 17 septembre 1914." 26 N 686. A shortened version of this report appears in the 5e DI *JMO*, where it is indicated that the report was written during Duchemin's captivity in Germany.

[86] In a supplement to Mangin's original report on the events at Brimont/Courcy, a note is attached indicating that the documents were to be saved "in case the commander of the Brimont battalion were at some time to be brought before a court-martial." "Rapport du Général Mangin, Commandant de la 5e DI, sur les Combats des 13, 14, 15, 16, 17, et 18 Septembre à Courcy, Château de Brimont, et Bois Soulains," 5e DI, 3e Bureau, 24 N 78.

Moreover, the soldiers marooned in the chateau now had no idea whether they would *ever* receive assistance. Duchemin did not know until after 0100 on 17 September (and then only through the efforts of a brave and fortunate runner) that the French still held La Verrerie, the only other position from which they could receive assistance.

This messenger brought what proved to be the last orders from Col. Henri Salle, commander of the 129e RI. Duchemin quoted from these orders (which contained no instructions particular to his battalion) in their entirety, and then outlined their irrelevance paragraph by paragraph. The first paragraph indicated that the mission of the 3e CA for 17 September was "to maintain the enemy on his front," a mission that Duchemin inferred precluded launching an attack to rescue the soldiers in the chateau. The second paragraph stipulated that the eastern section of the Bois de Soulain would be turned over to soldiers from the 1e CA. Duchemin remarked that this order did not take account of the loss of the woods, an event that "profoundly modified the situation." Duchemin concluded laconically that the third paragraph, which stated that "the battalions of the 129e RI will maintain until further orders their respective positions," simply "did not correspond to the situation."

As the German assault on the chateau began on the morning of 17 September, the utility of further resistance came to seem more and more questionable, though Duchemin took great pains to stress that he continued the good fight until the only alternatives were surrender or massacre. Between 0600 and 0700, the defenders of the chateau witnessed the last French attempt to retake the Bois de Soulain. One French column, deployed in extended order eight hundred meters to the south of the woods "melted away bit by bit and disappeared." The other French columns simply "turned around and disappeared in the direction of Reims."

By 0800, the chateau itself was under attack from three directions, the northwest, the northeast, and the southeast. Duchemin wrote that "we are between two pincers that are closing bit by bit." He described their situation late in the morning:

> Until now, the enemy infantry, held in place by our fire, could not get past the crests where they looked down on us on four sides. But we could not conceal how precarious our situation was. The defense of the fortifications facing the Bois de Brimont was disorganized by the bombardment that broke apart the garrets and the second floor of the chateau, where we had placed our sharpshooters.

The final assault came from the northeast, in the sector of the 2e Battalion of the 36e RI.[87] As the Germans approached through a small park adjacent

---

[87] No detailed account survives from the 36e RI of the Brimont episode.

to the chateau, "a great disorder reigned [and] the men, exhausted by five days of combat and bombardment without respite, offered no more resistance." Duchemin himself went to the northeast wall of the chateau, where he found some fifty men from his own 3ᵉ Compagnie still firing at the Germans only one hundred meters ahead of them. "One after another," he writes, "they showed me their empty cartridges. . . . No more resistance was possible. It was about 1600."

More details of the surrender came from a common soldier from the 129ᵉ RI taken prisoner who then escaped back to the French lines.[88] Joseph Pirot, attached to the 10ᵉ Compagnie and thus not part of Duchemin's battalion, arrived at the chateau shortly before the surrender and then mostly by accident. Assisting engineers trying to run a sap (trench) from La Verrerie to the chateau, Pirot's group of soldiers suddenly spied an unspecified number of Germans between them and La Verrerie. They followed the path of least danger by escaping to the chateau. Pirot recalled that "everyone was saying that the commander in the chateau had ordered the bugler to sound the 'cease fire' and had put out the white flag." At this point, a number of soldiers around Pirot put handkerchiefs at the end of their bayonets. Pirot claimed to want to fight to the bitter end, though he proved amenable to peer pressure: "I fired two or three times while they were advancing on us, and since my comrades insisted that I not shoot anymore, I didn't shoot anymore. The Germans gave the order to come out, and to leave weapons and equipment where they were."

Pirot's interrogators asked just how many Germans were in the vicinity when the defenders of the chateau surrendered, and were clearly dismayed to discover that by Pirot's estimate 450–500 Germans took some 900–1,000 French prisoners. He commented freely when asked what he and his comrades made of their lot as prisoners: "Now that we were prisoners, we were not afraid of the bullets anymore—we were saved from death." Upon his return to the ranks, this soldier was surely well situated to communicate to others in the division what had happened in the chateau.

Just what correct soldierly conduct was in such a situation proved subject to differences of opinion. The French numerical superiority mattered little if the French were out of ammunition and the Germans were not. The April 1914 infantry regulations barely mentioned the defense at all, much less what a soldier's obligations were if he found himself in a hopeless defensive situation. As noted in chapter 2, during the 1913 maneuvers, a surrounded company from the 36ᵉ RI simply charged *à la baïonnette*. With the stakes higher, the charm of such an approach diminished considerably.

[88] The account here draws from Pirot's interrogation by the 5ᵉ DI staff upon his return. "Procès-verbal d'interrogatoire du nommé Pirot, Joseph Léon," 23 September 1914, 5ᵉ DI, 3ᵉ Bureau, 24 N 78.

The soldiers of the 129ᵉ RI and the 39ᵉ RI reinforced the message that they had reached their limits for the time being in their panicked retreat at Courcy on the night of 17–18 September. Social scientists of battlefield behavior have observed that panic on the battlefield most often stems from a convergence of factors—a sudden and potentially "irrational" perception of overwhelming physical peril, combined with some external factor that weakens normal organizational demarcations, such as the mixing-up of soldiers from two regiments taking place during the relief at La Verrerie that night.[89] Command authority was highly devolved, inevitably the case when frontline troops were being relieved.

Even if the NCOs and junior officers had kept their heads while privates were losing theirs, the former really had only two options. They could either have attempted to enforce traditional discipline by vicious means (such as summary execution) or have consented to the flight and reimposed order later from some position of greater safety. Officers and NCOs taking the first option would have exposed themselves to responses in kind from soldiers who by definition were beyond reason. Taking the second option involved acquiescing in a highly explicit manner to a decision on the battlefield made by subordinates. The accounts of the panic at La Verrerie and Courcy showed that the officers and NCOs involved in the end chose the second option.[90]

A remarkable account of the role of the 39ᵉ RI appeared in the regimental *JMO*. The 1ᵉ Bataillon, commanded by Capt. Jean-Baptiste Dicharry, had orders on the night of 17 September to relieve the 129ᵉ RI in La Verrerie and to hold it "at any price."[91] As the battalion got within one hundred meters of the factory, a fusillade previously described as "sparse" suddenly became intense. When Dicharry went to the section closest to the fighting to see what was going on, "he had the men fix bayonets, and since the fusillade was getting closer and cries indicating panic were being heard along the side of the canal, he told the men to use their bayonets to encourage soldiers to go forward, and to reassure them by saying that help was on the way and that the surprise was for the enemy."

But instead of this scenario, Dicharry saw his authority evaporate before

---

[89] See, for example, Richard Holmes, *Acts of War: The Behavior of Men in Battle* (New York: The Free Press, 1985), pp. 224–29.

[90] See, for example, the reports from Col. Henri Salle (129ᵉ RI commander), Capt. Evelyn Mercier (3ᵉ Battalion commander), and Capt. Edouard Cabanel (12ᵉ Compagnie commander), in 5ᵉ DI, 3ᵉ Bureau, 24 N 79. These reports are examined further in Smith, "Command Authority," pp. 175–78.

[91] Dicharry had previously been La Chausée's company commander in the 7ᵉ Compagnie, 2ᵉ Bataillon. Dicharry must have played a substantial supervisory role in the rendering of the events that appeared in the *JMO*.

his very eyes. Order in his battalion began to break down as fleeing soldiers from the 129ᵉ RI got mixed in:

> At hearing the first shots, the Germans cried: "*Moi anglais, moi anglais, moi ami!* [Me English, me English, me friend!]" The men, tricked by these words and unable to distinguish the uniforms because of the darkness, cried resoundingly "Cease fire!" The fleeing soldiers flooded back pell-mell along with the Germans, pushing the battalion back to its first position, whereupon it ran into the 3ᵉ Bataillon. A great confusion reigned. Neither Lieutenant-Colonel Gibon-Guillheim, commander of the regiment, nor the officers were able to succeed in making the men advance.

Dicharry's explanation is less than convincing. British troops had never been anywhere near the 5ᵉ DI since the war began, and the idea that they had somehow taken the massif of Brimont from behind without the French knowing about it strains credulity. One can discount with some certainty the possibility that Dicharry's men were so oblivious to the overall situation that they really believed they faced British and not German soldiers. After all, it was clearly not the British that they had been fighting for the last four days. More likely, Dicharry's men were predisposed toward terminating their combative efforts, and did not need enormous persuasion to do so. But by blaming German perfidy for igniting the panic, Dicharry could also shift blame away from the officers, who had lost control over the situation.

The message of the panic—that no further offensive effort was to be expected for the time being—was reinforced the next day. Sometime on the morning of 19 September, when some order had been restored in the 39ᵉ RI, a Captain Hervlin "formed a company of volunteers to retake Courcy."[92] The notion that a village just lost by two regiments could be retaken by a single company was optimistic to say the least. Still, a particularly intrepid Sergeant Ludger from the 1ᵉ Compagnie got as far as a small wood east of Courcy. When he approached the outskirts of Courcy, though, his section came under heavy rifle and machine-gun fire, and could advance no further. Sergeant Ludgers looked for support from the other volunteers, but "could find no trace of the passage of the other sections." He would have continued searching, but "fire from the French artillery obliged him to retire." The sergeant and the men who accompanied him were cited for their "fine conduct" during this "sad affair."

In the wake of the drama of Brimont and Courcy, the command structure moved swiftly to prevent the recurrence of such episodes. Certainly, the command structure hastened to fill in the gap on surrender left in the 1914

[92] See 39ᵉ RI *JMO*, 19 September 1914.

infantry regulations. Mangin communicated his views on the matter in a statement dated 22 September, in which he observed that "brave men will estimate that a sacrifice is never useless and that action doomed in advance to complete failure could have, without their knowing it, a diversionary effect that could bring success to some other position."[93] In the 5ᵉ DI, only a romantic charge *à la baïonnette* would suffice in the future.

For his part, Joffre stated in an October 1914 memo: "In the most recent engagements . . . some men, deprived of their officers and believing themselves surrounded in a woods by the enemy, had the cowardice to surrender."[94] He claimed that the Germans had placed their disarmed prisoners in front of them as they retreated, so that they would be executed unwittingly by the advancing French. Any prisoners who missed this fate were allegedly shot by the Germans themselves.[95] Joffre wished the soldiers for the French army to "know the fate that awaits them if they lose their notion of military duty and deliver themselves to the enemy." Evidently the battalions from the 5ᵉ DI were not the only units to choose to terminate their efforts without proper authorization.

Mangin also proposed simply to order panics out of existence—no mean feat, since this meant regulating essentially involuntary behavior. In a memo on German trickery dated 25 September 1914, Mangin cited an enemy device of having a German dress up in the captured uniform of a French section leader and announcing to a captain that since the adjoining company was retreating, they should do the same.[96] Other similarly disguised Germans would simply cry "*Sauve qui peut!* [Every man for himself!]" In the future, stated the memo, "any man who cries '*Sauve qui peut!*' or any similar cry will be presumed to be a German agent and will be treated accordingly." Moreover, in the future, "any change of position to the rear must take place through a written order by an officer qualified to give it. The recipient of this order must be able to produce it upon request."

How seriously Mangin expected such a memo to be taken is of course a matter of speculation. As I will argue in chapter 5, Mangin was an unusually intelligent and articulate officer. He also had considerable combat experience in the colonies, which had to have taught him officers' need for flexibility in the field. But taken at face value, the Joffre and Mangin memos pointed to a polarization of views on correct soldierly behavior as the stalemate of force on the Western Front began to set in.

War planners before August 1914 had envisioned a conflict that would be nasty and brutish, but also decisive and short. What happened instead

[93] "Note," 22 September 1914, 5ᵉ DI, 3ᵉ Bureau, 26 N 77.

[94] G.Q.G., 3ᵉ Bureau, "Note pour toutes les Armées, No. 44," 5ᵉ DI, 3ᵉ Bureau, 26 N 78.

[95] This was certainly not the fate of Pirot from the 129ᵉ RI, who suffered nothing worse than rough handling well behind the German lines.

[96] 5ᵉ DI, 2ᵉ Bureau, 24 N 77.

involved stalemate and, for the combatants, a mosaic of experiences to sort out. At Charleroi, unreflective obedience to command authority spelled calamity and defeat, and would have led to massacre had not a reassessment from below intervened. At Guise, a peculiar and limited relationship seemed to exist between the French efforts and the outcome of the battle at all. After the fact, the fragments of the mosaic were pieced together to construct a victory. At the Marne, in contrast, a consensus existed between soldiers and commanders that aggression could have military utility after all. At Brimont and Courcy, this consensus broke down, as the command structure endeavored to push soldiers farther than they proved willing to go. A solution was determined in the field and imposed on the command structure. Never again in the war would the 5e DI encounter so much pitched battle in so short a time. Military stalemate after September 1914 meant that the French army had time on its hands—the time in short, to embark on a whole series of tacit negotiations among soldiers and commanders on how the unplanned-for war was to be waged.

CHAPTER IV

The New 5ᵉ DI and the New War

THE SOCIAL WORLD OF TRENCH WARFARE

As THE BATTERED REMAINS of the 5ᵉ Division d'Infanterie regrouped in St. Thierry in the days after the Brimont/Courcy disaster, the war of movement began to come to an end all along the Western Front. To be sure, the "race to the sea" would continue until November 1914, as a succession of attempted enveloping movements by the Allied and German forces extended to the front to the North Sea. But it soon became clear that neither side had sufficient reserves in either men or materiel to exploit a breakthrough, even if one occurred. With such French resources as were available siphoned off to the north, Vᵉ Armée commander Louis Franchet d'Esperey recognized his only option in his orders to his corps commanders for 20 September: "Endure and hold on [Durer et tenir]."[1] In practice, this meant beginning to dig the networks of trenches that would shortly run from the North Sea to the Swiss border.

In short, a new form of warfare had slipped in, unexpected and at first unrecognized for what it was. After a month of nearly constant maneuver and combat, the 5ᵉ DI took part in a total of only thirty-five days of pitched battles over the next seventeen months of the war, primarily in two attacks at Neuville–St. Vaast in the spring and fall of 1915.[2] During the rest of its time in the front lines, the division engaged in what Tony Ashworth has sensibly identified simply as "trench warfare," defined as what transpired in the frontline trenches between the major battles.[3] This chapter analyzes authority relations and confrontations therein during trench warfare. First, I will describe the new 5ᵉ DI, in the wake of reconstitution of the division after September 1914. Then, the new war will be examined through the venerable French social history model of "sociability," as a way to demonstrate both how battlefield experience was transmitted to new recruits and how alternative loyalties were created separate from the military authority structure. Finally, Ashworth's model of the "live and let live" system in trench warfare will be related to the argument about proportionality.

[1] AFGG, tome 1, vol. 4, p. 87.

[2] This figure was calculated from the list of engagements for the 5ᵉ DI appearing in the official French army history. See ibid., tome 10, vol. 2, pp. 40–41.

[3] Tony Ashworth, *Trench Warfare, 1914–1918: The Live and Let Live System* (New York: Holmes & Meier, 1980).

THE 5ᵉ DI IN OCTOBER 1914

When the 5ᵉ DI dug its first trenches in the new war, it comprised two main sorts of soldiers. The first included veterans of the liminal experience of the battles of August and September, in which conscripts and reservists became apprised early and so dramatically of the limitations of their prewar training. The second, socialized into the new war by the first, included diverse men completely new to the division, who often had a distant connection to prewar military life or no connection at all.

Oddly, data on personnel remained somewhat fragmentary throughout the war, despite the critical military importance of manpower issues. Certainly at the outset, bureaucratic structures in the French army were no more prepared for a protracted war than French munitions stockpiles. Daily casualty figures in the first phase of the war were hastily tabulated and certainly provisional, particularly concerning the large numbers of men reported missing. Regiments were reinforced over the course of the first month of combat, especially during the retreat. Unfortunately, the numbers of reinforcements received on the battlefield often are not reported in the JMOs or elsewhere. As a result, the most reliable demographic information turns out to be the (probably incomplete) paper trail left as units were being reconstituted in the fall of 1914.

At least the scope of the personnel change can be gleaned from the reports from the 1ᵉ Bureau of the 3ᵉ CA, responsible for keeping track of numerical strength or *effectifs*.[4] On 16 August, six days before the first contact with the Germans, the report gave a figure for the 5ᵉ DI of 382 officers and 17,479 NCOs and common soldiers; on 21 September, the respective figures were 201 and 9,807.[5] By 21 October, the division was up to what would be about its normal wartime strength, 313 officers and 15,543 NCOs and common soldiers.

That the 5ᵉ DI of August 1914 within two months after the fighting started found itself heavily diluted by conscripts lacking even a smattering of the prewar doctrine of the offensive is shown in a report on the reinforcements received as of 24 October 1914.[6] The report shows both the extent of the change and the diversity of personnel in the division. In the fall of 1914, a benchmark figure for an infantry regiment was 2,700 men.[7] In the 74ᵉ RI,

---

[4] "Situations: Rapports des 5 et 10 jours," 3ᵉ CA, 1ᵉ Bureau, 11 August 1914–December 1915, 22 N 90.

[5] These figures include all branches of service, such as artillery, engineers, etc.

[6] "Compte-Rendu concernant des derniers renforts arrivés, 29 Octobre 1914" (no author indicated), 5ᵉ DI, 1ᵉ Bureau, 24 N 76.

[7] The size of regiments declined steadily over the course of the war, as the French manpower situation worsened. A regiment at full strength would have been about 3,000 men at the mobilization, about 2,500 men in 1915, and about 2,200 men by 1918.

for example, 1,175 men (or nearly 44 percent) had arrived since 18 September. In the 129e RI (which lost no less than six of its twelve companies in the Brimont/Courcy disaster), the figure was 1,345 or nearly 50 percent. In the 36e RI, the figure was 698 men or 26 percent, though the regiment as of October had still not received nearly 500 of the 1,200 men it had requested. For the 274e RI, the reserve regiment of the 74e RI and the regiment least engaged in battles of August and September, the figure was 150 men or about 6 percent.[8]

The ages of the reinforcements also varied a great deal, though certainly the vast majority were old enough to have had considerably more distant contact with the military world than the men they replaced. In the 74e RI, 50 percent of the new personnel were from the classes of 1900–1904 (that is, between 34 and 38 years old). Another 20 percent were volunteers from Alsace and Lorraine, who of course would have had no previous exposure to the French military system at all.[9] In the 36e RI, on the other hand, all were between the ages of 21 and 26 (the classes of 1908 through 1913), and 70 percent were between 21 and 24 years old. In the 274e RI, all the new recruits were between the ages of 34 and 43 (the classes of 1881 through 1900), though 92 percent were between the ages of 35 and 37.[10]

Some information is included on wounded soldiers able to return to the front. The *blessés gueris*, though a tiny proportion this early in the war, would be perceived as a major destabilizing factor by the time of the 1917 mutinies. The seriousness of even most nonfatal wounds is revealed by the fact that according to the estimates provided, only 12 of 93 officers (13 percent) had returned by October 1914. The report called it "indispensable" in the future that as many recuperated soldiers as possible be sent back to the front.

The comments in the report on the training of the new recruits highlights their limited exposure to the martial world. The new men in the 74e RI, who came from the regimental depot in Rouen, had spent their time since being recalled to the colors in drill in the handling of rifles: "The instruction in combat is very rudimentary. Information on the present war seems totally unknown in the depot. The men claim that they fired rifles only once a week. The volunteers from Alsace do not know how to shoot." Roland Lécavelé (much better known to posterity as Roland Dorgelès, author of *Les Croix de bois* [Wooden Crosses, 1919]), reported that he was allowed to join the 39e RI at the front with no military training at all, simply

---

[8] For reasons not disclosed, no figures were provided for the 39e RI.

[9] An estimated 3,000 Alsatians and Lorrainers crossed the frontier before it was sealed to join the French army. See Pierre Miquel, *La Grande Guerre* (Paris: Fayard, 1983), p. 17.

[10] The human reinforcements in the 129e RI evidently arrived before the bureaucratic reinforcements, so no breakdown is possible for that regiment.

because he and his fellow volunteers insisted.[11] Of the reinforcements in the 36e RI, about one-third (229 of 698) were recovered wounded. These men, we are told in a language that has a double meaning in retrospect, had "a fine military instruction." The training of the other two-thirds was "nearly nil." Although no demographic information was known about the new men in the 129e RI, their training even in marching was rated "insufficient" and "the physical condition of the men they sent hardly seems always to have been sufficiently checked." The reinforcements sent to the 274e RI were "animated by a good spirit," but because of their age, were held to have "noticeably slowed down the regiment."

Reliable information on changes in the officer corps, perhaps surprisingly, is even more difficult to come by than for common soldiers. As discussed in chapter 2, the French army of August 1914 already confronted a severe shortage of junior officers, a shortage made much worse by the losses of the first month of the war. But the new officers were in the large majority promoted reservists and NCOs and thus do not appear in the regimental officers registers, which were for the most part restricted to career officers.[12] For only one regiment, the 39e RI, does the JMO provide a new *état nominatif* for the fall of 1914 (dated 1 November). Fortunately, the regimental JMO also provides a nearly complete list of promoted NCOs. It is thus possible to provide a basic reconstruction of the new officer corps based on what might be thought of as two snapshots, the *états nominatifs* of 5 August and 1 November.[13]

The most striking development is the precipitous decline in the number of professional officers just over two months into the war. To be sure, professional officers still commanded the heights. The 39e RI had a new commanding officer, who had previously served the regiment as lieutenant colonel. Two of the three August 1914 battalion commanders were still in place, and the third was a promoted captain from within the regiment. The deprofessionalization begins to become clear, however, in the profile of the company commanders. Ideally, each company should have been commanded by a career captain, and indeed four of the twelve captains from

[11] Roland Dorgèles, "Souvenirs et réflexions sur les 'Croix de bois,' " *Nouvelles Littéraires*, 24 November 1928.

[12] Exceptions were sometimes made when an outstanding reserve officer was given a commission in the regular army, but not enough of these exceptions occurred to make possible reliable generalizations.

[13] For the 36e RI and the 129e RI, both of which lost whole battalions at Brimont, the turnover in the officer corps was of course greater. For the 274e RI the turnover may be presumed to have been less, though the officers of this regiment would have been less professionalized to begin with. For the 74e RI, which had a roughly comparable combat record to that of the 39e RI, the turnover may be estimated as similar.

August 1914 were still in place in November.[14] Two other captains had been regular army lieutenants promoted within the regiment, for a total of six of twelve companies commanded by regular career officers. One other company commander was a reserve captain who did not leave Rouen with the regiment on 5 August. But of the other five company commanders, one was a reserve lieutenant and a second a reserve second-lieutenant promoted to lieutenant. The other three company commanders were actually former NCOs (adjudants-chefs) promoted to second-lieutenant for the duration of the war.

The professional junior officer corps in the 39e RI had practically ceased to exist. The two August 1914 lieutenants still with the regiment had been promoted to captain. Of the twenty-one second-lieutenants not commanding companies, only two (one active and one reserve) occupied the same or comparable position at the mobilization. Another fifteen were promoted NCOs (sergeants or adjutants). (No information is available on the other four.) While it is impossible to determine whether these promoted NCOs had held these ranks before the war or had been privates promoted under fire, the key point is that their formative military experience had been Charleroi, Guise, the Marne, and Brimont rather than Saint-Cyr or Saint-Maixent.[15]

Conspicuously lacking through the French army documentary record of the war is information about the class origins of men of all ranks. Certainly in the fall of 1914, all professional categories served together in the ranks, though over the course of 1915 skilled industrial workers (especially in metallurgy) began to be culled out to assist wartime production.[16] As for the officers, the états de services include no class information. Career officers' dossiers give fathers' professions, though these can be examined only 120 years after the officer's birth. Certainly some effort was made to recruit new officers from the middle classes, but the results were probably mixed.[17] It seems fair to observe, though, that the French military hierarchy remained far more heterogeneous in class origin than, for example,

[14] Normally, a captain was the highest ranking officer actually to live in the trenches.

[15] No dossier for an NCO survives unless he later received a regular army commission, and not always then.

[16] For a fine examination of French manpower policy see John Horne, "'L'impôt du sang': Republican rhetoric and industrial warfare in France, 1914–1918," Social History 14 (1989), pp. 201–23.

[17] General Mangin sought new officers from the middle classes, particularly those active and reserve NCOs who "in civilian life (such as supervisors in industry, directors of agricultural production, merchants, etc.) were accustomed to commanding. . . ." Note de Service, 16 September 1914, 74e RI, Opérations, 1914–1917, 25 N 52. But in a response noted at the bottom of Mangin's memo, the new 10e Brigade commander commented politely that "needless to say, a professional does not ipso facto meet the requirements, but the candidate must above all possess the qualities of a leader."

its British counterpart.[18] Demographically inferior France simply could not afford the luxury of high-class barriers.

SOCIABILITY AND AUTHORITY IN THE TRENCHES

The new 5ᵉ DI took shape in a new sort of battlefield environment in which conventional rules of battle no longer applied. Trench warfare inverted Clausewitzian principles of pitched battle, ideally of limited duration and decisive. In contrast, trench warfare was theoretically constant but inherently indecisive. The social world resulting from these inverted rules has been described most often in terms of its emotional impact on those who experienced it. The concept of the "brotherhood of the trenches," has described at best an ambiguously healthy response to the collective trauma induced by the horrors of the trenches. Eric Leed, for example, posited that "No Man's Land" became the very symbol of soldiers' alienated identities, even after the war. This symbol, their only remaining link with humanity, could only be shared with other soldiers.[19] Klaus Theweleit has argued that this concept of "brotherhood" described an annihilated male self-image, recast in a perverted form in the interwar paramilitary *Freikorps* in Germany.[20]

Antoine Prost, in contrast, contended in his extensive study of French veterans' organizations that the "brotherhood of the trenches," served mainly to distinguish survivors from the outside world while blurring the diversity of mentalities among the veterans themselves.[21] Moreover, the concept owed much to postwar tribulations such as chronic economic instability. Prost's work suggests that another model is needed to analyze soldiers' lives together during the war itself.

As a more subtle alternative, I propose here to adapt the venerable French social history concept of sociability, most often associated with Maurice Agulhon's analysis of the rapid diffusion of republican ideology

[18] From the British army, for example, a well-known story survives from R. C. Sherriff, the author of *Journey's End*. Sherriff found himself excluded from the British officer corps in August 1914 because his public school was not on an approved list. Even enlisted men whose backgrounds were considered too modest were excluded from some units early in the war. See Peter Simkins, *Kitchener's Army: The Raising of the New Armies, 1914–1916* (Manchester: Manchester University Press, 1988), chap. 8.

[19] Eric Leed, *No Man's Land: Combat and Identity in World War I* (New York: Cambridge University Press, 1979).

[20] *Male Fantasies, Volume 2: Psychoanalyzing the White Terror*, Erica Carter, Chris Turner, and Stephan Conway, trans. (Minneapolis: University of Minnesota Press, 1989 [originally published in German in 1978]).

[21] Antoine Prost, *Les Anciens Combattants et la société française, 1914–1939*, 3 vols. (Paris: Presses de la Fondation des Sciences Politiques, 1977).

FIG. IV-1. Frontline Trenches, 5ᵉ DI, 1915. Reprinted with permission of the Bibliothèque Nationale, Paris.

through the south of France in the first half of the nineteenth century.[22] In Agulhon's work, sociability relied on physical and institutional components that facilitated constant and informal interaction between social classes. To some degree, formal social hierarchies were obfuscated by the

[22] See Maurice Agulhon, *La République au village: les populations du Var de la révolution à la seconde république* (Paris: Plon, 1970).

rhythms of daily life. Through sociability, people from a wide variety of backgrounds found common social ground and acquired common political experience.

As adapted here, sociability serves two functions. First, it offers a way to explain how soldiers' experiences were collectivized and how the lessons drawn from that experience were transmitted to the new recruits. Second, sociability both drew from the fluid nature of the formal hierarchy in the fall of 1914 and functioned in ways that helped keep authority relations flexible among privates, NCOs, and junior officers.

The physical preconditions for the sociability of the trenches can be deduced from map IV-1, which shows the sector of the 5ᵉ DI on 2 August 1915. Anywhere on this map would have been considered the "front lines" as usually conceived. This map shows the trench system at its most complex, since it represents a sector in Neuville–St. Vaast in the Artois taken by the French in May, and from which new attacks would be launched in September and October. As a result, the remains of the previously German positions had French reorganization of the position superimposed on it. The first important feature to describe about this overview of the whole position is the set of spatial relationships among the various command centers (circled and labeled on the map). Concerning sociability, the spatial arrangements meant close proximity and nearly constant informal contact among men of different ranks.

The structure of the trench system also meant considerable physical distance between the "soldiers" exposed to physical risk and the "com-

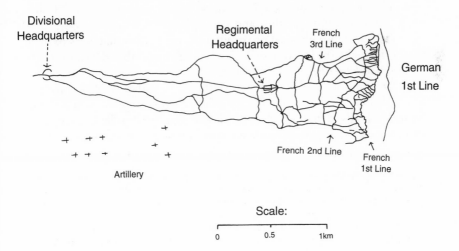

Map IV-1. 5ᵉ DI Sector, 2 August 1915

manders" at the rear of the position. The distance between the first line of trenches and the division command center is nearly three kilometers. Telephone lines provided communications between the front and rear of the position, a system that functioned well enough between major battles but that generally broke down completely during them. Communications during battles could be provided through cyclists and runners, or animals such as pigeons and dogs, all of whom suffered high casualty rates. As a result, once the shooting started, even a general as interested in providing a physical presence for his men as Mangin found his will difficult to communicate, let alone enforce. Even the regimental headquarters indicated on the map was just over one kilometer from the most forward position and about two kilometers from the divisional headquarters. The density of the forward part of the sector compared to the rear also bears pointing out. While the number of men posted in the first two lines of trenches would vary depending on the level of combat activity, there is certainly much to support the conventional literary image of thousands of men crowded together living like rats. Only after Verdun in 1916 would the density of men in the front lines be noticeably reduced.

A detailed picture of the frontline of trenches is provided in map IV-2. The normal delineation between three lines of trenches is somewhat blurred because of the French reorganization of the previous German position.[23] The whole spatial configuration fostered small-group interaction. The transverse structure of the trenches, which served to prevent enfilading fire along the whole length of the trench, grouped men together in earthen boxes. Perhaps even more important are the dugouts (marked on the map by "*A*" for *abri*.) The dugouts were the social centers of the frontline trenches, where common soldiers, NCOs, and junior officers could take refuge from the foul weather and eat, smoke, write letters home, and converse. The close physical proximity of company commanders to their men is shown by the location of the command posts (labeled P.C. for *poste de commandement*).

Apart from the combat of trench warfare, life in the trenches consisted primarily of building and maintaining the trench system and of sustaining the men who lived in it. Much of the dismal detail of this life has been well known since the time of the war, and need not be examined at great length here.[24] To be sure, even without the violence and even at its best, life in the

[23] In the top third of the map, the foremost line represents an attack trench, which would be manned only by snipers except during an offensive. As a result, the parallel trenches connecting the first two lines are not transversed, as would normally be the case, so that attacking troops could be moved forward as quickly as possible.

[24] The finest short survey for the French case remains Jacques Meyer, *La Vie quotedienne des soldats pendant la grande guerre* (Paris: Hachette, 1966). A short and comprehensive account in English is John Ellis, *Eye-Deep in Hell: Trench Warfare in World War I* (New York: Pantheon Books, 1976).

FIG. IV-2. Inspection Tour of the 5ᵉ DI Front Lines, Fall 1914. (General Mangin is third from the right.) Reprinted with permission of the Bibliothèque Nationale, Paris.

trenches was a dirty and dull experience. For much of the year, as anyone who has lived in northern France can confirm, it was also cold and wet. Frostbite in winter and trench foot year round beseiged soldiers' bodies. Sleep was irregular since many work details could only be performed at night, and was often interrupted by artillery bombardments. It is small wonder that soldiers felt more and more like the rats they spent so much time hunting.

But the dreary rituals of daily life in the trenches also fostered sociability. Much of a soldier's daily life was spent carrying out tasks in groups of varying sizes. A basic feature of trench life was the rotation of subunits within the division's sector. Companies would maintain subsectors for other companies, battalions for other battalions, etc. Especially in the first years of the war, a division could be in the "front lines" (in the sense of the whole sector shown in map IV-1) for months at a time. But soldiers rarely remained in the front line of trenches for more than four to five days at a stretch.[25] Considerable time was spent roaming on official duties in small

25 The 5ᵉ DI remained in the "front lines" broadly conceived until May 1915, when it was given nine days of rest before the offensive at Neuville–St. Vaast.

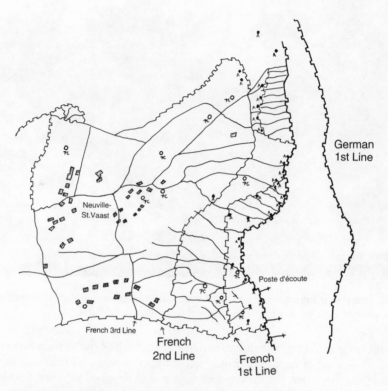

Scale:

0   100   200
meters

German
1st Line

Neuville-
St.Vaast

Poste d'écoute

French 3rd Line

French
2nd Line

French
1st Line

MAP IV-2. 5ᵉ DI Sector, 2 August 1915 (detail)

groups among sectors and subsectors. Building and maintaining the trench system itself was a time-consuming small-group activity, especially in the wet, chalky soil of the Champagne, so ill-suited to subterranean living. The various work details gave rise to a wide variety of friendships and disputes among men of different ranks.

Although the tireless drone of the trenches certainly remained the model, soldiers had a great deal of time on their hands to think and to exchange their thoughts with their comrades. As Jacques Meyer, a distinguished witness of the war (though not of the 5ᵉ DI), put it: "If sleeping, eating, and drinking, even miserably, were the only agreeable moments of life in the trenches, soldiers still had a great deal of time to occupy in the twenty-four hours of each day, when they were not guarding the battlements or sitting at the listening posts."[26] Much of this time, it seems reasonable to presume, was simply spent talking. During this conversation, I would argue, the sociability of the trenches took place. Particularly from 1915 on, a widespread movement of grassroots journalism in the form of trench newspapers appeared documenting sociability in daily life.[27]

A key function of the sociability of the trenches was to collectivize the lived experience of previous battles, and particularly to convey soldiers' rendering of that experience to new recruits.[28] A methodological problem exists, of course, in trying to document this largely oral process. Many of the conversations through which sociability took place survive only through literary accounts, upon which historians can cast many aspersions. A suggestive if particularly problematic source is by far the most famous account written by a soldier of the 5e DI, Roland Dorgelès's novel *Les Croix de bois*.[29] Dorgelès claimed to be writing the definitive statement on conveyed battlefield experience—"not *my* war," he wrote in 1928, "but *the* war."[30] Jean Norton Cru, after sixty years probably still the most important critic of French war literature, described Dorgelès as a shameless careerist who would stop at nothing to match the success of Henri Barbusse's *Le Feu* (*Under Fire*, 1916), and provided a withering point-by-point critique of the work's many distortions and factual errors.[31]

Still, even Cru did not fault the particular episode examined here, a convincing portrayal of how new recruits were assimilated into units.[32] Although one can pin down even the year in which the events depicted took place only by process of elimination, the novel appears to begin in November 1914, with the arrival of three new recruits to a unit resting behind the front lines. The novel is written in the first person, with the author pre-

---

[26] Meyer, *La Vie quotedienne*, pp. 131–32.

[27] See Stéphane Audoin-Rouzeau, *À travers leur Journaux, 14–18: les combattants des tranchées* (Paris: Armand Colin, 1986).

[28] Trench newspapers frequently dealt with battle experience, but not, as it turns out, the newspaper surviving from the 5e DI. See ibid., pp. 73–95.

[29] Paris: Albin Michel, Editeur, 1919.

[30] Roland Dorgelès, "Souvenirs et réflexions sur les 'Croix de boix,'" *Nouvelles Littéraires*, November–December 1928, quoted in Leonard V. Smith, "The 'Crisis of Masculinity' of World War I in the Fifth Infantry Division," *Proceedings of the Western Society for French History* 17 (1990), p. 450. See also idem., "Literary and Non-Literary Accounts of Battle: Roland Dorgelès at Neuville–St. Vaast in 1915" (paper delivered at the Annual Meeting of the Society for French Historical Studies, Vancouver, B.C., March 1991).

[31] Jean-Norton Cru, *Témoins: essai d'analyse et de critique des souvenirs de combattants édités en français de 1915 à 1928* (Paris: Les Etincelles, 1929), pp. 587–93.

[32] Dorgelès was classified as unfit for duty before the war, though he volunteered for service in August 1914. He was sent to the front with the 39e RI, and he remained with this regiment until he joined the aviators in the fall of 1915. See Roland Dorgelès, *Souvenirs sur les croix de bois* (Paris: À la cité des livres, 1929).

FIG. IV-3. Sociability: Rest during a Work Detail, 1915. Reprinted with permission of the Bibliothèque Nationale, Paris.

sumed to be a seasoned veteran. At first, the experienced soldiers and the newcomers looked at each other with mutual incomprehension:

> We were all standing and formed a curious circle around the three bewildered soldiers. They looked at us and we at them, without saying anything. They were just coming from the rear, they were coming from the cities. Just yesterday they were still walking the streets, they were eyeing women, tramways, and boutiques. Just yesterday they were living like men. And we looked at them amazed, envious, like voyagers arriving in a fantasy land.[33]

The newcomers were then mocked by the veterans, as a rite of initiation. A soldier named Sulphart picked out a particularly young-looking newcomer named Demachy. Upon inspecting him carefully, Sulphart discovered a large haversack made out of white imitation leather. Taunting the neophyte, Sulphart said: "Hey bud, did you have that game-bag made just to go into the trenches? If you're afraid that sometimes the Germans won't be able to spot you easily enough, maybe you could bring along a little flag

[33] Dorgelès, *Les Croix de bois*, p. 3.

and play a trumpet."[34] The newcomer was duly cowed and blushed. Having been ritually identified as an outsider, Demachy could now become an insider. Sulphart quickly added:

> I'm not saying this for you, you don't know any better yet. But as for those other fife-players who have you shine your mess tins with saber polish, don't you think they should all be shot? Don't they think you're enough of a target as it is? Come on, give me your bag, I'll burn some cork, and we'll pass your dixies, your *galetouses* and that bag over some smoke from burning straw, there's nothing better.[35]

Thereafter, world-weary Sulphart became Demachy's mentor. Toward the end of the afternoon, conversation among the group turned to the impending return to the front lines. The veterans started talking about their battlefield experience and whether Charleroi, the retreat, or the Marne was the single most difficult episode. Demachy commented that he would most liked to have been at the Marne, since it was a victory. Sulphart willingly conveyed the wisdom of his learned experience:

> Sure, it was a victory. . . . If you'd been there, you'd have slobbered like the rest of them, nothing more. Go find out from the boys what happened to them at Escardes. You just can't talk about it without knowing anything. Those assholes up there who write about it, they shouldn't have bothered. Me, I was there, I know what happened. Well, we went for more than fifteen days without even getting paid, since the end of August. Then, after it was all over, they paid us all at once. They gave us fifteen *sous* [15/100 of a franc]. That's the truth. So then, when guys talk to you about the Marne, you only have to say one thing to them. The Marne, it was a threshing machine that brought fifteen *sous* to the boys who won it.[36]

According to the model of sociability as applied here, experienced soldiers taught new recruits not only how to survive as well as they could in the trenches, but also the rules of the power dynamic between themselves and those who exercised authority over them. This produced a much more subtle situation, I would argue, than one in which lieutenants, sergeants, and corporals would simply show privates how to follow orders. Sociability was certainly facilitated by the transformation of the lower-level leadership structure. Yesterday's private became today's sergeant, and yesterday's sergeant today's company commander.

But the processes of sociability themselves lent flexibility to authority relations. Sociability created "horizontal" links among men of varying

---

[34] Ibid., p. 4.
[35] Ibid., p. 5.
[36] Ibid., p. 15.

ranks who shared common hardships and dangers. These links coexisted with and often competed with the "vertical" links along the institutional hierarchy.[37] Horizontal links among "soldiers" defined here also suggests that sociability need not be just the "trickle down" phenomenon from elites to nonelites. In the sociability of the trenches, junior officers, NCOs, and common soldiers could influence each other.

Positing ties of loyalty independent of institutional structures and based on shared experiences and hardships may seem a laborious way to assert a rather obvious point. Certainly, such ties are commonly explored in, for example, labor and rural history. Traditional military historians attach great significance to informal and emotional links among officers and common soldiers. But historians of peasants, artisans, and industrial workers have principally concerned themselves with attaching such social links to class structures. Military historians have applauded such links when they have served military efficiency, and labeled them part of Clausewitz's "friction" when they have not. My point here involves describing a self-defined military identity born of sociability, that of "soldier" as object of command authority, an identity that needs to be taken seriously in its own right.

La Chausée, the adjutant section commander from the 39e RI whose experience at Charleroi and Guise was explored in the previous chapter, was promoted to second-lieutenant just after he was wounded in September.[38] His memoir recounting his return to his regiment in November 1914 provided an unpretentious and even moving description of sociability. Upon his return, La Chausée assumed something of a dual identity, as both a "seasoned" battlefield veteran (such as the concept existed so early in the war) and a newly commissioned officer. His account illustrated the persistance of horizontal links alongside newer, vertical ones.

Indeed, La Chausée described a conversation that suggested closer links to the soldiers he had previously fought with than to the officer caste he had ostensibly just joined:

> I then received a visit from one of the two men who had come from the depot with me. They were no longer with their old section, and knew hardly anyone in the company, its personnel having changed so much. I took advantage of the situation to talk about the men still with my old section, several of whom had sent their news to me. The men wanted to stay with the same comrades and the same cadres, the others interesting them less directly.

This was a conversation among equals about a shared problem— assimilating into a new unit. Of course, normal conversation among men

[37] I am indebted to Professor Allan Silver of the Department of Sociology, Columbia University, for alerting me to the concept of competing horizontal and vertical social links.

[38] See Capitaine J. La Chausée, *De Charleroi à Verdun dans l'infanterie* (Paris: Eugene Figuière, no date, *dépôt légal* 1934), pp. 194–95.

of different ranks is not something any army authority structure would disapprove of under all or even most circumstances. What I am suggesting, however, is that this sort of conversation reflects the intermediary position of new officers like La Chausée. Mutual empathy behind the lines did not disappear in battle. On the contrary, this empathy helped give rise to tension between these officers' attachment to command aspirations and their attachment to the soldiers they commanded, and whose lives so closely resembled their own.

La Chausée simply but elegantly described his version of the comradery of the trenches. Despite all manner of literary conventions thoroughly developed by the time his account was published around 1934, he made no extravagant claim about "brotherhood of the trenches" as a conduit of any form of political ideology, let alone fascism. Also conspicuously absent was attention to ties based on military rank. As he showed time and again later in his account, La Chausée never forgot he had become an officer. But the very reason his account is so convincing in its simplicity is that he also never forgot he remained a human being:

> Wartime comradery, above all during trench warfare because it lasted so long, can be explained easily. In their lives together, men ended up grouping together according to like-mindedness. Thus, they formed small communities, in which it was not rare to see each one giving what he could, food, drink, tobacco, etc., and sometimes money.
>
> Those who sought solitude were rare, and were wrong, because everything about war affirms that no one can go it alone.

Again, personal attachments to comrades of varying ranks would be considered a key factor in any unit's "morale." Commanders have known throughout history that male bonding in its myriad forms has been one of the most powerful factors motivating men in war. The point from the command structure's perspective, however, would be to prevent horizontal links from taking on a life of their own in opposition to the command structure. In the British and German armies, the command structures worked toward this end by preserving class distinctions as much as possible, particularly in the selection of officers. Such a policy proved unworkable in the French army as early as the fall of 1914. As will be shown, the conflict between horizontal and vertical social links (which could also be described as sociability versus military discipline), proved a key factor in the negotiation of proportionality and command authority.

PROPORTIONALITY AND THE "LIVE AND LET LIVE" SYSTEM

The levels of violence in trench warfare are best thought of as a spectrum, ranging from a couple of shells or bullets lobbed each day in the general direction of the enemy trenches, to nearly constant shelling, sniping, and raids and counterraids. The point on this spectrum at which any given unit found itself at any given time depended on a number of factors, such as the reputation, leadership, and training of the unit, the strategic significance of the sector, and even the time of year.[39] However, a common feature of all points on this spectrum must be stressed. Whatever the level of violence, neither soldiers nor their commanders expected the outcome of the war to be determined by trench warfare. Nevertheless, as early as his orders for 17 September 1914, Joffre had made clear what he wanted to happen between pitched battles: "To maintain an aggressive attitude and to keep the enemy under constant threat of an energetic offensive, in order to prevent him from disengaging forces for movement from one part of the front to another."[40] This scenario frequently did not—and indeed given shortages in men and materiel could not—prevail in the field. The question to be negotiated among soldiers and commanders, then, concerned the appropriate level of activity under a given set of circumstances.

Because trench warfare was by definition stalemated in any strategic sense, Tony Ashworth's path-breaking model of the "live and let live" system, while a valuable conceptualization, needs to be rethought.[41] Ashworth argued that tacit truces, in which both sides would allow their nominal enemies to go about their daily activities in peace as long as they returned the favor, were an endemic feature of trench warfare. Moreover, the command structure found it could compel aggression in trench fighters only slowly and through extraordinary measures calculated to induce retaliation and counterretaliation.

Specifically, I wish to call into question two of Ashworth's assumptions that seem better explained through applying the concept of proportionality. First, Ashworth assumed that soldierly aggression was invariably imposed from above and against the naturally more pacific inclinations of the soldiers themselves.[42] Second, and as a corollary to the first assumption, Ashworth assumed that since soldiers always wanted peace or at least nonaggression, their commanders always wanted offensive violence and were willing to arrange such tactical situations and to take such disciplinary measures as were necessary to get it.

[39] In general, trench warfare was rather less deadly than literary convention would have posterity believe. The 274ᵉ RI *JMO* gave daily casualty figures for its time in the frontline trenches in Neuville–St. Vaast from July through September 1915. In this "active" sector *par excellence*, 30 men were killed and 69 wounded (23 of whom did not require evacuation) during a ten-day rotation in July. During another rotation in September just days before the French offensive, the figures were 16 killed and 65 wounded.

[40] G.Q.G., Instruction particuliére, no. 29, 17 September 1914, quoted in AFGG, tome 1, vol. 4, pp. 391–92.

[41] Ashworth, *Trench Warfare, 1914–1918.*

[42] See ibid., especially pp. 76–77.

The argument here operates on different assumptions. Although tacit truces probably were an endemic feature of trench warfare in the 5e DI, a way needs to be found to relate soldiers' willingness to engage in violence to their sense of what they were doing in the trenches in the first place. One need not choose, I believe, between primordial and coerced origins of soldierly aggression. It seems abundantly clear that most French soldiers between 1914 and 1918 wanted to win the war; the outcome of the mutinies of 1917 cannot be explained otherwise. The central argument of this study thus maintains that soldiers developed their own rules as to when their use of violence would and would not be useful toward this end, and over time proved able to impose these rules of proportionality on their commanders. This argument applies to trench warfare as well as to pitched battles. The live and let live system served to continue the process of negotiating the parameters of command authority that began in the pitched battles of August–September 1914.

The Christmas truce of 1914 in the 74e RI shows how this process worked.[43] Such a truce was of course the most extreme sort of example of the live and let live system—open fraternization with the enemy. But the incident provides important insights into how levels of activity in trench warfare were negotiated, both because of its unique character and in the way it was handled by the divisional command structure.

An intriguing account of the Christmas truce appeared in the memoir of Charles Toussaint, the bicycle messenger from the 74e RI whose memoir was cited in chapter 3.[44] The sequence of events was a familiar one along the Western Front.[45] On Christmas Eve, Toussaint reported, he could hear singing from both sides of the trenches, the French singing "Minuit Chrétien," the Germans "Weihnachten." The next day, a German soldier bearing a white napkin simply walked over to the French side and announced that the Germans "had decided to call a truce for Christmas Day and asked for reciprocity." The frontline soldiers of the 74e RI readily accepted. The result was a sort of "village fair," with the convivial exchange of items from Christmas packages sent from home—food, tobacco, beer, wine, etc.

While these events transpired, Toussaint was at the regimental command post, where he heard Lieutenant Colonel Brenot suddenly bark into the

[43] I am excluding fleeting episodes, the sort of which occur in all wars, such as the incident in the 39e RI in which the Germans allowed a French patrol to reclaim a wounded soldier, even though the patrol was in easy firing range. La Chausée, *De Charleroi à Verdun*, p. 119. The two sides also frequently allowed each other to bury their dead in No Man's Land, particularly at night.

[44] Charles Toussaint, *Petites Histoires d'un glorieux régiment: vécues par Charles Toussaint, soldat du 1ere classe au 74e Régiment d'Infanterie en guerre* (Montvillers [Seine-Maritime]: Binesse, 1973), pp. 53–55.

[45] On the British case, see Malcolm Brown and Shirley Seaton, *Christmas Truce* (New York: Hippocrene Books, 1984).

telephone: "If they don't want to go back, fire over their heads!" Understandably curious, Toussaint proceeded in great haste to the observation post. He found most surprising the sudden and dramatic transformation of No Man's Land, normally completely deserted during the day: "And now, all of the sudden, this landscape found itself peopled with all these men who wanted to forget the war, at least for Christmas Day." But quickly brushing aside his own empathy with the situation, Toussaint added: "But discipline and its requirements, which we might have ended up losing sight of, could not accommodate themselves to such a situation."

Brenot ostensibly ended the truce by ordering a few time-shells fired by the 75s, "high enough to avoid wounding our boys." It is worth noting that if the timed shells were fired into the air, they probably did not harm the Germans either. It seems reasonable to infer that Brenot's intent was to control the Christmas hiatus, but not pointlessly to make the sector of the 74e RI an active one. Moreover, discreet fraternization continued into the night: "One of our men, particularly curious or perhaps still under the influence of the nocturnal libations, let himself be carried away by the Germans. When night came, they brought him back, dead drunk, as far as the limit of our barbed wire, where we recovered him." A number of easily discerned subtexts are implicit in this passage. First, by wandering over to the German lines, the French soldier was technically guilty of a capital crime (desertion to the enemy), a fact overlooked at least by those of his superiors who knew about the incident and covered it up. Second, the Germans who returned him plainly were not inclined toward revenge, despite the shells that had been lobbed in their general direction earlier in the day. Finally, the Germans clearly had no trouble proceeding both to and from the French barbed wire.

That the command structure itself could be persuaded to accept the *dis*proportionality of demanding violence on 25 December 1914 is demonstrated by its restrained and even *pro forma* reaction. The fact that Brenot had to end the truce personally indicates that none of his subordinates had much interest in deeply engaging himself to end the festivities. His battalion and company commanders probably understood the irregularity of the situation, but preferred to let the lieutenant colonel take the blame for terminating it. There is also evidence of a lack of enthusiasm in disciplining the perpetrators. In a note of 28 December, Brenot chided an officer commanding either a battalion or a company for not naming as many NCOs as an earlier report by that officer indicated were involved.[46] When Mangin

46 74e RI, Opérations, 25 N 52. No reports on the incident survive, and this note survives only in a barely legible carbon copy scrawled into a notebook. For this reason, it is impossible to determine to whom the note is addressed. Evidently, the officer had earlier indicated that a number of sergeants were involved, though when the time came to name names, he identified only four corporals, one from each section of the 9e Compagnie.

THE SOCIAL WORLD OF TRENCH WARFARE 93

heard about the incident, his most important concern was to confiscate any photographic evidence of the episode and to prohibit cameras in the trenches in the future.[47] No courts-martial resulted from the incident. According to Toussaint, formal repression was limited to the demotion of a few sergeants and corporals and to assigning extra hours for some of the common soldiers involved in the listening posts (miserable and exposed dugouts ahead of the front line of trenches).

The point to stress here is that on Christmas Day 1914, the soldiers of the 74e RI challenged the parameters of command authority by venturing into the gray area between command expectations and their own inclinations, just as they ventured literally into No Man's Land. Officers had to have collaborated indirectly; the truce simply could not have continued as long as it did without second-lieutenants, lieutenants, and probably even captains and majors at the very least looking the other way. At the same time, all concerned, including Mangin, knew that the war was not going to be won or lost on 25 December. By challenging authority in a militarily harmless manner, the soldiers of the 74e RI presented their commanders with the choice of responding harshly, in which case they would appear mean-spirited and even foolish, or of acquiescing to one degree or another. The mild repression of the episode indicates a tacitly negotiated settlement that does not imply soldierly powerlessness.[48]

Indirect evidence suggesting that soldiers limited violence in trench warfare is substantial but of course more tenuous. Vague accounts, such as reports from the divisional artillery showing fire at unspecified times at unspecified targets or at targets with no apparent military value, can mean many things. In any event, obfuscation from below for ambiguous reasons is hardly a bureaucratic practice unique to the French army in World War I.

The best indirect evidence from the 5e DI indicating the limitation of violence from below is the constant stream of complaints running from the

[47] Note from Brenot, 26 December 1914 (not further identified), in ibid. No photographs of the incident survive in the archives. Mangin of course continued to take his own photographs, a number of which appear in this book.

In a letter to his wife dated 6 March 1915, Mangin described an incident in the 5e DI in which a battalion facing the Germans exchanged "shots from time to time, and bread and tobacco as well." Mangin reminded the errants that they "had in front of them a horde of the most dangerous assassins," and that any future episodes would result in executions. Charles Mangin, *Lettres de guerre*, Stanislaus Mangin and Louis-Eugène Mangin, eds. (Paris: Fayard, 1950), p. 44. Although Mangin claimed he went to some trouble to put his foot down, this is the only surviving documentary record of the incident.

[48] There is no evidence of a truce in the sectors of the other 5e DI regiments. Reports from patrols from the 8e and 9e Compagnies of the 36e RI simply reported that they heard Germans singing and celebrating. 5e DI, 3e Bureau, 24 N 80. Nor is there any evidence of fraternization at Christmas in 1915. A 5e DI report to the 3e CA reported that the Germans made overtures in the sectors of the 36e RI and the 129e RI that were "greeted with rifle fire." "Compte Rendu, 26 decembre 1915," 5e DI, 3e Bureau, 24 N 84.

FIG. IV-4. Indirect Evidence of the "Live and Let Live System": Original Label, "*Tranchée à 20m des Boches*" ("Trench 20 Meters from the Boches"), 1914 or 1915. Reprinted with permission of the Bibliothèque Nationale, Paris.

divisional command structure. To be sure, authority structures tend by nature to complain. In addition, senior officers appear to have had at least as much time on their hands as privates between major battles, and to have spent a good bit of it harassing their subordinates.[49] But the dynamic of the

[49] On 17 June 1915 (less than two weeks after the 5ᵉ DI attack at Neuville–St. Vaast),

complaints shows a negotiation of the parameters of command authority, much in the manner of the Christmas 1914 truce. I will examine two varieties of complaints here, about patrols and about general conditions in the trenches.

In the first two years of the war, patrols represented the major form of contact with the enemy between pitched battles, apart from the shells lobbed during artillery barrages.[50] Simply put, patrols were "search and find" missions, in which a group of five or six men (led by a junior officer and an NCO) would sneak out of the trenches after dark, cross No Man's Land, and provide intelligence reports on enemy positions and activity. Certainly, patrols were one of the least appealing features of trench warfare, given the great risk inherent in any foray into No Man's Land. Moreover, patrols could also have questionable military value, given the new possibilities of aerial reconnaissance and the fact that enemy positions often simply did not change much from day to day. The whole enterprise depended on the good will of the participants; patrols of course were unsupervised, and there proved no effective way to regulate the quality of the information they brought back.

A typical example of a strikingly anodyne but apparently "good faith" report resulted from a patrol undertaken by seven men from the 9e Cie of the 36e RI on the night of 5–6 February 1915[51]. The patrol comprised one second lieutenant, one sergeant, and five common soldiers. The patrol left French lines at 2300 and walked about 150 meters of the 250 meters between the French lines and the first German sentries. "Thanks to the clear moon and the calm of the night," the second lieutenant wrote, "I could observe perfectly everything going on around me." What he saw in over four hours of observation was no evidence whatsoever of serious work being done on the German side of the lines, nothing more than the standard nocturnal laying of more barbed wire. The second lieutenant did find a German rifle, a bayonet, and a cartridge in No Man's Land, booty he duly brought back to the French lines. Literally hundreds of such reports exist just for the 5e DI.

Some evidence exists that patrols were not always so devoted to duty, even when the division was posted in the highly active sector of Neuville–St. Vaast between the fall and spring offensives. A memo from 3e CA

Mangin complained to his wife that "I have never had so little to do." *Lettres de guerre*, p. 52. He took to rereading Shakespeare and Saint-Simon to pass the time.

50 Ashworth is correct to point out that the French had no systematic raiding policy before the 1917 mutinies. *Trench Warfare*, p. 225. But, unlike the British (who did not even adopt conscription until 1916), the French already had a huge army in the field, and believed they possessed the means for breaking through the German lines. It seemed reasonable then, for the French to conserve their resources toward that end. In 1915, Joffre did not need a raiding policy to convince his British counterparts that France was deeply committed to the war.

51 36e RI, 9e Cie., "Reconnaissance effectuée par le S/Lieutenant Neufville, du 5 Février, 23 heures au 6 Février 3 h 30," 5e DI, 3e Bureau, 24 N 81.

commander General Hache of 5 September 1915 complained that two patrols from the 39ᵉ RI comprised only one corporal and one private, and one corporal and two privates, respectively. Such tiny patrols "could not procure any serious information."[52] In the future, he added, patrols had to be constituted strongly enough "to give them vigor"; above all, an officer had to be included, "so that one can place absolute confidence in the exactitude of the information reported." Just a few days later, General Mangin complained that the 36ᵉ RI had not sent out any patrols at all on the night of 7–8 September.[53] The stated reason was a French artillery barrage on the enemy first lines given in retaliation for a German barrage earlier in the day. Mangin remarked tartly: "This fire certainly did not last all night, and an understanding with the artillery would have made possible the patrols formally proscribed by the general commanding the 3ᵉ CA." On 24 September (during a period of pitched battle), the 5ᵉ DI command complained of "superficial reports that contain no reference to numbers, such as the following: 'It has been noted that the German barbed-wire network had been seriously damaged; large gaps were cited.' A serious report must indicate the exact location, the number, and dimension of these breaches, as well as the source of the information."[54] In a quiet sector like the one inspected by the patrol from the 36ᵉ RI, information brought back by patrols did not matter much one way or the other, and probably engendered little tension along the chain of command. But even in an active sector, and indeed during a battle, the capacities of the command structure to compel the gathering of information to its liking proved limited. The nature of patrol reports did not vary fundamentally over the whole course of the war.

The physical condition of the trenches and the appearance of the soldiers who manned them proved constant bones of contention in the 5ᵉ DI as elsewhere, regardless of the level of activity in the sector. In addition to its other inconveniences, the work of maintaining the trench system was also often immensely frustrating, for officers and NCOs as well as for soldiers. The efforts of weeks preparing frontline positions could be washed away in few days of heavy rain. Lower-level authority figures found it a challenge to maintain turnout and (by implication) conventional discipline even between major battles. Nevertheless, conventional discipline remained a matter of some concern from above, on the theory that lassitude in the French lines would not encourage much aggressiveness toward the Germans in trench warfare, much less once pitched battle recommenced.

It will suffice here to cite two examples of a nearly constant stream of

[52] Note de Service, no. 2003/3, 5 September 1915, in 5ᵉ DI, 3ᵉ Bureau, 24 N 82.

[53] Note de Service, no. 6169/S5, 8 September 1915, in ibid.

[54] Note de Service, 24 September 1915 (signed by divisional Chief of Staff Brzumineski), in ibid.

complaints from above. In a surprise visit to the front lines on 13 November 1914, Lieutenant Colonel Brenot of the 74e RI found the sector of the 7e Compagnie far from his liking.[55] One section commander ostensibly on duty proved nowhere to be found. The listening post was far too close to the French frontline trench to be of any intelligence-gathering value. Brenot was most dissatisfied with the placement of the barbed wire, which he had previously explicitly ordered be moved: "No officer has inspected this trench over the course of the day, and the order that I had given thus remained a dead letter."

In a more sweeping memo of 17 May 1915, Lieutenant Colonel Jèze of the 36e RI condemned "on the part of nearly everyone a deplorable sense of *laisser aller* (letting things go), which the NCOs and even the officers for the most part make no effort to counteract."[56] Jèze continued:

Uniforms are slovenly, coats are unbuttoned, straps are not attached, hands are in pockets, képis are pointing down, etc., etc.

The turnout of the sentinels at stockade and at the colonel's command post would make reserve territorials blush.

The men show up in a ridiculous manner, heels apart, rifles held in any which-way. This is shameful. It must cease.

In an interesting mixture of "good cop/bad cop" rhetoric, Jèze pleaded that such conduct could "ruin irremediably the reputation of the regiment in the eyes of the superior authority." He added that he "counts on the good will of all" to remedy the situation. All companies should look out for each other, since all belong to the "same family." Should good will fail, he concluded, officers would henceforth be held personally responsible for the slack conduct of their men. This, of course, tended to confirm that officers acquiesced in their men's undisciplined conduct in the first place.

It should be stressed, however, that dissatisfaction did not just make itself felt in one direction, from above to below. In December 1915, the 5e DI was assigned a new sector at Frise in Picardy. This was a particularly miserable sector, with a large swamp in it that made organizing a good defensive position virtually impossible. Upon arriving in the sector, 10e Brigade commander Colonel Viennot asked subsector commanders to provide reports outlining the work that needed to be done, the means at their disposal, and the "relationship between these means and the extent of the effort required."[57] All three battalion commanders of the 129e RI commented in response that incessant rain and (implicitly) the lassitude of the previous occupants had left the sector in such a dreadful state that they did

[55] Untitled report from Brenot to 2e Bataillon commander, 13 November 1914, 74e RI, Opérations, 1914–1917, 25 N 52.

[56] Note de Service, 17 May 1915, attached to the 36e RI *JMO*.

[57] Note de Service, no. 2725, in 129e RI, Opérations, 1914–1918, 25 N 122.

not have enough manpower on hand both to defend the sector and to repair it quickly.[58] One commented bluntly: "It is doubtful that with the men at our disposition we can arrive at a really satisfactory result, even if the rain stops. In any case, if does not seem possible to ask for more work from the troops occupying the sector." Plainly, such a state precluded much harassment of the enemy trenches. If these three battalion commanders had anything to say about it, Frise would remain a quiet sector for the foreseeable future.

Most observers, when asked to describe the war of the trenches, would probably draw principally from the experience of pitched battle and the "over-the-top" assault across No Man's Land. To be sure, pitched battle certainly seems to have constituted soldiers' central formative experience. But by far, most of their measured time was spent in more mundane "trench warfare" between pitched battle. The adage that war comprises protracted periods of boredom and grinding discomfort punctuated by periods of incredible violence and terror certainly applies here. I have argued that authority relations came under negotiation between soldiers and commanders in trench warfare, just as they did in pitched battle.

The negotiation of violence in trench warfare, certainly in the first years of the war, proved relatively uncomplicated. Soldiers could effectively limit the theoretical command aspiration of constant aggression without provoking more than a stream of complaint from the command structure. Violence in trench warfare had certain propaganda functions, but in a military sense remained strictly a sideshow. Hopes remained high that a decisive breakthrough was in the grasp of the French army. Certainly in early 1915, soldiers and commanders, and indeed all of France, anticipated that trench warfare would prove a hiatus. A return to pitched battle, so high-command calculation predicted, could complete the work of the Battle of the Marne and carry France to victory.

[58] See the reports of the three battalion commanders in ibid.

CHAPTER V

From *Percée* to *Grignotage*

THE 1915 OFFENSIVES AT NEUVILLE–ST. VAAST

AT THE BEGINNING of 1915, confidence in "Papa Joffre" and the French high command had never been higher. Having rescued a grateful nation in the most impressive feat of French arms since Napoleon, the Hero of the Marne and his entourage fully anticipated completing their task by rupturing the German lines (the *percée*) in the Artois and then rushing through to complete the liberation of national territory. Careful planning, audacity, and a willingness to sacrifice, it was thought, could make the doctrine of the offensive workable in a new setting. But by the end of 1915, the command structure reluctantly concluded that the *percée* could be achieved only after the German reserves had been exhausted. This in turn could only be achieved by attacks designed primarily to kill Germans, a strategy known as "nibbling" or *grignotage*.

This chapter argues that this shift in strategy was not made in a vacuum, rather in response to a calculation of proportionality made by battlefield soldiers and imposed on the command structure. Such an outcome implies a considerable rethinking of what actually went on during a World War I battle. Posterity has come to understand pitched battle in World War I according to literary convention. Soldiers attacked in a hopeless situation, a horrible massacre ensued, and by some miracle a few traumatized soldiers survived. It is important to stress that such an interpretation is by no means wholly untrue. But neither does it tell us all we need to know. Indeed, if the conventional literary image told the whole story, we would be left wondering why *any* of the protagonists survived. As Jean Norton Cru observed in one of the quotes used as an epigraph of this study, had all orders been followed to the letter, the entire French army would have been massacred by the end of 1915.

In the 1915 offensives, soldiers and their commanders negotiated a more coherent configuration of the mosaic of battlefield experience that occurred in the summer of 1914. This process took place in two stages. In the first attacks in April and May 1915, soldiers fought ferociously, partly because of particular physical circumstances, and partly because the offensive seemed to offer some prospect of a *percée*. In the second attacks in September and October, however, a different scenario prevailed in a patently more problematic military situation. Soldiers went "over the top" at H-hour more or less in good faith, but simply stopped fighting when they perceived no additional utility in their efforts. Their commanders were then obliged to accept this outcome as adequate. This constituted the tacitly negotiated scenario of proportionality that held through the Battle of Verdun.

This chapter comprises two main sections. The first will outline the career and character of 5ᵉ DI commander Gen. Charles Mangin, who provided an unusually honest if grim version of command expectations. The second section illustrates the shift from *percée* to *grignotage* by providing a narrative of the 5ᵉ DI's engagements at Neuville–St. Vaast according to the "win/lose" and "experiential" framework established in chapter 3.

CHARLES MANGIN AND *OFFENSIVE À OUTRANCE* WITHOUT ILLUSIONS

Traditional military history has long been steeped in the cult of personality, nowhere more so than in Napoleon-worshiping France. Such history thrives on movement and heroic personality, traits ill-suited to World War I generals, whose records suffered from the effects of stalemate and frustrated dreams of glory. In strict win/lose terms, all senior commanders were "failures" for much of the war in that they failed to break the military stalemate. Historical legend and literary convention have tended to portray them as either fools or knaves, either criminally ignorant of the physical details of the war they waged or all but sadistically insensitive to them.

But if the analytical framework extends beyond how wars and battles are won or lost and assessing professional success or failure accordingly, the limits of this approach become clear. More important become questions such as how World War I generals came to determine the utility of soldierly aggression and how willing or reluctant they proved to enforce or revise their views on the matter.[1] Whether the commander of the 5ᵉ DI from September 1914 to June 1916, Gen. Charles-Marie-Emmanuel Mangin, was a knave is essentially a moral question removed from this study. Clearly, however, he was no fool. On the contrary, Mangin understood very well the nature of the technological stalemate of World War I and had specific if ferocious ideas of how to overcome it.

Mangin tended to defy military convention in general and, in particular, the unobjectionable homogeneity of the military notables described in

[1] A fine study raising new questions about World War I generalship using the case of Sir Douglas Haig of the British army is Tim Travers, *The Killing Ground: The British Army, the Western Front and the Emergence of Modern Warfare, 1900–1918* (London: Allen & Unwin, 1987).

chapter 2. He was born the son and grandson of state functionaries in Sarrebourg in 1866, just five years before this area became part of the "lost territories" of Alsace and Lorraine in 1871. Douglas Porch has observed that his career resembled that of one of his patrons, Hubert Lyautey.[2] Both attended Saint-Cyr, where both learned the art of defying military authority. No indication of class rank appears in his personal dossier, but a biography by Mangin's son gives a less than stellar graduation rank of 389 of 406.[3] Also like the outsider Lyautey, Mangin found his niche in the colonial army, which he joined upon graduation. As a lieutenant in 1898, he accompanied Col. Jean-Baptiste Marchand to Fashoda. His list of subsequent postings reads like a list of French imperial interests around the turn of the century—Senegal, Sudan, Indochina, Morocco. His famous victory at Sidi Bou Othmann in September 1912 helped the French convince themselves that they had conquered Morocco. But less than a year later, the mauling his troops received at the hands of the Moroccans at Casba Tadla in June 1913 resulted in Mangin's repatriation to the metropole.[4]

Nevertheless, as with Lyautey, it would be a mistake to overstate Mangin's position as an outsider. Mangin had an impressive ability to attract powerful patrons—Lyautey, Franchet d'Esperey, Robert Nivelle, and eventually Georges Clemenceau, who saved Mangin's career after the failed Chemin des Dames offensive in 1917.[5] Mangin could also impress metropolitan military notables, as shown in the evaluation of his time at the Centre des Hautes Études Militaires after his return from Morocco: "His great intelligence, his sure judgement, his zeal for work, and his previous experience will permit him to adapt himself very quickly to the conditions of continental war."[6] Not least, at a time when officers throughout Europe struggled to match financial means and social status, Mangin married in succession two wealthy women (his first wife died in 1905), both daughters of high state officials.[7]

---

[2] Porch, *The Conquest of Morocco* (New York: Alfred A. Knopf, 1983), pp. 263–64.

[3] Mangin personal dossier, no. 57/Gx.Div., 3ème Série, Troupes Coloniales. As is the case with all well-known military figures, the dossier has been specially processed by the archivists. Mangin's dossier no longer includes even the original *état de services*, which normally provides class rank. A purged typed version appears instead. The citation rank comes from Louis-Eugène Mangin, *Le Général Mangin, 1866–1925* (Paris: Éditions Fernand Lanore, 1986), p. 21.

[4] The losses were deemed enormous for a colonial operation: 77 dead and 170 wounded. Porch, *Conquest of Morocco*, p. 284.

[5] Unlike Lyautey, Mangin also had a knack for alienating these patrons. Even Clemenceau broke with him after the war, over his activities with Rhineland separatists.

[6] Fonds Joffre, Fonds divers, 14 N 1.

[7] His first wife was the daughter of a former *ministre plenipotentaire* in the foreign ministry who brought nearly 200,000 francs to the marriage. His second wife, Antoinette Cavaignac, was the daughter of former war minister Godfroy Cavaignac. She brought 100,000 francs to

Mangin has long attracted the attention of English-language historians, who perhaps have found themselves frustrated with the peasant inscrutability of Joffre and the cold aloofness of Pétain. Theodore Roosevelt is alleged to have concluded upon meeting Mangin before August 1914 that France and not Germany would win the next European war.[8] Winston Churchill called him the "fiercest warrior-figure of France."[9] Alistair Horne provided a memorable physical description that agrees closely with Mangin's photographs:

> Mangin was a killer, and he looked the part. His face was burnt and eroded by the Sahara; his square jaw seemed permanently set, like a terrier with its teeth clamped into a rat that it was vigorously worrying to death. His mouth was wide, thin-lipped, and cruel; his jet-black hair stood up fiercely *en brosse*. He walked with a quick, nervous gait, and had a Napoleonic habit of standing with his hands behind his back, his head thrust forward.[10]

Mangin's fundamental principles governing conduct of the Great War remained essentially unchanged to the end of his life in 1925. He maintained an unshakable belief in the constant necessity of the attack—in principle regardless of the extent of the results or even the cost at which gains were purchased. He wrote in a book published in 1920: "It is . . . evident that, by definition, passive defense can attain no positive result, because its sole function is to stop an attack. To make war is to attack."[11] As he showed in Morocco, where he formed "fighting squares" which the Moroccans assaulted with no success and much bloodshed, Mangin was not unable to fight a defensive battle.[12] But the Moroccan campaign was a war of conquest; the French maintained the initiative simply by being in the country at all. Continental war, on the other hand, was quite a different matter. Germany already occupied Mangin's birthplace, the "lost territories" of Alsace and Lorraine; the partial success of the Schlieffen Plan handed them industrial northeastern France as well. A negotiated settlement would have meant a de facto German victory.

Fate had thus handed France a life-or-death struggle with its ancient foe, in which the defense would sooner or later mean capitulation.[13] The per-

---

the marriage, with expectations of four times that amount. "Rapport du Lieutenant Corcuff commandant de l'arrondissement de Saint-Calais," 22 July 1905, Mangin personal dossier.

[8] Alistair Horne, *The Price of Glory: Verdun 1916* (London: Macmillan, 1962), p. 229.

[9] Quoted in ibid.

[10] Ibid., pp. 228–29.

[11] Charles Mangin, *Comment finit la guerre* (Paris: Plon, 1920), p. 7.

[12] See Porch, *Conquest of Morocco*, chaps. 19–20.

[13] Mangin discussed war aims frequently in his letters to his wife from the fall of 1914 through the spring of 1915 (although rarely thereafter until 1918). On 22 September 1914, for example, he advocated the annexation of Cologne, Aachen, and the Rhineland, as well as the destruction of the Krupp arms factories. Charles Mangin, *Lettres de guerre*, Stanislaus Mangin and Louis-Eugène Mangin, eds. (Paris: Fayard, 1950), p. 29. Mme. Mangin in turn served as her husband's political antenna in Paris throughout the war.

FIG. V-1. 5ᵉ DI General Staff (undated, probably 1915). Reprinted with permission of the Bibliothèque Nationale, Paris.

ceived moral need for the French army constantly to take the offensive, of course, had been presented by Grandmaison, Plan XVII, and the April 1914 infantry regulations. But followers of the fad of the offensive before the war tended not to dwell on the level of casualties such a strategy would involve, nor did they explain how demographically inferior France was to come up with enough men to replace them.

Mangin, in contrast, shared few illusions of the fad of the offensive. The existing military technology had simply enhanced the price in blood and treasure that France had to pay to prove its right to exist as a Great Power. In *La Force noire*, he argued that black African colonials provided the answer to France's demographic inferiority to Germany.[14] In the process, he gave black troops the dubious but unusual compliment of equality with white troops. If Mangin had ever believed in a short war, he divested himself of that belief quickly. As early as 15 October 1914, he wrote to his wife that "I see us in a deplorable and long stagnation."[15] Whatever he might have said in public (particularly before attacks), his belief in a long, bloody struggle persisted in letters to his wife throughout 1915. To be sure, Mangin did not acquire the historical sobriquet of *le boucher* (the butcher) without cause. But his problem was not so much that he was especially vicious as generals went, but simply more forthright about the implications of his military principles.

Mangin was unusually aware of the perils and hardships of World War I warfare (both trench warfare and pitched battles) and as far as possible sought to share these dangers with his troops. In the attack on Courgivaux during the Battle of the Marne, Mangin was held to have saved the day personally by "himself going into the firing line, and thanks to his energy and his presence among the troops, was able to keep them in place. . . ."[16] During the pitched battles of 1915 and 1916 he kept his command post within enemy artillery range. During periods of trench warfare, he made regular trips to the front lines and reported what he saw in gruesome detail to his wife.[17] At one point, according to Henri Dutheil, he publicly dared one (quaking) regimental commander to join him in raising his head above the parapet of a firing trench while enemy sniping was going on.[18] Mangin deplored as "colossal heresy" the conduct of staff officers who kept themselves "sheltered from the emotions of the battlefield, in order to maintain their freedom of spirit [*liberté d'esprit*]."[19] As will be explored further

[14] Paris: Hachette, 1911.

[15] Mangin, *Lettres de guerre*, p. 31.

[16] 5e DI *JMO*, 6 September 1914. This incident is also mentioned in several other sources.

[17] For example, in his letter of 29 May 1915, Mangin described stepping on the chest of a German recently buried by the French. Ibid., p. 51.

[18] Henri Dutheil, *De Sauret la honte à Mangin le boucher* (Paris: Nouvelle Librairie Nationale, 1923), pp. 184–85.

[19] Letter of 22 September 1914, in *Lettres de guerre*, pp. 27–28.

FIG. V-2. Sociability: General Mangin in the Frontline Trenches (probably early 1915). Reprinted with permission of the Bibliothèque Nationale, Paris.

below, Mangin also had a constant interest in innovation, as documented by hundreds of pages of reports and memos.[20]

But Mangin's letters to his wife also testify to immense professional frustration, some of which he took out on his troops. He lamented on 16

[20] Perhaps the most amusing recounted an episode in January 1915 in which a soldier who in civilian life had been "an entrepreneur in metallic construction" built a machine to run over barbed wire. It took the machine eight minutes to cross the forty-five meters to get to the barbed wire, whereupon it caught fire. This made the machine visible at least one kilometer away. It took the machine thirty-seven minutes to cut through three meters of barbed wire. It was estimated that had the apparatus been used in combat, all of the participants could have

July 1915 that he "remained the only general having taken part in operations since the beginning of the war who was neither deprived of his command nor advanced. . . ."[21] Particularly stinging was the upward mobility of Philippe Pétain (the other 3e CA division commander) who had been only a colonel in August 1914 (Mangin had been a brigadier), but who had been given a corps only two months later.[22]

The precise reasons for Mangin's professional stagnation certainly do not emerge from the glowing evaluations in the surviving version of his dossier. Mangin himself concluded after a conversation with Robert Nivelle in December 1915 that he had been held back because of the abiding prejudice in the metropolitan officer corps against colonials.[23] While this possibility cannot be discounted (though Joffre, Gallieni, and Franchet d'Esperey had also been colonials), it seems reasonable to suppose that the casualty rates of troops under his command also played a role. After all, Pétain may have only been a colonel in August 1914, but unlike Mangin, he did not lose over two whole battalions from his division near Courcy. Mangin, at least in his letters to his wife, never once conceded that he personally might have played a role in his limited success on the battlefield. The cause of the Brimont/Courcy disaster, he concluded to his wife, was the lackadaisical advance of the divisions to his right and left (the latter Pétain's 6e DI).[24] In 1915, Mangin explained in a similar manner the unfulfilled expectations at Neuville–St. Vaast.

In interpreting his limited military success, Mangin tended not to look very far down the chain of command. He did not hesitate to place blame on colleagues such as Pétain, or to demand the heads of brigade and regimental commanders when he felt the situation warranted it. But Mangin never blamed the junior officers, NCOs, and common soldiers he commanded for his professional frustrations—quite the reverse. He saw his men simply as an extension of himself and of his own will.[25] He never blamed them because he never blamed himself. He almost blithely assumed that they would do whatever he told them to, and if they did not that the cause lay elsewhere.

Mangin's approach to discipline via courts-martial supports the argument that he responded much more implacably to generals and colonels

---

been killed several times over. "Procès-verbal: établi à la suite de la mise en expérience d'un engin destiné à la destruction des réseaux de fil de fer," 5e DI, 3e Bureau, 24 N 80.

[21] Mangin, *Lettres de guerre*, p. 56.

[22] Letter of 18 November 1914, ibid., p. 34.

[23] Letter of 29 December 1915, in ibid., pp. 78–79.

[24] Letter of 13 November 1914, in ibid., pp. 32–33.

[25] How thoroughly this assumption permeated Mangin's historical image is powerfully illustrated in the statue to Mangin erected at the Place Denis Cochin in Paris and destroyed on Hitler's orders in 1940. An illustration appears in Louis-Eugène Mangin, *Le Général Mangin*.

than to privates. I have argued elsewhere that Mangin's disciplinary approach was never as ferocious as his historical image suggests, and indeed became less so over the course of 1915 and 1916.[26] To be sure, five of the seven executions carried out by the court-martial of the 5e DI during the entire war took place before September 1915. But only one of these took place under what could be construed as capricious circumstances under the letter of the law.[27] Over the course of 1916 and later, prosecutions for any infractions except abandoning a post and desertion became more and more rare. From the outset, a relatively lenient definition of "post" was decided upon, despite the theoretically constant combat and presence of the enemy in trench warfare. For the entire period of September 1914 through February 1916, only six of forty-five convictions for abandoning a post carried the aggravating circumstance of being in the presence of the enemy.[28]

For Mangin, in short, the politics of war remained the politics of generalship. Instead of attempting to enforce conventional discipline with ancien régime–style severity, Mangin attempted to overcome the stalemated war and his stalemated career through inventing ever-grander and more ambitious battle situations. This will be demonstrated in chapter 6 in his schemes for the 5e DI at Verdun, and is even more true once he became VIe Armée commander for the Chemin des Dames offensive of April 1917. The result was an ever-widening gap between what Mangin expected to happen on the battlefield and what the soldiers he commanded considered possible.

TOWARD THE PERCÉE AT NEUVILLE–ST. VAAST, MAY–JUNE 1915: THE ILLUSION OF PROPORTIONALITY

The French high command selected the Artois as a place where a *percée* could be exploited strategically, to liberate northeastern France and thus belatedly complete the Battle of the Marne. Despite the disappointing

[26] Leonard V. Smith, "The Disciplinary Dilemma of French Military Justice, September 1914–April 1917: The Case of the 5e Division d'Infanterie," *The Journal of Military History* 55 (January 1991), pp. 47–68.

[27] This case involved the execution of a private who had panicked during a bombardment not long before the division was to join the May offensive. The execution gave rise to considerable dismay even among Mangin's officers, and circumstantial evidence suggests a far more cautious approach to sending men to the firing squad thereafter. See Ibid., pp. 57–58.

[28] For "minor offenses" (ranging from hunting rabbits without authorization to being found asleep on duty in the presence of the enemy), less than one court-martial sentence in five from September 1914 to January 1916 was actually carried out. See Smith, "Command Authority in the French Army, 1914–1918: The Case of the 5e Division d'Infanterie" (Ph.D. diss., Columbia University, 1990), table IV-1, p. 237.

results of the British attack at Neuve Chapelle in March 1915[29], the French offensive must have seemed a most promising enterprise, at least on paper. A total of eighteen French divisions faced ten German divisions in the sector (six in the front lines, four in proximate reserve).[30] The French artillery comprised no fewer than 780 campaign artillery pieces and 293 heavy pieces, over an initial front of about twenty kilometers. In addition, clear French air superiority ensured good intelligence as to German strength and intentions.

Even stated in the most clinically succinct military language, the results tragically failed to fulfill this apparent promise. Although the fact is rarely recognized, 1915 proved rather a bloodier year for the French army than 1916—the year of Verdun and the Somme.[31] In the Artois offensive, the difficult terrain (chosen with some care by the Germans as they retreated after the Marne) and the unexpected facility with which the Germans reinforced their position with men and artillery during the battle itself were named in the official history as the principal factors limiting the French success.[32] The offensive produced gains over about eight kilometers of the twenty-kilometer front, and at certain points the French position advanced as much as three kilometers. Total casualties for the Xe Armée carrying out the attack were 102,500 men killed, wounded, or missing.[33] Even using the generous assumption that three kilometers were gained across the entire front, this meant that the Xe Armée took over 4,000 casualties per square kilometer. The German position, moreover, was not seriously threatened.

The part played by the 5e DI in this drama involved taking the village of Neuville–St. Vaast, which stood in one of the best approaches to the Vimy Ridge, from the southeast. The ridge constituted one of the few sectors of high ground in the area (some seventy meters above the plain). Its importance and that of the village leading to it were substantial. The Germans had heavily fortified the town with artillery, mortars, mines, machine guns, and underground shelters to protect their infantry during enemy barrages.

---

[29] On Neuve Chapelle, see Shelford Bidwell and Dominick Graham, *Firepower: British Army Weapons and Theories of War, 1914–1945* (London: George Allen & Unwin, 1982); and John Baynes, *Morale, A Study of Courage: The Second Scottish Rifles at the Battle of Neuve Chapelle, 1915* (London: Cassel, 1967).

[30] See Commandant Lefranc, "La Prise de Neuville-Saint-Vaast (9 mai–9 juin 1915), *Revue militaire française* 33 (1929), p. 332. Lefranc was one of the authors of the relevant volume of AFGG.

[31] According to figures established during the war, the French army suffered approximately 430,000 deaths in 1915 and 361,200 in 1916. Calculated from "Pertes des armées françaises" (Annexe VII-7[suite]), in Colonel Guinard, Jean-Claude Devos, and Jean Nicot, *Inventaire sommaire des archives de la guerre, Série N 1872–1919* (Troyes: Imprimerie La Renaissance, 1975), p. 213.

[32] See AFGG, tome 3, pp. 101–2.

[33] The exact figures are: 16,803 killed, 65,062 wounded, 20,635 missing.

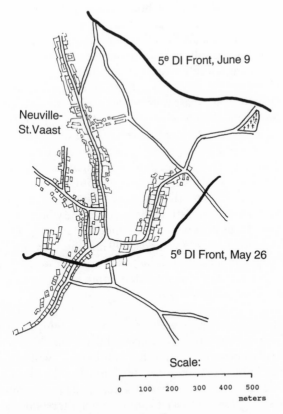

MAP V-1. Neuville–St. Vaast, May–June 1915

Neuville–St. Vaast had been a key objective since the French offensive began on 9 May. Three weeks of attacks by the 39ᵉ DI had brought the French only to the outskirts of the village (shown on map V-1).[34]

By the time the 5ᵉ DI arrived in the sector on 26 May, the topography and record of the offensive across the whole sector indicated that the village could be taken only by frontal assault, essentially house by house. The win/lose narrative of the 5ᵉ DI completing the conquest of Neuville–St. Vaast in June 1915 is at one level simple and straightforward. In short, the French took the village principally because they were willing to throw more bodies at it than the Germans. Throughout the attack, French artillery remained heavily engaged, and assaults on several houses were called off

---

[34] On these initial three weeks, see Douglas Porch, *The French Foreign Legion: A Complete History of the Legendary Fighting Force* (New York: Harper Collins, 1991), pp. 357–63.

because of insufficient preparation. But a variety of problems—getting the French artillery pieces close enough to fire on particular houses while not exposing them to German artillery fire, poor liaison between the artillery and the infantry, and the still-insufficient number of shells—the support to the infantry was considerably weaker than expected.

At the level of specifics, of course, the story of 5ᵉ DI's house-by-house conquest of Neuville–St. Vaast is extremely complex. Accounts of which buildings were taken when tend to vary widely among the *JMO*s, and no general summary need be provided here.[35] The division arrived in the sector on 26 May, and units posted in the front lines were more or less constantly in enemy artillery range until the village was taken. Upon taking the village by 9 June, trophies captured by the 5ᵉ DI included three 77mm artillery pieces, some fifteen machine guns, "thousands" of grenades, and some 1,000 German corpses left on the streets of the village. Casualties for the 5ᵉ DI were: 21 officers killed, 48 wounded, 3 missing; 586 NCOs and common soldiers killed, 1,228 wounded, 99 missing.[36] In other words, the division had taken about 2,000 casualties to conquer an area of less than one square kilometer, a ratio nevertheless approaching twice as favorable as that of the Xᵉ Armée as a whole.

In the "experiential" narrative, which describes that body of collective and collectivized experience through which soldiers and their commanders negotiated the parameters of each other's authority, I will explore what I have called the "illusion of proportionality" and how that illusion began to break down. Certainly, given the basic military situation as outlined, there was some reason before the fact to believe that aggression could prove useful in this first large-scale attack against entrenched positions. In addition, as will be explained, Mangin proved able actually to encourage the intensity of the fighting by exploiting a situation in which soldierly passivity would prove at least as dangerous as aggression. It turned out to be possible in the spring of 1915 to trap soldiers into fighting ferociously. But on the other hand, the meager military results led to the origins of what was refered to in chapter 1 as two "transcripts" of battlefield experience: an "official transcript" describing, in James Scott's words a "respectable per-

---

[35] The account from Mangin's report, "Historique des combats livrés par la 5ᵉ Division du 26 mai au 10 juin 1915 qui sont aboutis la prise de Neuville–St. Vaast," 23 June 1915, 5ᵉ DI, 3ᵉ Bureau, 24 N 83.

[36] These figures include only the 36ᵉ RI, the 39ᵉ RI, and the 129ᵉ RI. The 74ᵉ RI was under the orders of the 53ᵉ DI during this period and was attacking a set of German fortifications to the south of Neuville–St. Vaast so complex it was called the "Labyrinthe." Its casualties were 9 officers killed and 15 wounded, and 202 NCOs and common soldiers killed, 587 wounded, and 111 missing. The 274ᵉ RI was held in reserve and was not engaged at all.

formance," and a "hidden transcript," as yet unfocused, beginning to question the illusion of proportionality.[37]

In a strikingly candid letter to his wife on 9 June, Mangin explained his success at eliciting aggression from his troops:

> Nobody thought I would succeed, not even me, and in fact my attack on June 1 produced little. But my troops had tasted blood [*avaient mordu*] and I improvised a method, which imposed itself on the events: no attack from the sides, because of the machine guns our artillery could not destroy because they were too close to our lines, but instead attacking the houses one by one without stopping. A bombardment to the rear of the houses prevents reinforcements reaching the adversary, against whom one can always throw fresh troops if one takes the proper precautions. I was slowed down by the arrival of the means of action, but I succeeded much earlier than we were hoping; it was inevitable. We now hold the line from which we can continue the offensive without stopping. But my division, badly torn up, is going to regroup a bit behind the lines.[38]

Instead of endeavoring to encircle the village, Mangin sought to trap the German infantry in the village with French artillery fire falling behind the village. In the event, the German artillery fire did much the same to the French infantry. This had the effect of encircling the infantry on both sides, leaving them to fight it out with each other. This amounted to nothing less than the realization of the original objective of the prewar doctrine of the offensive—to transcend the superiority of defensive firepower by restoring the primacy of infantry-infantry combat. Here, aggression was restored by means of physical entrapment.

Mangin's official report included an annex comprising impressions and recollections of some of the company commanders.[39] In this piece of the "official transcript," junior officers recounted a tale of aggression reborn and instilled from above, with enthusiastic consent upon recognition of the results. To cite one of a number of examples, the report from the 12e Compagnie of the 39e RI described an attack on 9 June that recaptured the spirit of the April 1914 infantry regulations.[40] Mangin's call to arms was duly transmitted to the company: "*C'est une fuite en avant que je veux* [I

---

[37] See James C. Scott, *Domination and the Arts of Resistance: Hidden Transcripts* (New Haven: Yale University Press, 1990), chap. 3.

[38] Mangin, *Lettres de guerre*, p. 51. In a letter written on June 11, he proclaimed himself pleased with the results: "Despite the losses in officers, the division is worth much more now than when it arrived at the position." Ibid., p. 52.

[39] "Récits vécus des combat de Neuville–St. Vaast" (no date), 5e DI, 3e Bureau, 24 N 83.

[40] Lefranc emphasized the importance of the 1914 regulations in the decision to take the village in a frontal assault. See "La Prise," p. 346.

want an escape forward]." The author of the report described the motivation of the attackers at H-hour in just these terms: "To see the Boches, to kill the Boches, to conquer the Germans, is better than submitting to the shelling that obliges us to stay huddled up in the fox holes." The attack trench was only forty meters away from the Germans, and the attackers fell as one man upon the enemy, without "planned formations," and "like rabbits, bayonets on high, galloping forward like crazy people, rolling over the shell holes, bounding over the barbed wire." They evidently caught the Germans in the middle of a meal, and left behind ham, sausage, and loaded rifles, untended but pointed at the French. A corporal mounted the conquered parapet to cry "*C'est-y tapé ça, les enfants?* [We got them, didn't we boys?]" The victors responded in as one man: "*Ah, oui alors.*"

No evidence directly contradicts this textbook-perfect representation of events. As it happened, the memoir record was singularly thin for this particular engagement. Still, some observations even in this official rendering suggested that not all was quite what it seemed. The 10ᵉ Brigade commander oversaw similar feats of bravado, but observed that this came at a price. He wrote to Mangin as early as 6 June (three days before the village was finally taken): "Not only are the elements of my brigade incapable at present of cooperating in an offensive, but moreover my regiments are in such a state that I cannot guarantee the integrity of the front I am occupying."[41]

The one detailed memoir of the attack, La Chausée's *De Charleroi à Verdun dans l'infanterie* conspicuously downplayed aggression and even élan, through entrapment or otherwise.[42] La Chausée (by then a lieutenant commanding the 10ᵉ Compagnie) stressed two aspects of his experience at Neuville–St. Vaast—his sorrow at the intensity and extent of the human suffering and his concern with protecting his men from physical peril as much as possible.

La Chausée's memoir contains none of the bravado of the observations of the commander of the 12ᵉ Compagnie of the 39ᵉ RI, which was part of the same battalion.[43] At one point, a soldier told him that he had found two corpses (one French and one German) intertwined in a shell hole, and asked whether he should separate them for burial. "I responded no, and immediately went to see them. And by the light of a flare, I saw that they in fact were intertwined, face to face, as though they wanted to embrace

[41] "Lieutenant Colonel Viennot, commandant la 10ᵉ Brigade au Général commandant la 5ᵉ Division," 6 June 1915, 5ᵉ DI, 3ᵉ Bureau, 24 N 82.
[42] Capitaine J. La Chausée, *De Charleroi à Verdun dans l'infanterie* (Paris: Éditions Eugène Figuière, no date, depôt legal, 1934). Roland Dorgelès took part in the spring attack at Neuville–St. Vaast, though his account in *Les Croix de bois* (Paris: Albin Michel, 1919) is too loosely based and problematic to be used here.
[43] No report from La Chausée's 10ᵉ Compagnie appears in the "Récits Vécus."

FIG. V-3. Reconquered Neuville–St. Vaast, Spring 1915. Reprinted with permission of the Bibliothèque Nationale, Paris.

before dying. . . . And why should we separate them, since they had wanted to die as they should have been able to live."[44] He lectured his men at great length on the necessity of taking proper cover during bombardments, and told them: "If we have to die, we must die usefully."[45] He wishfully assured some desperately wounded men that he would hasten the arrival of the stretcher bearers, and that he had seen men recover who were much more badly wounded than they.

[44] La Chausée, *De Charleroi à Verdun*, p. 142.
[45] Ibid., p. 144.

On 9 June, the day the 5ᵉ DI completed its conquest of the village, La Chausée found it necessary to convey to his readers only two acts of aggression, one attempted ambush of a German reconnaissance patrol, and one incident in which he arranged retaliatory artillery fire after his shelter was hit by a shell. The purpose, he claimed, was not revenge but cover so that a new shelter could be built on the same spot. He observed almost in passing that his company's objectives were attained.

In time, even the "official transcript" of the conquest of Neuville–St. Vaast proved subject to revision. Another reconstruction deemphasizing aggression came from an unlikely source, a history by the division general staff published within weeks after the armistice, the *Pages héroiques de la 5ᵉ Division d'Infanterie*.[46] Like the company commanders who wrote the accounts appended to Mangin's report, the staff officers publishing the division history wished to emphasize the heroism of the 5ᵉ DI. But the officers who wrote the company accounts wrote of fearless, confident soldiers who prevailed because they could ignore danger; through their efforts, the *percée* was just a matter of time. In contrast, the subject of rupturing the German lines never even came up in the *Pages héroiques*. The implicit moral of the story was that the soldiers of the 5ᵉ DI won the war simply because they could suffer more than their enemies. The illusion of proportionality in the attempted *percée* faded into just another exercise in *grignotage*:

> It was at Neuville–St. Vaast that our troops for the first time were put to the test of the "war of attrition," a hideous term if we consider it in its literal sense but a term that evokes the grandeur of the sacrifices that were freely given and repeated daily by those who dream of heroic responsibility and those who had to submit to a war such as the one desired by those on the other side of the Rhine.[47]

THE CONSOLATION OF *GRIGNOTAGE*: SEPTEMBER–OCTOBER 1915

The strategic situation confronting France as it planned the fall offensive looked unpromising. The allies of France seemed unlikely to provide the decisive edge. Most seriously, the Russians had been driven out of Galicia and most of Poland in the spring of 1915, and struggled in the fall to restore a defensible position. The Italians had entered the war in May, but only against Austria-Hungary. Britain and its Commonwealth were diverted by the Dardanelles operation beginning in August. French planners reasoned

[46] Paris: S.T.D.I.5, 1918.
[47] Ibid., p. 34.

that a fall offensive would assist the hard-pressed Russians.[48] It would also enable the French to maintain the initiative of the Western Front, before winter set in and the Germans suspended their efforts in the East and again turned to the West (as they indeed were to do at Verdun in February 1916).[49]

But just what was to be gained by another major effort posed from the outset the problem of joining ends and means. Like the British in 1915, the French lacked a strategy that rendered respectable meager tactical results.[50] Both allies held out some hope based on broadening the attack front. The fall offensive was to be launched in two areas. The major effort took place in the Champagne, with a secondary effort in the Artois in association with the British. But on the French side, a difference of opinion was beginning to emerge within the high command as to whether the fall offensive should even try to achieve the yearned-for *percée*. Gen. Edouard de Currières de Castelnau, directing the attack in the Champagne, still believed a decisive rupture was possible. In contrast, Foch, directing the effort in the Artois, had already made the mental switch to *grignotage*. He believed that the *percée* of the lines could occur only after enemy reserves were exhausted by what amounted to siege warfare.[51] Joffre simply split the difference between his two highest-ranking subordinates and let each go his own way.

The Xᵉ Armée, which comprised the 5ᵉ DI, was to continue attacking the Vimy ridge, assisted this time by the British to its left. The 5ᵉ DI would continue its effort of June near Neuville–St. Vaast, which Xᵉ Armée commander General d'Urbal had christened "its sector."[52] The division would attack the ridge from the south, by continuing its advance to the Bois de la Folie, as shown on map V-2.

The Germans in the 5ᵉ DI sector had not remained idle since June. The two heavily fortified German lines of trenches are indicated on the map.[53] The first line, running south along the Vert-Halo road, was reinforced in its southern section by an advance network of trenches around the Tranchée Brune. The second line, as heavily fortified as the first, was located from three hundred to eight hundred meters behind the first line. In other words, the attacking troops had to cross a dense position over one kilometer long

---

[48] The offensive would also return the debt of Russia's offensive in August 1914, which had reduced the number of German divisions available to invade Belgium and France.

[49] See AFGG, tome 3, chap. 7, pp. 271–361.

[50] On the debate within the British army in 1915, see Bidwell and Graham, *Firepower*, chap. 5.

[51] See ibid., p. 275.

[52] Lecoc, *Pages héroiques*, p. 35.

[53] "Rapport sur les combats livrés par la 5ᵉ Division du 25 September au 4 Octobre 1915," 26 N 268.

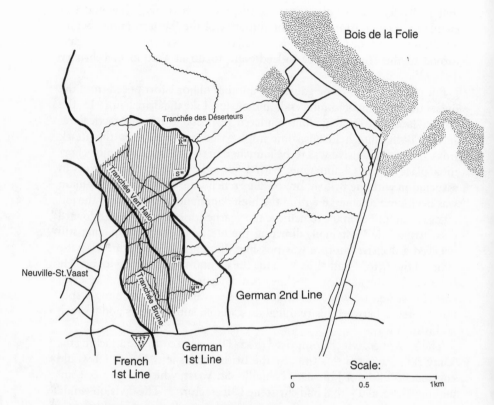

Bois de la Folie

Tranchée des Déserteurs

R"

S"

Tranchée Vert Halo

Neuville-St.Vaast

U"

W"

Tranchée Brune

German 2nd Line

French
1st Line

German
1st Line

Scale:

0   0.5   1km

MAP V-2. Neuville–St. Vaast, September–October 1915

before they even reached the Bois de la Folie, itself a natural barrier on an incline. The basic contours were easily enough discernable to the protagonists, even amidst the inevitable confusion of battle.

Essentially, the narrative of the fall efforts of the 5ᵉ DI recounts two days of costly French gains (25–26 September), six days of erratic battle in which the division consolidated and tried to extend these gains (27 September–2 October), and another week of violent trench warfare until the division was relieved beginning 6 October. Map V-2 indicates the extent of the 5ᵉ DI advance (the vertical lines). It should be kept in mind that the lines indicated are approximations, and that particular positions changed hands many times over the course of the offensive.

Serious operational errors accompanied the beginning of the 5ᵉ DI attack. Artillery preparation began on 20 September, which gave the Germans five days to bring up reinforcements before the infantry attack began on 25 September. A heavy rainstorm on 23 September further diminished prospects for a dash across No Man's Land. On 24 September, flame-throwers spewing fire at the Germans made a great spectacle without reaching the German front lines. The effort produced "ironical exclamations" from the Germans.[54] Tunnels had been dug toward the German lines, in which the French planned to place mines. However, they were being dug no less than four meters below the surface—so deep that they were not nearly finished when the infantry attack took place.

The 36e RI led the attack in the northern sector of the 5e DI front and the 129e RI in the southern sector. (The dividing line was the road between Neuville–St. Vaast and the Bois de la Folie.) The 74e RI and the 274e RI were deployed as reinforcements in both sectors over the course of the attack. Within minutes of the opening of the infantry attack at 1235, the attack of the 129e RI bogged down somewhere between the advance trench called Tranchée Brune and the main first-line trench at Vert Halo. To the north, the 36e RI met with more success. By 1330 much of the northern section of the Vert Halo trench was in its hands, and by 1630 some units had even reached the Tranchée des Déserteurs (the French name for the German second line). By the evening, and with the help of units from the 74e RI, much of the 129e RI section of the Vert Halo trench was also in French hands.

At 0600 on 26 September, the 274e RI launched an attack toward the line R"-S", as indicated on map V-2. A dense fog enabled the regiment to move into position relatively unnoticed, but also precluded any artillery preparation. Although this line was reached, the attack stalled there; the French line did not significantly advance in this sector for the rest of the offensive.[55] In the southern sector of the 5e DI front, the 74e RI had pushed the French line as far as U"-W"; this too would remain the farthest point of the French advance. At 1600, confusion resulting from a false report from the 24e DI indicated a breach of the German lines significant enough for the cavalry to ride through ultimately led to a loss of two hundred to three hundred meters in the southern sector of the 5e DI front.[56] On 27 September, the 5e DI was ordered to "install itself solidly on the conquered terrain."[57]

On 28 September, General Foch began to close down the attack in the sector of the 5e DI, ostensibly in order to free up resources to assist the British, who were meeting somewhat more success along the northern part

---

[54] Ibid. In the report, Mangin blamed these operational insufficiencies on the decision of his superiors over the summer greatly to enhance the scale of the effort in his sector. He argued that he had not been given sufficient time to prepare adequately for the offensive.

[55] Ibid.

[56] AFGG, tome 3, p. 450. The loss of ground is not explicitly cited either here or in the 5e DI report, and is instead inferred from a line drawn on the accompanying AFGG map.

[57] "Rapport sur les combats."

of the Vimy ridge. A general attack in the northern sector scheduled for 5 October was preceded first by heavy fog, then by rain. Because of the combination of the weather, the heavy casualties, and the physical exhaustion of the survivors, the attack was called off and the division began leaving the front lines the next day.[58]

The balance sheet for the offensive showed that the French would not *grignote* their way to the German border any time soon. The Xe Armée as a whole had taken 48,320 casualties to regain a strip or the Artois about nine kilometers long and at certain points as much as two kilometers deep.[59] Even with a generous assumption of two kilometers gained along the entire front, this meant 2,684 casualties per square kilometer—nevertheless an improvement over the spring figure of over 4,000 casualties per square kilometer. But the 5[e] DI fared much worse than the French army as a whole. Infantry casualties comprised 34 officers killed, 63 wounded, and 3 missing; and 971 NCOs and common soldiers killed, 2,091 wounded, and 578 missing. The 5[e] DI had gained a strip of the Artois a bit over one kilometer wide and from three hundred to seven hundred meters deep. In other words, the division had taken over 3,600 casualties to conquer less than half a square kilometer of ground. This compared to slightly more than 2,000 per square kilometer in the spring offensive. The division had also captured five trench mortars, three machine guns, sixteen rifles, and one grenade launcher. No estimate is provided in Mangin's report of German casualties.

In the "experiential" narrative, I will present an alternative to the conventional literary image of what happened in an "over the top" frontal assault, dealing not just with how such attacks began, but how they ended. In so doing, I will argue that the fall 1915 offensive represented an important turning point in the negotiation of the parameters of command authority. Both commanders and soldiers had to drop the illusion of proportionality that prevailed during the spring offensive, that a *percée* was even conceivably imminent. Given this situation, the individual companies of the 5e DI broke off their attacks once they determined they had done their bit and that additional effort would result only in pointless casualties. Consequently, the formal command structure in the end became a reactive rather than an active force in the field. Mangin and his superiors found themselves obliged to accept as militarily adequate an outcome that they had not been the central actors in determining.

To state this in the Clausewitzian terms noted in chapter 1, the formal command structure still controlled the *Zweck* or strategic goal of the war—the military defeat of the Germans through the *percée*. But the mea-

---

[58] Ibid., p. 511.

[59] AFGG, tome 3, pp. 540–42. The exact figures are: 8,939 killed, 29,663 wounded, 9,628 missing. The French put German casualties at 56,000, using German figures.

FIG. V-4. Trenches in the Neuville–St. Vaast Sector, Summer 1915. Re-printed with permission of the Bibliothèque Nationale, Paris.

ger results of the offensive, and more importantly the *way* in which the offensive came to a conclusion, demonstrated that commanders' control over the *Mittel* had become uncertain. This anticipated the dysfunctional relationship between the war of the commanders and the politics of the soldiers that emerged in 1916 and 1917.

Even more so than for the spring attacks, the "official transcript" for the 5e DI had to convey a narrative of a respectable performance, in which the consolation of *grignotage* was found in soldiers' going "over the top" as commanded and killing large numbers of Germans before they "were stopped." But there was much more to the sources of this standard narrative than meets the eye. Throughout the war, the less successful an engagement of the 5ᵉ DI, the more documentation was generated. Some account of the fighting survived for nearly every one of the fifty-six infantry companies of the division. The company reports for the most part were tactful, and went to some trouble to show that each company did the best it could. But they also admit more or less explicitly the point that both Mangin and the official history chose to avoid—that company commanders stopped attacking when they perceived no point in continuing.

Even the official transcript is filled with subtexts elaborating what had gone wrong. One representative if frankly stated example came from Second-Lieutenant Ansout, commanding the 17ᵉ Compagnie of the 274ᵉ RI.[60] On 29 September, the company took up a frontline position on the road between Neuville–St. Vaast and the Bois de la Folie. For the next two days, it worked at organizing the position, burying corpses at night when movements could be made more safely. At 1315 on 2 October, the company was ordered to evacuate the frontline trenches in anticipation of the French artillery barrage. The company was to attack the point S" at 1630.[61] Ansout wrote of the barrage: "From the first explosions, I let it be known that the artillery fire was falling short. Some shells fell on my first line of trenches, on my second line, and even behind that. *Eight times* I repeated this information, but the barrage continued in the same manner." (Emphasis in original.)

At 1625, Ansout ordered his men back into the assault trench. Shortly thereafter, a French shell landed in the trench, killing three men. That this appeared to make the *fuite en avant* an immediate matter of life and death for his men did not impress him. He noted sarcastically his "surprise that the German trench and its barbed wire seemed little damaged by the barrage, while our assault trench had suffered a great deal." At this point, "any advance seemed impossible" and "we could only remain in place and consolidate our position."

At 2330 that evening, Ansout's company was relieved by the 4ᵉ Compagnie of the 74ᵉ RI. The company commander, Second-Lieutenant Massé, likewise complained of an "absolute lack of liaison between the artillery and the infantry."[62] More specifically, he noted that artillery observers

---

[60] "Rapport du Sous-lieutenant Ansout Ct. la 17ᵉ Compagnie du 274ᵉ Régt. d'Infanterie sur les opérations auxquelles a pris part la compagnie du 26 septembre au 5 octobre 1915," 5ᵉ DI, 3ᵉ Bureau, 24 N 83.

[61] The 2 October attack along the line R"-S", it will be recalled, was the last serious effort made be the 5ᵉ DI in the sector.

[62] [Untitled report by] "Sous-lieutenant Massé, commandant la 4ᵉ Compagnie du 74ᵉ Régiment d'Infanterie," 30 October 1915. 74ᵉ RI, Opérations, 25 N 52.

were not at their post, that poor liaison with the rear when the observers were there meant that French shells could fall anywhere, and that requests for artillery support even by flares went unheeded.

Massé's report is part of a collection of similar reports from the 74e RI written in response to a note from Joffre dated 23 October requesting information on "the principal difficulties encountered by the troops over the course of the action," and in particular why the forward movement of the infantry stopped when it did.[63] Soldiers ceased to move forward at precisely the moment they considered themselves in the sort of situation that so dominated subsequent literary images of the war—one simply of bodies opposing technology.

The most prevalent reason given for ceasing to move forward was lack of friendly artillery support. As the commander of the 6e Compagnie put it:

> The preparatory fire from the artillery must be more violent, above all in the last minutes before the assault.
>
> The campaign artillery [the 75mm pieces] must target more precisely the accessory defenses of the enemy, which are always only partially destroyed.[64]

The commander of the machine-gun company noted that the machine guns were so numerous and cumbersome that they could not keep up with the attacking infantry, and that liaison with the infantry and even within the units of the company remained tenuous and "very difficult."[65] The 1e Compagnie commander, among many others, noted the breakdown in communications once the attack began.[66] He noted how important it would be in the future for each man "to know the point of the attack, the objective to reach, [because] no orders can be transmitted during the attack itself." This was perhaps a tactful way to indicate that command expectations in such situations should not be unlimited.

The evolving discrepancy between even these skeptical versions of the official transcript and individual experience can be examined for the 3e Compagnie of the 129e RI by comparing an official report with a personal memoir. The company commander's report conformed to the general pattern.[67] On 25 September, the company was assigned to the second attack

63 G.Q.G., État-Major, 3e Bureau, "Note pour les Généraux Cdt de Groupe d'Armées," no.12946, in 74e RI, Opérations, 25 N 52. These reports appear to be distinct in formula and content from those of the other regiments, though the explanation for this remains unclear.

64 Second-lieutenant [illegible], "Compte rendu relatif aux derniers offensives d'Artois," 31 October 1915, in ibid.

65 "Rapport du Lieut. Lagrola Commandant la Cie. de Mitrailleuses du 74e Régiment d'Infanterie, sur les enseignements tirés des récents offensives d'Artois," 31 October 1915, in ibid.

66 "Compte Rendu du Sous Lieutenant Desmaires commandant la 1ère Compagnie au sujet des renseignements à donner sur les attaques," 29 October 1915, in ibid.

67 "Rapport du Lieutenant Guillot Comt. la 3e Compagnie sur les combats livrés du 25 7bre au 5 octobre 1915," 12 October 1915, 5e DI, 3e Bureau, 24 N 83.

wave near the point where the sector of the 129ᵉ RI met the sector of the 36ᵉ RI (about the middle of the 5ᵉ DI sector). The 3ᵉ Compagnie did not even leave the trenches at first, because the company attacking in the first wave "was stopped by violent machine-gun and rifle fire." Although the company did leave the trench later, by evening "because of the lack of officers, a certain disarray manifested itself, and our line remained uncertain." On 26 September, the company commander stated that "not a single shell had been fired" on the trench the 3ᵉ Compagnie was supposed to be attacking, that the first wave was again stopped by machine-gun and rifle fire. He concluded that "it was impossible to advance, and we remained in place until nightfall. . . ." The company did not attack again during the offensive.[68]

An account by Second-Lieutenant Robert Desaubliaux provided some of the human drama behind his company commanders' official circumspection.[69] A conscript fulfilling his military service as a cavalry sergeant when the war broke out, Desaubliaux volunteered for the infantry in July 1915 because he wanted to make a more useful contribution to the war effort.[70] He wrote to his mother, whom he expected to be upset at his transfer: "Are we not put on earth to do our duty, all of it? . . . [To die] on the field of honor, an end so close to that of the martyr, is only glorious, Maman, it is not sad."[71]

It took only one battle for Desaubliaux to take a less idealistic view of the war, and in as yet an unfocused way to interrogate his situation. Like La Chausée in the spring offensive, Desaubliaux most vividly remembered the suffering of his fellow soldiers. His most graphic memory of the 25 September attack involved a sergeant severely wounded in the abdomen by a shell before the company even left its trench. The man clutched his exposed intestines and cried, "Let me through, I don't want to die here! Screwed [*foutus*], we are all screwed! Me, I'm going to die!"[72] Desaubliaux also had his idealistic notions of authority undermined on the battlefield. On 26 September, he saw a company from the 74ᵉ RI (not further identified) wandering without a commander toward his sector. He discovered that they fled before a large German patrol. Desaubliaux ran toward them, "revolver in hand, threatening to blow out the brains of the first one who kept retreating." Although this less-than-friendly persuasion convinced

---

[68] Guillot's report did not list casualties. The battalion commander's report lists figures for the 3ᵉ Compagnie of 11 killed, 24 wounded, and 5 missing for 25–27 September. However, the chart providing the figures has a large "X" drawn through it without explanation. If the figures are accurate, the company would have suffered casualties between 15 and 20 percent, about average for this sort of operation.

[69] *La Ruée: etapes d'un combattant* (Paris: Bloud & Gay, 1919).

[70] See ibid., p. 122. As of this point in the war, the cavalry had for the most part been kept out of the front lines, so that it would be able to exploit the anticipated *percée*.

[71] Ibid., p. 119.

[72] Ibid., p. 161.

them to return to their position, he was later chastised by a major from the 74e RI, who remarked, "Well then, second-lieutenant, when did you become a commander in my battalion?"[73]

For the most part, Desaubliaux left direct editorializing on the offensive to fellow officers, though he quoted them often and in some detail. For the attacks scheduled for 26 September, he quoted a lieutenant from his regiment as saying, "There are 200 meters to cover, barbed wire, and probably machine guns. The enemy has had since yesterday to put them there. It will be a massacre!"[74] On 1 October, Desaubliaux wrote to his mother that "we have beaten the enemy," though he confessed to his readers that "even to my mother, I did not have the courage to allow the suspicion that it had been a defeat."[75] Of the attacks scheduled for 5 October, he quoted a lieutenant from the 1e Compagnie as saying that "this attack is stupid. . . . The men can't do any more." When the attack was canceled because of fog, the elated lieutenant cried, "May the fog continue!"[76] We are left to imagine how vigorously these officers would have pursued the attacks if they had been launched. On 6 October, with the offensive discontinued but with the regiment still under regular bombardment, Desaubliaux provided a dialogue with his comrade from the 1e Compagnie. Although he did not indicate which officer said what, he plainly wished to present a concurrence of views: "This war will finish like this battle. There will be neither a victory nor a defeat. The two parties will both claim themselves the victors, and both will be the vanquished."[77]

In assessing the power relationship within the 5e DI by the end of 1915, it is important not to overstate the dichotomy between soldiers and commanders. The point here is not that the soldiers wanted to stop the offensive while Mangin wanted them to attack until every last one of them was annihilated. Even if Mangin was at heart the "butcher" his historical sobriquet indicated, he had discovered back at Courcy that commanders who lost too many men for too little ground did not get promoted. The point, rather, is that Mangin's control over his men's behavior diminished as the offensive proceeded. By the time his division was withdrawn, the attack had been stopped in the front lines and there was little Mangin could do to get it started again even if he had wanted to.

As early as 28 September (only four days into the attack), one of Mangin's own brigade commanders had informed him in writing that further offensive effort ought not to be expected from the soldiers.[78] The normal

[73] Ibid., pp. 172–73.
[74] Ibid., p. 173.
[75] Ibid., p. 192.
[76] Ibid., pp. 195–96.
[77] Ibid., p. 197.
[78] The 9e Brigade commander wrote to Mangin that the men "are not only gifted with a

124 CHAPTER V

diffusion of command authority during battle had been accentuated by the deployment of two regiments (the 74ᵉ RI and the 274ᵉ RI) as needed throughout the division's sector. As Desaubliaux discovered, command authority did not transfer easily among regiments. This further weakened the position of the divisional command structure, as had been noted as early as 29 September by Mangin's superiors.[79]

Mangin, then, had thus to decide how he would react to this fait accompli in the field. His personal version of the official transcript proved subject to revision. Mangin's initial reaction seemed glum. He wrote to his wife on 28 September that "the results in my sector are satisfactory, but they could have been complete and they are not. . . . I gained only 600 meters in all, at the price of considerable losses."[80] As at Brimont and Courcy, he placed the blame on others. Mangin's superiors were at fault for keeping the reserves too far back to be thrown into the attack, even though this would have made worse the mixing together of units. The French divisions to his flanks, as at Courcy, had proven their timorousness by stopping their advance.

But in the end, Mangin decided to declare at least a partial victory, just as Desaubliaux or his friend said he would. In his official report, he pronounced himself pleased with the "real success" of the operation, even though the assigned targets had not been attained.[81] He did manage to find some consolation in *grignotage*, at least until grander occasions for command heroism presented themselves.[82] In a letter to his wife on 11 October, Mangin seemed rather more sanguine about his accomplishment than he had been on 28 September: "However, the results are not bad; they show what we will be able to gain by the magnificent élan of our men, always admirable."[83] He altered his perceptions of the results in accordance with an outcome determined from below, but continued simply to assume that his men's attitudes reflected his own.

---

great capacity for resistance, but also with good will. [But] Their offensive capacity is limited by the degree of effort demanded of them, as much during the period of preparation as during the attack itself, which has produced an undeniable physical weariness." "Le Général de Thuy, commandant la 9ᵉ Brigade à M. le général commt. la 5ᵉ DI," 28 September 1915, 5ᵉ DI, 3ᵉ Bureau, 24 N 13.

[79] General Foch wrote to General d'Urbal that in the 3ᵉ CA in particular "heterogeneous groups are in the first line" and noted as a high priority the need "to restore order among the troops, that is to say to reconstitute the units." Groupe d'Armées du Nord, 3ᵉ Bureau, no. 1997/5, in AFGG, tome 3, Annexe, vol. 3, no. 2262.

[80] Letter of 28 September 1915, *Lettres de guerre*, p. 59.

[81] See the conclusion of "Rapport sur les combats."

[82] After the fall offensive, the disciplinary situation as reflected in the court-martial records became quite muddled. Given the circumstances of the cases, it becomes difficult to tell why several soldiers were convicted of desertion in the presence of the enemy (not a capital crime) and not of abandoning a post in the presence of the enemy (potentially a capital crime). See Smith, "Disciplinary Dilemma," pp. 58–59.

[83] Mangin, *Lettres de guerre*, pp. 60–61.

CHAPTER VI

The Crisis in Pitched Battle

VERDUN, 1916

IN THE CLAUSEWITZIAN TERMS cited in chapter 1, a profoundly dysfunctional relationship developed between politics and war in France over the
course of 1916. The strategic *Zweck* or ends had not changed—the liberation of northeastern France, the reconquest of Alsace and Lorraine, and the
permanent weakening of the German military threat. But the *Mittel*
(means) of "over the top" offensives as they had been negotiated between
French soldiers and commanders over the course of 1915 came to seem less
and less likely ever to produce these results. This is illustrated in the succession of French terms summarizing the *Ziele* (intermediate goal) that would
one day lead to a final victory—from the *percée* at the beginning of 1915,
to *grignotage* at the end of 1915, to *tenir* (holding on) by 1916.[1]

The Battle of Verdun, the dominating episode in the French war effort in
1916, exemplified this deterioration in military fortunes. Simply "holding
on" at Verdun meant nearly half a million French casualties to keep the
front lines just shy of where they were before the German siege began. The
Germans themselves took some four hundred thousand casualties with
little to show for it but the *grignotage* of the French. A.J.P. Taylor memora-
bly characterized the Battle of Verdun as "the most senseless episode in a
war not distinguished for sense anywhere."[2]

But from another and well-informed variety of contemporary historical
analysis, one might well draw just the opposite conclusion. If history
records the general and systematic assertion of power over the helpless,
Verdun could be understood as the *most* sensible episode of the war. Such
an analytical approach could be extrapolated from the work for which
Michel Foucault is best known, his writings before he became interested in
the sort of dialogical relationship between power and resistance that most
informs this study. This earlier Foucault is the *pur et dur* Foucault of
Discipline and Punish (1975).[3] Under such a system of analysis, one could

[1] Jean-Jacques Becker has explored the evolution of *tenir* in public opinion in *Les Français
pendant la grande guerre* (Paris: Éditions Robert Laffont, 1980).
[2] A.J.P. Taylor, *The First World War: An Illustrated History* (London: Hamish Hamilton,
1963), p. 123.
[3] Michel Foucault, *Discipline and Punish: The Birth of the Prison*, Alan Sheridan, trans.
(New York: Basic Books, 1979 [originally published in French in 1975]).

represent Verdun as carrying a central component of the history of Western civilization to its logical conclusion. Some nine hundred thousand French and Germans had to become casualties to demonstrate and reaffirm power relations in their respective societies.

The Verdun battlefield could be considered the teleological result of what Foucault called the "carceral archipelago"[4]—that collection of institutions and ways of thinking that generated the power relations of France, from the educational discipline of the Republican schoolhouse, to the work discipline of the fields and factories, to the military discipline of the army barracks and the trenches. The discourse of power relations, it could be argued, encompassed even Mangin, as professional imperatives drove him to promise victories he had good reason to know he could not deliver.

I will argue in the next two chapters that soldiers came to perceive their plight in just these terms, as they entered the valley of the shadow of what I will call foucauldian despair. The 1915 negotiated settlements of proportionality in the trenches, in which soldiers would engage in aggression up to a certain point and then cease, broke down in 1916 and 1917. This chapter explores the resulting crisis in pitched battle, the next a parallel crisis in trench warfare. But it will subsequently be argued that identification of these crises is not where the analytical usefulness of foucauldian despair ends, but where it begins.

SOLDIER-CITIZENS AND CITIZEN-SOLDIERS: THE 5ᵉ DI BEFORE VERDUN

Considering the manpower situation of the French army by 1916, *tenir* looked suspiciously like a necessity endeavoring to pass as a virtue. Most of the men in the French army of 1918 were in uniform before Verdun. Of the 8.4 million men France would mobilize in the entire war, 7.3 million (87 percent) had been mobilized by the end of January 1916.[5] Of these 7.3 million, over 900,000 (more than 12 percent) had already been killed, taken prisoner, or were missing.[6] At least as many and probably more were rendered noncombatants because of wounds.[7] Moreover, the French army

[4] See ibid., p. 301.

[5] Calculated from Col. Pierre Guinard, Jean-Claude Devos, and Jean Nicot, *Inventaire sommaire des archives de la guerre, Série N, 1872–1919* (Troyes: Imprimerie la Renaissance, 1975), pp. 204, 210. This source drew its data from a variety of parliamentary and general staff studies.

[6] Ibid., p. 213.

[7] Of course, the wounded represented a much more fluid population, and any figures probably do not go beyond reasonable guesses. A parliamentary report after the war estimated 2.8 million wounded over the whole course of the war, of which about half were wounded at least twice. Ibid., p. 209.

could expect only about 250,000 to 300,000 new recruits each year from new classes coming of age.[8]

"Replacing" casualties thus meant shuffling about a nearly fixed pool of mobilized men from less spent units to more spent ones, and strictly rationing those new recruits considered most militarily fit. Guy Pedroncini has observed that by 1916, the French army had become "a veritable army of professionals, of soldier-citizens and no longer of citizen-soldiers."[9] Even before Verdun, the homogeneous unshaven *poilu* of undeterminable age became an image generalized throughout the French army.[10]

While the surviving documentation permits no more than an educated guess as to the exact situation in the 5e DI, the 1915 casualties indicate that at least one-third of the men in the division in January 1916 were either new to the division or were recovered wounded. Oddly, information on officers remains even sketchier than information on enlisted men.[11] Regimental lists of officers became rarer and rarer, and so comparisons with the regimental registers become nearly impossible.[12] Still, a couple of available figures imply the magnitude of the change. In the 74e RI, for example, only four of the twelve company commanders by January 1916 had served in the regiment in any capacity before the war. In the 129e RI, only two of the twelve captains of the mobilization remained with the regiment in any capacity, and three of nine lieutenants, and two of sixteen second-lieutenants (both regular and reserve).[13]

The only remotely systematic investigation of the demographic evolution of the 5e DI over the course of the war appeared in June 1916, after the division's engagements at Verdun and against the background of increasing concern about manpower generally.[14] Although there are major gaps in the

[8] Ibid., p. 210. Relatively few new battlefield soldiers were previously exempted skilled factory workers—only about 90,000 by the winter of 1916–1917 in the entire French army. AFGG, tome 5, vol. 2, p. 22, n.4.

[9] "Le Moral de l'armée française en 1916," in *Verdun 1916: Actes du colloque international sur la bataille de Verdun, 6–7–8 juin 1975* (Verdun: Association national du souvenir de la bataille de Verdun, Université de Nancy II, 1976), p. 169.

[10] The term comes from *poil* (hair) from which French soldiers, like the biblical Samson, allegedly drew their strength.

[11] Certainly the officer corps as a whole reprofessionalized during the war. A 1920 parliamentary report provided a figure of 195,000 officers (regular and reserve) serving over the course of the war, 104,000 of whom received their commissions during the war itself. Guinard, Devos, Nicot, *Inventaire sommaire*, p. 209.

[12] Generally, an officer's *état des services* appeared in the regimental register only if he had a regular-army commission, and promoted NCOs almost always had commissions *à titre temporaire*, meaning for the duration of the war.

[13] "74e Régiment d'Infanterie, État d'encadrement, 10 janvier 1916," in 5e DI, 3e Bureau, 24 N 89. For the 129e RI, I used the état nominatif from the mobilization, JMO, 26 N 686. These lists were compared with names appearing in the regimental register.

[14] The following draws from a large untitled chart in 5e DI, 1e Bureau, 24 N 76. No information is provided on NCOs.

information provided by the study, the increasing dissatisfaction on the part of division general staff with the quality of the reinforcements stands out clearly.

The most detailed information exists for the 74ᵉ RI and the 274ᵉ RI. In the 74ᵉ RI, the reinforcements received through June 1915 (some 2,800 men in all) came almost entirely from the regiment's prewar recruitment areas of Normandy and Paris. Their military value was evaluated as "good" (*bon*). However, 900-men reinforcements received in June from Normandy and 300 men from the Auvergne and the South were classified only as "fairly good" (*assez bon*), while 200 recovered wounded received in September 1915 were considered only "*passable.*" On the other hand, 600 recovered wounded received in October were considered "good." The 1,000 men received by the 274ᵉ RI through October 1915, primarily reservists and territorials from Normandy, were considered "good." In October and December 1915, however, some 820 men from "old classes," as well as territorials and former customs officials, were classified as *mediocre.* Although no numbers were provided, reinforcements received by the 36ᵉ RI before January 1916 are described as "good," except for a contingent of southerners received in July 1915, and for the recovered wounded generally ("*très insuffisants*").

The most valued reinforcements were either dismounted cavalry or were from the youngest demographic cohorts. A contingent of 955 dismounted cavalry soldiers sent to the 129ᵉ RI in February 1916 was described as "excellent," though the admission of strategic despair behind redeploying the cavalry as infantry was probably not lost on either the former cavaliers or their new comrades. Recruits from the class of 1916 (300 men to the 74ᵉ RI, 100 to the 274ᵉ RI, and an unspecified number to the other two regiments) also received high ratings.

Surely the relative youth and physical resilience of both groups made them welcome additions. In addition, perhaps the command structure considered dismounted cavalry (like Robert Desaubliaux) and young soldiers relatively more amenable to "vertical" sociability of the command structure than to the "horizontal" sociability of battlefield soldiers. An unpublished memoir from one of the neophytes suggests that they were more carefully nurtured in their training than their counterparts had been before August 1914. Private Legentil of the 74ᵉ RI had been mobilized in April 1915.[15] He spent his first three months training in Rouen and another four months in a training camp in the Eure. He did not arrive in the zone of the armies until November 1915, and did not enter the front lines

[15] "Notes de campagne du 12 avril 1915 au 11 novembre 1918: au jour le jour, bons et mauvais souvenirs!" (Unpublished memoir, Fonds privés, 1 KT 86). Legentil's first name is not provided.

with his regiment until June 1916. A very different military education commenced shortly thereafter.

VERDUN AND THE LOGIC OF *TENIR*

Tenir served the same consoling purpose for French morale in 1916 as *grignotage* had in 1915, though on a yet more meager basis. In short, it equated winning the war with not losing it. The consolation of *tenir* had been under construction in the 5e DI well before it entered the Battle of Verdun. The pivotal event was a limited but highly successful German attack at Frise in Picardy at the end of January 1916.[16] One captain called the sector "a grotesque and untenable position, this peninsula in a laguna, with the Somme to our backs and communications impossible. . . ."[17] The Germans conquered an entire village and strip of Picardy about one kilometer deep in one day of fighting, only about one hour of which involved an actual infantry assault. It also captured an entire battalion from the 129e RI trapped in the village itself. The attack at Frise was exactly the sort of limited operation favored by the French after the 1917 mutinies.

The French in early 1916, however, had the challenge of reconstructing victory out of this relatively small but clear defeat. The French, it turned out, had won because the Germans had not achieved a *percée* (not that any evidence existed that this in fact was their intention). "*Tenir*," the *Pages héroiques* proclaimed, "it is at Frise that this word which at Verdun will become a symbol already takes on its real significance. French tenacity is a new virtue that manifests itself as greatly, as beautifully, as our legendary "*Furia*."[18] Robert Desaubliaux, who had given up hope of the *percée* back at Neuville–St. Vaast, now embraced with equal passion the rhetoric of finding victory in not losing: "'*Tenir*' means to stay where you are, despite the Boches, despite the bullets, even if you are isolated and surrounded. '*Tenir*' means to die where you stand, while giving up your life as dearly as possible."[19]

For his part, Mangin claimed to his wife after the fact that Frise had always been "a very bad position that they [his superiors] obstinately

---

[16] The town is located along the Somme River some 28 kilometers east of Amiens. The attack is described in more detail in Leonard V. Smith, "Command Authority in the French Army, 1914–1918: The Case of the 5e Division d'Infanterie" (Ph.D. diss., Columbia University, 1990), pp. 298–322.

[17] Quoted in Robert Desaubliaux, *La Ruée: étapes d'un combattant* (Paris: Bloud & Gay, 1919), p. 219.

[18] *Pages héroiques de la 5e Division d'Infanterie* (Paris: S.T.D.I.5, 1918), p. 53.

[19] *La Ruée*, p. 233.

insisted on holding despite the advice of the sector and corps commanders, French and English."[20] After the attack, he went on, "I continued to regain step by step all that was useful to us, without getting into a dangerous position." None of this could obscure, however, a fresh professional humiliation. Embracing the logic of *tenir* could serve as a form of damage control. But *tenir* could not win Mangin a higher command any more than it could win France the war. The Battle of Verdun, which began on 21 February, became for Mangin his best and perhaps his last chance professionally to redeem himself.

New French army infantry regulations issued sometime around the middle of the nine-month Battle of Verdun codified the logic implicit in *tenir*.[21] In some respects, the contrast with the 1914 regulations is striking. The regulations accepted the 1915 negotiated settlement of proportionality more or less explicitly. "The infantry," the manual reads in bold letters, "by itself has no offensive power against obstacles defended by fire protected with accessory fortifications." The sort of romantic infantry charges against whatever lay ahead, considered indispensable in the 1914 regulations, now were held "to have no chance of taking the position: they will simply raise casualties." Official doctrine seemed to reconcile itself to the conclusion reached in the field: "One cannot fight with men against materiel."[22]

But on the other hand, the logic of *tenir* had turned *offensive à outrance* into *défensive à outrance*, with the attending lack of attention to a principle of proportionality. The manual stated in bold letters: "All troops assigned to the defense of a piece of terrain must never abandon it, whatever happens."[23] Indeed, section commanders were forbidden to retreat at all unless they had received a formal order to do so by their superiors, preferably in writing. Should this mischance occur, "all lost terrain is to be retaken by an immediate counterattack carried out by troops designated toward that end."

This encapsulated at the tactical level the strategic implications of *tenir*. Defending Verdun came to symbolize at the most basic level the entire French war effort. Even though there was never much question of the Germans achieving a *percée* at Verdun, losing what cooler heads might have seen as an awkward salient in the French line would have meant that

[20] Letter of 14 February 1916, in *Lettres de guerre*, Stanislaus Mangin and Louis-Eugène Mangin, eds. (Paris: Fayard, 1950) pp. 92–94. In a letter of 26 January, however, he had praised his own efforts organizing the sector. Ibid., p. 89.

[21] G.Q.G., 3ᵉ Bureau, *Manuel du Chef de Section d'Infanterie* (Paris: Imprimerie Nationale, 1916). The month of publication is not provided, though because of references in other army publications, it seems to have appeared sometime between the middle of April and September.

[22] Ibid., Titre IV, chap. III, p. 198.

[23] Ibid., Titre VII, chap. I, p. 345.

tenir failed in 1916 just as the *percée* and even *grignotage* had failed in 1915. If Verdun fell, it followed that not only could France not win the war, it could not avoid losing it. Consequently, Verdun had to be defended to the end, *coûte que coûte* (at whatever cost).[24] Moreover, defending Verdun to the end meant blurring the distinction between the offensive and the defensive. If the defensive aim of holding Verdun were to be achieved, every possible inch of the sector that had fallen into German hands had to be regained by counterattacking.

The battle had already reached epic proportions some time before the 5e DI arrived in the sector at the beginning of April. The German attack began on 21 February, and the fort at Douaumont (the most important fortification seized by the Germans during the whole battle) fell virtually without a fight on 25 February. On 26 February, General Pétain took command of the IIe Armée, assigned to carry out the defense of Verdun. By April and May, the battle had entered a back-and-forth phase, with both the German attacks and the French counterattacks meeting little success. By April, a rift had developed between Pétain and Joffre over the former's *Noria* system of rotating fresh troops through the Verdun sector as quickly as possible, a system Joffre felt wasted troops needed for his own brainchild, the British-French effort at the Somme scheduled for that summer. On 19 April, Pétain was "promoted" to command of the Army Group Center, and the key IIe Armée command was given to Robert Nivelle.[25]

In the French army as a whole, only in April 1916 did the casualty figures noticeably exceed those of 1915.[26] Yet at the time and historically, Verdun has been perceived as the most bloody and tragic episode endured by the French during the entire war. The change involved the way French society, military and civilian, came to view the levels of casualties, and the relationship between 1915 levels and what the various protagonists considered a "successful" prosecution of the war.

In win/lose terms, the engagement of the 5e DI at Verdun resembled its engagement at Neuville–St. Vaast. Its ultimate objective in two large-scale attacks was a clear and militarily significant target, the fort at Douaumont, which dominated the whole center of the Verdun position. In the first phase

---

[24] This was exactly what Gen. Erich von Falkenhayn predicted when he proposed the Verdun offensive to Kaiser Wilhelm his famous memo of December 1915. See Alistair Horne, *The Price of Glory: Verdun 1916* (London: Macmillan, 1962), chap. 3. Despite its thinly concealed Anglo-Saxon chauvinism, not to mention several factual errors concerning the record of the 5e DI, Horne's book remains the best short survey in English or French.

[25] This was at best a lateral move for Pétain, since operations at Verdun would henceforth be under the direction of Nivelle. See ibid., pp. 230–31.

[26] The French army suffered about 50,000 casualties (killed, wounded, and missing) in April 1916 and about 40,000 in May 1916. Between February and September 1915, casualty figures ran between 35,000 and 45,000 per month. See Devos, and Nicot, *Inventaire Sommaire*, p. 212.

(2–17 April), the division had the mission of regaining ground recently lost in a German attack. Its success was small and costly, but arguably real. In the second phase (22–24 May), the division was to retake the fort itself. This effort proved far more costly and far more unambiguously a failure.

The remainder of this chapter will argue that for the combattants of the 5ᵉ DI, the logic of *tenir* at Verdun precipitated a crisis in pitched battle, as the negotiated settlement of proportionality worked out in 1915 broke down. It had been demonstrated at Neuville–St. Vaast in June 1915 that soldiers could be physically trapped into fighting aggressively if passivity could be rendered at least as dangerous. The same would prove true in the short run at Verdun, as the logic of *tenir* temporarily dictated. But after the fact, a "hidden transcript" continued to emerge, in which soldiers reconstructed their experience as foucauldian despair, meaning control toward no end proportional to what their commanders expected them to suffer. This reconstruction of the experience of Verdun would have considerable implications for the dynamic between soldiers and commanders later. After Verdun, the soldiers of the 5ᵉ DI would not be content simply to close down a pointlessly murderous offensive once it had begun.

The Bois de la Caillette, 2–17 April

The 5ᵉ DI arrived at Verdun on the evening of 2 April, in a greatly endangered sector of the front (see map VI-1). A German attack earlier in the day had taken the Tranchée Morchée in the western part of the sector and had opened an (unexploited) hole several hundred meters wide in the French line at the Ravin de la Caillette.[27] Pétain's *Noria* system meant that fresh troops could counterattack immediately, before the Germans had time to consolidate their gains. Mangin assigned three main objectives for the division: the recapture of the Tranchée de Morchée; the recapture of the Ravin de la Caillette; and the capture of the ridge along the Ravin de la Fausse Côte. These three targets would then create a position of departure for an attack on the fort itself.

This three-pronged attack met with varying degrees of success between the time it began on 2 April and the time it ended on 17 April, as shown on map VI-1. On the night of 2–3 April, the 74ᵉ RI was thrown in to seal off the gap in the French line at the Ravin de la Caillette. After a march of some eighteen kilometers that night, the 2ᵉ Bataillon attacked at 0610. By the end of the day, the 2ᵉ and 1ᵉ Bataillons had sealed off a large section of the gap. The 3ᵉ Bataillon continued this progress on 5–6 April, despite an

[27] The main source for this "win/lose" account is Mangin's "Rapport sur les combats livrés par la 5ᵉ Division d'Infanterie devant Douaumont du 3 au 17 avril 1916," 5ᵉ DI, 3ᵉ Bureau, 24 N 86.

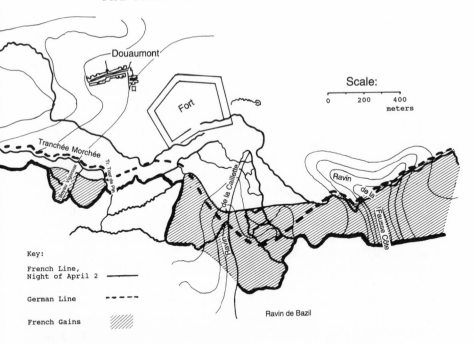

Key:

French Line,
Night of April 2   ———————

German Line   - - - - -

French Gains   ▨▨▨

MAP VI-1. Verdun Sector, 5ᵉ DI, April 1916

episode that will be examined shortly in which a retreat ordered by the battalion commander incurred Mangin's wrath. The center of the division's sector was reinforced by the 274ᵉ RI and the French gains sealing the gap were consolidated, despite a strong German counterattack on 11 April.[28]

On 6 April, the 129ᵉ RI attacked on the left portion of the division's sector, in the direction of the Tranchée Morchée. Some 150 meters of the Tranchée Morchée were regained initially, along the Tranchée Tour de Pin, and about 60 meters of the Boyau Vigoroux. But a German pillbox or *Blockhaus* located at the intersection of the Tranchée Morchée and the Boyau Vigoroux and filled with German infantry and machine guns prevented the recapture of the remainder of the German first line. The third and most successful phase of the April effort by the 5ᵉ DI took place on 15 April in the western part of the division's sector, in the direction of the Ravin de la Fausse Côte. Assisted by the 120ᵉ RI (on loan from the 6ᵉ DI), the 36ᵉ RI took and held a line reaching across the ravine, despite a German counterattack in the early morning of 16 April . By the time the 5ᵉ DI was

[28] 9 April, the date of Pétain's famous IIᵉ Armée order of the day concluding with "*Courage, on les aura!*" was described in Mangin's report as "relatively calm."

relieved on 17 April, the French position assumed the line shown on map VI-1. The 5ᵉ DI had certainly left the French position stronger than it had found it. But infantry casualties had comprised over twenty-eight hundred officers and men, and the dearly purchased gains were lost again not long after the division left the sector.[29] In short, the attack at the Bois de la Caillette was a typical Verdun engagement.

The "experiential" narrative of the April attack at Verdun will compare two episodes in which official and individual accounts of the fighting survive. I will argue that the differences between the "official transcript" of the engagements and the "hidden transcript" of individual combatants grew both more serious and more focused. Official reports show little change from comparable accounts of Neuville–St. Vaast. Soldiers departed as commanded, did what they considered their best to fulfill command expectations, and stopped their efforts when they seemed likely to result only in pointless annihilation. But the individual accounts begin to show a serious questioning of the 1915 settlement of proportionality and of the parameters of command authority behind it. These accounts pointed toward the descent into foucauldian despair in the second series of attacks at Verdun in May.

The 74ᵉ RI *Journal de Marches et d'Opérations* (*JMO*) entries for 4–5 April recounted a typical "good faith" effort on the part of the 3ᵉ Bataillon to continue advancing up the Ravin de la Caillette toward the fort at Douaumont.[30] An order from the division to attack at 1830 arrived only at 1815, which in the event delayed the attack until 1930. Once the attack got under way, the 3ᵉ Bataillon found its path "very difficult" because of a combination of mud, debris from the forest (which had after all been under bombardment for over one month) and the "extremely dark night." The entire regiment was also under periodic artillery fire. After several hours, further difficulties arose to both its right and left, since on one side units were mixing in with units from the 2ᵉ Bataillon (which generally meant the disintegration of formal command authority), and on the other side, contact with the 1ᵉ Bataillon had been lost completely. Finally, in the early hours of 5 April, "the situation seemed critical" to 3ᵉ Bataillon commander

[29] The breakdown is as follows:

Regiment	Killed	Wounded	Missing	Total
74ᵉ	132	591	63	786
274ᵉ	110	430	41	581
36ᵉ	169	461	137	767
129ᵉ	172	494	54	720
Total	583	1,976	295	2,854

[30] 74ᵉ RI *JMO*, 26 N 660.

Fɪɢ. VI-1. The Bois de la Caillette, April 1916. Reprinted with permission of sɪʀᴘᴀ/ᴇᴄᴘᴀ France.

Paul Lefebvre-Dibon, who feared that his unit would be caught in an "unfavorable position" once day broke. On his own authority, he ordered his battalion back to its original position, and two other battalion commanders followed his example.

Lefebvre-Dibon's memoir of the incident was written from a prison camp in Germany and published after the war. This senior officer began expressing skepticism toward *défensive à outrance* in a utilitarian manner that strained but did not fully break with the official language. But he did evoke a thinly veiled contempt for the decision to launch the attack in the first place: "I had no knowledge of the position, not having had the time to have made any reconnaissance, as proscribed for all night operations and reiterated in the most recent instructions from the G.Q.G."[31] Upon himself visiting the front line, Lefebvre-Dibon's observations revealed considerable empathy for his soldiers: "The men are exhausted from this disordered march, which has lasted for five hours. They are dying of thirst, not having had a drop of water because they have not been resupplied for forty-eight hours."[32]

His decision to retreat earned him Mangin's ire. In a stinging memo issued on the morning of 5 April, he maintained that although Lefebvre-Dibon apparently did not have enough control over his men to keep them advancing, "he nevertheless had no difficulty rallying them when he decided to bring them back to the initial position."[33] Lefebvre-Dibon's decision to "abandon" four hundred meters of terrain constituted a "real failure of command." In such a situation, Mangin continued, "one stops where he is and organizes the terrain conquered. . . ." Even when the battalion attacked later in the day on 5 April under more favorable conditions and with rather greater success, Mangin personally delayed the 74e RI commander's recommendation that Lefebvre-Dibon be made a chevalier of the Légion d'Honneur.[34]

Lefebvre-Dibon, in short, took up "soldiers'" cause of proportionality in opposition to one of his superiors. When the moment of decision came, Lefebvre-Dibon sought, in his words, "to spare, as much as possible, the lives of my men,"[35] a decision he would reaffirm in a much more dramatic

---

[31] Commandant Paul Lefebvre-Dibon, Chef de Bataillon de Réserve, *Quatre Pages du 3e Bataillon du 74e RI: Extraits d'un carnet de campagne*, 2d ed. (Nancy: Imprimerie Berger-Levrault, 1920), p. 41.

[32] Ibid., p. 43.

[33] "Note pour les officiers supérieurs de la 9e Brigade," No.34/5 Confidentiel, 5 April 1916, 5e DI, 3e Bureau, 24 N 85. Mangin's wrath had cooled considerably by the time the official report on the attack appeared.

[34] Note in Mangin's easily identifiable hand at the end of "Le Chef de Bataillon Lefebvre-Dibon, Ct. le 3e Bon. du 74e RI à monsieur le général commandant la 5e Division d'Infanterie," 20 April 1916, 5e DI, 3e Bureau, 24 N 86.

[35] Lefebvre-Dibon, *Quatre Pages*, p. 50.

situation the next month. In the end, he felt more responsibility to his men than to the designs of his divisional commander: "I risked a great deal on April 4; the decision that night was grave. I recognize this. If I deserved the painful reproach I received the next day, I nevertheless felt from the officers and men of my battalion more of that absolute confidence that they give to a leader who knows how to take responsibility."[36]

The attack at the Bois de la Caillette was the only engagement in the entire war for which I found an account from another unit describing combat by the 5e DI. Jean Tocaben's company from the 269e RI was positioned to the right of the ravine, and had a good position from which to observe the proceedings.[37] Most World War I combat on the Western Front took place over terrain too flat to make possible this type of eyewitness account. Moreover, the rapid rotation of units meant that such readings of events could be rapidly disseminated to men entering and leaving the Verdun sector. Tocaben described the attacking 9e Brigade (comprising the 74e and 274e RI) as an "elite troop, evidently under the command of quite a leader [Mangin], brave among the brave."[38] Yet he perceived the situation into which the brigade was thrown as less than sanguine: "I considered the Germans, dug into our lines since the day before, as unmoveable without a preliminary hammering of the artillery. There was no question of using artillery in this affair."[39]

Strikingly, Tocaben provided an account of a 5 April attack not only more grim than that of the official rendering, but also that of Lefebvre-Dibon. He noted that the attack did not begin until 0620, by which time the sun was already coming up: "It was just like 1914, the assault à la baïonnette under the withering fire of the waiting machine guns."[40] As the 274e RI followed the 74e into the furnace, "it went blindly into the massacre. . . . The morning sun on the burnished helmets into spattered rays of light, and, covering in splendor the men, the young men going toward death, surrounded them with glory and crowned them with a crest of fire."[41] He concluded that the attack created "only a diverting spectacle" for the Germans: "It was even a rare stroke of fortune [for the Germans] to see troops coming at them deployed in maneuver order and to shoot them at their ease, without running the slightest risk."[42]

In the 129e RI, the discrepancy between the official transcript and Robert Desaubliaux's personal account illustrated evolving soldierly despair. The

---

36 Ibid., p. 49.
37 Jean Tocaben, *Virilité (au front de la grande guerre)* (Paris: Flammarion, 1931).
38 Ibid., p. 264.
39 Ibid.
40 Ibid.
41 Ibid., p. 269.
42 Ibid., p. 271.

129ᵉ RI arguably took more casualties for less ground gained than any of the other regiments in the division, although the fighting at Verdun was so confused and so compressed in physical space that calculations become particularly problematic.[43] Nevertheless, the official reports remained upbeat. Lieutenant Colonel Valzi, commander of the 129ᵉ RI, wrote of his regiment: "Under continuous bombardment night and day, officers and men outdid each other in commitment and endurance."[44] The 3ᵉ Bataillon, moreover, "had gained ground." Battalion commander Pourel affirmed this tribute: "Without weakening and for eight long days, the battalion remained at its post, realizing gains it was able to hold. . . . The moral ascendancy over the enemy has been very clearly maintained."[45] Pourel continued that the machine-gun section of Lieutenant Desaubliaux (supporting the 3ᵉ Bataillon), "survived eleven long days in placements where trenches no longer existed, under incessant bombardment, under direct and enfilading rifle and machine-gun fire, with extremely difficult communications with the rear."[46] The machine gunners gave the infantry "all the support that was expected of them."

Desaubliaux's own account of the engagement poignantly continuated his emotional journey from the idealistic ex-cavalier to the despondent infantryman trapped in the trenches. He had been given a clear idea of what to expect at Verdun from soldiers being relieved. He described his emotions and those of his men in intriguingly contradictory terms. On the one hand, before entering the sector, he claimed to hold on to the rhetoric of *tenir* that he had embraced with such fervor after the German attack at Frise. The Battle of Verdun had become nothing less than a pure contest of French and German masculinity: "The two races have put all their youth into the furnace, to test which is strongest and most virile."[47] But the internal contradictions of this language proved too prominent to ignore. He wrote of a walk he took before the battle on a beautiful spring night, on a night just like the one during which he decided to join the infantry. He recalled saying to himself, "What an absurd decision!"[48] His men before the attack displayed the same confused sentiments. They were either "drunk, howling out patriotic airs, or in contrast weeping with emotion or despair." One had the temerity to remark within earshot of the company commander:

[43] Total casualties were 720 men for an area of less than 600 square meters.

[44] "Rapport du Lieut.-colonel Valzi, comt. le 129ᵉ sur les opérations auxquelles pris part le régiment du 3 au 12 avril 1916," 18 April 1916, 5ᵉ DI, 3ᵉ Bureau, 24 N 86.

[45] "Rapport du Chef de Bataillon Pourel Cdt. le 3ᵉ Bon. sur les événements du 4 au 11 avril," 14 April 1916, 5ᵉ DI, 3ᵉ Bureau, 24 N 86.

[46] "Rapport du Capitaine Thomas Ct. la 2ᵉ Cie de Mitrailleuses de Brigade sur les événements du 4 au 14 avril (Secteur de Gauche-Pourel)," 16 April 1916, 5ᵉ DI, 3ᵉ Bureau, 24 N 86.

[47] Desaubliaux, *La Ruée*, p. 254.

[48] Ibid., p. 253.

"Baa. . . Baa. . . I am the sheep on his way to the slaughterhouse."[49]

Desaubliaux's section, like many units at Verdun, spent more time hiding as best it could from the incessant shelling than actually fighting. To behave "aggressively" meant simply being there at all. At night, when movement became marginally safer, the soldiers took up new and theoretically more advantageous positions, though these positions were invariably extremely difficult to find and sometimes did not exist at all except on a map. Nevertheless, on the rare occasions when enemy soldiers were sighted, the gunners had no reservations mowing them down.[50] But most of the time during the battle, Desaubliaux felt quite helplessly surrounded by death, with his body and soul thoroughly controlled by foucauldian despair. In the wake of an unsuccessful German counterattack on 11 April, Desaubliaux described his situation: "Nearly all of our trench has caved in. In what remains, we have scraped out niches in the walls. We huddle up in them to get at least a bit of shelter from the explosions, but we are so tightly packed that our sore limbs can't move."[51]

At the same time, Desaubliaux described the deterioration in his faith in even the immediate command structure. Despite the intense control of soldiers in the sense of the general physical situation, communications with immediate commanders at Verdun remained tenuous even by World War I standards.[52] At one point, Desaubliaux remarked, "At first I felt disgusted, these orders and counterorders exasperated me."[53] He let the facts speak for themselves when during a bombardment in which both French and German shells were falling on his position, he tore open a note from the company commander, only to find that the note contained nothing more helpful than instructions to propose some of his men for citations.[54]

Desaubliaux succinctly identified soldiers' plight in a conversation on 12 April. This was his section's eighth day in the sector. By this time, all the men around him saw their chances of emerging alive diminishing by the minute:

—"I'd like to toss everything away and get the hell out of here, no matter where," declared Claron.

---

[49] Ibid., p. 255.

[50] Ibid., pp. 280–81. Little sorrow was expressed one morning when daybreak revealed some thirty German corpses, the result of the French response to a small-scale nighttime raid.

[51] Ibid., p. 288.

[52] Jacques Meyer, himself a World War I veteran, maintained that "commanders of regiments, battalions, and sometimes even companies no longer knew where their men were, or the men, where their lines were." *La Vie quotidienne des soldats pendant la grande guerre* (Paris: Hachette, 1966), p. 300.

[53] Desaubliaux, *La Ruée*, p. 268.

[54] Ibid., p. 287.

140   CHAPTER VI

I shook my head. . .

—"Come on!" I said, "my friends, do not forget that we are here for France!"

Also, how could one really think of running away with the barrage pinning you to the bottom of the trench?[55]

Actual Verdun combat, once entered into, indeed resembled Foucault's carceral situation in important ways. As in 1915, commanders could create a situation in which soldiers' simply staying put or retreating proved just as dangerous as moving forward. But behind the front lines, more soldiers opted for resistance. The court-martial records for the period around the April attack show that experienced and hitherto reputable soldiers were beginning to question their situation.[56] The prospect of simply stopping their efforts *coûte que coûte* would occur to many more in the spring of 1917.

For his part, Mangin gave no indication of having learned or forgotten anything since 1915. He accepted with alacrity *défensive à outrance* and its attending blurred distinction between defense and offense. Mangin wrote to his wife on 2 April: "We are now convinced that we cannot allow ourselves to be *grignotée* and that we must defend ourselves by attacking."[57] After the fighting, he wrote a memo contrasting the "defensive" counterattack of the 74e RI on 2–5 April with the "offensive" attack of the 36e RI on 15 April.[58] The 74e RI, responding to the German initiative of 2 April, had regained only a part of the lost ground with casualties of 26 officers and 620 NCOs and common soldiers. The 36e RI, on the other hand, had advanced two hundred meters across a front of three hundred meters, and even after a German counterattack had suffered casualties of "only" 7 officers and 336 NCOs and common soldiers. Moreover, the number of artillery shells consumed over the division's front (some 26,000 shells just for the 75s) was approximately the same on the days of the French attack and the German counterattack. "In offensive operations," Mangin argued, "the commander chooses his men and his terrain. He controls the timing, he can act by surprise." Such operations "exalt the morale of our troops and depress that of the adversary."

[55] Ibid., pp. 290–91. Ellipses in original.

[56] None of the twenty-one soldiers convicted for abandoning a post or desertion was a recidivist. No less than four of the eleven soldiers convicted for abandoning a post were NCOs (three sergeants and one corporal). Of the twenty-one soldiers convicted, fourteen had been with their regiments since the mobilization. (One soldier was convicted of both desertion and abandoning a post.) See Leonard V. Smith, "The Disciplinary Dilemma of French Military Justice, September 1914–April 1917: The Case of the 5e Division d'Infanterie," *The Journal of Military History* 55 (1991), p. 61.

[57] Letter of 2 April 1916, in *Lettres de guerre*, p. 102.

[58] "Remarques sur les combats livrés au sud de Douaumont du 3 au 17 avril 1916" (no date), 5e DI, 3e Bureau, 24 N 86.

Such a rendering of what had transpired, I would suggest, proved possible only with a chilling detachment from his soldiers' experience. Mangin clearly was not unaware of his growing reputation as a squanderer of France's ever-dwindling supply of manpower. He wrote to his wife on 8 May:

> The people—civilian or military—who say in Paris that I get too many people killed are misinformed. They would not dare to say that here. In point of fact, the bombardment is horrible and shelters nearly non-existent. Whatever you do, you lose a lot of people. If the combat is between the infantries, you lose fewer through the cannons and more through the rifle and the grenade. But the number of casualties is about the same.[59]

But Mangin almost blithely assumed that his soldiers shared his calculation of the relationship between ends and means at Verdun.[60] "The state of morale is excellent," he wrote to his wife after the fighting, "quite exalted by our success because we did not cease to gain ground."[61] He asserted to Pétain that "in a month, the troops will be even better than when they arrived on the battlefield."[62] The inculcation of aggression through entrapment, he stubbornly believed, would provide the French moral superiority that one day would prove the key to success.

Douaumont, 22–24 May: Die beste französische Division

In a win/lose contest, the 5e DI endeavor to reclaim the fort at Douaumont constituted an act of desperation, based on an absolute imperative of instant results. Gen. Robert Nivelle had been given the key operational IIe Armée command on 16 April 1916 because he had promised Joffre to obtain through sheer offensive ardor more gains with fewer men than the cautious Pétain. Nivelle needed a speedy demonstration of the benefits of his more aggressive approach to the Verdun campaign. Mangin seemed the perfect instrument. Not only was Mangin one of the most professionally frustrated division commanders in the French army, but he had also demonstrated that ground could be gained at Verdun if the French were willing to entrap enough bodies there.

As to the results, Mangin's own report concluded that in retrospect, the

---

[59] Mangin, letter of 8 May 1916, *Lettres de guerre*, p. 112.

[60] Mangin's disciplinary hand had lightened considerably since Neuville–St. Vaast, though new legal restrictions probably played a role. No soldiers were shot for their conduct at Verdun, not even five who were found guilty of abandoning a post in the presence of the enemy (and who were not even sent to prison). See Smith, "Disciplinary Dilemma," pp. 50, 61–62.

[61] Letter of 19 April 1916, in *Lettres de guerre*, pp. 104–5.

[62] Letter of 20 April 1916, in ibid., p. 105.

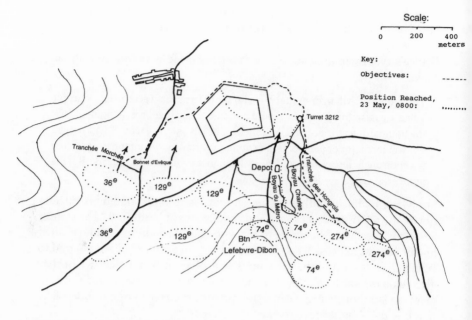

MAP VI-2. 5ᵉ DI Attack on the Fort of Douaumont, 22 May 1916

failure of the attack had been essentially over-caused.[63] Map VI-2 shows that the division had virtually the same starting line as in the April attack, though this time it had the objective of taking the entire fort in a dramatic *fuite en avant*. It was reinforced by one brigade from the 36ᵉ DI, though the brigade was kept some forty kilometers from the front lines until the evening of the first day of the battle, and could not be thrown into the fight until the morning of the second day, by which time the French position had already begun to deteriorate. Once again, the German position at the fort was never seriously compromised by the French artillery before the infantry assault began, despite one of the most intensive and best-planned barrages since the war began, backed up with an unprecedented amount of high-quality reconnaissance from the air. German machine guns could fire virtually at will.

In the end, the attack proved the victim of its initial success. At 1150 on 22 May, the division attacked as a whole with "remarkable *élan*" along the whole front. The line marked on map VI-2 as indicating the French position at 0800 on 23 May was actually reached more or less by 1400 on 22

---

[63] "L'Attaque de Plateau de Douaumont par la 5ᵉ Division d'Infe. (22–23–24 Mai 1916)," 31 May 1916, 5ᵉ DI, 3ᵉ Bureau, 24 N 87. The win/lose narrative is based on this report.

May. Troops from the 129e RI had actually entered the fort from the south and west, and a key turret at the point 3212 east of the fort had been taken as well.

But appearances deceived. The French had indeed entered the fort, but while the Germans could be reinforced in relative security through tunnels coming from the north, the French could be reinforced only across open ground. In any event, the entire French effort in the fort could be threatened from both flanks, since the 5e DI attack was not accompanied by a major effort from any other unit. To cite one example that will be explored further shortly, Lefebvre-Dibon's 3e Bataillon of the 74e RI had reached the turret at point 3212, but the 2e Bataillon (Schaffer) to its right had secured neither the Tranchée des Hongrois, the Boyau Charles, nor the Boyau du Métro. Lefebvre-Dibon's battalion, then, thus risked being taken from behind.

The situation of the 5e DI began deteriorating from the morning of 23 May. The entire division had been committed to the attack by that time, and the brigade from the 36e DI was being fed into line only slowly and to no good effect. The news got worse over the course of the day. In the afternoon, a report trickled back that the French now had only about fifty men in the fort and that the hope of taking it ought to be abandoned. Worst of all, the colonel commanding the 74e RI reported that all contact had been lost with Lefebvre-Dibon's battalion.

At 0700 on 24 May, soldiers from this battalion who made their way back to the French lines reported that it had surrendered after a "heroic resistance" had been offered. A German counterattack beginning at 0950 between the Tranchée Morchée and Bonnet d'Evêque and extending throughout the morning along the whole of the division's line completely ground the French effort to a halt. Mangin's report noted with a certain understatement that "if the situation was critical on the left, it was not brilliant on the right." The loss of the 3e Battalion of the 74e RI left a hole in the French line along the Ravin de la Caillette, just as there had been when the 5e DI arrived at Verdun back in April. Fortunately for the French, the Germans were again too spent to exploit their success. Mangin turned over command of the sector at 1530 on 24 May, and the 5e DI was withdrawn over the course of the next day.

The Douaumont attack remained the single best-known engagement of the 5e DI during the entire war, a symbol of the dramatic, courageous futility that characterized the Battle of Verdun as a whole. A German communiqué of 24 May 1916 referred to it as *die beste französische Division*.[64] A scene in Jean Renoir's film *La Grande Illusion* (1937) portrayed French prisoners and their German captors competing in song as informa-

---

[64] Cited in Louis Lecoc, *Pages héroïques de la 5e Division d'Infanterie* (Paris: S.T.D.I.5, 1918), p. 77.

tion on the 5e DI attack at Douaumont trickled into the prison camp. Alistair Horne called the attack "an incomparable display of the *Furia Francese*," though it exemplified the price the French paid for glory at Verdun.[65] The Douaumont attack proved by good measure the single bloodiest operation of the 5e DI during the entire war. Infantry casualties for the four regiments comprised 894 killed, 2,857 wounded, and 1,608 missing—for a total of 5,359 infantrymen out of approximately 12,000 taking part in the assault.[66] No ground had been gained at all. Only Mangin himself advanced; he attained his long-sought promotion, to a corps command in June 1916 and to an army command in December.

In the experiential narrative of the Douaumont attack, I will argue that the discrepancy between the official and "hidden" transcripts of the engagement became so large as to precipitate a real crisis in pitched battle. For his part, Mangin could not have been more pleased. He claimed that the Germans had had to call in three divisions to face his one, and that he had thus preempted a major attack along the Meuse.[67] But at a more fundamental level, he found his faith affirmed in the inducement of aggression through entrapment. For that reason, it would appear, the Douaumont attack constituted a moral victory, as he equated the wish for military success with its fulfillment. His men, he asserted, would pay any price to prove him right, as he wrote to his wife: "My *poilus*, reduced by half, want more. They say that with their general they would go back there. They have been magnificent."[68] Moreover, even Mangin's own commanders did not hold the Douaumont debacle against him. Mangin quoted his old rival Pétain (even then known as the *poilu*'s general) in a letter to his wife: "You did your duty and I cannot blame you. You would not have been the man you are if you had not acted as you did."[69]

But soldiers surviving the Douaumont attack told quite a different tale. Although the soldiers of the 5e DI faced the prospect of a horrible death

[65] Horne, *The Price of Glory*, p. 235.
[66] The regimental breakdown from Mangin's report is as follows:

Regiment	Killed	Wounded	Missing	Total
74e RI	448	896	620	1,964
274e RI	121	473	135	729
36e RI	181	692	459	1,332
129e RI	144	796	394	1,334
Total 5e DI	894	2,857	1,608	5,359

The corresponding figures for the Battle of Charleroi, hitherto the most costly engagement, were 49 officers and 3,891 NCOs and common soldiers for a total of 3,940 casualties.
[67] See letter of 30 May 1916, *Lettres de guerre*, pp. 115–16.
[68] Letter of 19 May 1916 in ibid., p. 115.
[69] Letter of 29 May 1916 in ibid., p. 115.

FIG. VI-2. 5e DI Soldiers in the Front Lines before the Douaumont Attack. Reprinted with permission of SIRPA/ECPA France.

every time they went into battle, the accounts from Douaumont differ considerably from those of 1914 and 1915, and for that matter from those of 1918. These narratives contain a paradox between soldiers' behavior on the spot and the soldiers' written response once they left the unique logic of the Douaumont battlefield. What Mangin took to be soldiers' virtually frantic efforts on the spot to fulfill his wishes and their written accounts emphasizing despair and near obsession with death, I would suggest, really reflect two sides of the same coin. Soldiers responded in two different ways to a situation of foucauldian control in the compressed physical conditions of Verdun combat, situated at two different points in time.

Lt. Robert Desaubliaux was wounded in a shell explosion along with two other soldiers on the night of 20 May. At the time, his machine-gun company was being moved into position for the attack. Except for these casualties, the company commander reported, movement of the company into the attack trenches "was achieved without great incident."[70]

Desaubliaux's version, in contrast, recounted a descent into foucauldian despair. He recorded a flurry of emotion as the company began its march to the attack trenches on 19 May, some of them contradictory. Desaubliaux wrote: "I had the impression that I am marching in front of Death. It made me afraid, but a mysterious force pushed me forward all the same."[71] He read the same "confused sentiments" in the faces of his men. But in the next paragraph, he tried to put up a brave front of sincerely wishing to do his duty. The sense of death, he maintained, "transforms one, ennobles one." Patriotism made its last appearance in the memoir: "The soul of our race sings in us, the soul of the brave knights of old, the soldiers of the Revolution and the *grognards* of the Empire, the soul of a people shaped by twenty centuries of struggle. . . ."[72]

This brave front faltered as Desaubliaux got closer to the front lines, and disintegrated entirely as he confronted death personally. During the night march, his men followed him "silently, resigned."[73] But as they got closer and closer inside shell range, each explosion made them march faster and bump up against the soldiers ahead of them. Ironically, they could find some shelter, however inadequate, only once they were in the attack trenches: "Although loaded up like beasts of burden, we march fast, hurried, as though there were less danger and less terror up there."[74]

[70] "Rapport du Capitaine Thomas, commandant la C.M.3 sur les événements du 20 au 24 Mai 1916," 26 May 1916, 5e DI, 3e Bureau, 24 N 87. Desaubliaux's account gives a date of 19 May, but the date on the commander's report is more likely.

[71] Desaubliaux, *La Ruée*, p. 300.

[72] Ibid. *Grognard* comes from the verb *grogner* (to grumble). The reference is to an adage attributed to Napoleon describing his seasoned troops: "*Ils grognent, mais ils marchent encore* [They grumble, but they still march]."

[73] Ibid., p. 301.

[74] Ibid.

FIG. VI-3. The Assault on Douaumont, 22 May 1916. Reprinted with permission of SIRPA/ECPA France.

Suddenly the men heard a shell fly by, followed by a deafening explosion. Afterward, someone handed Desaubliaux a handkerchief and asked if he was wounded. Gradually becoming aware of what had happened, he realized that blood flowing from his head had blinded him, and that he could feel the warmth of the blood down his fingers to his feet. His teeth started to chatter and for a moment he could not speak. He wiped his eyes and saw the men lying down along the road; he was convinced they were all dead. A soldier assigned to help him to the first-aid station assured him otherwise, and they were shortly left alone to make their way back.

Desaubliaux does not reveal the precise seriousness of his wounds, though in addition to the head wound he also sustained a shrapnel wound in the chest and shortly became unable to walk on his left leg. He obviously lived to tell the tale, however, and could endure the two-kilometer walk to the first-aid station.[75] But at the time, he was clearly convinced he would die. He told the soldier accompanying him (perhaps himself relieved to have the chance to avoid battle temporarily) that he was too grievously wounded to survive and that the soldier should let him die there. The soldier refused, and the two continued their three-legged hobble. As they got closer to the first-aid station, Desaubliaux felt himself drawn toward life as he was earlier drawn toward death and the logic of *tenir*. He concluded his memoir with the following:

> Still a few hundred meters. I feel myself weaken, but I cannot stop. If I stop, I will never be able to start again.
>
> I want to get there! I want to be saved! I want to live![76]

Of course, Desaubliaux was neither the first nor the last World War I soldier to have presentiments of death before a battle or to be convinced that he would not recover from a serious wound. But the same obsession with death as a metaphor for helplessness and control from above on the battlefield appears in two memoirs by two soldiers who took part in the *fuite en avant* stage of the attack—Guy Hallé and Paul Lefebvre-Dibon, both of the 74e RI. Both, it is worth noting, did not report suffering physical harm in the attack.

In the 5e Compagnie of the 74e RI, the company commander provided a version of the Douaumont attack that followed the basic formula established back in 1915 at Neuville–St. Vaast.[77] The 5e Compagnie, part of the 2e Bataillon unsuccessfully securing the right flank of the 3e Bataillon

---

[75] Indeed, according to his *état de services*, he was released from the hospital by 25 May, though he continued to have health problems. He never returned to the front, and served out the remainder of the war in staff positions.

[76] Ibid., p. 304.

[77] Lieutenant Maridet, "74e Régiment d'Infanterie, 5e Compagnie, Compte-rendu sur les opérations de la Cie. du 20 au 24 mai 1916," 5e DI, 3e Bureau, 24 N 85.

THE CRISIS IN PITCHED BATTLE

attacking the fort itself, attacked the Boyau Charles at 1150 on 23 May. Shortly thereafter, the company was stopped by enemy grenades, as well as rifle and machine-gun fire. Over the next twenty-four hours, the company renewed the attack to no particular effect, though enemy counterattacks failed as well. The company was relieved at 0200 on the morning of 25 May. Casualties were certainly grave—3 of 4 officers, and 65 of some 250 NCOs and common soldiers. But the 5e Compagnie was far from the most stricken unit to fight at Verdun.

Sergeant Guy Hallé of the 5e Compagnie provided a description of the attack that explains both the élan with which it commenced and the despair after the fact as two sides of the same coin of reactions to helplessness and control on the carceral battlefield.[78] The work is set up as a series of vignettes. One described Hallé's emotions as his company prepared to go "over the top."

The *fuite en avant* of leaving the trenches marked the culmination of an almost clichéd four-stage process of denial, rage, despair, and acceptance. One hour before the attack, Hallé recounted an emotional state of denial. Although he and his men knew full well that they had been sent into the sector to attack the fort, until the written orders were received and the watches synchronized, he wrote: "My poor mind doubted, hoped. For what? I don't know myself—a counter order, a relief, a postponement of the operation, who knows?"[79] Thirty-five minutes before the attack, their position was detected by the German artillery, meaning that the Germans knew that a French infantry assault was imminent. In his anger and frustration, he lost any identification with the purpose of the war and could think only of a horrifying scenario of his own death:

> Oh, to get out of here, to save myself, to run like a hunted beast, anywhere, to the corridors of the Fort de Souville, to the Ravin de Bazile, no matter where, but not to stay here. . . . There will be a huge flame, a cry, then I will have smashed legs, my chest all torn up and bloody, eyes open wide and my face completely white.[80]

Anger shortly gave way to total despair. Before the war, Hallé used to wonder how the condemned found the strength to walk to the guillotine. "Now I know," he wrote, "and for us it is even more terrible. We have the suffering to fear, which for the executed is never long."[81] But in the last minutes before the attack, his calm and sangfroid returned. He recalled

---

[78] *Là-bas avec ceux qui souffrent* (Paris: Garnier, 1917). Its overall pessimism is especially remarkable considering that it was published in October 1917, a time of significant wartime censorship. Some twenty-three lines of text were censored, all marked by ellipses.

[79] Ibid., p. 31.

[80] Ibid., pp. 33–34.

[81] Ibid., p. 34.

that twenty minutes before H-hour, "I am in a hurry for the time to advance. We must attack, attack now, or we will be crushed without budging."[82] Five minutes later, he inspected the twenty meters of trench occupied by his men, nearly all of whom greeted him with some kind of quip or joke. By the time he went over the parapet, he accepted the *fuite en avant*, even if it meant escaping into death. He concluded the vignette with his call to his men, "*En avant, en avant, nom de Dieu*!! [Forward, forward, for God's sake!!]"[83]

In another vignette, he completed the link among helplessness, control, and death, by describing the death of a comrade alongside his narrative of the conclusion of the attack. As his company commander noted, the attack had been "stopped," much as had been the case in 1915. Hallé cowered near a barricade with a sergeant from another company and some other men unknown to him. He soon heard someone calling to him. Hallé described the man as a comrade rather than a friend, and admitted that he had not even been particularly fond of him. Nothing joined them except their shared wartime experience: "He was a companion in misery. We were both sergeants."[84] He wrote: "I wish very much he weren't there, I can't take care of him; also, I know what's wrong. I saw my brother die of the same wound."[85] The next five and a half lines were censored, though we shortly learn that the man was wounded in the abdomen.

Hallé experienced death vicariously through his comrade. He recalled that just yesterday, before the attack, they shared the same quarters. Like Hallé, the comrade was convinced he would not survive the attack. Hallé was all too aware that the doomed man could just as easily have been him. His indirect encounter with death rendered him completely paralyzed with fear, as he frankly confessed: "I cannot budge, I am too afraid. If I turn my head, a grenade will fall on my neck, on my back. All of us are there lying down, quite visible from the air. . . . There is nothing to do but wait."[86]

At the point when Hallé and his comrades felt completely immobile, the command structure that put them there accepted this outcome as adequate, and told them to dig in. This meant that they would not be asked to attack again. If they could stay alive for a few more hours, they would be liberated from the battlefield:

Its over, we're getting out of here, we'll be relieved without attacking. Others are coming and will take the barricade. As for us, those who are spared the shells, we will get out of here. We will be saved, one by one, during the night,

[82] Ibid.
[83] Ibid., p. 115.
[84] Ibid., p. 39.
[85] Ibid., p. 41.
[86] Ibid., p. 43.

sneaking out, our backs hunched over, our ears attentive to the whistle of the passing shells, sneaking out to the Ravin du Brazil, cursed yesterday, so yearned for today.[87]

Hallé closed the vignette by observing that his mortally wounded comrade found his own release when he died upon arrival at a hospital.

Paul Lefebvre-Dibon's entire 3ᵉ Bataillon was captured near Douaumont. His account sought to reconcile the official language of a senior commander endeavoring to carry out orders with his personal empathy with his soldiers, whose physical and emotional perils he shared. The resulting narrative has striking similarities to that of Hallé. But Lefebvre-Dibon's account also testified to the logic of *tenir* coming apart, as he tried to negotiate his roles as the author and subject of command authority in a nearly impossible situation. Lefebvre-Dibon, it will be recalled, had felt a conflict between his two roles before, when he incurred Mangin's wrath back in April by calling off an attack along the Ravin de la Caillette he deemed too ill-conceived. Here, faced with the choice between explicitly giving up on *tenir* and annihilation whose benefit could only be symbolic, he located his own emotional exit from the battlefield.

Like Desaubliaux and Hallé, Lefebvre-Dibon recounted a painful transition back to pitched battle at Verdun. He opened his account at the moment he received the order to begin the movement back to the front lines. He found the transition all the more painful because his battalion had spent the past month resting in a "delightful" village only about fifty kilometers from the front lines. But the village plainly belonged to another world, characterized more by horizontal than by vertical sociability. For Lefebvre-Dibon, the high point of the sojourn was a small revue portraying a soldier trying to explain himself after returning six months late from a leave because he had "lost" his regiment. Lefebvre-Dibon himself portrayed the errant *permissionaire*: "I felt that it would so much amuse my *poilus* to see their battalion commander as a common soldier, kidding around and complaining incessantly about the whims of the commander, I could not resist playing the role."[88]

Just twelve days later, the 3ᵉ Bataillon found itself on its way back to the front lines. "If the memory [of Verdun] still persists," he wrote, "the impression of course blurred after a time. But a return to that wretched place brought back the memory in all its acuity."[89] The poor state of the French lines did not bode well for the attack. Supply details would still require a fifteen-kilometer return trip, through virtually nonexistent communications trenches. The lack of communications trenches furthermore meant

[87] Ibid., pp. 44–45.
[88] Lefebvre-Dibon, *Quatre Pages*, p. 61.
[89] Ibid., p. 55.

no shelter from the bombardment for the troops moving into the attack trenches, which themselves were "completely insufficient."[90]

Lefebvre-Dibon provided a description of going "over the top" as a desperate attempt to escape entrapment, much as had Hallé. As he waited for H-hour in the attack trench, the wounded from the 129e RI began filtering through Lefebvre-Dibon's trench as the least dangerous path back to the first-aid station. He wrote that "the spectacle is not only demoralizing, it signals our position to the enemy." Nevertheless, he saw that the 129e RI was "much more afflicted than us," and had to let them pass.[91] With the German shells getting ever closer, Lefebvre-Dibon wrote: "All my men were running into each other, trying to get out faster, some leading the others, singing, crying, hurling themselves forward filled with enthusiasm." Lefebvre-Dibon witnessed "a spectacle that made me feel an unforgettable sensation," as he cried to his men upon bounding into No Man's Land, "*Bravo, mes amis, et vive le 3e Bataillon!*"

Ironically, given Lefebvre Dibon's experience at the Bois de la Caillette, his battalion followed Mangin's stated orders all too closely: "The assault troops must have only one thought, to reach the assigned objective. Liaison with units to the right and the left must be sought only upon arrival at the conquered position. Conquered terrain may never be abandoned without orders."[92] Temporarily, the 3e Bataillon simply had the good fortune to find less resistance in front of it than the 2e Bataillon of the 74e RI to its right or the 2e Bataillon of the 129e RI to its left. As ordered, Lefebvre-Dibon concerned himself with liaison only as he began setting up his command post at the depot at the end of the Boyau du Métro. "To my left," he wrote, "to my great shock, I do not see the unit next to me. Decimated during the [artillery] preparation, what could have happened to it?"[93] Ironically, the exit of the battalion from the logic of *tenir* at Verdun through surrender was set up by its strict adherence to that logic at the outset.

Like Hallé near his barricade, Lefebvre-Dibon found himself marooned on a tiny island of relative security in a sea of pain and gruesome death. Even as he set up his command post in the depot, which the Germans had been using as a shelter during the French bombardment, "one imagines the German cadavers surging out of this indescribable disorder, here a head, there a foot."[94] Also like Hallé, Lefebvre-Dibon experienced death vicariously. On 23 May, he received a report from one of his captains carrying what proved to be the last set of orders from the regimental commander. The colonel ordered the battalion (now virtually surrounded and with

[90] Ibid., p. 71.
[91] Ibid., p. 76.
[92] "L'Attaque du plateau du Douaumont."
[93] Lefebvre-Dibon, *Quatre pages*, p. 79.
[94] Ibid., p. 82.

casualties mounting) to continue the attack on the fort. The captain cleverly responded that "since this is an order he will carry it out," but that "the attack seemed doomed and no one will come back alive."[95] We will never know if the captain would actually have carried out the attack, since he was killed upon rejoining his company. Lefebvre-Dibon, for his part, pursued no further offensive action despite his colonel's wishes.

As hope inside the depot for reinforcement diminished, Lefebvre-Dibon recounted with remarkable candor how his soldiers persuaded him to surrender through recognizing a situation effectively determined by them. By the afternoon of 23 May, both machine guns defending the depot were out of action, and requests by flare for artillery support were answered by too few shells too late. The battalion was nearly out of grenades and ammunition, as the Germans began to break down the barricade barring the entrance to the depot. Lefebvre-Dibon described his thoughts as death and helplessness converged:

> Everyone looks at me. They wonder what I'm going to do. Fight, fight to the end, wait for reinforcements or a counterattack from our lines. There can be no question of surrender. But trying to break out *en masse* is useless, we'd be killed to the last man by the machine guns trained on us. Alongside the vision of a general massacre, I see on everyone's face panic, spreading like wildfire on human animals sensing themselves hunted, lost, powerless. They beg me to surrender, I refuse. It is impossible.[96]

To the moment he surrendered, Lefebvre-Dibon felt caught between his roles as soldier and commander. Without orders, a soldier in the depot put a white handkerchief on the tip of his rifle. Lefebvre-Dibon threw himself on him, revolver in hand, ready to strike the man down. He wrote that one of his own captains "stopped me, it seems." We are left to imagine how much further this miniature mutiny would have gone had Lefebvre-Dibon pursued the point. Finally, after taking one final look outside the depot, only to see a double circle of Germans preparing to attack, Lefebvre-Dibon concluded that "We are taken, definitely taken. I am completely aware of the most horrible responsibility a soldier can bear. I must take it, and I remain fully responsible."[97]

Upon leaving the special logic of the Verdun battlefield, Lefebvre-Dibon became only more convinced that he had decided wisely. He wrote that "the memory of my poor annihilated battalion . . . haunts my long days of captivity and will never leave me."[98] Still, he found comfort in what amounted to a doctrine of proportionality, which provided his emotional

[95] Ibid., p. 90.
[96] Ibid., p. 92.
[97] Ibid., p. 93.
[98] Ibid., p. 95.

release from the guilt he felt by surrendering. The 3ᵉ Bataillon, "losing 50 percent of its men . . . reached the position it was supposed to take. . . ."⁹⁹ The day of the surrender, the battalion "did its duty one last time," in resisting vastly superior forces "to the last extremity." Just what this constituted had been determined by his subordinates. Having done its best, the soldiers of the battalion could surrender with a clear conscience.

This chapter has explored a crisis in the approach to pitched battle, as the logic of *tenir* began to come apart at Verdun because of its internal contradictions. The principle itself sent contradictory signals to soldiers. On the one hand, as evidenced by the 1916 infantry regulations, some explicit recognition began to take shape within the command structure that there was more to the present war than the "mind over matter" characteristics of the prewar doctrine of the offensive. But on the other hand, the politics of *tenir* made further territorial losses unacceptable, regardless of their inherent military utility. Putting *tenir* into practice at Verdun presented soldiers with little to choose between *défensive à outrance* and *offensive à outrance*. Indeed, the former seemed to promise less than the latter, since the best scenario could provide only a return to the status quo. Soldiers' responses, I would argue, were twofold. Induced aggression on the battlefield was followed among the survivors by a demonstrable sense of despair and helplessness. It will be shown subsequently that the negotiation of proportionality and command authority did not end with this nadir of foucauldian control on the Verdun battlefield. But for the time being, more distance separated calculations of military utility between soldiers and commanders than at any time since August 1914.

⁹⁹ Ibid., pp. 93–94.

CHAPTER VII

The Crisis in Trench Warfare

LES EPARGES

La Chanson des Eparges[1]
(Air: Si tu veux, Marguerite)
Connaissez-vous les Eparges?
C'est le pays du carnage.
Y'a pas d'erreur
Mon Dieu, quel' terreur
C'est pas l'filon, ce secteur.
Pour ne pas que l'on roupille
Les Boches balancent des torpilles;
Quatre-vingt kilos
C'est guère rigolo
Quand ça vous tombe sur les dos.
Si en perme vous le racontez,
Les Civils sont épatés.
Refrain:
Les Journaux ne parlent point
Des Eparges (bis)
Il est vrai que dans ce coin
C'est les Boches qui trinquent le moins?
—*Le Canard de Boyau*, March 1917

AS THE BATTLE OF VERDUN by the fall of 1916 came to what French military and civilian leaders insisted could pass for a successful conclusion, the policy of *tenir* delivered all it had promised. Stalemate masqueraded as victory, sustained by the Micawberish hope that if France could avoid

[1] Translation, *The Song of Les Eparges*: Do you know Les Eparges?/It is the land of carnage/Make no error/My God, what terror/It is no cushy post this sector./So that we don't doze off/The Germans toss heavy mortars at us;/Eighty kilos/It's not too cute/When they fall on your back./If you talk about it on leave/The civilians are astounded. *Refrain*: The newspapers never talk about/Les Eparges (again)/Is it true that in that part of the world/It is the Germans that get the better of it? *Le Canard de Boyau* was a semimonthly published by the 74e RI beginning in the summer of 1916. On World War I slang in French see Albert Dauzat, *L'Argot de la guerre: d'après une enquête des officiers et soldats* (Paris: Librairie Armand Colin, 1918).

losing the war for long enough, something would turn up enabling it to win it. The British-French offensive along the Somme from July through November (which did not involve the 5ᵉ DI) proved another costly failure, though more at British expense than at French. Ironically, the French achieved the best "offensive" success on their "defensive" front, at Verdun. Although the last major German assault in June brought them to within five kilometers of the gates of the city of Verdun, the French resumed the attack in the fall, and by October had retaken the forts at Douaumont and Vaux. The heroes of this success proved none other than Robert Nivelle and Charles Mangin. They attributed their victory to an alleged tactical breakthrough called the "rolling barrage."[2] Nivelle replaced Joffre as *generalissimo* in December 1916, and Mangin was given an army command. The duo promised still greater miracles for the offensive planned for the spring of 1917, after the French army regrouped and restocked yet again.

In the meantime, *tenir* continued in the front lines, though the command structure expressed a greater interest than previously in harassing the enemy in trench warfare than had been the case in 1915. Nowhere was an aggressive posture more symbolically significant than in the sector around the village of Les Eparges, some fifteen kilometers south of Verdun, the sector occupied by the 5ᵉ DI from June 1916 through February 1917.[3] Located on the periphery of the Verdun salient, Les Eparges could not be allowed to become a "quiet" sector, as close as it was to the very symbol of French tenacity.

This chapter will argue that the negotiated settlement between soldiers and commanders of proportionality in trench warfare broke down during the time the 5ᵉ DI spent at Les Eparges, much as the analogous settlement of proportionality in pitched battle had broken down at Verdun. The problem was not so much that the characteristics of trench warfare had changed. Indeed, senior officers were more implicated than ever in limiting militarily indecisive violence in the front lines. Rather, the problem was more that soldiers were beginning to view themselves as incarcerated in the trenches, potentially in perpetuity. In short, trench warfare at Les Eparges was coming to bear a conspicuous resemblance to pitched battle at Verdun. Soldiers responded with the same sense of foucauldian despair. This connection has considerable importance, since the military situation precipitating the 1917 mutinies in the 5ᵉ DI resembled that of Les Eparges far more than that of Douaumont.

---

[2] This involved simply moving the artillery barrage and the infantry forward at the same predetermined speed, so that the attacking soldiers always had artillery cover in front of them. The *barrage roulant* was indeed an effective innovation as long as the enemy was not expecting it, though the Germans proved quick learners when the trick was tried in April 1917 along the Chemin des Dames.

[3] The sector is best known through the work of Maurice Genevoix, who was posted there in January–April 1915. See *Les Eparges* (Paris: Flammarion, 1923).

TRENCH WARFARE AT LES EPARGES

The manpower of the 5e DI remained essentially constant from the summer of 1916 through the mutinies. As noted earlier, the division suffered approximately 5,500 casualties in the Douaumont engagement, over 40 percent of its entire strength. Although given the surviving documentation one can make only a reasonable approximation concerning the replacements, probably one-third of them were recovered wounded and about two-thirds new recruits (these a mixture of soldiers from the youngest classes and men previously classified as unfit for active duty).[4]

In such documentation as survives, the age distribution in the division seemed a matter of the foremost concern, despite the image of the bearded, ageless *poilu*. The division had indeed aged since August 1914, even allowing for differences in perceptions of age between that time and the present.[5] By March 1917, for the three regular-army regiments (the 74e RI, 36e RI, and the 129e RI), approximately 40 percent were between 19 and 24 years old, some 50 percent between 25 and 35, and about 10 percent between 36 and 42.[6] For the one reserve regiment (the 274e RI), the respective figures are 17 percent, 45 percent, and 38 percent. Some 60–70 percent of the soldiers in the division came from the prewar recruitment areas of Normandy and Paris and its suburbs, the remainder from other parts of France.

The 5e DI sector at Les Eparges varied between about seven and ten kilometers during its time there.[7] Considering that according to the 1916 infantry regulations, only about one-third to one-sixth of the troops were supposed to be in the front line of trenches at any given time, this meant a thin disposition of manpower throughout the sector.[8] At least as the French told it, in no area of the sector did the terrain work in their favor. To be sure, they held much of the high ground. But given the abiding weakness of French artillery, this proved less of an advantage than might be expected. Indeed, high ground could actually work to their disadvantage, given the German skill at digging tunnels for high explosives under enemy positions, known simply as mining. In other areas of the sector, such as around the village of Les Eparges itself, both French and Germans held high ground,

---

[4] These were proportions of recovered wounded and new recruits from French army estimates for the fall of 1916 and the winter of 1916–17. AFGG, tome 5, vol. 1, p. 32, n. 2.

[5] As noted in chap. 2, all of men in the 5e DI were twenty-seven years old or less, and one-half were between twenty and twenty-three. See chap. 2, pp. 34–35. Men in their thirties would be considered rather older in 1917 than men the same age in the 1990s.

[6] Général Henri de Roig-Bourdeville, "Notice sur la 5e Division d'Infanterie," 22 March 1917, 5e DI, 1e Bureau, 24 N 76.

[7] This compared to about 1 km of front at Neuville–St. Vaast, 12 km at Frise, and 1.5 km at Douaumont.

[8] See G.Q.G., 3e Bureau, *Manuel de chef de section d'infanterie* (Paris: Imprimerie Nationale, 1916), p. 350. The rationale involved limiting and keeping as many soldiers as possible ready for supposedly decisive pursuits.

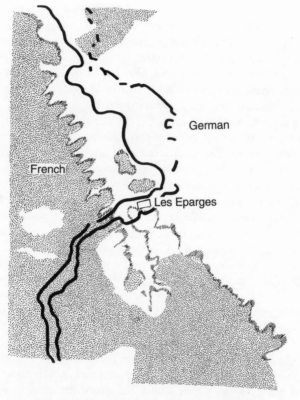

MAP VII-1. Les Eparges Sector, Winter 1916–17

with the low ground as No Man's Land between them. This put frontline soldiers in an unusually exposed position. In the southern part of the sector, the Germans had a heavily wooded area to their rear, which made it difficult for the French to gauge the extent of their defenses.

Command interest in what transpired in trench warfare proved inversely proportional to hopes for decisive results during pitched battle. British commanders had a particularly keen interest in constantly harassing the enemy *before* they had a large field army on the continent; French commanders acquired this interest after they had spent much of theirs. Tony Ashworth's description of World War I high-command expectations— constant barrages, mining, or raids of enemy positions—is thus more accurate for the time the 5ᵉ DI spent in the Eparges sector than had been the case earlier.

The 1916 infantry regulations reflected this emphasis on aggression between pitched battles. A section requiring constant fire by snipers stated in bold letters: "Trench warfare is neither a truce nor guard service; it is a phase of the battle."[9] The most minute enemy movements were to be watched closely, and every opportunity taken to inflict casualties. "The adversary must feel in front of him a vigilant hatred," the regulations continued, "and must know that we want no rest before his defeat."[10]

Orders dated 26 July 1916 from Nivelle, at that time the IIe Armée commander in charge of the entire Verdun sector, further underscored these expectations.[11] He sought to "render our front inviolable" through maintaining an aggressive defense, a sort of "offensive defense," in which the defender kept the initiative by continuously harassing the enemy. Three ways existed of doing this: artillery, digging mines under the enemy positions, and raids. Concentrated and precise artillery, Nivelle argued, could prevent the installation of new trench mortars (the feared *Minenwerfer*), and immobilize those already in place. Mining and raids could "take advantageous positions whose possession would reinforce our defensive organization and would menace other enemy positions."

The man in charge of carrying out Nivelle's orders was Mangin's successor, Gen. Henri de Roig-Bourdeville. Although he and Mangin were approximately the same age and shared some similarities in their career paths, in other respects the contrast was notable. General de Roig had risen from the ranks without the drama of Mangin's more erratic record. A volunteer in the colonial army, he graduated (without distinction) from Saint-Maixent, the school for promotable NCOs.[12] He spent ten years in the North African colonies before the war, and was posted in metropolitan France thereafter. He commanded a reserve infantry regiment that served ably in August 1914, and by January 1915 had been given a brigade. General Lebrun, the 3e CA commander, praised him in his evaluation of September 1916 as "extremely active, conscientious, and hard-working. Sure judgment." Apart from his personal dossier, information on the personality of de Roig does not abound. Henri Dutheil, the 5e DI staff secretary who had such an unwholesome fascination with Mangin, remarked simply: "He had the methodical, slow, calm manner of the director of a

[9] G.Q.G., 3e Bureau, *Manuel de Chef de Section*, p. 351.

[10] Ibid.

[11] Note No. SC-1673, quoted in "Rapport du Colonel de Monthuisant, Ct. la 10e Brigade d'Infanterie à Mr. le Gal. Ct. la 5e Division d'Infanterie," No. 1917, 3 August 1916, 5e DI, 3e Bureau, 24 N 89.

[12] His rank was 361 of 499. De Roig-Bourdeville personal dossier, Gx/4 308. His early career was marked by continuous debt problems, however, until in 1894 he made a marriage as financially successful as those of Mangin, to a woman who received fifty thousand francs on her wedding day, with expectations of another two hundred thousand.

factory. But the flame, ah!, where was it, the claws of the lion, the talons of the eagle?"[13]

Whatever his anatomical or spiritual defects, de Roig played a role in consistently endeavoring to scale down the expectations of his superiors of constant aggression in the Eparges sector. He clearly understood how little harm his artillery could inflict on the Germans. Considering the number of shells consumed at Verdun and along the Somme, and with another major offensive planned for the spring, a division not engaged in pitched battle inevitably found itself on short artillery rations. In a report of 22 December 1916, de Roig noted that "without having a very great density, the barrages are sufficient" for countering enemy barrages.[14] But the division's ability to defend itself would be "very much too weak," however, if the enemy attacked along the whole 5e DI front. He called "dangerous" a proposal to remove some 240mm cannons, whose range and size made them "an element of the moral support of our troops." Brilliant aggressive results were plainly not to be anticipated from the 5e DI artillery.

Mining held no more promise. As noted, though the French held a considerable amount of high ground at Les Eparges, this meant that it was actually much easier for the Germans to mine than the French, which they did in the fall of 1916 with impunity, given the weakness of the French artillery. In a report stinging to the point of impertinence, the major in charge of construction in the front lines explained his decision to order all mining stopped on 18 December 1916.[15] Given the insufficient supply of both men and materiel, he considered further effort simply pointless. Two acetylene lamps requested three weeks previously had still not arrived, and "the lack of mining tools has already rendered this type of work particularly difficult and has paralyzed all productivity." In his comment on the report, the brigade commander added that "we must not forget that the front in the Eparges sector represents 7km of front lines . . . and that I have only one incomplete company on average of every half kilometer to occupy, maintain, rebuild the multiple lines and communications trenches within that half kilometer."[16]

[13] Henri Dutheil, *De Sauret la honte à Mangin le boucher: roman comique d'un état-major* (Paris: Nouvelle Librairie Nationale, 1923), pp. 324–25.

[14] General Henri de Roig-Bourdeville, "Mesures à prendre en vue d'augmenter la capacité défensive des troupes dans le secteur," 22 December 1916, 5e DI, 3e Bureau, 24 N 88.

[15] "Zone des Eparges, major des tranchées, compte-rendu," in 5e DI *JMO* (Pièces annexées), 26 N 272.

[16] This translation largely preserves the syntax of the original. To begin to thin out the numbers of men in the front lines and to establish instruction centers close to the front, Joffre ordered Depôts Divisionnaires established in the fall of 1916. Approximately one company of men per battalion was supposed to be posted to the depots at any given time. See AFGG, tome 4, vol. 2, p. 92.

This left raids. The basic problem of raids in the Eparges sector was outlined by 10ᵉ Brigade commander Colonel de Monthuisant in August 1916.[17] As noted, the area south of the village of Les Eparges was mostly heavily wooded, concealing what were presumed to be thick and complicated defenses. An attack on either side of the salient around Les Eparges, Monthuisant noted, "would no longer be a question of a raid, but an offensive on a front of 1,000 to 1,200 meters by at least two regiments side by side, without counting the reserves needed." He concluded that "personally, I do not think that the military results . . . are worth the effort of an enterprise on the scale indicated above." He suggested raids involving one or two battalions at most, "no longer to gain an advantageous position, but simply to gain a foothold in the enemy lines, to create there a threat that would prevent the free disposition of the reserves."

By November 1916, senior officers resisted even this. Battalion commanders from the 10ᵉ Brigade cited the onset of winter and the basic militarily pointlessness of the enterprise. The commander of the 1ᵉ Bataillon of the 36ᵉ RI, for example, commented bluntly that "the terrain in which the raids would have to operate is truly a chaotic one in which, after the mortar fire, it is impossible at night to walk for twenty meters without the risk of sinking twenty times."[18] Now that the forest had lost its leaves, it was possible to see from aerial reconnaissance that the enemy trenches were "well-organized," and that "a raid would only have a chance of success if it could be executed quickly, which is impossible." Moreover, he went so far as to say that the French themselves had an interest in maintaining the "live and let live" system for the time being: "At the moment, our situation is so precarious that a violent reaction on the part of the enemy could be fatal." De Roig duly reported this conclusion to his own superiors.[19]

Militarily speaking, then, the 5ᵉ DI in the Eparges sector proved at least as much and perhaps more the object than the perpetrator of aggression in trench warfare. During the eight months the division spent there, it suffered approximately 1,000 casualties, an average of some 125 per month (just under 1 percent of the total strength).[20] Although these figures do not compare with losses during pitched battle, they are certainly "active sector" figures. They certainly sufficed to keep soldiers' minds focused on the ubiquitous possibility of death and serious injury. But as the next section

[17] "Rapport du Colonel Monthuisant."

[18] "Rapport du Commandant Ménager sur les coups de main à éxécuter dans le quartier," 1 November 1916, 5ᵉ DI JMO (Pièces annexées), 26 N 272.

[19] See "Le Général de Roig, commandant la 5ᵉ Division d'Infanterie à M. le général cdt. le Groupement G," No. 8940, 5ᵉ DI, 3ᵉ Bureau, 24 N 88.

[20] De Roig, "Notice sur la 5ᵉ Division d'Infanterie," 22 March 1917.

will argue, and like the casualty figures at Verdun for the French army as a whole, the significant change is not so much in the absolute numbers of casualties, but how those casualties were perceived.[21]

SOLDIERS' DILEMMA: ENTRAPMENT VERSUS DEFEAT

Simply put, the crisis in trench warfare involved an increasing sense on the part of the soldiers of the 5e DI that trench warfare at Les Eparges had no more military utility than pitched battle at Verdun. *Tenir* held little for them but incarceration in the trenches and the constant and pointless danger. The problem, however, centered around finding an alternative given existing military technology and the fact that the Germans continued to hold northeastern France and Belgium hostage. Recognizing the military uselessness of their efforts meant recognizing that France had lost the war. This dilemma—entrapment versus defeat—became more and more clearly focused in the months before the 1917 mutinies.

Guy Hallé of the 74e RI provided a moving account of a new descent into foucauldian despair at Les Eparges. Immediately after Douaumont, Hallé sought almost desperately to find meaning in the division's efforts there. One day, the regiment was ordered to assemble for a distribution of decorations. Hallé sought a special link in the ceremony to those killed at Verdun. As the survivors assembled, they looked to him like "phantom companies, with so few men in them that once the regiment was brought together, our hearts were torn by sorrow."[22] His own words best describe the ceremony itself:

> The colonel gave the command: "*Au drapeau* [To the flag]." The bayonets glistened motionless and the clarions sounded. One often laughs at military parades, me like the others, for all their artificiality, their showiness, and their staged poses. I assure you that no one wanted to smile at that moment.
>
> The thoughts of all were over there, on the slopes of Douaumont, in the grey smoke of the power, with the dead.[23]

But once Hallé's unit entered Les Eparges, the same sense that he felt leaving the trenches in front of Douaumont of helplessness in the face of ubiquitous death returned. In a vignette set in August 1916, his company was posted in the southern part of the Eparges sector. All of a sudden, a

[21] Indeed, deaths in the French army as a whole declined from 44,700 in July 1916 to 6,500 in January 1917 (the lowest figure in the war up to that time). Pierre Guinard, Jean-Claude Devos, Jean Nicot, *Inventaire sommaire des archives de la guerre, série N 1872–1919* (Troyes: Imprimerie La Renaissance, 1975), p. 213.

[22] Guy Hallé, *Là-bas avec ceux qui souffrent* (Paris: Garnier, 1917), p. 82.

[23] Ibid.

German shell came flying out of the woods on the other side of No Man's Land. At first the veterans of the unit thought nothing of it: "The Germans often fire by surprise like this, the only danger in a reasonably tranquil part of the sector."[24] Shortly however, a soldier showed up in shock and so badly wounded in the legs that his shoes were soaked with blood: "Without him saying anything, we understand that there are dead over there."[25]

This indeed proved the case, as the shell fell among a group of men playing cards. As with his comrade killed back at Verdun, Hallé was all too aware that he could just as easily have been the victim. A group of men new to the unit became quickly socialized to life at Les Eparges. "Around us the men are troubled and shaking," he wrote. He continued somewhat callously, showing the rapid deterioration of the special link with the dead back at Douaumont: "Its a good thing we have the rookies of the section, who arrived after Verdun and who haven't seen much yet. We disperse them, because this isn't a very nice place, and right away we busy ourselves carrying away the corpses, to remove as much as possible the traces of the horrible, stupid death of these three unhappy men."[26]

By October, with poor weather setting in, Hallé linked trench warfare in the Eparges sector in October 1916 more closely than ever to incarceration on the battlefield. By that time a lieutenant commanding a company, Hallé described a closed-off world of semihumans. They were cut off not only from "real life" back home, but even from the war itself, in the sense of war as some comprehensible exercise of force toward some justifiable end: "What are we doing there, we poor numbed creatures, our hearts broken and crying with our very blood for peace, for love, for light, and the sweetness of seeing again everything that is so far away, so far away. We feel separated from all this by distance without limit and by infinite suffering."[27] Per Hallé's title and insistent use of the term *là-bas*, the world of the trenches has become simply "out there somewhere," identified principally by the suffering of the men incarcerated there (*avec ceux qui souffrent* [with those who suffer]).

When the "real world" of the civilian society and the closed world of the trenches collided, Hallé proved unable to cope with it. In November 1916, he received a letter from the wife of a man reported missing. Such letters always arrived, he complained, "on a fine day when we are resting, when the nerves loosen up a bit, and we feel ourselves becoming alive again."[28]

---

[24] Ibid., p. 49.

[25] Some sixteen lines of text were censored from this vignette, it would appear because of the graphic nature of Hallé's description of the wounded and dead.

[26] Ibid., pp. 52–53.

[27] Ibid., p. 57.

[28] Ibid., p. 66.

The woman was aware that mine explosions had been reported in the sector of the 74e RI. Hallé knew the whole story. A mine explosion at the base of the ridge made a crater at least 180 meters long, and caused a landslide that buried one whole section (some 40–50 men). But since only two bodies were recovered and no physical evidence existed of the death of the others, regulations required them to be classified as "missing."

Although Hallé sincerely liked and admired the soldier whose wife wrote the letter, he decided not to respond, consciously numbing himself to the human tragedy of the situation. For the time being, he chose an almost unfeeling detachment, not only from the world behind the lines, but even from the dead man himself. He rationalized that officers were not formally obliged to answer private letters. He continued with remarkable candor: "One often responds even so out of sympathy. But me, I never had the courage. . . . When all's said and done, I think that sometimes it's better not to respond. This unhappy woman will understand that he is dead. It is useless to tell her in so many words what has happened. No, truly, it is better not to say."[29]

By this time, absolute numbers of casualties in the 5e DI mattered little. Hallé scarcely cared that over the course of the whole time the 5e DI spent in the Eparges sector less than 1 percent of his men would become casualties each month, and that very few of these would suffer the fate of being buried in a mine explosion. What counted was that the possibility of horrible death without useful military purpose existed everywhere, just as it did at Verdun. Looking at his men one day, he wondered, "who will be the first to fall?"[30] He was well aware that he was as likely a candidate as anyone else, since as he wrote: "We are all equal before death, and my hide is worth the same as yours, you poor fools who mutter and murmur as I pass."[31] At one point, he dreamt of being able to release each of his men from the trenches. He provided an intriguing glimpse into what may have been passing through officers' minds in May 1917, when having left the special logic of the trenches, they were now expected to order their openly resisting men back there: "Go on, you're free, go home. If back there, you still suffer sometimes, at least you can try to forget, draw from the good life, all that will make your body happy, all that will set your heart at rest, in making you forget your sorrow."[32]

Two other memoirs, by men new to the 74e RI, provide a striking contrast in ways soldiers could be socialized into life in Les Eparges and the dilemma facing soldiers there. Private Legentil, of the Class of 1916, joined

[29] Ibid., p. 69. Ellipses in original.
[30] Ibid., p. 60.
[31] Ibid., pp. 60–61.
[32] Ibid., p. 61.

the 74ᵉ RI as a machine gunner just after Douaumont.[33] He began learning the role of the *poilu* even before he entered the trenches for the first time in the Eparges sector. During an extended medical inspection while his unit was out of the front lines, he wrote: "We got to know the old-timers of the section, who were quite few, having left many comrades on the slopes of the fort of Douaumont. There was nothing to do [during the inspection], and these survivors of Verdun occupied themselves just getting drunk."[34]

Also before he actually entered the front lines, he learned from his new comrades the difference between battlefield soldiers and others in uniform, and the art of cleverly defying authority when exercised by the wrong sort of person. During his company commander's leave, an ex-cavalier second lieutenant who had not been at Douaumont had been left in charge: "He did his work with zeal, and wanted to order the old-timers around as though they were back at the barracks. This didn't work at all."[35] Somehow, the second lieutenant was able to get his mistress into the encampment, and as Legentil recalled, "for several nights, we had a veritable *charivari* underneath the windows of his bedroom. We avenged ourselves a bit." When the company commander returned, "we only had to do some parade marches and some practice fire."

Once in the lines after 23 June, Legentil was just as quickly socialized into disillusionment with the bleak prospects of trench warfare in Les Eparges. At first, he could still hear the battle raging at Verdun to his north. But in his sector "the days passed quite monotonously, marked only by some small artillery exchanges or an encounter with a night patrol that would provoke a short alert.[36] When violence did come, it was often unpredictable and deadly. He described a mortar barrage on 23 June, just after he entered the sector:

These are curious projectiles, launched by small trench mortars. You can follow their capricious trajectory, and they fall to earth pirouetting in a great snort. You often have time to take cover, because they only come one at a time, and they don't always explode. On the other hand, wounds from these projectiles are often very grave, because they explode into a small number of very large pieces of twenty centimeters or even more![37]

He found a mine explosion even more frightening. On the evening of 27 September, a huge explosion went off like an earthquake in Legentil's

[33] Private Legentil (no first name provided), "Notes de campagne du 12 avril 1915 au 11 novembre 1918: au jour le jour, bons et mauvais souvenirs" (unpublished memoir, Fonds Privés, Côte 1 KT 86).

[34] Ibid., p. 5.

[35] Ibid., pp. 5–6.

[36] Ibid., p. 6.

[37] Ibid.

subsector, followed by a violent artillery barrage. Some thirty men were killed outright or buried alive. The explosion created a huge crater; by the eerie light of flares, Legentil could see French and Germans scurrying to occupy its rim. He remarked: "An epic struggle, as cruel as it is murderous, for very meager results."[38]

When the weather deteriorated by October, he had to endure another form of entrapment—the mud. Legentil described an unusually painful trip moving his machine gun to the front lines. The men had to crawl for three hours through a "thick and glutinous bed of mud" to get to the assigned position. Dragging bulky and heavy ammunition proved especially painful: "How will we get there? Good will, human resistance, has its limits. We stop every hundred meters, despite the comments of the liaison agent, who is in a hurry to get us into position so he can go take a nap."[39] On days when the "live and let live" system did not prevail, their dehumanizing situation became complete: "In fact, once day broke, you had to sit down, and a big devil like Caron [a comrade] had to lie down so as not to be seen from the front. Painful hours, interminable days, without even being able to stand up to take a couple of steps, not even for bodily functions. Naturally, you relieve yourself the best you can, where you are."[40]

Another newcomer to the division, Capt. Paul Rimbault, socialized himself very differently.[41] Indeed, his is the only memoir from the 5e DI, in which the author identified more with the official language of "commanders" than that of "soldiers," as those categories have been used here. Like Hallé, Rimbault commanded a company, and actually lived in trench conditions similar to those of his soldiers. But if Hallé and Legentil reacted to the dilemma of trench warfare in Les Eparges with a sense of helplessness bordering on despair, Rimbault struggled to maintain continuity with values he expressed before the war on military society and military authority. The result is an almost schizophrenic account, in which he juxtaposes sympathy with his men with considerable alienation from and disillusionment toward them.

According to his military resume, Rimbault had joined the army as a volunteer back in 1896. In 1904, he graduated from Saint-Maixent (the officer training school for NCOs) as a second lieutenant in 1904, and was promoted to lieutenant in 1906. He was still a lieutenant at age thirty-two in August 1914. The fact that he had remained at the same rank for eight years suggests that had the war not intervened, his professional status would not have changed.

[38] Ibid., p. 9.
[39] Ibid., p. 11.
[40] Ibid.
[41] *Propos d'un marmité, 1915–1917* (Paris: L. Fournier, 1920).

In 1912, Lieutenant Rimbault had published a pamphlet for soldiers about to complete their two years of military service.[42] The pamphlet outlined soldiers' continuing military duties and provided a guide to the preferred attitudes toward the army and toward war as conscripts prepared to reenter civilian life. Rimbault left no doubt that he considered the military hierarchy the sole source of legitimate authority on the battlefield: "To follow his leader everywhere, this is the first virtue of the soldier in combat."[43] He appears also to have been a true believer in the doctrine of the offensive. Rimbault gave his readers the surprising assurance that "if you flee [on the battlefield], you will certainly get killed. If you go forward, you have 90 chances out of 100 to get out of it without a scratch."[44]

Before joining the 74e RI, Rimbault had served several extended stretches in trench warfare, though his record does not indicate experience in major pitched battles. He arrived with the regiment in late October 1916, that is, after the onset of bad weather and in a period of heightened German activity.[45] Hallé and Legentil by this point clearly suffered from the spiritual malady so closely identified with French soldiers in World War I, le cafard.[46] Upon first inspecting the listening posts in advance of the front lines, he observed that "the existence of these poor devils who live over there is terrible. They are no longer men, they are piles of mud."[47] But even his description of his first efforts to socialize with his men suggests that he was much more interested in maintaining emotional detachment from them than was Hallé (also a company commander): "Finally, one chats with them for a bit, gives them a cigarette, a bit of drink. It gives them pleasure; it also proves to them that one is thinking of their misery."[48]

For his own part, he concluded stoically that his part of the Eparges sector "isn't of such a bad character; apart from the mortars, one can live his life here."[49] Although his own living conditions could not have differed greatly from those of Hallé, Rimbault wrote much more of "their" suffering in the trenches than "our" suffering. He also differed from a number of more senior officers in the division cited previously in seeing some advantage to conducting raids as late as January 1917. Rimbault described the planning of one raid in some detail, though he said nothing about its

---

[42] Rimbault, Le Soldat dans la guerre de demain: causeries morales sur la guerre, fait à ses hommes libérables par un officier d'infanterie (Paris: Berger Levrault, 1912).

[43] Ibid., p. 79.

[44] Ibid., pp. 87–88.

[45] His memoir maintains that he commanded the 3e Compagnie, whereas his dossier records that he commanded the 6e Compagnie.

[46] The term literally means "the cockroach." Figuratively, the term was employed to express discontents ranging from dissatisfaction with the wine to calls for a socialist revolution.

[47] Rimbault, Propos, p. 71.

[48] Ibid.

[49] Ibid., p. 73.

execution. His concluding statement on the raid rather blithely asserted that it pleased his men as much as himself. But it also showed that he was not completely unaware of the concept of proportionality at Les Eparges: "The men like these little operations a lot, in which there is little risk and much profit. At the same time, one must not abuse them, lest a sector be wrecked uselessly and the time there be rendered, if not untenable, at least difficult."[50]

Rimbault's memoir was divided into two parts, one a rudimentary diary that without explanation covered only the period from July 1915 to July 1917, the other a series of short commentaries on topics ranging from diplomacy to war profiteers. The most revealing expression of his complicated views on French soldiers after Verdun was an essay written in February 1917 called "The Simple *Bibi*."[51] On the one hand, he praised the tenacity of the French soldier: "He is there, now and forever, armed and ready, looking the Boche in the eye without flinching." Indeed, this capacity for accepting *tenir* "has saved the country."[52]

But on the other hand, Rimbault believed that the French soldier of February 1917 had passed his military prime. He maintained somewhat naively that back in 1914, the French soldier "had faith in his bayonet, that is to say in his valiance. He ignored the terror of the machinery of modern warfare."[53] By 1917, however, "the simple *bibi* has lost fifty percent of his value."[54] Rimbault believed that the French soldier had been worn down by disappointment, through fruitless offensives, wartime propaganda laden with untruths, and the impersonal nature of trench warfare itself. Most remarkably, this prewar professional officer maintained that they had become "more citizens than soldiers. . . . They are egalitarians, who bear a strong grudge toward their commanders and those behind the lines, who shun serried ranks, military fashion, everything that gives the appearance of an army."[55] Like Mangin, he suggested that the hope for the renewal of the *furia francese* lay with black African and other colonial troops.[56]

If Hallé and Legentil responded to the dilemma of stagnated warfare by early 1917 with an internalized sense of entrapment and despair, Rimbault responded with an externalized sense of disillusionment with the soldiers he commanded. He continued to have great faith in his own commanders' capacity to win the war, and with the exception of the essay just cited, he had far more to say about his military superiors than his military inferiors.

[50] Ibid., p. 77.
[51] *Bibi* is a very familiar term for "individual."
[52] Ibid., p. 144.
[53] Ibid., p. 138.
[54] Ibid., p. 143.
[55] Ibid., pp. 139–40.
[56] Ibid., p. 143.

Rimbault's identification with the military hierarchy became even closer in the spring of 1917.

Beginning in late 1916, a new documentary source emerged for examining opinions of the soldiers of the 5ᵉ DI, reports from the mail censors or *Contrôle Postal*. Soldiers' letters had been opened and read by their superiors at least since 1915. Mangin referred to them with some regularity in letters to his wife as evidence of his men's high morale. But over the course of 1916, surveillance of correspondence became centralized under a new office attached to the General Staff, the Service de Renseignement aux Armées (SRA).[57] SRA records comprise primarily reports on samples of letters read, with summaries and many direct quotes.

These reports seem too linked to a prearranged bureaucratic agenda for them to be analyzed quantitatively, despite frequent attempts to do so both during the war and subsequently.[58] Staff officers, I would suggest, wrote the reports more to please than to inform. They tended to find "morale" invariably holding up well, whatever external evidence might have existed to the contrary. Displeasing sentiments were frequently cited, but most often as exceptions that prove the rule of soldierly docility. In short, postal censorship records are neither more nor less "representative" than published memoirs, though for very different reasons. They serve most usefully as another form of literary evidence, in that they put words to phenomena suggested by broader circumstances. As Annick Cochet observed, "family correspondence of the common soldier in fact situates itself at the meeting point between the individual and the collective,"[59] that is, where individuals describe collective experiences. Letters constitute a unique form of literary evidence, since they were not intended for publication and were not written by literary figures. As letters were destined for a personal rather than a collective readership, they tended to be shorn of the public artistic ambitions that influence even the most self-consciously humble published accounts.

[57] On the development of postal censorship, see Jean-Noël Jeanneney, "Les Archives des commissions de contrôle postal aux armées (1916–1918): une source précieuse pour l'histoire contemporaine de l'opinion et des mentalités," *Revue d'Histoire moderne et contemporaine* (Janvier–Mars 1968), pp. 209–33.

[58] For example, a report on the 5ᵉ DI of 4 March 1917 reported with bizarre precision that 6.1 percent of the letters read expressed "good" sentiments and 3.7 percent "poor"; the remaining 90.2 percent were simply "without interest." "5ᵉ DI, Rapport du Contrôle Postal," 4 March 1917, G.Q.G., 2ᵉ Bureau, SRA, 16 N 1392. Since all reports are found among the SRA documents, they will henceforth be identified simply by title, date, and carton. One more recent attempt at quantitative analysis is Annick Cochet, "L'Opinion et le moral des soldats en 1916 d'après les archives du contrôle postal," 2 vols. (Thèse pour le doctorat, Paris X-Nanterre, 1986).

[59] Cochet, "L'Opinion et le Moral," p. 495. Unfortunately, the dissertation ends rather than begins with this intriguing observation.

I propose here simply to illustrate echoes of views expressed by Hallé, Legentil, and Rimbault. Like the three authors of memoirs, soldiers in the ten months preceding the mutinies were thinking deeply about the dilemma of entrapment versus defeat. Two mutually contradictory sentiments appeared consistently in the reports: the sense expressed by Hallé and to a lesser degree Legentil that the principle of *tenir* in trench warfare had come to signify nothing more than control, misery, and death; and the abiding interest in winning the war so critical to understanding Rimbault. Most soldiers, I would suggest, held both views simultaneously. In the spring of 1917, soldiers had to choose which of these sentiments was more important.

Of course, deep concern that the war might never end was hardly new, and surfaced in the first reports citing soldiers from the 5e DI. A report of 1 July 1916 quoted a soldier from the division (not further identified): "There is reason to despair, truly. . . . The newspapers lie to us and will lie to us again, because they are not better placed than the combattants to judge certain things greatly embellished by the journalists."[60] Expressions of misery figured more prominently in the reports beginning in October and November 1916, as the weather deteriorated and as German activity in the sector increased. "I am not blind," wrote a sergeant of the 274e RI to his mother, "and I see very well that this is not the last winter of the war. For a long time, the government and the civilians have sacrificed the *poilus*, as they say. As long as there are still *poilus*, the war will continue. We are caught in the machinery; sooner or later we will all pass through it in our turn."[61]

Moreover, a strain of opinion existed that matters on the Western Front would get worse rather than better. A stretcher bearer from the 129e RI wrote to a friend: "You say that the hardest part is over. I don't share this opinion, because the longer the war lasts the worse it gets. After more than eighteen months of battles, Verdun passed all preceding battles; this summer the Somme—even more horrifying! In this way, the spring of 1917 will surpass Verdun and the Somme for the belligerents of the two camps."[62] Even though they knew their letters were being read by the authority structure, some soldiers expressed clear premutinous opinions. A soldier from the 274e RI, whose letter was described in the report as "the most outrageous" of its genre, made an unfavorable comparison between the lot of the frontline soldier and that of the convict. He wrote in January 1917:

[60] "IIe Armée, compte-rendu hebdomadaire du contrôle des correspondances," 1 July 1916, 16 N 1391.

[61] "5e DI, Compte-rendu: contrôle de la correspondance," No. 9.303, 14 Novembre 1916, 16 N 1391.

[62] Report of 28 November 1916, No. 10.007, in ibid.

Considering the way we are led, convicts are happier than we are, and back there they don't risk their lives. It is disgusting to be French. . . . The real criminals aren't under fire. . . . The law protects them, while the fathers of families get their heads broken. We are only old men, and I assure you that our reflections are more bitter than enthusiastic.[63]

But many soldiers never entirely rejected *tenir*, even if they accepted it simply as the worst alternative except for all the others. "As far as I'm concerned," wrote a corporal from the 74e RI in August 1916, "I have decided to carry it through to the end, understanding very well the sacrifice that France demands of me, making to her willingly the sacrifice of my life."[64] Such sentiments appeared as regularly as sentiments of despair in SRA reports, and were construed by the staff officers writing them as confirmation of the identity between soldierly and command expectations.

Perhaps the most curious manifestation of soldiers' abiding interest in winning the war involved expressions of actual enthusiasm for the offensive planned for the spring of 1917. A sergeant from the 129e RI wrote in January 1917 that "we have confidence in the great spring offensive, which we *must hope* will be decisive, because, with Nivelle, we have an amazing man from the artillery who has proved himself at Verdun and in whom we have confidence."[65] A soldier (not identified but probably an officer or an NCO) whose views were reported as indicative of the "dominant impression," went further in March 1917, when the 5e DI was behind the lines in the last stages of training for the offensive:

The celebrated formula "*On les aura*! [We shall have them!]" begins to become "*On les a*! [We have them!]." The retreat of the Germans is noted by all the men as a certain sign of their weakness, and has raised in their ranks the hope of a striking revenge that they foresee on the horizon; all burn with desire to join their comrades attacking first for this offensive, so much yearned for. Their morale is excellent, completely up to the situation.[66]

Soldiers could imagine a leap of faith in the early spring of 1917, not dissimilar to Rimbault's faith in the command structure, and Nivelle and

63 "Contrôle postal, rapports des commissions, IIe Armée," 13–20 January 1917, 16 N 1392. This letter evidently was not even seized. Seizure of a letter in fact rarely occurred unless the authors expressed openly socialist sentiments.

64 "IIe Armée, compte-rendu hebdomadaire du contrôle des Correspondances," 4 August 1916, 16 N 1391.

65 Ibid., 27 January 1917, 16 N 1391. Emphasis added.

66 Ibid. (Rapports, VIIIe Armée), 26 March 1917, 16 N 1433. The retreat refers to the German withdrawal in February 1917 to the Hindenburg Line (referred to by the Germans as the Siegfried Line), from fifteen to forty kilometers behind the previous line. The Germans in fact retreated to a much stronger defensive position, which virtually doomed the Chemin des Dames offensive in advance.

Mangin's faith in the *barrage roulant.* The key concept is the notion expressed by the sergeant from the 129ᵉ RI that soldiers *had to* hope that the next offensive would prove conclusive. Their most basic hope, perhaps, was to reconcile their despair with trench warfare with their abiding interest in winning the war.

In a different idiom, the courts-martial also underscored the impasse between soldiers and commanders at Les Eparges, which paralleled the impasse between the French and the Germans. Beginning in November 1916, by which time Hallé and Legentil noticed a serious decline in their spirits, convictions for desertion rose to their highest levels yet. The previous records had been set during the Battle of Verdun, 12 for April 1916 and 13 for May. After declining to 6–7 per month for the summer of 1916, convictions rose sharply—16 in November, 19 in December, 17 in January 1917, and 18 in February.[67] Only in March 1917 did they decline, after the division had been withdrawn from Les Eparges. The argument of this chapter suggests that deserters came to regard the closed world of trench warfare at Les Eparges as providing many of the emotional and physical hardships of pitched battle. But many more opportunities to resist by deserting existed at Les Eparges than at Verdun—notably the physical dispersion of the division along a seven- to ten-kilometer front, and the granting of leaves.[68]

In this context, the court-martial evolved into an instrument for the management (as opposed to the repression) of desertion. Although this meant that the *conseil de guerre* in many ways functioned more coherently than had been the case previously, it also meant an institutional confession that the disciplinary dilemma of just what to do with errant soldiers had worsened considerably.[69] The particular disciplinary approach at Les Eparges seems clearer than had been the case earlier. Recidivists and those considered likely in some way to "contaminate" otherwise obedient soldiers had their sentences carried out. Of the fifty sentences carried out

[67] See Leonard V. Smith, "The Disciplinary Dilemma of French Military Justice, September 1914–April 1917: The Case of the 5ᵉ Division d'Infanterie," *The Journal of Military History* 55 (January 1991), p. 65. These numbers refer to the month in which the soldier deserted.

[68] From June 1916 to April 1917, 53.4 percent of desertion convictions were for leaving a unit directly and 46.6 percent for failing to return from some sort of authorized absence, most often a leave.

[69] This dilemma involved the fact that because of legal restrictions put in place over the course of the war, soldiers normally could be executed only after a cumbersome and time-consuming appeal process. Since soldiers could not be shot quickly, this became in disciplinary terms tantamount to not being able to shoot them at all. A "dilemma" ensued because deserters sent to prison in effect had their desertions rendered successful. See ibid., pp. 49–51. By late 1916, the ambiguity between abandoning a post and desertion had for the most part been clarified. Those who left their units but remained in the Zone of the Armies were convicted of abandoning a post, and those who left the zone were convicted of desertion.

between June 1916 and April 1917, thirty-five (or 70 percent) were for soldiers already convicted by a *conseil de guerre* in wartime. No soldiers were executed, or even given death sentences. It thus bears pointing out that carrying out sentence for desertion had the paradoxical effect of rendering the desertion successful. Although a special *section de discipline* had set up in December 1916, its effect seems to have been minimal.[70] The line dividing service in the trenches at Les Eparges from incarceration continued to obscure.

One 5e DI officer recognized this situation even before the dramatic rise in desertion convictions. In a report dated 19 September 1916, Major Ménager, commanding the 1e Bataillon of the 36e RI, explored the causes of the "moral depression and lack of military spirit" in the front lines."[71] The first factor he cited was the incorporation into each company of five or six men found guilty by courts-martial. He commented that "they are nearly all certain to profit from an amnesty at the end of the war, and they boast about it. . . . It is regrettable that the courts-martial are not more severe." Particularly galling for Ménager and his men was the practice of sending soldiers from the rear into the front lines for limited periods (about thirty days) in lieu of a prison sentence. Not surprisingly, this had "an absolutely deplorable effect" on the rest of the soldiers. Ménager noted one incident in which the men complained to their officer: "The rest of us, we foot soldiers, they consider us convicts! So will they send us to the rear to be punished?"

This being the case, the question to pose in concluding this chapter is not so much why so many soldiers were deserting from the 5e DI at Les Eparges, but given how low the potential risk was, why so few. Memoirs, letters, and military justice records indicate that soldiers plainly were developing serious reservations about what they were doing in the trenches. But for the vast majority, the ill-tempered compromise between soldiers and commanders of *tenir* had not been pushed to the breaking point—at least not yet. Ménager brought to bear the old Napoleonic axiom of *"ils grognent mais ils marchent encore* [They grumble but they still march]" to insist that his men still wanted to resolve the dilemma of entrapment versus defeat. Under conditions he probably could not have foreseen, the 1917 mutinies would prove him correct: "But one thing is certain. If they grumble, they still march and they will always march because their hearts are all in the right place, because above all they love their country, because they love their regiment, and they want to support its glorious reputation. I affirm that one will never call in vain on their fine sentiments."

[70] See ibid., pp. 64–65.
[71] "36e Régiment d'Infanterie, 1er Bataillon: Compte Rendu," 19 September 1916, 5e DI, 3e Bureau, 24 N 88.

Indeed, after the division had left Les Eparges in February 1917, General de Roig made the considerable leap of faith that all was well. Now that the division had left the sector and its various encumbrances, nothing remained to inhibit the exercise of command authority. "The long sojourn in the trenches," he admitted, had indeed raised the possibility of "a diminution in the combative value of the troops of the division."[72] But after a period of rest and training in a camp in March 1917, he added hopefully, "the bad habits have disappeared." He concluded with a less than prophetic statement of the division's role in the "final" offensive planned for April:

> The maneuvers of the division have proven that everyone, commanders and soldiers [*chefs et soldats*], has not lost anything of their qualities of intelligence, endurance, and discipline. . . . The morale of all, enhanced by the present events, is excellent, and the 5e Division will certainly know how to show itself worthy of its past in the coming battles.

[72] De Roig, "Notice sur la 5e Division d'Infanterie," 22 March 1917.

CHAPTER VIII

The Implicit Struggle Becomes Explicit

THE MUTINIES OF 1917

IN HIS CLASSIC interpretive essay on World War I, A.J.P. Taylor observed that if Napoleon had suddenly come back to life at the beginning of 1917 "he would have found nothing which surprised him or which, at any rate, he could not understand," but that if he had come back at the end of the year, he would have been "bewildered."[1] Although Taylor referred principally to the Russian Revolution and to United States intervention in the war, Napoleon would have been equally surprised at changes in the relationship between war and politics in France.

In 1917, politics regained control over war in France, though in ways that Napoleon or Clausewitz perhaps would not even have recognized, much less felt comfortable with. Georges Clemenceau established a neo-Jacobin dictatorship in November 1917, declaring his only policy was to "make war."[2] But Napoleon (though perhaps not Clausewitz) would certainly have found perplexing Clemenceau's other most quoted adage, that war had become too serious a matter to be left to generals. Henceforth, civilians would keep French generals on a much shorter leash than they had Joffre or Nivelle. But politics also constrained war in a very different sense. In the French army mutinies following the failure of the Chemin des Dames offensive in the spring of 1917, the politics of citizen-soldiers at last made itself explicitly felt on the authority structure at the highest levels—and months before the Clemenceau ministry assumed power.

This chapter will explore ways a close examination of the mutinies in the 5e DI can help illuminate the particulars of this much larger process. In the wake of the Chemin des Dames offensive, a convergence occurred of the two crises of foucauldian despair examined in chapters 6 and 7—the crises in pitched battle and in trench warfare. The mutinies constituted what James Scott called "the public declaration of the hidden transcript,"[3] the moment at which soldiers passed from manipulating formal authority

---

[1] A.J.P. Taylor, *The First World War: An Illustrated History* (London: Hamish Hamilton, 1963), p. 165.

[2] See Jean-Baptiste Duroselle, *Clemenceau* (Paris: Fayard, 1988), chaps. 9–11.

[3] James C. Scott, *Domination and the Arts of Resistance: Hidden Transcripts* (New Haven: Yale University Press, 1991), title of chap. 8.

relations to openly rejecting them. This "saturnalia of power," to borrow another term from Scott, resulted from an open confrontation between soldiers and commanders in the power relationship. An effective reversal of the relationship existed, as soldiers became for a time essentially free political actors. This chapter will explore the complex internal dynamic of the mutinies, which revolved around the ways soldiers articulated, prioritized, and asserted their demands, as well as how the command structure received, resisted, and in the end partly accepted them. At the heart of the confrontation lay a struggle with the paradox of popular sovereignty, the paradox of soldiers being expected to obey a source of authority originating in themselves.

"POLITICAL" MUTINIES AND THE PEDRONCINI THESIS

Historians of the mutinies of 1917 have been most concerned with whether they were "political." Because France, unlike Russia, did not experience revolution in its 1917 rethinking of politics and war, most have concluded comfortably that they were not. The need to continue posing the question came partly from the dearth of sources. For nearly fifty years after the war, most archival evidence remained sealed. Consequently, the only sources for researching the mutinies had some "political" origin—journalistic accounts (many directed toward reform of the military justice system) and memoirs from politicians.[4]

Gen. Philippe Pétain, the successor to Gen. Robert Nivelle as *generalissimo* and the man charged with resolving the mutinies, wrote an account for French army consumption in 1926.[5] Pétain cited three main causes, some of which subsequent observers have deemed were "political" and others not. The first factor cited was the "launching and exploitation of a pacifist propaganda campaign."[6] Beginning in the winter of 1916–1917, soldiers in the trenches found themselves bombarded by "antimilitarist and anarchist leaflets," and found their confidence in their commanders further undermined by the "reprehensible habit" in the civilian press of

---

[4] The account in the official history is brief and frequently vague, and emphasizes the role of factors external to the army. AFGG, tome 5, vol. 2, chap. 4. Among journalistic accounts see Paul Allard, "Les Mutineries de l'armée française," *L'œuvre*, 26 August–1 September 1932; and Joseph Jolinon, "La Mutinerie des Cœuvres," *Mercure de France*, 15 August 1920. Among the relevant memoirs from politicians are Raymond Poincaré, *Au Service de la France*, 10 vols. (Paris: Plon, 1926–1933); Paul Painlevé, *Comment j'ai nommé Foch et Pétain* (Paris: Alcan, 1923); and David Lloyd George, *War Memoirs of David Lloyd George* (Boston: Little, Brown & Company, 1934).

[5] "A Crisis of Morale in the French nation at War," Rivers Scott, trans., in Maj. Gen. Sir Edward Spears, *Two Men Who Saved France: Pétain and De Gaulle* (London: Eyre & Spottswoode, 1966). The report was published for the first time in France in the same year.

[6] Ibid., p. 72.

editorializing on military operations.[7] Second, Pétain cited the poor physical conditions at the front, especially capricious leave policies and bad food. Third, Pétain faulted "a fantastic strategic over-confidence," exemplified by Nivelle's and Mangin's irresponsible claim that they had discovered the formula for the *percée*.[8]

Pétain maintained that French soldiers in their vast majority remained well-intentioned, but exhausted and easily misled. First led to false optimism by the Nivelle-Mangin public relations machine, they proved in their disappointment all the more susceptible to seduction by pacifists and other traitors from the interior. But to Pétain, soldiers remained conspicuously incapable of genuinely autonomous action. He argued that in a few regiments, such as the 129e RI, the mutiny was "premeditated and methodically planned," and that such treachery deserved little indulgence.[9] But for the most part, soldiers became "politicized" only when they felt let down by their leaders. Restoring apolitically correct soldierly behavior, also known as "morale," remained principally a matter of restoring appropriate leadership.

Most subsequent historians of the mutinies seem not to have known of the existence of Pétain's report, though they generally arrived at similar conclusions about the three main causes of the mutinies. French historians have tended to minimize the role of subversion from the rear. Jean Ratinaud wrote in 1960 of a "quasi-professional strike," that ceased when "intelligence and friendship took their place alongside discipline and order."[10] R. G. Nobécourt in 1965 pointed to a convergence of subversion, material hardship, and command overconfidence, and agreed with Ratinaud that Pétain was the right man at the right time.[11] But English language historians, always on the lookout for early symptoms of the moral collapse of France in 1940, have focused on the disease of subversion infecting soldiers at the front. John Williams in 1962 wrote of "weary and demoralized *poilus*" who found themselves "egged on to rebellion by home-front traitors and pacifists," though he concluded charitably that any army might have behaved similarly under the same "intolerable strain."[12] Richard Watt in 1963 made essentially the same argument; no one, he concluded, should dare call treason this "convulsion of exhausted troops."[13]

French historian Guy Pedroncini transformed the historiography of the

[7] Ibid., pp. 73, 75.

[8] Ibid., p. 82.

[9] Ibid., pp. 89–84.

[10] Jean Ratinaud, *1917 ou La Révolte des poilus* (Paris: Fayard, 1960), pp. 15, 19.

[11] R. G. Nobécourt, *Les Fantassins du Chemin des Dames* (Paris: Robert Laffont, 1965), pp. 219–19.

[12] John Williams, *Mutiny 1917* (London: William Heinemann Ltd., 1962), pp. ix–x.

[13] Richard M. Watt, *Dare Call It Treason* (New York: Simon and Schuster, 1963), p. 303.

mutinies in 1967, when he published the first study based on archival evidence, particularly the all-important military justice records.[14] Pedroncini plotted the exact course of the mutinies and their repression. He concluded that mutinies were a limited and sophisticated protest against three years of tried-and-failed offensive tactics, brought to their nadir in the Chemin des Dames debacle. He conclusively situated the incidents in "active" sectors—that is, where soldiers believed they would be ordered into fruitless assaults.[15] Pétain succeeded in resolving the mutinies because he alone recognized that war had become fully industrialized, and that against this physical reality the question of pacifist subversion became secondary.

The significance of subversion from the rear had been wildly exaggerated, Pedroncini concluded, and had been used as an excuse by failed commanders such as Nivelle and Mangin. Pedroncini argued that the mutinies remained strictly military protests, and hence "nonpolitical." Rhetoric from soldiers that to the untrained eye appeared revolutionary exemplified simply a "more human desire to save one's life. The revolution, according to the evidence, was simply something to cling to, without thereby taking on a great significance."[16]

Some twenty-seven years after its publication, *Les Mutineries de 1917* remains a classic, by good measure the most impressive study of the mutinies to date. But it remains as well a book with a "high politics" agenda—the rehabilitation of Pétain. By 1967, the fog of historical amnesia around his memory had finally begun to lift, a process in which Pedroncini's work has plainly sought to play a role.[17] But in the process, Pedroncini greatly underestimated Pétain's own concern with subversion from the interior, particularly in the 5e DI.[18] Moreover, Pedroncini did not adequately explain why the mutinies reached their zenith well *after* the Chemin des Dames offensive was being wound down and *after* Pétain had been made commander-in-chief. Based on the mutinies in the 5e DI, I contend that the Pedroncini thesis is not so much wrong as skewed and incomplete because of its focus on Pétain.

Recent thinking on what constitutes "political" history also suggests the need to reconsider Pedroncini's "nonpolitical" interpretation of the muti-

---

[14] Guy Pedroncini, *Les Mutineries de 1917* (Paris: Presses Universitaires de France, 1967).

[15] Ibid., pp. 71–89.

[16] Ibid., p. 125. In this passage, Pedroncini specifically referred to the mutinies in the 5e DI, which he considered among those most easy to misinterpret as "political."

[17] Pedroncini's subsequent work has continued in this direction, notably with *Pétain: général en chef: 1917–1918* (Paris: Presses Universitaires de France, 1974), and *Pétain: le soldat et la gloire, Tome I, 1856–1918* (Paris: Perrin, 1989, tome 2 in preparation).

[18] Oddly indeed, Pétain's "Une Crise morale" is not cited in Pedroncini's chapter titled "L'Interprétation de Pétain," though it is cited elsewhere in the book. *Les Mutineries de 1917*, pp. 302–7.

nies. New work on the history of women has shifted attention from a strict focus on state institutions toward the ways power is negotiated and exercised in its social contexts and in people's daily lives. In particular, Joan Scott has drawn on poststructuralist theory to redefine the "political" history of women. "By studying power as it is exercised by and in relation to formal governmental authorities," she has contended, "historians unnecessarily eliminate whole realms of experience from consideration."[19] Politics, for Scott, must encompass nothing less than "the process by which plays of power and knowledge constitute identity and experience."[20]

The risk of such a sweeping approach, of course, involves expanding the term "political" past coherence. At the very least, making all aspects of everyday life political begs an important question. All struggles may be political, but few historians would conclude that all political struggles are equally significant in all contexts. No scholar grants equality to all bits of knowledge—certainly not poststructuralists. If the term "political" is to maintain intellectual integrity, ways must be found to determine why particular political struggles matter in well-defined contexts.

The interpretation here of the mutinies in the 5ᵉ DI will explore one way the empirical might help clarify the theoretical. Expanding a definition of "political" is certainly a worthwhile enterprise if state institutional structures do not accurately describe actual power relations. By 1917, the real balance of power between soldiers and commanders in the French army proved profoundly less unequal than the institutional structures implied. During the course of the mutinies, soldiers explicitly figured this out. The mutinies are thus best understood as the complex "political" renegotiation of the parameters of command authority.

THE STRUCTURE OF THE MUTINIES

Conventional military historians have long concluded that the failure of the Chemin des Dames offensive, like that of the 5ᵉ DI attack on Douaumont, was essentially overcaused.[21] The "rolling barrage," which had worked such wonders at Verdun in the fall of 1916, proved a one-time trick. The attacking barrage could not roll forward indefinitely, and the Germans simply kept the bulk of their infantry well to the rear, protected

[19] Joan Wallach Scott, *Gender and the Politics of History* (New York: Columbia University Press, 1988), p. 26.

[20] Ibid., p. 5.

[21] In addition to the works cited earlier on the mutinies, see Henri Contamine, "De quelques Problèmes militaires en 1917," *Revue d'histoire moderne et contemporaine*, no. 1 (1968), pp. 108–21; General J. Roquerol, *Le Chemin des Dames* (Paris: Payot, 1934); and Maj. Gen. Sir Edward Spears, *Prelude to Victory* (London: Jonathan Cape, 1939).

and fresh for the counterattack once the frontline defenders had slowed the French down. To make matters much worse, the German withdrawal to the Hindenburg Line in February and March 1917 had removed the salient that was Nivelle's first objective and had given the Germans a stronger position. Nivelle's refusal to abandon or even alter his plan provoked War Minister Hubert Lyautey's famous remark that the plan had become worthy of light opera, of "the army of *The Grand Duchy of Gerolstein.*"[22]

The relationship between the offensive and the mutinies is more complicated than generally recognized. Militarily speaking, the Chemin des Dames offensive recapitulated the 1915 transition in the Artois from *percée* to *grignotage*. Once the *percée* proved quite unobtainable, the high command hastily scaled down extravagant expectations and proclaimed the results a success. This process began on 22 April—well before Pétain assumed supreme command on 15 May. On that day, Nivelle announced to his army group commanders that henceforth the goals of the offensive would be limited to occupying the high ground near Reims and the complete occupation of the plateau along the Chemin des Dames.[23] Nivelle thus proved willing to settle for the very sort of "tactical success" that Joffre proclaimed rendered his own offensives triumphs back in 1915.

Pétain's opposition to Nivelle's original scheme was well known in "high-politics" military circles.[24] But in the event, Pétain held a key operational command—Army Group Center, attacking in the Champagne. The government appointed Pétain its chief military advisor on April 29, as a form of damage control after the Chemin des Dames offensive floundered.[25] In a meeting with the British on 4–5 May, Pétain affirmed French intentions to continue the offensive, albeit with limited objectives.[26] Upon succeeding Nivelle on 15 May, Pétain's first directive affirmed the goal of *grignotage*: "the wearing down of the enemy, while wearing down ourselves as little as possible."[27]

But by that time, the matter proved not so simple. The irregular gains made by the offensive resulted in a highly unstable position. There is much

22 Quoted in Watt, *Dare Call It Treason*, p. 163. I am indebted to Professor Sir Michael Howard for explaining to me this initially puzzling remark.

23 AFGG, tome 5, vol. 1, pp. 707–9. One of the key objectives was the massif at Brimont, where the 5ᵉ DI had been stopped back in September 1914.

24 Pétain spoke especially frankly at the famous 6 April meeting of senior members of the government and senior commanders during which Nivelle obtained final approval for the offensive after threatening to resign. See Watt, *Dare Call It Treason*, pp. 168–70. Watt drew primarily from the memoirs of Painlevé.

25 The expanded duties of this position (the Chef de l'État-Major de l'Armée) involved advising the government on the feasibility of high-command schemes. See AFGG, tome 5, vol. 1, pp. 713–14.

26 Ibid., tome 5, vol. 2, p. 58.

27 G.Q.G., Directive No. 1 (pour les commandants de groupes d'armées et d'armées seulement), No. 17356, 19 May 1917, quoted in ibid., pp. 85–86.

to be said for the argument that Pétain had been called in to repair the ruin spread by others at the Chemin des Dames, just as at Verdun in February 1916 and at Vichy in June 1940. When he assumed supreme command, the partial conquest of the Chemin des Dames plateau either had to be consolidated (which could only be done by further if limited attacks) or abandoned. If the highest aspiration of the *pétainisme* of the trenches was to save soldiers' lives, the logical choice might have been to withdraw to safer positions (as the Germans themselves had done along the Hindenburg Line) and to throw no more live bodies after dead. But abandoning the gains meant admitting to all the world and particularly to increasingly volatile French soldiers and workers that the whole spring offensive had been a colossal waste of blood and treasure. Accordingly, Pétain felt obliged in May and June 1917 to continue consolidating the position subject to the uncertain means at his disposal.[28]

Pétain's limited options had important implications for battlefield soldiers. In a nutshell, the crises in pitched battle and trench warfare converged at the Chemin des Dames. For soldiers, an order to attack meant assaulting well-prepared positions of principally symbolic military utility. This recapitulated their experience at Verdun. But as will be shown in the case of the 5e DI, given the irregular nature of the French gains in the sector, even trench warfare had to be conducted from dangerous and precarious positions. This recalled the 5e DI's experience in the Eparges sector. Chapters 6 and 7 suggested that once soldiers entered the closed world of the trenches, pitched battle and trench warfare operated according to their own logic of control and entrapment. Soldiers reasoned, then, that the useful moment to resist was before they entered the trenches at all.

Incidents of "collective indiscipline," as the official expression had it, had been occurring in the French army for over a month before incidents in the 5e DI began on May 28. Both the scale of the incidents and the demands made by the soldiers had been escalating. Pedroncini has identified a useful breakdown of five phases of the crisis.[29] During the first month after the beginning of the Chemin des Dames offensive (16 April–15 May) some twenty-six incidents broke out. These were considered a nuisance rather than a dire threat by the command structure, since they involved relatively small numbers of soldiers and were limited solely to regiments directly involved in the attacks.

During the second phase (16–31 May) some forty-six incidents broke out, many involving whole divisions. Some units (such as the 5e DI) had not been involved in the Chemin des Dames fighting at all. Meetings of repre-

---

[28] Pétain considered this objective accomplished (and the crisis of indiscipline ended) in October 1917, after the successful French attack at Malmaison. See "A Crisis of Morale," p. 126.

[29] See *Les Mutineries de 1917*, chap. 4.

sentatives from several regiments took place that came suspiciously to resemble soldiers' councils or soviets in Russia. Demonstrators now spoke openly of ending the war by marching to the Chamber of Deputies in Paris. Pedroncini considered the third period (1–6 June) the paroxysm of the crisis, because of the threats of violence in many units and several incidents in which mutineers and their commanders passed from words to deeds (though notably not in the 5e DI).[30] During the fourth phase (7–30 June), Pedroncini concluded that Pétain's cure of reform coupled with judicial firmness finally began to take hold, though dispersed collective incidents of lessened intensity continued through a fifth phase lasting until January 1918.

An interpretation of the events in the 5e DI must go beyond a direct causal link between the Chemin des Dames offensive and the mutinies. The division was never engaged in the Chemin des Dames offensive, and was not even ordered into the front lines until 28 May, well after the winding down of the offensive had begun. In fact, when the mutinies broke out, the 5e DI had been out of the trenches entirely for over three months, its longest period during the entire war. Soldiers had spent enough time outside the enclosed world of the trenches profoundly to question the utility of returning there.

The 5e DI had been designated as part of the "exploitation" force for the Chemin des Dames offensive, those units assigned the task of charging through the *percée* scheduled for the first hours after the beginning of the attack.[31] The division had been training for this role since 12 February, the day it left the Eparges sector. After the *percée* failed to materialize, the 5e DI was sent further to the rear on 18 April. Soldiers spent nearly a month working as laborers repairing roads and working in fields. On 13 May, the division was sent for further instruction (toward undisclosed ends) much further behind the lines, to Nogent l'Artaud near Paris. On 27 May, the division was returned to an area southeast of Soissons, the main debarkation point for the Chemin des Dames sector. The mutinies broke out on 28 May, the day it was ordered to reenter the front lines. Despite its conspicuously nonviolent military record in the spring of 1917, the 5e DI proved by Pedroncini's reckoning the most mutinous in the entire French army.[32]

---

[30] Pedroncini found evidence of only three deaths outside the military justice system, though he conceded that there could have been more. Ibid., p. 132, n. 6. If the reaction of the commanders of the 5e DI is at all representative of the French army as a whole, I am inclined to support his conclusion that no substantial numbers of soldiers were shot out of hand.

[31] The source for this chronology is "Le Général de Roig-Bourdeville, Comt. la 5e DI à M. le Général Ct. la IIIe Armée," 2 June 1917. G.Q.G., Service Spécial Morale, 16 N 1521. Hereafter cited as De Roig report, 2 June.

[32] Pedroncini, *Les Mutineries de 1917*, p. 62. Pedroncini counted sixteen "incidents," though some ambiguity exists in his use of the term.

Although many historians have disdained the term "collective indiscipline" as an official euphemism, it is in some respects more accurate than the term "mutiny" because it reflects the fluid nature of the events themselves. Most simply described, the key events involved antiwar demonstrations, collective airings of soldierly grievances whose content will be examined in the next section. Legally, of course, these demonstrations were also "mutinous," for three reasons. First, they involved a collective and categorical refusal of orders to take up positions in the front lines. Second, for the most part, the demonstrations concluded with soldiers leaving for other units to encourage further resistance, first to other units in the 5e DI and then beyond. Third, soldiers' stated demands—sometimes including peace through revolution if necessary—went well beyond boundaries of expression normally conceded even citizen-soldiers.

But the mutinies in the 5e DI in other respects remained highly restrained. The institutional structures of the French army were bent but not broken because in the end they proved flexible. Officers remained not only unharmed, but almost universally treated with respect (probably because they returned the compliment). Perhaps even more significant, the demonstrations in the 5e DI were constrained from within by the very nature of soldiers' demands. At no point, according to the evidence, did external force play the determining role in breaking up the demonstrations. The repressive apparatus of the command structure did not function until after the mutinies were essentially over.

The first mutiny in the 5e DI took place in the 1e Bataillon of the 129e RI on 28 May.[33] The previous day, which happened to be the Sunday of Pentecost, the battalion had suddenly been ordered to leave by truck for Soissons. According to Colonel Boucher, a staff officer investigating the events, the soldiers were particularly upset because a number of wives and children had made the trip from Paris to Nogent l'Artaud to spend the holiday with their loved ones. These soldiers' annoyance did not abate when upon their arrival they were told that they would be marooned there for the next three days, pending the arrival of their logistical train. At about 2000 on 28 May, the first meeting took place, at which an estimated 150 to 180 unarmed protestors demanded an immediate peace and formed a cortege marching toward the billets of the rest of the regiment. Battalion commander Auberge tried to stop the cortege as soon as he heard of its existence, though neither he nor the officers under his command made any

[33] The description here of the mutinies in the 129e RI and the 36e RI draws from Colonel Boucher, "Rapports d'ensemble sur les événements qui se sont deroulés le 28 et le 29 mai au 129e RI," 9 June 1917, IIe Armée, 1e Bureau, 19 N 305. Boucher, a staff officer from the 35e DI, led the inquest into the events in the 129e RI, and this report summarized six previous reports beginning on 2 June.

attempt to stop the demonstrators by force. According to Boucher, Auberge's "intervention had no effect. The demonstrators arrived at the village, where they dispersed without incident."

Despite what were claimed to have been exceptional measures of surveillance, the demonstrations recommenced early on the morning of 29 May. In addition to some 250–300 men from the 1e Bataillon, some 110 men from the 3e Bataillon and a "certain number" of men from the 2e Bataillon joined the cortege. Boucher noted that some demonstrators wore flowers in their buttonholes and that many left their jackets unbuttoned, "to make themselves appear like strikers." He himself referred to them as strikers (*grèvistes*) at several points.

At about 1400, a joint demonstration involving some 750–800 men took place near the billets of the 36e RI. By that time, units of at least two regiments were involved, the 129e RI and the 36e RI. For some five hours, speakers aired collective grievances. But at the 29 May meeting, an extraordinary encounter took place between mutinying soldiers and their commanders about which disappointingly few details are known. The regimental commander, the division infantry commander, the division commander, and even the corps commander appeared to exhort the men to end their demonstrations. At least in the short run, however, their efforts showed no effect, since as Boucher noted, "the strikers had made up their minds." But these officers made no attempt to use force, and the demonstration gradually dissipated by around 1900.

A demonstration involving the entire 5e DI was planned for 0800 on 30 May. Rumors began to circulate that soldiers from the 129e RI and the 36e RI were planning to go to Paris bearing arms to demand that the Chamber of Deputies make peace, and that sympathetic military truck drivers had arranged to take them there. Although the demonstration did not take place, a number of soldiers from the 74e RI carrying their rifles presented themselves without authorization to the regimental commanders to enquire what had become of their comrades.[34] In any event, the entire 129e RI was ordered at 0300 on 30 May to new locations farther behind the lines, where it was put under the command of a different army corps. The transport of the regiment took place amid considerable drama, since the men were understandably reluctant to get into trucks to be transported they knew not where toward unspecified ends. But junior officers played a critical mediating role, and persuaded the men to go along. A similar removal of the 36e RI took place the same day. At no point was force used.

The next series of incidents took place on 5–7 June, the next time the 5e DI was ordered into the front lines. Although both mutineers and com-

[34] The only documentation of this incident comes from the military justice records, since ten soldiers were court-martialed as a result of the episode.

manders behaved in a more complicated and potentially explosive manner, the basic structure of the events remained the same. On 5 June, a number of men from a variety of units of the 74ᵉ RI showed, in the words of Lieutenant Colonel Brenot, "a certain reluctance to take up arms and go forward."[35] These soldiers began their trip to the front lines only after the personal intervention of Brenot.[36] On 6 June, when Brenot and a group of officers from the 2ᵉ Bataillon returned at about 1450 from their reconnaissance of the position along the Chemin des Dames that the division was about to occupy, they discovered that a demonstration by the 2ᵉ Bataillon was about to take place in a nearby meadow. Battalion commander Schaeffer spoke directly to about three hundred assembled men, "calling on their best sentiments, showing them the cowardice of their conduct, the grave consequences to which they were exposing themselves, the crime they were committing against the *Patrie*, and advising them to be on time for the assembly for the departure for the sector."[37] Schaeffer was greeted with the unanimous cry: "*Nous ne monterons pas aux tranchées!* [We will not advance into the trenches!]"

At this point, both soldiers and officers raised the stakes for potential confrontation. The demonstrators returned to their billets, only to reemerge shortly thereafter with their rifles. They could scarcely have indicated more strongly the seriousness of their intentions without crossing the line into violence. Their immediate intention, Brenot believed, was to spread the movement among the other two battalions. "All the officers," according to Brenot, attempted to stop the mutiny from spreading. A number of officers, courageously under the circumstances, stood in the road to bar the route to the demonstrators, who for their part declared that they wished these officers no harm. Some of the demonstrators stopped, though they moved forward again as soon as the officers got out of the way. Neither side was willing to push the situation to the point of violent confrontation.

At this point, the commanders of the 74ᵉ RI adopted a "divide and conquer" strategy. The authority structure attempted to diffuse collective disobedience by individualizing it. A number of soldiers were ordered by name to return to their billets. Some obeyed, and some others who did not had their names taken down. When this did not halt the march toward the other two battalions, Brenot himself ordered the cortege to stop. The collective refusal of this direct order enabled him to estimate the number of rebels at 230, an attrition of about 70 of the original 300. In a less than

[35] "Rapport du Lt. Colonel Brenot Comt. le 74ᵉ RI sur les actes d'insubordination ayant eu lieu dans la journée du 6 juin 1917," G.Q.G., 2ᵉ Bureau, Section Spécial Morale, 16 N 1521. Perhaps less than truthfully, Brenot attributed the activity in his regiment in part to "the unawareness of the sanctions taken against" the 36ᵉ RI and 129ᵉ RI.

[36] A group of soldiers was nevertheless tried later for revolt resulting from this incident.

[37] Brenot report.

successful attempt to prevent the "infection" of collective indiscipline from spreading to the other two battalions, Brenot sent one cavalry sergeant and four mounted scouts to guard the column comprising the two battalions. Of course, such a force could have only symbolic significance among hundreds of armed infantry.

It must be stressed here that any numbers appearing in the documentary record must be treated with caution. The mutinies in the 5e DI involved thousands of individual decisions made and remade over a period of about ten days. Any number, no matter how precise, can represent no more than a snapshot of the inclinations of a given group at a given time.[38] Although the memoir record of the mutinies in the 5e DI is slender indeed, one can easily demonstrate that soldiers who claimed no sympathy whatsoever with the demonstrations in fact had more confused loyalties than they wished to let on. Charles Toussaint, a bicycle messenger from the 74e RI, blamed the mutinies on "crybabies" newly arrived with the regiment.[39] Nevertheless, he found himself interceding with the colonel on leave policy after he met a cortege of actual demonstrators. Private Legentil, a machine-gunner also of the 74e RI, referred to the mutinies as an "evil virus," but confessed that he was unsure that he could have fired on his comrades if asked.[40]

Two points bear keeping in mind here. First, however many they were, the demonstrators were too numerous for everyone to be punished—and both soldiers and commanders knew it. Second, the "good" soldierly majority was also a silent one that did little or nothing to stop the more effervescent minority. For many soldiers as well as officers, one of the most important forms of action was inaction.

On the evening of 6 June, an incident occurred in the 274e RI.[41] One of the battalions, the 5e, took up its positions in the front lines without incident. But in the other battalion, the 6e Bataillon, 193 men categorically refused to advance to the front lines. Similarities in the form of the protest and the demands made by the soldiers convinced regimental commander Lieutenant Colonel Houssais that the movement had to have been organized from the home front. Again, the protesters "declared that they had no animosity toward the officers, who shared their dangers." Their frankly stated desire was to "attract the attention of the public powers." No force was applied by the command structure, and the demonstrations dissipated

---

[38] To give one example of the difficulty, on 2 June, Colonel Jèze of the 36e RI reported that of the 2,373 men under his command, 1,926 had a "moral value [*valeur morale*]" rated as "good"; 285 as "doubtful"; and 162 as "bad." Jèze did not explain these categories further, however, nor how he placed men in them. "Résultats de l'enquête faite au 36e sur la valeur morale des hommes," G.Q.G., Service Spécial Morale, 16 N 1521.

[39] Charles Toussaint, *Petites Histoires d'un glorieux régiment: vécues par Charles Toussaint, soldat de 1e classe au 74e Régiment d'Infanterie en guerre* (Montvilliers [Seine-Maritime]: Binesse, 1973), pp. 153–54.

[40] "Notes de Campagne du 12 avril 1915 au 11 novembre 1918: au jour le jour, bons et mauvais souvenirs," S.H.A. Fonds privés, 1 KT 86, p. 20.

on their own. At the moment Houssais was writing the last page of his report on 7 June, twenty of the protesters had already returned to their duties; by the time he had written the last paragraph, all had done so.

The last incident of collective disobedience in June 1917 for which documentation survives took place in the 3e Bataillon of the 74e RI on the afternoon of 7 June.[42] The pattern of the mutiny closely resembled that of the 2e Bataillon on 6 June. The battalion commander and a group of officers returned from their reconnaissance of the front lines to discover that some four-fifths of the men in the battalion were departing south (that is, away from the trenches) bearing their rifles and tents. The officers and NCOs, according to de Roig, made every effort to halt the column of marchers.[43] Officers again tried standing in the road, and were physically removed by the demonstrators, "however without violence." Little else is known of the incident, since de Roig's hastily written and fragmentary document is the only surviving report. At some point in their trip south, the demonstrators were stopped by colonial troops, though evidently without the use of force.[44] The 1e Bataillon took up its positions in the trenches during the night of 7–8 June, though the military justice records indicate that some soldiers from this officially untouched battalion were involved in the events. The other two battalions took up their positions within the next twenty-four hours, and by 9–10 June the 74e RI found its interest in continuing the war sufficiently revived for it to be holding a sector of the line subjected to intermittent but severe enemy artillery bombardment.[45] The judicial repression of the mutinies got underway just as soldiers' consent to the war was beginning to appear restored.

OUT OF THE CARCERAL TRENCHES:
THE DEMANDS FROM BELOW

When the time came to advance to the front lines, an incident happened in the army corps in which we demanded our rights in the following things:

[41] "Rapport du Lieut.-Colonel Houssais commandant le 274e Rég. d'Infie. sur les incidents survenus au régiment," G.Q.G., 2e Bureau, Service Spécial Morale, 16 N 1521.

[42] Untitled report by General de Roig, 7 June 1917, in ibid.

[43] Some ambiguity in the facts exists here, since de Roig estimated the column at 250 men, which conflicted with his earlier estimate that four-fifths of the men in the battalion were taking part in the demonstration. It could have been that the commanders were partly successful.

[44] Regimental and divisional reports conspicuously failed to mention colonial troops at this point, though Legentil reported that the demonstrators were halted by Moroccan sharpshooters and spahis. Legentil, "Notes de campagne," p. 22. Mention was also made in one court-martial case of a soldier's reluctance to surrender his rifle to Moroccan cavalry. Dossier 552, J 439.

[45] See 74e RI JMO, 9–10 June 1917, 26 N 660.

1. Peace and the right to leaves, which are in arrears.
2. No more butchery; we want liberty.
3. On food, which is shameful.
4. No more injustice.
5. We don't want the blacks in Paris and in other regions mistreating our wives.
6. We need peace to feed our wives and children and to be able to give bread to the women and orphans.

We demand peace, peace.

—Soldier of the 36ᵉ RI to his uncle, June 1917[46]

This representative example shows the striking diversity of soldiers' demands during the mutinies. Demands that would probably have required the overthrow of the Third Republic, such as that for an immediate peace, took their place alongside others that in comparison seem trivial, such as better food and more leaves. The circumstances of the mutinies do much to explain this diversity. When soldiers refused point-blank to enter the front lines and instead held antiwar demonstrations, and their commanders decided that for the time being they could not or would not stop them, a unique situation emerged. When the formal structures of command authority proved suddenly inoperative, the distinction between the "public" and "hidden" transcripts vanished. Soldiers had an unprecedented chance to consider all of their demands, publicly and simultaneously.

The most important source for examining soldiers' demands is the postal censorship records, which proliferated during the mutinies. These records offer a useful way to finesse the partly artificial problem of determining the numbers of "participants" in the mutinies. If an entire regiment could not take up positions in the trenches because, say, 10 percent of its men were demonstrating, the remaining 90 percent had the same opportunity as the demonstrators to air their grievances to each other and, through letters, to civilians behind the lines. The reports rarely made any distinction between soldiers who participated in the demonstrations and those who did not. They suggest essentially the same concerns among the "mutineers" and the waiting, and otherwise silent, majority. Making sense out of the 1917 mutinies involves methodological problems analogous to those involved in making sense out of a battle—not a surprising observation if one considers the mutinies as an implicit struggle between soldiers and commanders suddenly rendered explicit. A mutiny, like a battle, exists at first only in fragments over which the historian must impose some conceptual order. I offer here a line of analysis documented through the

---

[46] IIIᵉ Armée, 2ᵉ Bureau, Service de Renseignement, Rapport No. 334/A, 3 June 1917, in Guy Pedroncini, ed., *1917: les Mutineries de l'armée française*, Collection "Archives," no. 35 (Paris: Juillard, 1968), p. 122.

words of particular individuals that makes the outcome of the mutinies more comprehensible.

By the time the first incident broke out in the 5ᵉ DI on 28 May, the division had been out of the front lines for over three months. During that time, soldiers had been encouraged to believe that they would never have to enter the trenches again, since they were being trained in mobile warfare in preparation for their planned role in the spring offensive. When contrary to these expectations they were summoned back to the trenches, they fought against a return to the logic of *tenir* along the Chemin des Dames. A critical part of this process involved asserting their peacetime identities as human beings, as fathers and sons, and as citizens. Their demands covered the "political" spectrum, from the international to the personal.

As illustrated in the quote beginning this section, soldiers demanded first and foremost immediate peace. Despite command insistence on the importance of external subversion, it must be stressed that no evidence exists of an actual link between the events in the 5ᵉ DI and any civilian pacifist movement. Rather, I would suggest, demanding peace enabled soldiers to reach out to civilian compatriots behind the lines. In doing so, soldiers envisaged an alliance of citizen-soldiers and citizens that would end the war, an alliance that proved unworkable once their different agendas became clearer.

"The government does not yet want peace," wrote a soldier from the 129ᵉ RI on 3 June, "very well, but let's not forget that there are in France other voices that have a say in the matter."[47] Soldiers especially identified with the *midinettes*, women textile workers striking in Paris and other large cities.[48] A machine-gunner from the 74ᵉ RI remarked cautiously, "I am ready to go into the trenches, but we are doing like the *midinettes*. We have gone out on strike, everyone has really had enough."[49] A corporal from the same company added, "I see that in Paris things have come to a standstill. This makes me happy, because it is already a beginning! If only all this can shorten the war!"[50]

But despite this apparent affinity across male and female spheres, the gender politics of the mutinies provided one significant source of internal constraint. Even as they claimed to identify with their striking *com-*

---

[47] "5ᵉ Rapport sur le Sondage spécial effectué le 4 juin 1917 pour le 129ᵉ Régiment d'Infanterie, Secteur Postal 62," IIᵉ Armée, 1ᵉ Bureau, 19 N 305.

[48] On women's strikes in the spring of 1917, see Jean-Jacques Becker, *Les Français pendant la grande guerre*, (Paris: Éditions Robert Laffont, 1980), pp. 192–219.

[49] "Compte-Rendu, Objet: Contrôle postal," 5 June 1917, in G.Q.G., 2ᵉ Bureau, Service de Renseignements des Armées, 16 N 1522. All SRA reports will subsequently be identified only by title, date, and carton. Other reports will be identified by full references.

[50] Ibid. In his summary of the report, dated the day before demonstrations in the 74ᵉ RI recommenced, General de Roig noted an overall "great amelioration in the state of morale of the civilians as well as the military personnel."

patriotes in Paris, soldiers sought to reassert traditional male roles as protectors and providers for their families. Soldiers reclaimed patriarchal roles in their demands to the patriarchal Third Republic, which had so stubbornly denied women the vote and other basic civil rights. This Republic, in the guise of its generals and politicians, proved able to hear them.

Soldiers found most threatening apparently untrue rumors that the government had called in colonial troops to break up women's strikes.[51] A soldier from the 74e RI saw both strike breaking by colonials and continuing the war as an attack on the family: "When will the war be over? If it lasts much longer, there won't be any French left, and it will be the foreigners who come in to be the police in France and to mistreat the women and the children, according to our information."[52] Using foreigners to suppress strikes, soldiers believed, not only trampled on their "private" rights as fathers and protectors, but on their "public" rights as French citizens. A soldier from the 129e RI saw little to choose between colonials outside the body politic of the French Republic firing on civilians and the Germans shooting at him. Both could be stopped only by citizens reclaiming their right to influence the political process:

> We demonstrated because we knew that Paris was on strike and that to stop this they [the government] had machine guns installed and the agents had then uncovered them, knowing that we refused to go into line and get ourselves killed while foreigners were killing civilians in Paris. We were asking the minister of war to make the necessary overtures as promptly as possible for peace because there are enough dead as it is.[53]

Soldiers often immediately juxtaposed a demand for peace to reforms in leave policy, again as shown in the quote beginning this section. At first this seems bizarre, since immediate peace would presumably have made any leave policy irrelevant. The two demands become more compatible, however, if they are both seen as attempts to reestablish links with the interior, links institutionalized in soldiers' leaves. Although they were occasions inevitably charged with joy, pain, and acute apprehension, leaves constituted soldiers' main connection to life beyond the war.[54] Consequently, the "political" significance to soldiers of this link can scarcely be overestimated. Considering demands for an immediate peace and demands for an

---

[51] Laura Downs found no evidence that colonial troops had actually been used. "Women in Industry, 1914–1939: The Employers' Perspective, A Comparative Study of French and British Metals Industry, 1914–1939" (Ph.D. diss., Columbia University, 1987).

[52] "Analyse de la Correspondance Militaire" (74e RI), 12 June 1917, 16 N 1418.

[53] "129e RI, Secteur Postal 63," 3 June 1917, 19 N 305. As much as possible, I have tried to preserve the syntax of the original prose in my translations.

[54] The psychology of leaves as represented in trench newspapers is examined in Stéphane Audoin-Rouzeau, *À travers leurs Journaux: les combattants des tranchées* (Paris: Armand Colin, 1986), chap. 5.

improved leave policy as two sides of the same coin offers insight into how soldiers eventually were able to rank order their demands. Once links to the home front were guaranteed by leave reform, soldiers could give up their demand for immediate peace.

Leave policy before the mutinies was not so much harsh as unpredictable.[55] The percentage of men allowed leave at any given time varied widely according to the military situation, as perceived by unit commanders. According to the French army official history, figures could vary from 10–20 percent within the same division. All leaves had been canceled, of course, at the beginning of April for units taking part in the spring offensive. In the uncertain military situation that followed, leaves were restored only gradually and erratically, and of course a substantial backlog had developed. In the 5e DI as of 22 May, the percentage of NCOs and common soldiers on leave was 14.2 percent (well within limits proscribed by Pétain) and no significant variations existed among regiments.[56] Just before 28 May, de Roig reduced this figure to 5 percent, with the division about to enter the front lines. This reduction and the backlog proved the immediate bones of contention, as well as the explicit acknowledgment of leaves as a right rather than a privilege.

A fascinating, rambling letter from a soldier of the 36e RI to his wife showed how dissatisfactions with leaves came to symbolize a whole variety of grievances with both the military and the home fronts:

> They delight us with one leave per year, while they are supposed to give them every four months, and here we are five months have gone by, and since we have been out of the lines for a long time, it is because of the meanness of the commanders; but the officers go on leave every four months, and then they forget all about us, whether we get to go or not. We can't allow it.
>
> Its like how long the war has lasted. The capitalists who aren't at the front and whose money earns three times as much as before the war, the ones who keep it going to annihilate the worker.
>
> A soldier on leave told me that things in Paris are heating up and that today there is supposed to be a general strike there, so much the better as long as nobody gets killed and it can bring this Hell to an end, which for three years has tormented us physically and morally, because we all know very well that to send the Boches back where they came from there is nothing to be done—kill people in chaos and that's all.[57]

Slipping effortlessly from complaints about leave policy to the inequities of capitalism, this letter shows how quickly soldiers' demands could escalate

[55] See AFGG, tome 5, vol. 2, pp. 200–202.

[56] Untitled report, 22 May 1917, 5e DI, 1e Bureau, 24 N 76. Pétain's reforms are outlined in G.Q.G., "Instruction, 1080," 2 June 1917, quoted in AFGG, tome 5, vol. 2, p. 201.

[57] Rapport No. 334/A, quoted in Pedroncini, ed., *1917: Les Mutineries*, p. 123.

and even become "political" in the conventional sense. Leave, a precious form of property to the wartime soldier, had in this soldier's mind accumulated in the hands of the strong at the expense of the weak.[58] Workers striking in Paris and soldiers striking at the front were fighting the same struggle to redress the balance, which both for a time thought must necessarily lead to peace.

Soldiers' asserting themselves as citizens brings an expanded use of the term "political" close to the conventional one. Theoretically, conventional military discipline prohibited even citizen-soldiers from making significant judgments about the execution and outcome of the war. In fact, the collapse of this discipline during the mutinies meant that soldiers could make such judgments pretty much as they chose. Colonel Boucher quoted (or more likely paraphrased) the sentiments of the mutineers of the 36ᵉ RI and the 129ᵉ RI on their meeting of 29 May:

> We want peace, . . . we have had enough of the war and we want the deputies to know it. . . . When we go into the trenches, we will plant a white flag on the parapet. The Germans will do the same, and we will not fight until the peace is signed. We want the deputies to know about our demonstration; it is the only means we have at our disposition to make them understand that we want peace.[59]

Most threatening to the military authorities, not to mention the civilian ones, was the notion of soldiers marching to Paris to bring their demands directly to the Chamber of Deputies—a scheme particularly associated with the mutinies in the 5ᵉ DI.[60]

Pedroncini's skepticism that such publicly displayed threats constituted serious plans is well founded, though dismissing them out of hand would distort their point. Soldiers demanded that the civil authorities be aware of

---

[58] The author's unfavorable reference to the officers is practically unique. His allegation was also incorrect. In the 22 May report cited previously, 14.2 percent of NCOs and common soldiers were on leave; for officers, the figure is 13.6 percent.

[59] Boucher, "Rapports d'ensemble." At least some Germans knew that the mutinies were taking place. Gen. Erich Ludendorff wrote in his memoirs: "We heard but little about them, and that by degrees. Only later did we learn the whole truth." *My War Memories: 1914–1918*, 2 vols. (London: Hutchinson & Company, 1919), p. 426. But the liberal newspaper *Landauer Anzeiger* on June 30 quoted a French soldier of the 119ᵉ RI who wrote: "Morale is very low and they aren't managing to raise it. The infantry regiments numbers 36 and 129 refused to go into the trenches and the 74th shortly after that. Comrades came over to where we were staying to invite us to disobey." G.Q.G., 2ᵉ Bureau, Service Spécial Morale, 16 N 1522.

[60] A general staff memo credited undercover police spies with alerting the authorities in time to prevent the march of the 36ᵉ and the 129ᵉ RI. "Note sur l'emploi des inspecteurs de police des armées & agents auxiliaires de police pendant les troubles militaires de mai-juin 1917," État-Major Général, Bureau des Services Spéciaux, 29 January 1918, Fonds Clemenceau, Dossiers Personnels, 1917–1919, 6 N 54.

THE MUTINIES OF 1917 **193**

their plight, and knew that they had the means at their disposal to make sure this happened. "Do not forget," wrote a soldier of the 274ᵉ RI to a member of the Chamber of Deputies, "that we hold in our hands the destiny of the country. If by this winter you [deputies] have not shown your willingness to negotiate [with the Germans], we will give way."⁶¹ The author went on specifically to reject Pétain's promise "to spare French blood" as insufficient. Instead, he demanded nothing less than a comprehensive reconciliation of the home and military fronts, on the soldiers' terms:

> A mountain separates us. You want a peace of the capitalists, of the same ones who saw the war coming and put their capital abroad because of the bogey man of business taxes. . . . We, the *poilus* of the front, who in our vast majority belong to the proletariat, we envisage a peace that will guarantee the liberty of the peoples. After three years of great massacre, we suppose that it is now possible to negotiate.

I would argue that the significance of soldiers making their demands to their deputies can scarcely be overestimated. In calling on their legally constituted representatives, they tacitly recognized the legitimacy of the Third Republic. By reclaiming the right to make demands on their government, soldiers expressed their power and made their choices *as citizens*. The question of the rights and responsibilities of French citizenship became the point at which the "hidden transcript" of gathering frustration and despair met the "public transcript" of the national need to endure. Even in their darkest hour, the soldiers' concept of the "nation" remained defined in terms of the French Republic, and the Republic in terms of popular sovereignty. In the 1917 mutinies, French soldiers directly confronted the paradox in military authority under a system of popular sovereignty—of being expected to obey a military command structure that drew its legitimacy from a citizenry that included the soldiers themselves. They accepted this paradox even as they asserted themselves as a source of legitimate authority when politics regained control over war in 1917.

Unlike their counterparts in Russia, the *poilus* of 1917 still considered themselves part of the national polity.⁶² France was still their country, and they reclaimed their rights to make demands on their government. However incompletely from a late twentieth-century vantage point, the French Revolution and the Third Republic had done their work. Socialism, I would suggest, provided a language of protest already in place, and use of it by mutinous soldiers did not necessarily indicate a foreordained longing

⁶¹ "Compte-Rendu" (5ᵉ DI), 20 June 1917, 16 N 1418.

⁶² On the political evolution of soldiers in the imperial Russian army, see Alan Wildman, *The End of the Russian Imperial Army*, 2 vols. (Princeton: Princeton University Press, 1980 and 1987).

for socialist revolution. In the end, soldiers chose to operate within the power relationship of the army of the Third Republic when little prevented them from doing otherwise. The consent of soldiers proved an important part of the power relationship.[63] As a soldier of the 36e RI put it: "We refused to march not to bring about a revolution, which would be inevitable if we continue the movement, rather to attract the attention of the government in making them understand that we are men, and not beasts to be led to the *abattoir* to be slaughtered, that we want what is due to us and that we demand peace."[64]

But if the mutinous *poilus* still felt themselves a part of the French nation and of France, it followed that they had to have an interest in whether France lost the war. Most fundamentally, soldiers had to reconsider what they wanted from the war, and what they were willing to sacrifice toward that end. The immediate questions the mutinies begged, of course, were what soldiers wanted to happen next, and just what would prove the consequences of an immediate peace. When a military police investigator named Chapuy asked soldiers from the 36e RI and the 129e RI what they wanted from a peace settlement, he reported an entirely self-contradictory response: "They demand Alsace, Lorraine, and the maintenance of the status quo (no indemnity, no annexations)."[65] Presumably, Alsace and Lorraine did not qualify as "annexations" because the soldiers considered them French. Unfortunately, Chapuy did not pursue how soldiers expected the Germans to surrender the lost provinces (not to mention most of northeastern France) without military victory. He did, however, pose the question of what would happen if the Germans took advantage of a movement such as theirs to launch an attack: They responded, remarkably, in the language of Verdun: "as long as they are there, *les Boches ne passeront pas* [the Boches shall not pass]."

---

[63] Foucault considered this sort of "consent" not really a matter of choice on the part of a totally free individual will, rather the result of internalized aspects of the self created through the historical construction of power relations. This phenomenon is explored in Graham Burchell, Colon Gordon, and Peter Miller, eds., *The Foucault Effect: Studies in Governmentality* (Chicago: University of Chicago Press, 1991).

To the end, Foucault declined to incorporate consent as usually understood into power relations. In his 1982 essay "The Subject and Power," he put consent in the same category as physical violence: "But even though consensus and violence are the instruments or the results, they do not constitute the principle or the basic nature of power." Herbert L. Dreyfus and Paul Rabinow, eds., *Michel Foucault: Beyond Structuralism and Hermeneutics*, 2d ed. (Chicago: University of Chicago Press, 1983), p. 220. In a May 1984 interview, the month before his death, Foucault doubted the existence of even a preexisting intellectual or academic consensual community. See "Power, Polemics, and Problematizations," in Paul Rabinow, ed., *The Foucault Reader* (New York: Pantheon Books, 1984), p. 385.

[64] "Rapport No. 334/A," quoted in Pedroncini, ed., *1917: Les Mutineries*, pp. 129–30.

[65] "Le Commissaire de Police Mobile Chapuy à monsieur le commissaire spécial chef du Service de Sûreté de l'Armée," 31 May 1917, in G.Q.G., 2e Bureau, Service Spécial-Morale, 16 N 1521.

Two letters cited earlier also reflect soldiers' reluctance to opt for peace at any price. The soldier from the 274e RI who warned a deputy not to forget "that we hold [in our hands] the destiny of the country" wrote: "What does the French army ask for? (1) To remain on the defensive. (2) To ask the Boches their intentions. If the Boches do not want to accept a peace corresponding to the sacrifices that we have made and satisfactory to our honor, we will push them out ourselves." The soldier from the 36e RI who demanded that the deputies know "that we are men and not beasts" continued that at a certain point they could no longer continue their refusal to march, because "we will be obliged to sign shameful treaties, which will bring us ruin and misery, of which we have already seen too much in France."

The *vox populi* of the mutineers and those who shared their sentiments did not reveal the secret to military victory that had eluded Joffre, Nivelle, and Mangin—and for that matter Pétain and Foch until the last months of the war. Nor did it reveal the diplomatic solution that eluded the would-be socialist peace makers at the Stockholm conference planned for May 1917. French Socialists proved no more willing to give up Alsace and Lorraine than their German counterparts.[66] The only option for immediate peace without victory—the general European revolution advocated by V. I. Lenin—found no large constituency in France, either at the front or in the interior. In the end, neither workers nor soldiers proved much interested in the requirements of a classic Marxist historical narrative. For their part, striking workers proved easily enough mollified by wage increases. It is likewise problematic to fault soldiers for not having an adequate "consciousness."

At some point over the course of the mutinies, a moment of decision arrived for every soldier in the French army. Soldiers' self-perception as citizens in the end had opened the door to tacit negotiations with Pétain. Contrary to the Pedroncini thesis, Pétain's offer of repression, reforms, and proportionality was not necessarily what soldiers had wanted all along, but proved what he and French soldiers could persuade each other to accept. Pétain's success in presiding over a resolution of the mutinies, I would suggest, lies in his willingness to accept a changed balance of power not just between infantry and artillery, but between soldiers and commanders.

THE RESPONSE OF THE OFFICERS: THE CASE OF THE 129e RI

Of course, the *poilus* of the 5e DI did not work out the issues of the mutinies in a vacuum. The formal authority structure of the French army remained

---

[66] The Stockholm conference in any event proved stillborn, in part because Pétain sabotaged French Socialists' chances of getting passports.

in place, and attempted constantly to regain control over events. This structure reached the discontented soldiers through the officers. Much has been made throughout this study of the dual role of the officers of the 5e DI as both soldiers and commanders—those who exercised command authority but who to one degree or another shared the physical hardships and perils of the soldiers they commanded. The officers of the 5e DI had been key figures in determining proportionality ever since the beginning of the war, as the first links in the chain of command to acknowledge and legitimate the cessation of attacks when further effort seemed useless.

The evidence strongly indicates that at the moment of decision during the mutinies, the officers made their choices as commanders. No good evidence exists that any officers in the division ever openly sided with the protest movement.[67] Indeed, as will be shown below, they pursued effectively the ugly task of identifying "leaders" within their own units. But substantial indications also exist of empathy with the demonstrators that went beyond simple tactical caution. The officers played a critical role mediating between the restive soldiers and the command structure. To them fell the task of negotiating with the soldiers explicitly, even as Pétain negotiated with them implicitly. The response of the officers says much about how the mutinies in the division were resolved without violence. In response, the senior command proved thankless and even hypocritical— all the way up to Pétain. Tensions between soldiers of varying ranks and their commanders persisted to the end of the war.

The sources permit a much more thorough examination of what officers did than of what they thought. The memoir record practically evaporated, and officers were almost never mentioned in the postal censorship records.[68] But an extensive collection of documents survives recounting the response of the officers from the 129e RI. The first mutiny in the division took place in this regiment, which thus became the perceived leader (*meneur*) of the disorders, the gangrened limb that infected the body of the

[67] A captain from the 74e RI accused a captain from the 129e RI of muttering on the train back from their leave: "The men have had enough of the war, and us as well." Nothing appears to have come of the allegation. "Le Général Lebrun, commandant le 3eme Corps d'Armée au général commandant la VIe Armée." G.Q.G., 2e Bureau, Service Spécial Moral, 16 N 1521.

Evidently some loose talk was also bandied about the 3e Bataillon of the 129e RI about electing new regimental and battalion officers. A captain in question remarked of the project: "I took the thing as a joke, as I should have done." Untitled statement before the IIe Armée *conseil de guerre*, 9 July 1917, in ibid., 16 N 1522.

[68] Legentil's brief comments have already been noted, and Hallé's account ends without explanation in February 1917. Paul Rimbault's account becomes extremely brief and elliptical, and also ends without explanation shortly after the 74e RI entered the Chemin des Dames sector after the mutinies. He showed himself a true believer in outside subversion, attributing the mutinies, to the "*cafard*, carefully nourished by traitorous Frenchmen from the interior and by Boche spies." *Propos d'un marmité* (Paris: L. Fournier, 1920), p. 92.

THE MUTINIES OF 1917 197

division. The documentation includes running commentary on the conduct of the officers of the 129ᵉ RI and depositions by officers themselves.

From the first, officers in the 129ᵉ RI, as well as their superiors in the division command, chose negotiation and persuasion over attempted coercion. Major Auberge learned of the first demonstrations in the 1ᵉ Bataillon on the evening of 28 May, evidently with some surprise.[69] He and his officers personally met the demonstrators, who were marching "in the greatest order," in a column four abreast.[70] The intervention of the officers, according to Auberge's statement as reported by Colonel Boucher, "consisted of stopping the column, which obeyed without difficulty, and of trying to bring the men together again by groups and to make them understand reason."[71] The men shortly thereafter returned to their billets without further trouble and even "very correctly saluted the major and the officers present."[72]

Auberge shortly informed regimental commander Lieutenant Colonel Genet, division infantry commander Colonel Martenet, and division commander de Roig of the unrest in his unit. The three then went to discuss the situation with General Lebrun, the 3ᵉ CA commander. The meeting lasted until after 0500 on 29 May.[73] These officers collectively reaffirmed the decision to respond gently to the demonstrations, an attitude they maintained throughout that day. Genet concluded in a report of 29 May that "it is difficult at the moment to identify the leaders and to arrest them; only when calm returns will we know through reliable men who the leaders are and what measures we can take against them."[74] In an annex attached to Genet's report, Martenet agreed: "No rigorous measures must be taken. We must do our best to dilute the movement by persuasion, by calm, and by the authority of the *officers known by the men*, and acting above all on the good ones to bring the strikers toward the best sentiments." General de Roig concurred in the same annex that "we cannot think of reducing the movement by rigor, which would certainly bring the irreparable."[75]

The reasons given by these three officers for a restrained approach turns

[69] Technically, since the reports cited hereafter are found in the Série N archives and not in Série J (military justice), names may legally be used. However, I will follow here Pedroncini's practice of citing names only when they have already been published elsewhere. Any pseudonym will be identified as such.

[70] "Le Général de Roig-Bourdeville, commandant la 5ᵉ Division d'Infanterie à M. le général commandant le 3ᵉ CA," 29 May 1917, in IIᵉ Armée, 1ᵉ Bureau, 19 N 305. Hereafter cited as De Roig report, 29 May.

[71] "2ᵉ Rapport du Colonel Boucher à monsieur le général commandant la 2ᵉ Armée sur l'enquête en cours au 129ᵉ RI," 2 June 1917, in ibid.

[72] De Roig report, 29 May.

[73] "2ᵉ Rapport du Colonel Boucher."

[74] "Rapport du Lt.-Colonel Genet, commandant le 129ᵉ Régiment d'Infanterie sur les incidents des 28 et 29 Mai 1917," 29 May 1917, in ibid.

[75] De Roig report, 29 May. Emphasis in original.

the notion of "apolitical" mutinies on its head. All three considered the movement a *political* demonstration rather than a conventionally conceived mutiny. A "mutiny" would have implied a considerably less deferential attitude toward officers such as themselves. Accordingly, they considered the movement actually *less* dangerous than if it had been strictly military. At least for the time being, they were willing to treat the mutineers simply as fellow Frenchmen. Indeed, the demonstrators actually asked their commander's help in pressing their demands on the civilian authorities. Genet paraphrased the demonstrators: "We want the government to know all this and, *mon colonel*, if you would be so good as to put it all in your report; this is for us the most sure means of knowing that the government will learn of it." Martenet expressed open relief at the "political" character of the demonstrations, if with a surprising choice of words: "It is a veritable revolutionary movement, and not a military one. I spoke at length with the men who knew me when I was the colonel commanding the 129e RI; several swore to me that they would not let the Boches pass, that despite their slogans, they will go into the trenches."

De Roig concurred that the movement was "uniquely political," and rank-ordered its causes:

The length of the war, which has created lassitude at the front.

Increasing cost of living, which has engendered poverty back at home.

The use of a foreign workforce, which has made many fear that they will not get their jobs back when peace comes.

Only then did de Roig mention soldiers' reading newspaper accounts of the Russian Revolution and the strikes in Paris, as well as pacifist propaganda. Subversion had clearly played its role, and from the first he believed that "this movement is organized." He argued that the 129e RI also had to be removed from the Chemin des Dames sector and kept from the Paris region. But he stressed the demonstrators' continuing respect for the military institutional framework as the command structure's most valuable asset. His warning that excessive rigor could bring about the "irreparable" expressed his concern that the demonstrations might spill over from the political realm into the military. Protesting citizen-soldiers could easily enough become an armed mob.

The eventual significance of this early command choice of restraint can scarcely be overstated. Command restraint meant that discontented soldiers could sort out and prioritize their demands with the authority structure temporarily in abeyance. But in the short run, restraint probably did encourage the spread of the demonstrations. After the fact, the newly assertive high command would construe this as great error.

The 2e and 3e Bataillon commanders on 29 May showed no reluctance carrying out their orders not to push the men too far. Both were also eager to place as much blame as possible on "leaders" from the 1e Bataillon. 2e Bataillon commander Maguin reported that only eleven men were led astray during the first attempt at proselytization, and that these returned to their billets upon his personal intervention.[76] With the second attempt, however, some 195 men from his battalion "escaped our surveillance," as the impulse toward solidarity among demonstrators overcame the personal links between those soldiers and their officers. Maguin concluded: "My officers and I did everything we judged possible, while remaining within the note of instructions we had received from the command encouraging us to act with gentleness [*douceur*] and to avoid extreme measures." Once again, the demonstrators reciprocated this respect, as a colonel investigating the events in the 2e Bataillon observed: "There was unanimity on the part of the men in affirming their respect and their affection for their officers and their NCOs, and declaring that the only objective of their demonstration was to attract the attention of the government."[77]

In the 3e Bataillon, according to another outside investigator, Major Pourel received notification by telephone of the impending arrival of instigators from the 1e Bataillon.[78] Pourel immediately brought together all his officers and ordered them and their NCOs to stick close to their companies. Pourel and his adjutant personally met the column of demonstrators in an attempt to dissuade it from "contaminating" his unit. Although the demonstrators simply walked around the two officers and proceeded to encourage soldiers from the battalion to demonstrate, "the personal action of the officers kept everyone in the line of duty." At about 1130, regimental commander Genet and division infantry commander Martenet reiterated their instructions "to avoid any collision." Not long thereafter, the officers of the 3e Bataillon retired to have lunch, believing the situation stabilized. During their absence, demonstrators from the 1e Bataillon reappeared and departed with some one hundred men from the 3e Bataillon.

Perhaps the best indication of the degree to which officers of the 129e RI sympathized with the demonstrators appears in the explanations they gave to Colonel Boucher of the causes of the mutinies. Statements survive from all three battalion commanders, all three machine-gun company commanders, and eight of the twelve infantry company commanders. Of these, *not one* mentioned instigators outside the army or subversion from pacifists in the interior.

Officers described these causes compassionately and often poignantly, in

[76] "4e Rapport du Colonel Boucher à monsieur le général commandant la 2e Armée sur l'enquête en cours au 129e Régiment d'Infie.," 3 June 1917, in ibid.
[77] "Le Colonel Balagny, commandant le Groupement Central à Monsieur le Général Putz, commandant le 4e Corps d'Armée," 6 June 1917, in ibid.
[78] "Rapport du Colonel Chabord, Ct. l'I.D. 16 rélatif à l'enquête qui a été faite sur les faits réprochés au 3e Btn. du 129e RI," 7 June 1917, in ibid.

language strikingly similar to that of the discontented soldiers themselves. 2e Bataillon commander Maguin recalled the seven months the regiment spent in the Eparges sector as "very painful."[79] But as the April offensive approached, spirits lifted, and "the men had the enthusiasm of the beginning [of the war]." But when the promised *percée* failed to materialize, "their sense of disappointment was great; they understood that their hopes had melted, vanished, and there resulted an accentuated decline in their morale." 3e Bataillon commander Pourel affirmed that "the defeat of the April 16 attack and the obligation to return to the rear at the very moment when they were hoping to deliver a decisive pursuit was for them the cause of a great disappointment."[80] Some officers were also struck by the precipitous departure of the 129e RI for the front lines on 27 May, just when a number of soldiers were counting on spending the Pentecost holiday with their families. When they had to separate prematurely, noted Maguin, "this was also a disappointment in the minds of some of them." The 5e Compagnie commander added that the men believed the suddenness of the departure could only have meant "that we were being brought into position to attack."[81] He concluded that "if we are called on to hold a sector, I have good confidence that the men will follow me."[82] It is not difficult to discern here a subtle warning about the perils of ordering a more aggressive course of action.

Officers indeed attempted to persuade soldiers to return to their duties throughout 29 May. According to Colonel Boucher, the regimental, division infantry, and even corps commanders actually spoke at the meetings of the demonstrators. Not surprisingly, given the dim view of such things taken by the senior command after the fact, the 5e DI reports did not mention them. A letter from a soldier from the 129e RI mentioned an apparently chance meeting on 29 May between the cortege of demonstrators and 3e CA commander Lebrun. The soldier wrote:

Along the way, we encountered the general commanding the army corps, who was passing by in his car and in seeing this whole crowd descending made a morale-boosting speech to us in which he asked us what we wanted. We responded that we had had enough of the war and that there had been enough victims. He tried in vain to get us to return. He got back into his car with tears

[79] "4e Rapport du Colonel Boucher."
[80] "2e Rapport du Colonel Boucher." Disturbances reportedly were minimal in Desaubliaux's former company, the 3e Compagnie des Mitrailleuses, thanks to Pourel's success in seeing off "instigators" from the 149e RI.
[81] Ibid.
[82] Most company commanders, many of them lieutenants and second-lieutenants, were rather more circumspect in their statements. Officers had refused earlier to talk at all to police investigator Chapuy.

in his eyes. This is the first time I have seen a general go out among the *poilus* without obtaining any success.[83]

During the night of 29 May, 129ᵉ RI commander Genet received an alarming report from division infantry commander Martenet.[84] According to the report, whose source was two NCOs from the 36ᵉ RI, a detailed plot had been hatched within the 129ᵉ RI to march on Paris. At 0900 on 30 May, the soldiers of the 129ᵉ RI were to assemble with their rifles, and to proceed from there to the billets of the 36ᵉ RI, where they were to "compel, if necessary by force, the men of this regiment to follow them."[85] They would secure transport by trucks and cars, and the men were to find food along the route. To emphasize the seriousness of the plans, the alleged plotters forbade soldiers to carry wine in their canteens. Martenet ordered Genet to assemble the companies, inform them that the command structure had become apprised of their plans, and "show them the enormity of the crime they were ready to commit in running the risk of shedding French blood." Genet was ordered to "make the most desperate efforts, without violence, up to the last minute, to hold them back."

The moment of decision arrived at about 0300 on 30 May, when the 129ᵉ RI received an order to assemble for transport by truck further behind the lines. This proved a shrewd move on the part of the command structure, as the order actually granted the demonstrators' demands that they not go into the front lines. But soldiers getting into the trucks had many implications of its own. The soldiers of the 129ᵉ RI had good reason to believe that they would be headed toward some form of repression, which seemed all the more likely given the presence of cavalry near the transit point.[86] In short, getting into the trucks meant ending the mutinies, and, at least for the time being, unconditionally accepting command authority.

Not surprisingly, the soldiers of the 129ᵉ RI demonstrated a certain reluctance to leave their billets. A soldier from the 5ᵉ Compagnie wrote that the officers assured them that they were going to the rear to rest and had given their "word of honor that there would be no consequences." According to a soldier from the 2ᵉ Compagnie, Genet had given his word of

---

[83] "5ᵉ Rapport sur le Sondage," 5 June 1917.

[84] "Rapport complementaire sur les incidents qui se sont déroulés les 28 et 29 Mai au 129ᵉ Régt d'Infie," 3 June 1917, in IIᵉ Armée, 1ᵉ Bureau, 19 N 305.

[85] This report was not necessarily accurate. The colonel investigating events in the 3ᵉ Bataillon reported that the demonstrators returned to their billets on the evening of 29 May "without having a very clear idea of what was supposed to be done the next day." "Rapport du Colonel Chabord."

[86] The role of the cavalry in concluding the mutinies in the 129ᵉ RI remains something of a mystery. It is difficult to imagine that the numbers of cavalrymen in place would have been sufficient had the infantry been determined to resist.

honor that the backlog of leaves would be eliminated.[87] Although officers were not really in a position to guarantee such promises (and the soldiers perhaps knew it), the promise of increased leaves at least was clearly made in good faith.[88] Officers could still speak with credibility to their men.

The captain commanding the 1e Compagnie described the drama of the departure in his company:

> During the night of the 29th–30th, the order arrived to prepare for the embarkation by truck. We sounded the reveille at 4h. Getting the men up was painful. For the first time, I made my men face reality. I said to them that there was still time for them to regain control of themselves, and if they did not obey, they would cause the shedding of French blood. My efforts and those of my officers were finally crowned with success. My men decided to take up their packs and get into the trucks.[89]

When the moment to decide came, I would argue, the soldiers of the 129e RI agreed to get into the trucks to go they knew not where because they felt they could trust their officers. According to one report the men were persuaded to get into the trucks only when the officers threatened to leave without them.[90] This trust, furthermore, was based in officers' sharing their privations and perils—and not least, in soldiers' role in shaping the parameters of command authority. In the end, comradeship made deference possible.

A report by Colonel Martenet described a dramatic ceremonial end to the mutinies in the 129e RI, when the three battalions were loaded into separate trains going in different directions.[91] He had cavalry and gendarmes posted near the station, though they were ordered to remain as discreetly placed as possible. Standing at the station, Martenet noted their arrival "in perfect order. . .I have never seen men march and turn their heads to the left [facing himself] more correctly." He was struck by "the way they rendered the honors with dignity and by the way the men saluted

[87] Both from "5e Rapport sur le sondage" (129e RI), 5 June 1917.

[88] On 30 May, Genet received orders from acting IIIe Armée commander General de Maud'huy to increase the percentage of leaves in the 36e RI and 129e RI to 25 percent. This order was countermanded in the 129e RI on 1 June when the regiment came under the orders of IIe Armée commander General Guillaumat. See Genet, "Rapport complementaire," 3 June 1917.

[89] "3e Rapport du Colonel Boucher à monsieur le général commandant la 2e Armée sur l'enquête en cours au 129e R.I.," IIe Armée, 1e Bureau, 19 N 305. The captain quoted was the same one who had been accused by his unfraternal brother officer of muttering that the officers had had enough of the war. See n. 67.

[90] "Rapport du Général de Maud'huy sur les incidents survenus aux 36e et 129e RI" (2130) 30 May 1917, in Pedroncini, ed., 1917: Les Mutineries, p. 135.

[91] "Rapport du Colonel Martenet, Cdt. l'I.D.5 sur les conditions de l'embarquement du 129e Régt. d'Infie.," 31 May 1917, in IIIe Armée, 3e Bureau, 19 N 551.

me from the cars as I watched the trains leave." He expressed full confidence in the officers of the 129ᵉ RI, though he added that "all of the officers are absolutely heartbroken. . . . Many had trouble hiding their tears when the time came to bid farewell." The mutinies in the 129ᵉ RI, as least so far as they concern a study of authority relations in the 5ᵉ DI, had come to an end.[92]

With the reacceptance of formal command authority, a new "public transcript" began to take shape reflecting the realigned power relationship between soldiers and commanders. For senior commanders, this implied a need to reinterpret what actually had happened during the mutinies. For if they were convincingly to portray themselves in the narrative of a "respectable performance," senior commanders needed to escape from a logical trap in a professional military ethos. If soldiers' behavior simply reflects their commanders' wishes, officers become logically responsible for their men's conduct. Nivelle and Mangin could take the blame for the strictly military calamities of the Chemin des Dames offensive. But their successors, who could not in the short run manage operations much differently, needed to find other candidates. As the senior command structure began to reassert itself, the search for scapegoats began. The civilian press and pacifists proved irresistible targets. Day by day, senior officers sought more expedient explanations of the mutinies. The junior officers who had done so much to diffuse the mutinies were forgotten, and by some openly reviled.

As early as 2 June, Colonel Martenet and General de Roig had begun to change their explanation of the events in the 5ᵉ DI, including even the unit principally responsible for "contaminating" the others. Writing after the departure of the 129ᵉ RI and the 36ᵉ RI but before the demonstrations in the 74ᵉ RI and the 274ᵉ RI, the two no longer viewed the mutinies as "political" rather than truly threatening military protests. Nor could they any longer explain the mutinies principally as the result of war-weariness, along with vaguely defined subversion from the rear. Martenet and de Roig had some incentive to shift blame away from the 129ᵉ RI. Regimental commander Genet, highly praised by the investigators and only in command of the regiment since February 1917, proved an unpromising scapegoat. One of his predecessors (from July to September 1915) had been none other than Martenet himself. Martenet now came to the unsurprising conclusion that "the 129ᵉ RI was a regiment well commanded and with

[92] Particularly in the 1ᵉ Bataillon, relations between soldiers and their commanders quickly deteriorated thereafter. On 3 June, the captain commanding the 1ᵉ Compagnie observed that "the bonds of affection uniting our men and us are tending to disappear. . . . If they were to receive an order to go into line now, they would not follow us. If it were a question of work details in the second positions, perhaps they would follow us." In the end, four men from the 129ᵉ were shot. Pedroncini, *Les Mutineries de 1917*, p. 226.

good cadres . . . exterior discipline was very good."[93] The chief source of weakness now became the 36ᵉ RI. In the 36ᵉ RI, Martenet observed, "discipline had been let go."

De Roig agreed. He considered the 129ᵉ RI "the best in the division, perfectly officered, commanded by a leader of the first order."[94] He observed that in the 36ᵉ RI, in contrast, "I have had, on several occasions, to make observation to the regimental commander that turnout was neglected, that the marks of respect and honors were poorly rendered, and that the action of the NCOs did not make itself sufficiently felt." More generally, de Roig attributed more influence than previously to inappropriate press accounts and "above all to the occult action of certain agents on turbulent elements," particularly in the otherwise impeccable 129ᵉ RI.

But emphasizing *both* outside agitation and differences between the 36ᵉ RI and the 129ᵉ RI encouraged a bizarre interpretation of the demonstrations. One might suppose that subversive agents would likely have been more drawn to the 36ᵉ RI than to the 129ᵉ RI, as the weaker of the two vessels. But the first mutineers indisputably came from the 129ᵉ RI. On 3 June, IIIᵉ Armée commander General Humbert tried to resolve this difficulty by letting yet more of the fog of outside subversion descend over the narrative. Given the record of the 129ᵉ RI, he argued, "it is surprising that such a unit could let itself be led to such a grave act of indiscipline. . . . Only the press and a powerful occult organization, established in Paris, could, in my opinion, have realized such effects."[95] The key factor in both units, he believed, was outside subversion. To deemphasize the differences between the two regiments, he observed that in the 36ᵉ RI there proved to be more "good" soldiers and fewer "doubtful" ones than he had previously believed.

A 12 June report on events in the 129ᵉ RI by IIᵉ Armée commander General Guillaumat exemplified the ingratitude expressed by the senior command for the work of the 5ᵉ DI officers in defusing the mutinies. In a blistering indictment, Guillaumat blasted the "weakness, not to say more, that the command at all levels displayed during the night of 28–29 May, and in the days that followed."[96] Major Auberge of the 1ᵉ Bataillon had begun the vicious circle by "beginning immediately to negotiate with the mutineers, as one man to another, with a disconcerting ingenuity, considering them as 'strikers.'" By spending much of the night of 28–29 May at 3ᵉ

---

[93] "Compte-rendu du Colonel Martenet, cdt. l'ID 5 au sujet des renseignements demandés par la lettre 157 secrète du général cdt. la 3ᵉ Armée," 2 June 1917, G.Q.G., 2ᵉ Bureau, 16 N 1521.

[94] De Roig report, 2 June.

[95] "IIIᵉ Armée, EM, Cabinet no. 23," in Pedroncini, ed., *1917: Les Mutineries*, p. 141.

[96] "Rapport du General Guillaumat sur les résultats de l'enquête faite sur les événements qui se sont passés les 28 et 29 mai au 129ᵉ RI, alors à la IIIᵉ Armée," in ibid., pp. 143–50.

CA headquarters deciding upon a policy of restraint, "the battalion commander, the colonel, the colonel commanding the division infantry, and the general commanding the division abandoned their posts to go seek reasons to excuse their inertia at a higher level of command." Army Group North commander Franchet d'Esperey agreed with Guillaumat's assessment of the conduct of de Roig and Lebrun, and had a note inserted into both officers' personal dossiers that faulted them for negotiating with the demonstrators instead of "knowing how to rally around them the healthy elements among their troops."[97]

But ironically, Guillaumat took such an extreme position that he nearly came full circle back to the truth. He at least understood the complex loyalties of the officers. He lamented that throughout 29 May, "there was nothing but empty chatter between officers of all grades and the soldiers, chatter such that certain of the latter ended up wondering if the officers were not at heart on their side." Alone among senior commanders commenting on the 129e RI, Guillaumat hesitated to hide behind scapegoats outside the army:

It is probable that a plot existed and played a role in the rebellion. But I do not believe that an organization was the only determining cause. . . . I see it much more in the spirit of cowardice that, incontestably, reigned within the 129e RI for a long time. In fact, these pacifist sentiments did not reveal themselves until the moment came to go get hurt.

There was, of course, something hypocritical in all this. Guillaumat held the officers of the 5e DI complicitous in the "cowardice" of the mutineers because they chose to persuade rather than confront the demonstrators. Pétain likewise faulted the officers of the 5e DI for looking on the demonstrators "naively, as mere strikers whom words would certainly soon restore to a better way of thinking."[98] But essentially, these officers no more than did explicitly what Pétain and his subordinates did implicitly. Soldiers' power to close down offensives before all the battlefield soldiers got killed had been unofficially recognized since 1914. In initiating a principally defensive strategy until the Americans and the tanks gave France a clear military superiority, Pétain tacitly recognized that soldiers had the power to stop doomed offensives before they had begun. His reforms in leave policy, rotations in the front lines, and food distribution were proudly displayed as attempts to respond to the grievances of the mutineers while keeping France in the war. In their way, and under much more perilous circumstances, the officers of the 5e DI had done no differently. Both had

[97] "Le General Franchet d'Esperey, commandant le Groupe d'Armées du Nord, au général commandant la VIeme Armée," 25 June 1917, 18 N 37. The note was annulled on 20 September 1917, though it remains in de Roig's personal dossier, Gx/4 308.
[98] Pétain, "A Crisis of Morale," p. 91.

been compelled to realize that command authority did not operate only in one direction.

THE COURTS-MARTIAL AND THE SEARCH FOR LEADERS

The court-martial records have provided the empirical bedrock supporting the Pedroncini thesis. Pedroncini argued that by preserving normal judicial procedures (that is, the *conseil de guerre* rather than the summary *cour martiale*) and above all by executing only a relative handful of soldiers out of thousands involved in the demonstrations, Pétain made clear his firm but prudent and insightful approach to the mutinies. According to Pedroncini's calculations, courts-martial throughout the army convicted 3,427 soldiers for offenses resulting from the mutinies. Of these, 554 received death sentences, and 49 were actually shot.[99] Certainly, the Pedroncini thesis is correct if the context is the historical reputation of the *conseil de guerre* or what Pétain's rivals would probably have done under the same circumstances.

But the argument of the present study suggests an alternative interpretation. The power relationship between citizen-soldiers and their commanders became one of explicit confrontation during the mutinies. But that relationship was never annihilated—even though soldiers had the opportunity to do so. When they decided instead to end the mutinies by accepting conventional command authority, a new "public transcript" had to take shape describing the new parameters of the power relationship. In this new transcript, symbols played a key role in demonstrating the conquest of war by politics.[100] Part of the new public transcript was described in the previous section, as senior commanders rewrote their own official narrative of just what the mutinies had been about.

Another part of the new public transcript involved regenerating a narrative of a "respectable performance" through symbolic repression of the mutinies through courts-martial. The courts-martial illustrate especially clearly the four particular characteristics of the public transcript identified by James Scott.[101] The courts-martial provided a "concealment" of real changes in the conduct of the war behind a facade of reasserted, one-directional command authority. Second, they served as something of an institutional "euphemism," in that they purported to constitute an impartial and fair series of judicial procedures. Third, the courts-martial "stig-

[99] Pedroncini, *Les Mutineries de 1917*, pp. 194, 215.

[100] When Georges Clemenceau completed the reconquest of war by politics at the national level in November 1917, he engaged in an assertion of his authority analagous to that of the courts-martial by the judicial silencing of his two principal political rivals, Louis Malvy and Joseph Caillaux. Malvy was tried and Caillaux was imprisoned on highly dubious charges related to "defeatism." See Duroselle, *Clemenceau*, pp. 646–51.

[101] Scott, *Domination and the Arts of Resistance*, pp. 50–58.

matized" a particular group of men who appeared to have behaved no differently from dozens of others who were not prosecuted, but who could nevertheless conveniently bear responsibility for the collectivity. Finally, the courts-martial provided an illusion of "unanimity," in that no one, soldiers or commanders, publicly contested their legitimacy. The symbolic repression of the mutinies showed the power relationship between soldiers and commanders at its ugliest. Officers and NCOs selected those singled out for punishment, and their comrades in effect abandoned them.

After the mutinies, the *conseil de guerre* in the 5ᵉ DI in the wake of the mutinies became exactly what it had *not* been previously—an ancien régime–style instrument for symbolically asserting sovereign power. The Foucault of *Discipline and Punish* provided an intriguing discription of this phenomenon: "Its aim is not so much to re-establish a balance as to bring into play at its extreme point, the dissymmetry between the subject who has dared to violate the law and the all-powerful sovereign who displays his strength."[102] In principle, military justice has always lent itself to ancien régime displays of power. Far more than civilian justice, or at least far more explicitly, military justice aims at disciplining a subject population. When soldiers agreed to accept command authority without immediate preconditions, they accepted redefinition as a subject population. An element of arbitrariness became not only possible, but part of the point of demonstrating a public transcript of hegemonic sovereign military power. The collective offense of *révolte* called for a strikingly different disciplinary strategy from that of the individual offense of desertion.[103]

Against the backdrop of a mass upheaval that did not overthrow the existing institutions, but that involved too many people for them all to be prosecuted, the concept of "leaders" became a pretext label applied to the group identified to pay the price for everyone. As early as 8 June, Pétain clearly stated his intention to identify "leaders" of the mutinies.[104] He observed that "certain officers have hidden from their superiors the poor

[102] Michel Foucault, *Discipline and Punish: The Birth of the Prison*, translated by Alan Sheridan (New York: Vintage Books, 1979, originally published in French in 1975), pp. 48–49. For a more general historical survey, see the essays in Sean Wilentz, ed., *Rites of Power: Symbolism, Ritual, and Politics Since the Middle Ages* (Philadelphia: University of Pennsylvania Press, 1985).

[103] The management of the individual offense of desertion did not change during and after the mutinies, despite the most dramatic increase in convictions in the entire war.

Convictions were handed down for twenty-eight desertions that took place during June 1917, a figure more than 50 percent higher than the previous record set in December 1916. This figure is all the more striking given than the 5ᵉ DI now comprised three rather than four infantry regiments. Of the twenty-eight soldiers convicted, only nine had their sentences carried out. See Leonard V. Smith, "Command Authority in the French Army, 1914–1918: The Case of the 5ᵉ Division d'Infanterie" (Ph.D. diss., Columbia University, 1990), pp. 525–37.

[104] "Télégramme chiffré, général commandant en chef à l'État-Major, No. 2.433 et 2.434," 8 June 1917, in G.Q.G., 2ᵉ Bureau, Service Spécial Morale, 16 N 1522.

spirit that has been reigning in their regiments. Others have not shown in the repression the initiative and energy desired." He warned that "inertia equals complicity" and left no doubt as to how such insufficiencies were to be overcome in the future:

> In order to avoid fulfilling their duties, certain officers and NCOs have hidden behind the fact that since the movements have a collective character, they found it difficult to unmask the leaders. Such a reason is not valid. It is always possible, in fact, to transform a collective act into an individual one. It suffices to give a few men (beginning with the unmanageable ones) an order to execute.

As had been the case throughout the war, the cases trying soldiers for *révolte* did not brazenly manipulate the letter of the law in a technical sense. For their part, the soldiers prosecuted admitted taking part in the demonstrations. But to a man, they stubbornly protested being singled out for exemplary punishment. Individuals probably did exist who put the match to the tinderbox of discontent. But these proved nearly impossible to identify, and officers from the 5ᵉ DI used many dubious criteria to do so. In any event, the immediate instigators bore little more "responsibility" for the mutinies than matches for forest fires—and Pétain knew it. If the real problem did not go beyond a few hotheads, Pétain would have had no reason to offer anything to the soldiers but repression, lest the malleable mass of soldiers perceive concessions as a sign of command weakness.

The courts-martial following the mutinies opened a new phase in the history of authority relations in the 5ᵉ DI. After 1 June, following the removal of the 36ᵉ RI and the 129ᵉ RI, the infantry of the 5ᵉ DI comprised the 74ᵉ RI, the 274ᵉ RI, and two new units, the 5ᵉ RI (formerly of the 6ᵉ DI, the other unit besides the 5ᵉ DI in the 3ᵉ CA), and the 114ᵉ Bataillon de Chasseurs à Pied (114ᵉ BCP). Only the mutinies in the 74ᵉ RI and 274ᵉ RI were tried by the 5ᵉ DI *conseil de guerre*, and these are the only cases that will be examined here. By the time the trials took place, the division had taken up positions in the front lines along the Chemin des Dames.

In all, the court-martial tried 100 soldiers from the two regiments, 9 from the 274ᵉ RI, and 91 from the 74ᵉ RI.[105] In the 274ᵉ RI, all of the soldiers tried were privates; in the 74ᵉ RI the breakdown is 19 corporals and 72 privates. As shown in the data presented for the 74ᵉ RI in table VIII-1, the heaviest concentrations of convictions are in the 2ᵉ and 3ᵉ Bataillons, and five companies (the 5ᵉ, 6ᵉ, 7ᵉ, 10ᵉ, and the 11ᵉ) account for 78 of the 91 convictions (86 percent).

---

[105] Série J 439, Dossiers 542–44, 546–53, 555–60. Four additional soldiers from the 274ᵉ RI were convicted in the case corresponding to Dossier 545. However, the Conseil de Révision of the VIᵉ Armée overturned the convictions on 22 June, and the soldiers were retried by the *conseil de guerre* of the 77ᵉ DI. The dossier no longer appears with the 5ᵉ DI records, and is not considered here.

TABLE VIII-1
Court-Martial Convictions for Revolt:
74e RI, June 1917

Unit	Date of Offense			
			30 May	
1e Bataillon				
1e Compagnie			5 privates	
3e Compagnie			5 privates	
		5 June	6 June	7 June
2e Bataillon				
5e Compagnie		4 privates	11 privates	
6e Compagnie			4 corporals	
			10 privates	
7e Compagnie			6 corporals	
			8 privates	2 privates
Compagnie Mitrailleuse₂			3 privates	
3e Bataillon				
10e Compagnie				5 corporals
				13 privates
11e Compagnie				4 corporals
				11 privates

Total Convictions
(By Unit)
1e Bataillon   10 (all privates)
2e Bataillon   48 (10 corporals, 38 privates)
3e Bataillon   <u>33</u> (9 corporals, 24 privates)

Total   91

The demonstrations in the 74e RI and 274e RI had less focus than the mutinies in the 129e RI and the 36e RI. The mutineers gave no indication of wanting to march on Paris, and indicated their direction simply as "south." But the demonstrations in the 74e RI and 274e RI had run a much greater risk of exploding into violence. The demonstrators, well aware of the precipitous departure of the 129e RI and the 36e RI, had their rifles in hand from the outset. The court-martial thus charged the "leaders" with revolt bearing arms under Article 218 of the military justice code.

Comparing the numbers of soldiers tried with the numbers of soldiers reported involved in the demonstrations provides some indication of the size of the groups selected for punishment. The variations between the 274e RI and the 74e RI and even within units of the 74e RI are striking and suggest a good deal of discretion in the naming of "leaders." The 30 May demonstration, in which soldiers from two companies of the 74e RI appeared before the regimental commander demanding to know what had become of the 129e RI and the 36e RI, involved about 60 soldiers each from the 1e Compagnie and the 3e Compagnie.[106] Of these, a total of 10 soldiers were tried, or 8.3 percent. No information exists of how many soldiers were involved in the 5 June incidents, apart from the regimental commander's mention of a "certain number."

In the 6 June demonstrations, 274e RI commander Houssais reported that 194 men had refused, rifle in hand, to take up positions in the front lines. Of these, 13 men were tried (6.7 percent), including 4 whose verdicts were overturned on 22 June. In the 74e RI on 6 June, 2e Bataillon commander Schaeffer reported speaking to about 300 men, of whom 234 remained with the column of demonstrators after regimental commander Brenot ordered them to desist. Of these 234, 43 (18.4 percent) were tried.[107] Three of the four infantry company commanders provided information on the numbers of men involved in their units. In the 5e Compagnie, 57 men demonstrated, of whom 11 were later tried (19.3 percent).[108] In the 7e Compagnie, 7 corporals and 60 privates were reported involved, of whom 6 corporals and 8 privates were tried (86 percent and 13.3 percent, respectively).[109] In the CM$_2$ (Compagnie Mitrailleuse$_2$ [Second Machine-gun Company]), 15 soldiers demonstrated, of whom 3 were tried (20 percent).

The figures for the demonstrations of 7 June highlight the problems of determining the number of "participants" in the mutinies. General de Roig wrote of "four-fifths" of the 3e Bataillon heading south in its protest (some 700–800 men). The 33 men tried represent only 4.4 percent of the total if 750 is used as the base figure. A report in a court-martial dossier by battalion commander Paul gave a figure of 74 men from the 10e Compagnie and 78 from the 11e Compagnie missing from the evening call, just before the battalion entered the front lines.[110] If these figures are used as indications of the most determined mutineers, the results are 18 tried of 74 men (24.3 percent) in the 10e Compagnie and 15 tried of 78 men (19.2 percent) in the 11e Compagnie.

The evidence from the 74e RI and the 274e RI confirms Pedroncini's conclusions on the socioeconomic diversity of those prosecuted.[111] Among the 100 men tried in the two regiments, no less than 51 different occupations appeared across a wide variety of economic activities. The only concentrations were 23 farmers (*cultivateur*), 8 day laborers (*journalier*), and 6 bakers (*boulanger*). The rest include, among others, artisans (shoe-

---

[106] Dossiers 543 and 544.
[107] Dossier 553.
[108] Dossier 552.
[109] Dossier 553.
[110] Dossier 549.
[111] Pedroncini, *Les Mutineries de 1917*, p. 204.

makers, stonecutters, and masons) and a variety of domestics and gardeners. Conspicuously absent were industrial workers—only about 10, using the most generous definition. At least as many gave unambiguously middle-class professions, such as architecture student, accountant, and businessman or banker.

This is not to say, however, that the men cited as "leaders" were selected at random. Three company commanders from the 74ᵉ RI gave some indication in their reports of how this was done. The captain commanding the 11ᵉ Compagnie provided some surprising criteria for the men held accountable for the events of 7 June.[112] Only one of several men to whom the captain gave a personal order to cease their demonstration figured among the accused. Among the others, four corporals stood out as obvious candidates. But four privates were apparently selected strictly on principle, soldiers who "by their poor spirit and their usual manner of service must be [*doivent être*] among the leaders." The tenth soldier was identified simply as "intelligent, having much authority over his comrades and who could be [*peut être*] considered among the principal leaders."

The 10ᵉ Compagnie commander applied similar criteria in selecting fifteen soldiers.[113] Five corporals were identified, one of them held particularly culpable because his family lived in the occupied areas. As in the 11ᵉ Compagnie, only one soldier was named because he refused a direct order from the company commander. Five more were named because they were considered "bad soldiers" or had "poor antecedents." One other soldier was heard directing the movements of the demonstrators, and another was overheard by the company commander saying "they want me to raise my head, but I would rather lower it, I am so ashamed to wear this uniform." Two other soldiers who demonstrated were perceived as leaders because they were "intelligent and well-instructed."

The lieutenant commanding the 5ᵉ Compagnie, who identified ten privates held accountable for the events of 6 June, showed unusual honesty.[114] Although he contended that the demonstrators from his company had been "ordered" to appear with all their equipment for their march south, "the investigation did not permit the discovery of the author of this order." One soldier was named because he refused three times to turn over his rifle to a Moroccan cavalryman when the column of demonstrators from the

---

[112] "Rapport du Capitaine G----, commandant la 11ᵉ Compagnie du 74ᵉ Régiment d'Infanterie, tendant à la comparution de militaires de sa compagnie devant un conseil de guerre," 10 June 1917, Dossier 549.

[113] "Rapport du Lieutenant G-----, A-----, commandant la 10ᵉ Compagnie du 74ᵉ Régiment d'Infanterie sur les événements du 7 juin tendant à faire traduire les militaires de la compagnie devant un conseil de guerre," 8 June 1917, Dossier 550.

[114] "Rapport du Lieutenant M------, commandant la 5ᵉ Compagnie du 74ᵉ Régiment d'Infanterie concernant 10 hommes de la compagnie traduités devant un conseil de guerre pour rébellion par les militaires armés," 8 June 1917, Dossier 542.

74e RI was stopped. Another was named because he refused a direct order from his battalion commander. Another, although "normally a good soldier, showed so much activity in the wrongdoing that he merits an exemplary punishment." One soldier qualified because he had already been convicted for desertion in May 1916.[115] But six others found themselves among the accused simply because they were "bad soldiers, who by their conversation and their attitude, encouraged their comrades to rebellion."

As a descendant of the inquisitorial system of justice, a case that actually made it to a *conseil de guerre* carried a general presumption of guilt. Only two of the one hundred soldiers tried from the 74e RI and 274e RI were acquitted. If serious questions arose as to the guilt of the accused, the case was more likely to be dismissed before trial by a declaration of *non-lieu*. This meant that insufficient evidence existed that a crime had taken place.

The defense normally did not figure prominently in a court-martial, and probably figured even less prominently during the mutiny trials. One man, a corporal from the 74e RI who had been the principal counsel for the defense in the 5e DI since 1914, defended all but one of the one hundred men accused.[116] All of the mutiny trials took place within a four-week period, from 16 June to 12 July. The responses of the defendants were so similar that some defense strategy could have existed, at least to keep the defendants from saying anything particularly likely to get them shot. They all admitted participating in the demonstrations, but denied leading them, or even knowing who led them. More implausibly, the defendants denied knowing anything of the objectives of the demonstrators. When asked why they participated, virtually all responded at one point or another "*J'ai suivi les camarades* [I followed the comrades]."

The prosecutors attempted to connect a few soldiers to pacifist movements in the interior. One such soldier, Alphonse Boneau, was identified because of an imprudent conversation he had with a Lieutenant Castile (both names pseudonyms) of the 5e Compagnie on 5 June.[117] According to Castile, Boneau refused to do his duty because of "an order from the minority Socialist Party," and advocated peace without annexations or indemnities and a plebiscite in Alsace-Lorraine. The two conversed "as comrades," according to the lieutenant, after Boneau had been persuaded to rejoin the company. Castile observed that "movements like the one he

---

[115] In the division as a whole, of the one hundred soldiers tried, twenty-one had already been convicted by a court-martial in wartime.

[116] The remaining defendant, a lithograph engraver from Versailles, hired a trial lawyer from Paris at his own expense. He was tried individually and his dossier included more statements from witnesses, but the outcome was not noticeably different from the cases of his comrades. The accused was found guilty of revolt but not of being an instigator. His sentence (the length of which is unknown), was suspended by order of the Sous-Secrétaire d'État in April 1919. Dossier 559.

[117] Dossier 542.

was involved in did not serve to obtain the goal he desired." Boneau, he claimed, advocated instead "demonstrating in the army and bringing the troubles to the countryside." Castile gave his somewhat tenuous reason for claiming that Boneau took orders from a subversive organization: "He always employed the term 'we.' 'We wanted this, we wanted that,' and after this conversation, it follows that he along with his comrades, received instructions coming from an organization in the interior."

Boneau, of course, told quite a different story and responded mostly according to the formula used by the defenders. He said he knew nothing of any prearranged protest movement, though he admitted taking part in the demonstrations. Eventually, he admitted entering into a political conversation with Castile, though he pleaded entrapment: "It was only at the solicitation of the lieutenant that we entered on this subject." He also protested that "of about thirty men of my section, given the facts put forward in the same situation, I am the only one incriminated." The court-martial found Boneau guilty both of revolt and of being an instigator. It sentenced him to death, though the sentence was commuted to twenty years in prison and was reduced to ten years in January 1918. There is no record of whether he eventually received an amnesty.

Statistically, the repression of the mutinies in the 74e RI and 274e RI was more severe in most respects than in the French army as a whole. Using Pedroncini's figures cited earlier for the entire army, 16 percent of all convictions resulted in death sentences. In the 5e DI, of the 96 convictions for which the sentences are certain, 33 resulted in death sentences (34 percent).[118] Of the other 63 sentences, 54 (or 86 percent) came under Pedroncini's category of "heavy sentences [peines graves]," of more than five years in a labor camp (atelier de travaux public). Pedroncini's figures gave a breakdown for non-death sentences of 48 percent "heavy sentences" and 52 percent "less heavy [moins grave]."[119] On the other hand, Pedroncini arrived at a figure of 8 percent of all death sentences actually carried out (49 of 554); in the 5e DI, the figure is only 3 percent (1 of 33). The other death sentences were commuted to prison terms of fifteen to twenty years, and virtually all of those imprisoned were released by 1922.[120] With the war safely over, the group selected to bear responsibility for the whole had lost its raison d'être.

The case of the one soldier actually executed appropriately summarizes the symbolic repression of the mutinies by the courts-martial.[121] This

[118] Of the other four cases, the outcome of one is uncertain, the sentence for the other is unknown, and the other two were acquitted.

[119] Pedroncini, Les Mutineries de 1917, p. 215.

[120] Probably because of postwar administrative oversight, not all remissions of sentence are noted in the dossiers, but it seems safe to make this assertion given the data that are there.

[121] Dossier 546.

soldier's most extraordinary characteristic is that there is nothing extraordinary either about his military antecedents or his case as it evolved over the course of events leading to his execution. The accused was twenty-four years old, unmarried, and listed in different documents in the dossier as a linen-worker and a chimney sweep from Le Havre. He had served with the 39ᵉ RI in August 1914, and over the course of the war had been wounded three times. Transferred to the 274ᵉ RI at the end of May 1916, he had been involved in perhaps the most harmless of the mutinies in the 5ᵉ DI. In the mutinies in the 274ᵉ RI, it will be recalled, all of the protesting soldiers returned to their duties before the regimental commander had even finished his report of the incident.

The company commander did consider the accused the premier "leader" in the company: "He went from group to group, encouraging his comrades to take part in the movements, giving directions and holding together the indecisive ones." Similar statements were made about a number of men who were out of prison by 1922 or even earlier. The accused gave mostly single-word responses and followed the pattern used by the defendants of admitting participating in the demonstrations but denying having led them, and volunteering to go back into the trenches. His appeal for mercy was denied by President Raymond Poincaré on 30 June, and he was shot on 2 July. He proved to be the last soldier from the 5ᵉ DI executed during the war. At least symbolically, the command structure had made its point.

The Grandeur and Miseries of Proportionality

JUNE 1917–NOVEMBER 1918

GEORGES CLEMENCEAU, who presided over the conquest of war by politics at the national level in France, titled his memoirs *Grandeur et misères d'une victoire.*[1] This chapter argues that much of the title equally well applied to the renegotiated parameters of command authority in the French army after the mutinies. The symbolic significance, even the grandeur, of Pétain renouncing *offensive à outrance* can scarcely be exaggerated. By publicly admitting the *dis*proportionality of attempting a *percée* until tanks and American reinforcements gave France a decisive edge, Pétain tacitly reopened the lines of communications between the high command and battlefield soldiers. By extending a policy that began before the mutinies of *défense en profondeur* (defense in depth) and by improving policies on leaves, rotation in the front lines, and food distribution, Pétain also sought to mitigate the worst physical risks and deprivations of trench warfare.

But the brute fact remained that in the short run, the conquest of war by politics did little to alter the military situation. The politics of proportionality indeed restrained further quixotic attempts at offensive violence, but the stalemate of the trenches remained. For French soldiers, defeating the likes of Nivelle and Mangin brought them no closer to defeating the Germans, a goal to which they had nevertheless rededicated themselves by ending the mutinies. The misery of proportionality lay in the fact that the new settlement between soldiers and their commanders could not in itself end the war. Most immediately, accepting Pétain's recalculation of proportionality necessitated a return to the miseries of the trenches. In time, it would also mean resuming the attack. Accordingly, the tension within the power relationship between soldiers and commanders persisted for the duration. With the grand gestures of the mutinies and the symbolic repression of them complete, it remained to negotiate the finer points of the new public transcript for trench warfare and pitched battle.

This negotiation occurred in the context of greatly restructured 5e DI. This restructuring, not uncommon among restive divisions, constituted an effort to enhance the formal distance between soldiers and commanders.

[1] 4 vols. (Paris: Plon, 1930).

Two new regiments were brought in to replace the 36e RI and the 129e RI, the 5e RI and the 114e Bataillon de Chasseurs à Pied (114e BCP). The 224e RI replaced the 114e BCP in November 1917.[2] The 274e RI was dissolved in December 1917, though not, it would appear, for disciplinary purposes. Rather, the manpower crisis in the French army had become so acute that the command structure cannibalized some units to top up others.[3] Only the 74e RI served with the 5e DI from August 1914 to November 1918. Sources of continuity existed between men new to the division and those already serving, as had been the case throughout the war. The 5e RI had previously served with the 6e DI, the other division besides the 5e DI in the 3e CA. Although it had served with different army corps, the 224e RI, like the 5e DI, originated in the 3e Région Militaire in Normandy.

General Lebrun, 3e CA commander, wrote optimistically if less than accurately on 18 June 1917 that the new regiments "have proved of excellent morale, and do not seem to have been touched by recent events."[4] "General indiscipline" in the 5e RI was noted on 1 June (the day the regiment joined the 5e DI) and a "sort of strike with crossed arms [*sort de grève des bras croisés*]."[5] A postal censorship report from the 5e RI written the same day the regiment joined the 5e DI listed demands remarkably similar to those of the mutineers of the 5e DI.[6] In the 224e RI, after the regiment had served in the front lines along the Chemin des Dames, a number of soldiers attended a meeting of demonstrators from three regiments on 26 May, and went to a fourth regiment on 28–29 May to make converts. Apparently only one soldier from the 224e RI was actually prosecuted (not by the 5e DI *conseil de guerre*) for abandoning a post in a war zone and for the "propagation of alarmist information."[7]

The change in the composition of the division presents both problems and opportunities for the methodology of this study. Certainly, it bears reemphasizing that the narrative here recounts not so much the history of a

[2] Since the 114e BCP served with the 5e DI for a relatively short time and not even a *JMO* survives, the experience of this unit will not be examined in great detail here.

[3] On the dire manpower situation by the end of 1917, see AFGG, tome 5, vol. 2, pp. 1197–1206.

[4] "Le Général Lebrun, commandant le 3e Corps d'Armée au général commandant la VIe Armée, No. 5869/3," 18 June 1917, G.Q.G., 2e Bureau, Service Spéciale Morale, 16 N 1522.

[5] "Actes d'indiscipline dans les régiments d'infanterie, 1 à 60, 1917–1918," in ibid., 16 N 1526.

[6] "Unité contrôlé par sondage: 5e Régiment d'Infanterie," 30 May 1917, G.Q.G., 2e Bureau, Service de Renseignement des Armées (SRA), 16 N 1388. As in previous chapters, all subsequent SRA reports will be identified only by title, date, and carton.

[7] See "Actes d'indiscipline dans les regiments d'infanterie, 61 à—[sic], 1917–1918," in G.Q.G., 2e Bureau, Service Special Morale, 16 N 1527; and "Rapport du S/Lieutenant B------, Commissaire Rapporteur prés de Conseil de Guerre de la 158e Division s'Infanterie, sur l'Affaire P------," in ibid., 16 N 1522. See also Guy Pedroncini, *Les Mutineries de 1917* (Paris: Presses Universitaires de France, 1967), pp. 119–20.

particular group of individuals as the history of a body of experience and of authority relations drawn from that experience. In many senses, Mangin's 5e DI no longer existed by the summer of 1917. But as has been shown, the demographic composition of "Mangin's 5e DI" had undergone dramatic change with some regularity ever since 1914. The changes in personnel after the mutinies also presents an unusual opportunity, that of comparing the experience of the new regiments with the old under near-laboratory conditions. The evidence presented here suggests that the experience of the soldiers new to the 5e DI followed a path consistent with that of the old. A similar dynamic, perhaps, had emerged between the battlefield soldiers and commanders throughout the French army.

THE PUBLIC TRANSCRIPT OF SYMBOLIC AGGRESSION: TRENCH WARFARE AFTER THE MUTINIES

Tony Ashworth argued in his landmark study of tacit truces in trench warfare between the British and the Germans that the opposing command structures proved able to break down the "live and let live" system in the last two years of the war.[8] Through centralizing control over artillery fire and the planning and execution of raids, British and German commanders could provoke militarily indecisive but selectively lethal experiences that would incite countermeasures. The commanders thus engineered an escalating spiral of violence, and indirectly but effectively coerced their soldiers into behaving aggressively.

Certainly, the evidence presented here points to greater central control over the use of violence in trench warfare. But here as previously, a negotiated settlement of proportionality seems to provide a more effective way of understanding trench warfare. Ashworth tended to consider violence in the trenches as an exogenously imposed phenomenon, almost like the weather. Left to their own devices, Ashworth's argument implied, commanders would always advocate violence and soldiers would always resist it. But an explanation involving proportionality allows for any number of other possibilities, including a decision by battlefield soldiers in favor of violence if that violence could be construed as having some military purpose.

That purpose, I would suggest, could be principally symbolic, provided that casualties did not seem to rise out of control—as they did in the largely symbolic pitched battle at Verdun, and threatened to at the Chemin des Dames. Violence in trench warfare revolved around a set of symbols agreed upon between soldiers and their commanders—and perhaps even between

[8] Tony Ashworth, *Trench Warfare, 1914–1918: The Live and Let Live System* (New York: Holmes & Meier, 1980), chaps. 4–5.

the French and the Germans. Through these symbols the protagonists conveyed to each other their interest in continuing the war until the return to the war of movement.

In an indirect way, such a modus vivendi agreed with the wishes of the Pétain regime. In principle, the 1916 regulations on trench warfare stipulating constant aggression in the front lines remained in effect. But new regulations on pitched battle bearing Pétain's name and issued in January 1918 suggested a type of authority relationship between soldiers and commanders that could easily accommodate managed and symbolic trench warfare.[9] Implicitly, the new regulations recognized that soldiers and commanders exercised some authority over each other.

"The commander who knows his job," the regulations observed, "will ask only useful efforts from his troops. . . ."[10] Agreement on what soldiers and commanders considered "useful" would be guaranteed through close and constant communication between them. Officers should take great care to "explain the general military situation" and "make them understand the grandeur in the effort that the country still expects from its army."[11] But communication was clearly to take place in two directions: "[Officers must] apply themselves to understanding at all times the emotions of their men, to care about them, to reward them, to tend to their needs of all kinds, to exercise authority with justice."[12] The advice to officers subtly blended traditional tensions expressed in traditional military language, some of it taken directly from the 1916 regulations: "The rank and file are the reflection of their leader. . . . They demand only to admire him and to follow him blindly."[13] But by January 1918, few in the French army remained unaware that the word "blindly" would not be taken too literally.

The linchpin of Pétain's attempt to mitigate the miseries of trench warfare revolved around *défense en profondeur*, a concession to proportionality that had actually been evolving for some time. By the fall of 1916, divisional depots had been created, partly to provide centers for instruction close to the front lines, but also to thin out the numbers of men actually in the trenches. Pétain expanded upon the concept of defense in depth when he assumed supreme command. Defense in depth, as he noted in his instructions of 4 June, "avoids the tendency to pack together the infantry in the front lines, which only uselessly augments casualties."[14] The key for

---

[9] G.Q.G. des Armées du Nord et du Nord-Est, *Instruction sur le combat offensif des petits unités* (Paris: Imprimerie Nationale, 1918).

[10] Ibid., p. 13.

[11] Ibid., p. 103.

[12] Ibid., p. 14.

[13] Ibid.

[14] Quoted in Guy Pedroncini, *Pétain, General en chef: 1917–1918* (Paris: Presses Universitaires de France, 1974), p. 73.

Pétain involved regaining operational flexibility by creating a large strategic reserve. This could be accomplished only by keeping as many troops as possible out of militarily inconclusive duty in the front lines. Those remaining there would satisfy expectations by keeping up appearances by demonstrating symbolic aggression as best they could.

From the point of view of battlefield soldiers, the problem remained that some sectors showed themselves far better suited to defense in depth than others. The 5e DI spent approximately eight of the last seventeen months of the war in the trenches.[15] It occupied three sectors during these eight months. Immediately after the mutinies, the 5e DI took up positions along the Chemin des Dames, a sector most unsuited to defense in depth. It remained there until September, including one month of rest in the middle. The other two sectors proved much quieter, and hence better suited to the 1918 version of symbolic aggression.[16]

Theoretically, *defense en profondeur* began to be applied in the 5e DI within days of the end of the mutinies. A memo of 12 June 1917 from 3e CA commander Lebrun specified three lines of resistance.[17] The purpose of the first line was simply to maintain an observational perspective to guide fire from the 75mm guns and to provide a line of infantry fire. Only one quarter of the men assigned to defend the first two lines were to be placed in the first line. The second line was "the principal line of defense" and had to be maintained "at any price." A part of the garrison was to be assigned to the defense proper of the second line. The remainder, as well as all of the men positioned in the third line, were to be maintained as a reserve available for immediate counterattack if portions of the second line fell. In the event of a German attack, the purpose of the first line was to slow down rather than immediately to stop an assault. Counterattacks were to restore the militarily vital second line, but not to waste casualties for the principle of regaining every lost centimeter of French soil as an end in itself.

In practice, however, the matter proved not so simple. The basic military situation the 5e DI faced in the Chemin des Dames determined that the public transcript of symbolic aggression would take shape through a process rather than through an event. Map IX-1 shows the exposed nature of the 5e DI's position in June 1917. The division occupied about two kilometers of the sector, with No Man's Land less than one hundred meters wide

---

[15] The remainder of the time it was either resting behind the front lines or (after July 1918) engaged in pitched battle.

[16] From September 1917 to June 1918, the division occupied a sector near where the French and British armies met near Saint-Quentin. The last sojourn of the 5e DI in trench warfare was in the Champagne from March to June 1918, which was mostly a quiet period apart from a German attack in March designed as a diversion from the main effort against the the British.

[17] "Plan d'organisation défensive de la première position," 12 June 1917, in 3e CA, 3e Bureau, 22 N 122.

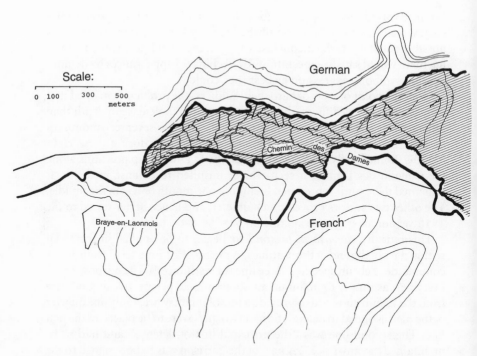

MAP IX-1. Chemin des Dames Sector, 5ᵉ DI, June 1917

in most places. Both the French and the Germans occupied high ground above the trenches, which meant that both could shell at will the helpless infantry below. As indicated, the Germans retained a deep defensive position even after the French offensive that spring. Despite evidence presented below of restrained aggression, the time the 5ᵉ DI spent in the Chemin des Dames proved its bloodiest period of trench warfare during the entire war. In just over eight weeks in the sector, the 5ᵉ DI suffered some 1,500 casualties.[18] In contrast, the division suffered 1,038 casualties in nearly eight months in the Eparges sector. In four months in a quiet sector to the north from September 1917 to January 1918, it suffered only 169 casualties.

The problem of "liquidating" the Chemin des Dames offensive limited the degree to which commanders could mitigate the dangers and stress of life in an active sector. In a report of 29 June 1917 protesting a proposal to lengthen the sector of the 5ᵉ DI, General de Roig argued that "the sector is far from calm," and that "it does not have the solidity of the front in a sector where work has been taking place for a long time."[19] Moreover,

[18] General de Roig-Bourdeville, "Renseignements sommaires de la 5ᵉ Division d'Infanterie," 1 February 1918, IVᵉ Armée, 3ᵉ Bureau, 19 N 746.
[19] Idem., "Étude de l'extension du secteur de la 5ᵉ D.I. vers la droite, No. 2891," 29 June 1917, in 5ᵉ DI, 3ᵉ Bureau, 24 N 90.

he bluntly stated that level of activity in the sector rendered the sort of deployment advocated by Lebrun ill-advised for the time being: "One cannot consider, without exposing ourselves to unpleasant surprises, extending the front of the companies of the first line to create reserves in depth."

The need to continue stabilizing the Chemin des Dames sector resulted in a small echo of the mutinies on 30 August 1917. Some units of the 114e BCP were scheduled to take part in a small-scale attack alongside the 151e DI. When the time came for the 1e Compagnie to assemble, "the men made themselves difficult picking up their equipment, showing little turnout and clear ill-will, without, however, going so far as to disobey the order given to them."[20] As the *chasseurs* (light infantrymen) proceeded to the front lines, they passed by a line of soldiers from the 3e Bataillon of the 74e RI, which was being relieved in the sector.[21] The soldiers of the 74e RI began loudy to refer to them as "the Sénégalais of the division," implying that they were to be used as they perceived black colonial troops to have been used—as cannon fodder. The hecklers invited the *chasseurs* to join them in leaving the sector, without authorization if necessary. The *chasseurs* of the 1e Section of the 5e Compagnie then sat down alongside the road leading to the front lines, though they shortly thereafter obeyed a direct order to reassemble. The attack took place as scheduled, apparently successfully.[22]

Army Group North commander Gen. Louis Franchet d'Esperey did not wish to let the matter rest there.[23] He showed particular displeasure with de Roig, for having only one *chasseur* court-martialed and no soldiers at all from the 74e RI. Recalling de Roig's initial restraint during the mutinies, Franchet d'Esperey added that "this is the second time that I have noted this state of mind in this general," and proposed a more thorough inquest into de Roig's attitude. But within a week of his first report, Franchet d'Esperey modified his views and selected a new scapegoat. It turned out that "the affair did not have the grave character" he had earlier supposed, and that "the responsibility of General de Roig in particular is diminished."[24] Showing the same ingratitude toward junior commanders that characterized high-command responses to the mutinies, he suggested that the company commander from the 114e BCP might have been at fault for

20 "Le Général de Division Duchêne, commandant la Xe Armée, à monsieur le général commandant le G.A.N. No. 528K," 3 September 1917, in Groupe des Armées du Nord (G.A.N.), 1e Bureau, 18 N 37.

21 It will be recalled from chap. 8 that the 3e Bataillon was one of the two most deeply engaged in the demonstrations of 6–7 June.

22 74e RI *JMO*, 31 August 1917, 26 N 660.

23 "Le Général Franchet d'Esperey, commandant le Group d'Armées du Nord à monsieur le général commandant en chef, No. 7148," 4 September 1917, G.A.N, 1e Bureau, 18 N 37.

24 "Le Général Franchet d'Esperey, commandant le Groupe d'Armées du Nord à M. le général commandant la Xe Armée, No. 7790," 11 September 1917, in ibid.

not heading off the incident. The captain in question was given thirty days in prison and appears to have been relieved of his command.[25]

Pétain's concern with increasing the quantity and quality of artillery support required more centralized control at all levels.[26] A memo from de Roig dated 18 June 1917 set down procedures centralizing his own authority to regulate artillery fire.[27] A small barrage of a few shells to silence, say, an enemy machine gun could be ordered by a battalion or even a company commander using a flare. For fire involving some sort of reprisal, however, the zone commander had to report to the artillery group commander the exact reason he requested the fire, and the exact location of the targets. If the infantry commander sought a reprisal of a more general sort (*tir de punition*) requiring fire from heavier pieces than the 75mm gun, he had to provide an even more thorough explanation. The third and most extensive category of fire, designed to counter an enemy barrage believed to be preceding an attack, could be ordered only by the division commander himself. Ashworth has argued that the main purpose of this sort of "bureaucratization" of violence was to break up the "live and let live" system of tacit truces. Making infantry commanders specify the location and utility of targets provided one way to make sure that a worthy target really existed. But it also involved the division commander in negotiating the meaning of "worthy."

The last entry in the diary portion of Paul Rimbault's *Propos d'un marmité* shows that this sort of centralization did not always result in constant aggression.[28] Rimbault, who pointedly refused to comment at length on the mutinies, broke his silence to describe remarkably brazen "live and let live" arrangements along the Chemin des Dames. The entry for 1 July 1917 identified an "unedifying sector [*secteur peu brillant*], without shelters or communication trenches, in which at points only eight meters separated the French and German listening posts."[29] Rimbault himself used the term "tacit truce," in which "the Boche smokes his pipe while sitting on the parapet, and the Frenchman writes his letter in the same position." French and German soldiers would actually exchange materiel they had on hand to fortify their respective positions.

[25] "Compte-rendu à monsieur le général commandant le Groupe d'Armées du Nord" (from General Humbert, IIIᵉ Armée commander), 20 September 1917, in ibid.

[26] On Pétain's use of artillery in his limited offensives at Verdun on August 1917 and at Malmaison in October 1917, see Pedroncini, *Pétain: général en chef*, p. 43; and Lt. Col. M. Aublet, "L'Artillerie française de 1914 à 1918," *Revue militaire française* 33 (July–September 1929), pp. 249–51.

[27] "Note de Service, No. 2545," 18 June 1917, in 5ᵉ DI, 3ᵉ Bureau, 24 N 90.

[28] Paul Rimbault, *Propos d'un marmité* (Paris: Fournier, 1920), pp. 96–97. He does not explain why his memoir ceased at this point, even though according to his *état des services* he served with the 74ᵉ RI until January 1918.

[29] Ibid., p. 96.

The war of symbols described by Rimbault could occasionally prove comic. If the German sitting on his parapet happened to spy a commander (*chef*, probably either French or German), he would notify his counterpart so that both could scurry into more bellicose positions. Holding up a grenade signaled an impending raid, and that the protagonists "did not want to take part in the bloody celebration."[30] He recalled that the Germans would sometimes call their own artillery gunners "assassins," when they knew that German fire would shortly provoke a French response.

Rimbault provided no indication that he (or for that matter his superiors) ever went out of their way to disrupt these arrangements. For his part, Rimbault exceptionally took the part of battlefield soldiers over such command expectations as may have existed of constant aggression. He concluded that the problem lay not so much in some nefarious passivity on the part of soldiers, but in commanders insisting that the opposing lines remain so close together. This would only bring back conditions found at Les Eparges, a "murderous, demoralizing, terrible war, without appreciable tactical result."[31] If the command structures required that French and German soldiers face each other eight meters apart, these soldiers really had only two choices: "to kill each other, or make friendly arrangements."[32]

Ashworth described raids as the single most important element in the breakup of the "live and let live" system, as teams of specially trained commandos struck erratically to disrupt quiet sectors and thus incite revenge all along the front.[33] But again, the advent of a systematic raiding policy in the French army after the mutinies seems best understood according to symbolic aggression. Raids were where Pétain's solutions to crises in pitched battles and in trench warfare met. Raids in trench warfare were simply his limited offensives carried out on a yet smaller scale.

Raids, like artillery fire, became more bureaucratized in the last year of the war. True to the French bureaucratic tradition, raid reports assumed a formula in which the objectives, resources, and results of operations were provided week after week in the same format. These reports described the raids almost invariably as successful, though as with patrol reports it is difficult to evaluate the quality of the intelligence gathered. It is improbable, though, given improvements in air reconnaissance by late 1917, that the information gathered by raids was often vital to the security of the French front. The evidence suggests that "success" could simply mean carrying enough smoke and noise to the enemy to convince French and German soldiers and commanders that France at least symbolically continued the fight.

[30] Ibid.
[31] Ibid., p. 97.
[32] Ibid.
[33] Ashworth, *Trench Warfare*, chap. 8.

Simply put, raids after the mutinies served more theatrically the same symbolic function served by patrols as examined in chapter 4. Patrols, it will be recalled, were described as "search and find missions," that placed a premium on not being noticed by the Germans. Like patrols, raids were intelligence-gathering missions, though intentionally much more obtrusive. In the 5e DI as elsewhere, raiders (all volunteers) were offered special arrangements by the command structure. In exchange for exposing themselves to extraordinary risks in inherently indecisive operations, raiders were allowed extra leaves and exemptions from guard duty in the trenches.[34]

A group of men from the 1e Bataillon of the 5e RI conducted a generic "successful" raid on 31 March 1918, when the 5e DI occupied a quiet sector in the Champagne.[35] The perpetrators planned and executed the raid with the precision of a railroad timetable. The report stated three goals of the operation: taking prisoners to confirm the identity of the German units facing them, examining the German defensive positions, and preventing "the Boche from moving his reserves, by proving that he has before him active and prepared troops." The 32 men carrying out the raid were divided into no less than 15 groups, with 4 actually attacking, 8 providing covering fire, and 3 providing support and covering the retreat. The raid was supported by artillery, with the fire directed to the right and left of the actual zone of the raid to make possible an element of surprise.

The raiders fulfilled their mission—they came, they saw, and they departed. The artillery gunners performed their function "with a precision of which they should be proud," enabling the raiders to reach three successive German lines while suffering only three casualties (all wounded, though one seriously by a German 77mm shell). The raiders shot some half dozen Germans, and took an NCO machine gunner prisoner. When the attacking groups encountered serious resistance from enemy grenades at the fourth German line, they launched a flare giving the signal to retreat, which occurred without incident.

The raid "confirmed" the identity of units facing the 5e DI (which implies that this information was already known). It also "confirmed" that the French were not the only ones to practice defense in depth. The author of the report concluded that in the event of an attack the Germans intended to evacuate the first three lines of trenches, which meant that there were at

[34] "Le Général de Roig, commandant la 5e Division d'Infanterie à monsieur le général cdt. le 3e Corps d'Armée," no. 3974, 31 July 1917, 5e DI, 3e Bureau, 24 N 90.

[35] "Rapport du Chef de Bataillon Venesson Cdt. le I/5 sur le coup de main exécuté le 31 mars 1918 (dans les lignes allemands, devant S/Secteur Cameroun)," 31 March 1918, 5e DI, 3e Bureau, 24 N 94. In a memo issued the day before the raid, General Lebrun complained that "the most recent raids attempting to take prisoners have produced no results," because the Germans had developed the reflex habit of retreating deep into their many lines of defenses. Lebrun counseled that the solution lay in "organization and audacity." "Note de Service, No. 624/3-OP," 30 March 1918, in 3e CA, 3e Bureau, 22 N 122.

least four lines and probably several more. Indeed, the first line seemed quite unoccupied except by barbed wire. The second line was protected by a barbed-wire network from ten to twelve meters thick, and the communication trenches joining the first two lines (through which the raiders had to pass for maximum cover) had been filled in with barbed wire as well. The second line contained numerous grenade launchers, which stopped the French raid with little difficulty. The Germans, for their part, had well-established lines of retreat; the author of the report observed that "only surprise" made possible the taking of the single prisoner. Whatever the symbolic significance of the French raid, it was not the sort of thing seriously to disrupt the stalemate of force on the Western Front.

The soldiers of the 5e DI reacted to the resumption of trench warfare after the mutinies in a predictably broad variety of ways. The key choice had been made during the mutinies—to return to the trenches rather than lose the war. In so doing soldiers explicitly gave their consent to the military authority governing them, and thus resigning themselves at some level to the hardships and perils of trench warfare. But while the evidence does not suggest a new descent into foucauldian despair, soldierly dissatisfaction with life in the trenches diminished slowly, with great difficulty, and never completely.

To the extent that court-martial convictions serve as an index of resistance to command authority, the results suggest an imperfect but workable arrangement between soldiers and commanders. The "disciplinary dilemma" between sending soldiers to prison and sending them back to the front never disappeared.[36] Rather, it faded in significance. I noted in chapter 8 that despite the high incidences of desertion convictions during the time the division spent in the Chemin des Dames sector, the policy continued of removing only those soldiers deemed likely to contaminate the otherwise obedient majority. More desertions took place in the 74e in June 1917[37], but thereafter the discrepancies between the old and new regiments basically canceled each other out.[38] After the division left the Chemin des Dames sector, the numbers of convictions generally de-

[36] See Leonard V. Smith, "Command Authority in the French Army, 1914–1918: The Case of the 5e Division d'Infanterie" (Ph.D. diss., Columbia University, 1990), pp. 525–42.

[37] Overall, Guy Pedroncini found higher rates of desertion in divisions "lightly touched [peu touchée]" by collective incidents than in divisions "touchée," though the lowest incidences occurred in divisions without collective incidents. Les Mutineries de 1917, pp. 67–71.

[38] Convictions for desertions committed in the summer of 1917 were as follows:

	June	July	August
74e RI	19	6	8
274e RI	5	1	6
5e RI	4	7	2
Total	28	14	16

clined.[39] In the last seventeen months of the war, the *conseil de guerre* sufficed to keep "good soldiers" good after they had backed away from the specter of revolution during the mutinies.

A mosaic of responses from individual soldiers appears in the postal censorship records, much as before the mutinies. Reports continued to emphasize opinions at the extremes of the spectrum, those either highly optimistic or highly pessimistic. But like raid reports, postal censorship reports became more formulaic in the last seventeen months of the war. The reports perhaps best serve the function of illustrating a variety of individual strategies for coping with marginally improved but still dismal conditions of trench warfare.

Like soldiers throughout history, the soldiers of the 5e DI continued to complain about their food. Dissatisfaction proved especially acute in the Chemin des Dames sector, it would appear because of the difficulty of getting hot food to soldiers in such an active sector. A soldier from the 274e RI commented in July 1917: "for forty-five days, we haven't had any hot food. Always cold, and served in oil and vinegar."[40] But once the division left the sector, complaints diminished in intensity, and were counterbalanced by some expressions of outright contentment. A soldier of the 74e RI wrote in September 1917: "Happily, we are fed well enough, because the kitchens are close by and our food arrives hot."[41]

Anything perceived as capricious drew especially resentful observations. A soldier from the 74e RI writing in late July 1917 had his own explanation why his regiment had been kept in the front lines so long: "Here we have the third day that the regiments from our division have been relieved, and the 74e is still in line. Everyone gripes, probably even the officers. It's like a punishment, because the regiment rebelled before entering the sector."[42] A plan to institute ten-day leaves every four months (up from seven days previously) was supposed to take effect on 15 September 1917.[43] But it was delayed until 1 October, presumably because the 5e DI was in the process of taking up frontline positions in a new sector. A corporal from the 274e RI considered this an unfair infringement of the tacit contract between soldiers and commanders.

> It's been fifteen days already, and I have the number 3, and we still don't know yet when we'll be leaving. You know, to put off for fifteen days the beginning of

---

[39] Exceptions to this pattern were the worst months of bad weather and pitched battle respectively, January and July 1918. See Smith, "Command Authority," fig. VII-1.

[40] "Rapport" (274e RI), 21 July 1917, 16 N 1442.

[41] "Correspondance des militaires pour la France: semaine du 22 au 28 septembre 1917" (74e RI), 16 N 1400.

[42] "Rapport" (74e RI), 24 July 1917, 16 N 1442.

[43] On the new leave regime, see G.Q.G., *Réglement général du 5 september 1917 rélatif aux permissions et congés, avec les rectifications du 20 septembre et suivi de la circulaire du 12 août 1917 rélative aux titres de permissions* (Paris: Berger Levrault, 1920).

the 10-day leaves might make some people unhappy. I can't say anything, because liberty is forbidden to us [a reference to postal censorship], but it's always tough to be thanked like this because when we are in the lines and they ask something of us, we are ready to do it.[44]

General disgust with the prosecution of the war, so prominent during the mutinies, certainly never disappeared. A soldier from the 274e RI wrote in July 1917: "We are carrying out the war as a succession of injustices. No one is where he belongs, and the shirkers will remain shirkers until the end."[45] A letter seized by the authorities written by a sergeant from the same regiment in August 1917 could have been written during the mutinies:

I would like to know what is preventing our leaders from trying to make peace. What do they hope for in continuing the struggle? They could certainly end up exterminating the whole French race if this goes on. Here it is real butchery, and I hesitate to think of the men who are leading such a life in the middle of death and hell.

May the end come![46]

On the other hand, two soldiers from the 74e RI wrote just a few days later that all was as well as could be expected.[47] "In the area of the Chemin des Dames," wrote one, "I can assure you that we are holding off the Germans well." Another observed that "morale is holding up, because this is the idea of everybody: 'Keep trying.'" Many soldiers simply conveyed cynicism. A soldier from the 74e RI remarked wryly in September 1917: "We are leaving for the trenches, supposedly in a tranquil sector, but marshy. Once again we will be up to our bellies in water. It seems that it is a good sector for rheumatism."[48] The officer writing the censorship report concluded that "optimism strictly speaking does not exist, we can only call it resignation."

Postal censorship records after the mutinies devoted more attention to soldiers' views of the international political context of the war. Certainly, this was partly because the entry of the United States and the exit of Russia changed that context so dramatically. But one might also suppose that the censors had became more aware that the *poilus* were actually "political" animals after all. Opinion on France's allies, new and old, remained as diverse as soldiers' views of the war generally. A soldier from the 74e RI wrote in July 1917: "Victory is no longer in doubt now, the great demo-

[44] "Correspondance des militaires pour la France" (274e RI), 16 September 1917, in 16 N 1400.
[45] "Rapport" (274e RI), 21 July 1917, in 16 N 1442.
[46] "Rapport" (274e RI), 20 August 1917, in ibid.
[47] "Rapport" (74e RI), 22 August 1917, in ibid.
[48] "Correspondance des militaires pour la France" (74e RI), 15 September 1917, in 16 N 1400.

cratic ideas having gained a lot of ground in the last two months, notably in Russia, Spain, the United States, and in Greece. We see them now breaking loose in Austria. The day when the central empires are won over to this cause, the war will be over, and that day is not far off."[49] But few of his comrades shared this expectation that the end was near. A soldier from the 5ᵉ RI mentioned in the same report did not expect much from *les dough-boys* in the near future: "It looks like the war is going to drag slowly into another year, and that the Americans will not be ready before winter. It might not even be over next year."

In the wake of fresh disasters for the British in the Ypres salient and Paschendaele in the late summer and fall of 1917, expressions of confidence in the ally across the channel became even more rare. From a sector adjacent to the British, a soldier from the 74ᵉ RI wrote in October 1917: "As for the 'Tommies,' I don't know what they are capable of. . . . They are with us, but we would like them better back were they came from."[50] As the military skies continued to darken in the fall of 1917, with a second revolution in Russia and the Italian calamity at Caporetto, French soldiers found it more difficult to maintain confidence in their allies. By that time, soldiers generally showed little sympathy for the revolution in Russia, or at least felt themselves restrained from expressing it. A chaplain from the 5ᵉ DI wrote that at best, the American entry and the Russian exit would cancel each other out: "With the Americans, we will no doubt be able to hang on. But the war will be prolonged!"[51] The Italian defeat provoked the following comment from a soldier from the 5ᵉ RI: "Only the English and ourselves are left to go after the Boches, and we can only count on ourselves. . . . No doubt the Italians have done the same thing as the Russians, and must be completely disorganized. Let's hope that this offensive opens their eyes and that they will come back after this defeat."[52]

This collection of emotion and opinion is represented as a roller coaster of optimism and pessimism in the one thorough memoir from the 5ᵉ DI that continued to the end of the war, that of Private Legentil, the machine gunner from the 74ᵉ RI.[53] In the summer of 1917, he described the Grelines subsector along the Chemin des Dames as "constantly shelled and full of poisonous gas," but wrote with optimism of visits by the first American observers. He proclaimed that "the crusade of liberty has just renewed

[49] "Analyse de la correspondance étrangère, périod du 30 juin à 6 juillet" (VIᵉ Armée), 16 N 1419.

[50] "Rapport" (IIIᵉ Armée), 27–31 October 1917, in 16 N 1401.

[51] "Correspondance des militaires allant à l'étranger et correspondance venant de l'étranger pour les militaires" (IIIᵉ Armée), 1–7 December 1917, 16 N 1401.

[52] "Correspondance des militaires pour la France" (5ᵉ RI), 2 November 1917, 16 N 1401.

[53] "Notes de campagne du 12 avril 1915 au 11 novembre 1918: au jour le jour, bons et mauvais souvenirs," Fonds privés, 1 KT 86, pp. 22–33.

itself." He continued: "May they [the Americans] hurry up to join us in the lines; that will lighten our load, and we won't be jealous!" By August, Legentil was posted in a quieter subsector, though one night his highly esteemed section commander was killed by a German sniper. A small retaliatory raid took place the following night. Legentil did not hide his satisfaction when, in his words, "we clearly heard a cry, a Boche who had been hit, almost certainly right in the head! This consoled us a bit." It is worth noting that however sweet Legentil may have found revenge, violence in the sector did not escalate further thereafter.

By September 1917, Legentil was more happily installed in a much quieter sector near Saint-Quentin, "very tranquil and, it seems, rarely bombarded." His spirits were also raised by his new status as commander of a machine gun, which he obtained after a special training course behind the lines. Still, by October he grumbled that "the weather is horrible. It rains without stopping and the positions are transformed into a lake of mud!" By November, the success-turned-failure of the British at Cambrai further lowered his spirits, despite continuing improvements in food distribution. He wrote: "Frequent visits began by the hot food wagons, and we quickly saw things get better. They needed to and even so, how long can this last?"

On 16 January 1918, the 5ᵉ DI was posted to Camp de Saint Ouen in the Aube for a "*grand repos* [major rest]." The *grand repos* was at the heart of Pétain's plans to make life in the trenches as bearable as possible for the *poilus*, enabling soldiers to look forward to regular, complete, and comfortable respites well behind the front lines. Legentil's expectations were not fulfilled, to say the least. To get to the camp in the first place, the soldiers were herded into "unpleasant wagons for farm animals," in which they were packed together and slept on straw. He described the camp as more like a prison carefully separated from the civilian world than an area of rest and relaxation:

> The impression on our arrival was of feeling sad and disappointed. There was a big agglomeration of Adrian barracks, symmetrically aligned and big enough to receive the whole division. The nearest village house was in Saint Ouen, more than 2km away. All around, a great uncultivated plateau, all white and chalky, with only a few rickety fir-trees in a few places, trying to provide the air of a veritable oasis. At that time of the year, it was even worse. A very cold thaw transformed the soil into a lake of white and gluey mud that stuck to our boots. As a *grand repos*, we were hoping for better.

As if this were not enough, soldiers' days were filled with exercises and maneuvers that they found of dubious value. The crowning glory was a lecture on maneuver by a former reconnaissance pilot turned infantry consultant. He drew on prewar methods, as Legentil put it, "methods long since outdated, whose absurdity has been demonstrated by three years of war." While Legentil did not exactly look forward to going back in the trenches, he concluded of the *grand repos* that "the time dragged on, very monotonously."

One theme runs most consistently through the documentary record of the 5ᵉ DI in trench warfare after the mutinies. Few of the protagonists, soldiers or commanders, predicted an end to the war in the foreseeable future. The painfully negotiated settlement of repression, reforms, and proportionality had restrained certain miseries of trench warfare, yet the war continued. *Le Canard de Boyau*, the trench journal published by the 74ᵉ RI, quipped in the fall of 1917 that the war would end "when all the regiments know all the sectors," and perhaps more tellingly, "when all the shirkers are at the front and all the *poilus* of the front are shirkers."[54]

PROPORTIONALITY AND AGGRESSION: THE END OF THE WAR

A discouraging strategic situation greeted the Western Allies in the first quarter of 1918. Well-informed individuals in the senior French command agreed with the 5ᵉ DI chaplain cited previously—that American participation in the war would just about cancel out the final departure of the Russians after the Bolshevik call for an armistice in December 1917. Guy Pedroncini has convincingly shown that by early 1918, with Germany fighting on only one front, Pétain himself had largely lost faith in a total allied victory.[55] Pétain concluded that the most cost-effective approach would be to launch a major offensive in Alsace and Lorraine in 1919. A success there would enable France to realize its one concrete war aim—regaining the "lost territories." The theory was that possession would have proven nine-tenths of the law had peace broken out.

But just when Pétain had begun elaborate plans to win at checkers, the Germans kicked over the board and resumed playing chess, for the first time since 1914. In a dazzling display of surprise and tactical innovation, Gen. Erich Ludendorff's soldiers finally obtained the *percée*, first against the British in March and April and then against the French in May. The restored chess game of the war of movement brought in its wake the professional resurrection of Gen. Ferdinand Foch and the emergence of a more unified allied command.[56] After the spring of 1918, Foch commanded the allied reserves, one division of which was the 5ᵉ DI. Despite ever more desperate cries for help first from the British and then from Pétain, Foch

[54] *Le Canard de Boyau*, October–December 1917.
[55] Pedroncini, *Pétain: Général en chef*, pp. 110–38.
[56] Foch's star had faded with that of Joffre in late 1916. He had been put to work studying the unlikely prospect of a German invasion of Switzerland.

held back the reserves until July 1918, when he determined that they could be deployed to maximum effect. His success kept the front from recongealing, right up to the armistice on 11 November.

In the process, Foch acquired the reputation of a military genius comparable to Napoleon. All over Europe and in the United States, Foch's newfound and numerous admirers dusted off copies of his 1903 École de Guerre lectures, published as *Des Principes de la guerre* [*On the Principles of War*]. In the book, Foch could scarcely have stated more clearly the spiritual foundations of the prewar doctrine of the offensive: "War = the domain of moral force. Victory = Moral superiority of the victors; Moral depression of the vanquished. Battle = the contest between the two wills."[57] Given Foch's historical aura, one might believe that the war had come full circle. After some 1.3 million French soldiers lay dead, perhaps "moral superiority" had led the French army to victory after all, just as the proponents of the doctrine of the offensive had predicted before the war. The French high command, such an argument would continue, had managed to reimpose "high morale" on French soldiers after their bout with military vertigo during the mutinies.

But I will argue in the battle narratives provided here that the components of the "high morale" of the 5e DI in the pitched battles of 1918 proved far more complicated and ambiguous. Whether the command structure thought it was playing checkers or chess, soldiers continued to calculate the utility and the proportionality of aggression on their own terms. Their commitment to aggression never became open-ended. The old and new soldiers of the 5e DI would fight aggressively only as long as they perceived that this aggression supplemented rather than replaced the army's physical resources. In the end, mutual recognition of the real balance of power between soldiers and commanders provided the foundation of the 5e DI's "morale" in the last months of the war. A.J.P. Taylor wisely observed of Foch's ascendancy over the Germans that "he had to take success as it came, not as he wanted it."[58] The same could be said of what posterity has construed as Foch's "ascendancy" over the dynamic between soldiers and their commanders.

The 5e DI took part in three attacks, or more accurately, the two attacks and one pursuit. From 18 July to 26 July, the division fought the Second Battle of the Marne, the first of the French counteroffensives. From 26 August to 18 September, the division participated in the push toward the Hindenburg Line, in the Chemin des Dames sector of unblessed memory.

---

[57] The version cited here is the first English edition, with a new preface by Foch dated 1 September 1918. Marshal Foch, *The Principles of War*, Hilaire Belloc, trans. (London: Chapman and Hall, 1918), p. 287.

[58] A.J.P. Taylor, *The First World War: An Illustrated History* (London: Hamish Hamilton, 1963), p. 231.

Finally, in the last weeks of the war (14 October–11 November) the division pursued the retreating Germans alongside the Belgian army in Flanders east of the former Ypres salient.

The Second Battle of the Marne: 18–28 July

The Second Battle of the Marne shared strategic circumstance as well as location with its 1914 namesake. As at the First Battle of the Marne, the French struck back at an overextended and exhausted enemy who had made dramatic territorial gains without destroying the opposing armies. Foch, like Joffre before him, drew the Germans into a sack, then hit them from all sides. The 5e DI formed part of the Xe Armée, commanded by the rehabilitated Gen. Charles Mangin, attacking the western side of the German salient.

The 5e DI played the part in the Second Battle of the Marne that it was supposed to have played in the Chemin des Dames offensive.[59] On 18 July, the first day of the battle, it charged through a break created by the 128e DI in the still-fluid German position. As shown on map IX-2, the first objective was the Buisson de Hautwisson, a plateau surrounded by a wooded area. To achieve surprise, no preparatory artillery barrage took place, only a rolling barrage accompanying the attackers.

The 18 July attack took place successfully; the Germans were thoroughly surprised, and caught in the middle of a relief in the front lines. By the end of the day, the plateau had been taken. The Germans had set up "islands of resistance," mostly machine-gun nests in the wooded area, but since they did not have enough time to prepare the whole position in depth, they could be surrounded and conquered by the French without seriously slowing down the attack.

This pattern of combat continued for the next three days. On 19 July, the attack began at 0400, and proceeded across open fields filled with German machine guns. Although this made the 5e DI's task "extremely difficult," in de Roig's words, the French were able to use their own machine guns effectively to cover the attacking foot soldiers. However, by 22 July the attack had slowed, the result of cumulative casualties and general weariness. Although some additional progress toward Oulchy-le-Château took place on 23 July, by 24 July the division had come to a halt.

The all-out effort made by the 5e DI on 25 July to take Oulchy-la-Ville and Oulchy-le-Château proved Pétain's adage that the artillery conquers and the infantry occupies. The division artillery expended 5,500 heavy

---

[59] This win/lose narrative is based on "Rapport sur les opérations de la 5e Division d'Inf. du 18 au 28 juillet 1918 (characteristiques et particularités), No 8904/3," 5e DI *JMO*, 26 N 269.

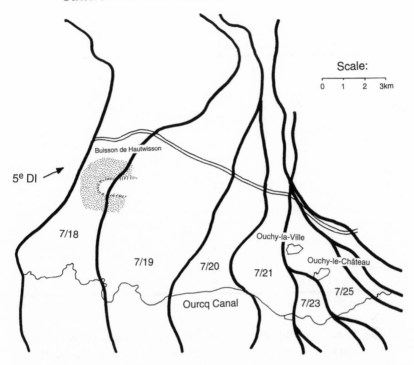

Scale:

0   1   2   3km

Buisson de Hautwisson

5ᵉ DI

7/18

7/19

7/20

7/21

Ouchy-la-Ville

Ouchy-le-Château

7/25

7/23

Ourcq Canal

MAP IX-2. The Advance of the 5ᵉ DI, 18–25 July 1918

artillery shells and 20,000 campaign artillery shells (principally from 75mm pieces) along an attack front of 6.2 kilometers. This corresponded to one heavy shell per 1.16 meters of attack front and 1 campaign artillery shell per 32 cm of front (or 3 shells per meter).[60] This broke an already malleable German position.[61] The 5ᵉ DI occupied the villages the next day with relatively few casualties, and spent 26 July consolidating gains. It was relieved on the night of 27–28 July.

In the Second Battle of the Marne, the 5ᵉ DI conquered a total of fourteen kilometers in seven days. It also captured seventy cannons and an "enormous" amount of materiel. That the Germans should leave so much precious firepower behind suggested a retreat in haste and disorder. But the battle also proved an immensely costly engagement for the 5ᵉ DI. Total

[60] The calculations are my own, based on a measurement of the front shown in map IX-2, divided by the numbers of expended shells provided in de Roig's report.

[61] The relative fluidity of the German position in the restored war of movement remains the key distinction here. In the failed May 1916 attack on the fort at Douaumont, for example, the French expended 7,587 heavy artillery (155 C.) shells on the day of the attack, over a front of just over 1.1 km. See Mangin's report, "L'Attaque du Plateau de Douaumont par la 5ᵉ Division d'Inf. (22–24 Mai 1916)," 5ᵉ DI, 3ᵉ Bureau, 24 N 87.

TABLE IX-1

Casualties, 5e RI and 74e RI: 18–26 July 1918

(All Ranks Combined)

	7/18	7/19	7/20	7/21	7/22	7/23	7/24	7/25	7/26
5e RI:									
Killed	7	22	26	11	21	13	6	2	—
Wounded	69	193	89	88	100	48	17	32	7
Missing	5	7	2	17	—	1	—	—	—
74e RI:									
Killed	6	6	14	20	13	25	5	18	2
Wounded	57	191	116	124	91	117	82	51	12
Missing	1	1	—	4	1	7	2	4	4
Daily Total	145	420	247	264	226	211	112	107	25
Cumulative Total	145	565	812	1,076	1,302	1,513	1,625	1,732	1,757

Source: JMOs, 5e RI, 74e RI.

casualties comprised 80 officers and 3,300 NCOs and common soldiers. Daily and cumulative figures are provided in table IX-1 for the 74e RI and the 5e RI, the two regiments for which such survive. Total casualties are all the more striking considering that the division comprised only three infantry regiments, compared with five at the first attack at Neuville–St. Vaast in 1915 and four at Verdun in 1916. Plenty of *grignotage* accompanied the *percée*.

The "experiential" narrative of the Second Battle of the Marne will argue that proportionality by no means precluded aggression, even with very high casualties.[62] But soldiers' commitment to aggression never became open-ended. They continued to communicate to their commanders when they perceived no additional utility to their efforts, and compelled the latter to take notice. Indeed, this communication became more explicit than ever. In the end, soldierly aggression in 1918 was not so much reimposed from above as repurchased with massive amounts of materiel.

Soldiers seemed well aware from the outset that the offensive beginning 18 July took place under qualitatively different circumstances. For the first time since 1914, they did not have to advance against withering enemy fire

[62] The documentary record for the Second Battle of the Marne remains about as sparse as that of its namesake. As had been the case throughout the war, the 5e DI's most militarily successful operations generated the least documentation. The entire documentary record comprises little save the JMOs supplemented with a smattering of brief reports and ever more formulaic postal censorship accounts.

from entrenched positions. Quite the contrary, they perceived that the French had finally gained the upper hand. One soldier wrote in a letter that "the effects of our explosives are terrifying," another that "I'm sorry that you haven't been among us to see the drive of everybody in feeling the Boche begin to break."[63] The use of infiltration tactics against the disrupted German positions, particularly by the 5e RI shooting through the "door" opened up by the 128e DI, demonstrated that aggression did not necessarily depend on strict command surveillance.[64]

The figures in table IX-1 show that daily casualties declined substantially over the course of the engagement. But the high cumulative totals make it necessary to interrogate the resilience of the consensus between soldiers and commanders. Soldiers never relinquished the right to determine their own solution in the field. The evolution of the dynamic of authority relations was perhaps best described by an unlikely source, an officer writing a postal censorship report dated 4 August: "If the enthusiasm of the first hour is a bit attenuated, a *reasoned satisfaction* has substituted itself, increasing as the results expand in importance and significance."[65] Soldiers' reasoned satisfaction, of course, could be reasonably withdrawn. "Their problem," the officer concluded, "is weariness, very great weariness, the inevitable consequence of prolonged combat and privation." One letter he quoted agreed: "We are waiting impatiently to be relieved, and I think this cannot be far away for us."

The command structure, for its part, took pains not to push too far soldiers' consent to aggression in 1918. By 23 July, messages began to be transmitted up the command structure that the division was coming to the end of its offensive capacities.[66] Major Dubois of the 224e RI reported to General de Roig that one of his companies had been reduced to four soldiers and one corporal.[67] In the 5e RI, Lieutenant Colonel Roustic reported that in his 3e Compagnie, only one second lieutenant and about thirty men were able to conduct further combat. He requested tanks (evidently unavailable) to keep the attack going. Lieutenant Colonel Sabaton, the 224e RI commander, stated the point more bluntly: "Further progress does not seem possible with the means we have, despite the heroism of the survivors."

General de Roig's report to his own superiors for 23 July drew the necessary conclusions. He chose his words carefully, though, as he had

[63] "Rapport de la Sous-Commission de Contrôle de la correspondance metropolitaine (Période du 26 juillet au 2 août)" (Xe Armée), 4 August 1918, 16 N 1466.

[64] See 5e RI *JMO*, 18 July 1918, 26 N 577.

[65] "Rapport de la Sous-Commission" (Xe Armée), 4 August 1918. Emphasis added.

[66] The following draws from an untitled series of short reports for 23 July in Xe Armée, 3e Bureau, 16 N 1656.

[67] A company at full strength would comprise about two hundred men. While it is certainly possible that all but five of them had become casualties, it is more likely that Dubois made a grim estimate based on inadequate information.

good reason to know how Mangin dealt with faint-hearted subordinates. De Roig observed that the "casualties have been very heavy and have reduced considerably the fighting personnel." He continued that "although the combat capacities" of the division were "necessarily diminished" by the casualties, "the division will continue its mission in the evening of 23 July; the orders have been given for the progression to continue. But the attack will be pursued with very reduced means and with weakened troops."

But something clearly had changed since the "stopped" offensives of 1915. The next major assault was delayed for two days and took place under the French artillery avalanche noted earlier. General de Roig could not have been more pleased with "reasoned satisfaction" supporting the efforts of the division. He congratulated his artillery for "crushing the enemy with rapid and precise fire."[68] He praised his infantry as "supple in maneuver, unshakable before counterattacks, irresistible in the assault. . . . I thank you and congratulate you from the bottom of my heart." One of his soldiers quoted by the postal censors returned the compliment: "Our general went to a lot of trouble, working day and night without stopping, going himself to the observation posts and from time to time to the front lines to distribute chocolate and cigarettes."[69]

But in a memo issued even before the last 5e DI attack, Pétain hinted ominously that the new consensus between soldiers and their commanders was based on a level of shell consumption that might not prove sustainable.[70] Pétain observed that "the habit has been established of firing daily five or six times the number of projectiles fired by the Germans, and no one dares claim that the results are worth the expenditures of shells. . . . This bad habit must not continue." The available stock of 75mm shells shrank dramatically, from 28 million in March 1918 to 8.5 million by October.[71] In the summer of 1918, it remained far from certain that commanders would be able to keep their part of the bargain in the negotiated settlement of aggression in pitched battles.

The Threat of Grignotage: Toward the Hindenburg Line, 28 August–18 September

The 5e DI attacks along the Aisne River toward the Chemin des Dames proved its last extended phase of pitched battle in the war. It took place

---

[68] "Ordre général No. 510," 30 July 1918, 5e DI, 3e Bureau, 24 N 93.

[69] "Rapports de la Sous-commission," 16 N 1466.

[70] "Note pour les groupes d'armées et les armées, No. 23546 (à repartir jusqu'à l'echelon division)," 19 July 1918, in Xe Armée, 3e Bureau, 19 N 1656.

[71] Aublet, "L'Artillerie française," p. 245.

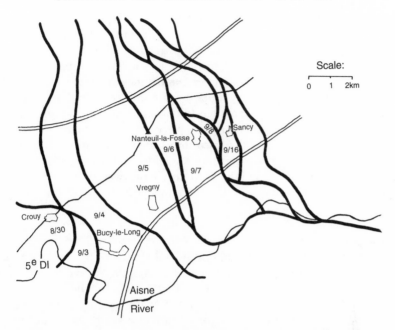

MAP IX-3. The Advance of the 5ᵉ DI, 30 August–16 September 1918

against the background of accelerating Allied military success, as the Germans lost piece by piece the gains made since the spring offensive. General Ludendorff referred to 8 August as the "black day of the German army," as British and Commonwealth forces advanced to the northeast from Amiens. By the end of September, continuing Allied attacks restored the battle lines before the German offensive along most of the front. The German High Command concluded that the war had been lost, and prevailed on the government by 4 October to appeal directly to President Wilson for an armistice based on the Fourteen Points.

The 5ᵉ DI made a worthy contribution to the Allied success in the field, under far more difficult conditions than the counterattack the preceding July. The terrain shown on map IX-3 presented considerable difficulties. The French and German infantries were squeezed between two ridges, in the basin of the Aisne River. Soldiers thus could be pounded by the opposing artilleries with no natural protection. The river itself, of course, constituted a significant natural barrier to the French advance. Moreover, the French knew that any progress simply brought them closer to the Hindenburg Line, toward some of the best-prepared positions anywhere on the Western Front.

The map indicates three main phases of the attack. The first phase (28 August–4 September) involved taking and maintaining a foothold on the right bank of the Aisne.[72] In the second phase (5–8 September), the "war of movement" proceeded much as it had in July. In the third phase (9–18 September), the division took one additional village, Sancy, and withstood several German counterattacks before it was relieved in the sector. Although the German position never crumbled, the combination of infiltration tactics and strong artillery support again showed their worth.[73] In all, the 5ᵉ DI had progressed some ten kilometers, and had captured some seven hundred prisoners, ten artillery pieces, and two thousand rifles.[74] French casualties were less than two-thirds their totals for the July offensive, at least for the two regiments for which figures exist. Combined casualties for the 74ᵉ RI and the 5ᵉ RI during the twenty days the division spent in the front lines were 1,015 (compared with 1,757 for the July offensive).[75]

If the win/lose narrative of the push of the 5ᵉ DI toward the Hindenburg Line recounted hard-won though considerable success, the "experiential" narrative will recount a far more stern test than the Second Battle of the Marne of the compromise on pitched battle between soldiers and their commanders. Refighting the Battle of the Marne in July 1918 could be construed as having a certain heroic aura. Once again, the French army could rescue the nation in its darkest hour and show that it could still attack after four years of bloody stalemate and a serious mutiny. But a different and more trying situation presented itself by the end of August. Legentil, the machine gunner from the 74ᵉ RI was not the only soldier to find it "not reassuring" that the French were attacking from the positions 1915—that is, behind even the modest gains made by the 1917 Chemin des Dames offensive.[76] The success of the division in the sector proved a near thing—and the protagonists knew it. The narrative here suggests that Foch's "moral force" had a different and more limited meaning than it had

---

[72] No comprehensive survey exists comparable to General de Roig's report for the July counteroffensive. The win/lose narrative here draws from three sources: the skeletal narrative in the *Pages héroiques*, the 74ᵉ RI and the 5ᵉ RI *JMO*s, and an incomplete series of daily reports from de Roig, "Compte Rendue des événements," 28 August–8 September 1918, in 5ᵉ DI, 3ᵉ Bureau, 24 N 95.

[73] Based on calculations from de Roig's daily reports, shell consumption was running about one 75mm shell per meter of attack front and one 155mm shell per eight meters of attack front. On two days of exceptional activity (29 August and 3 September), consumption approximated those of the 25 July attack.

[74] Louis Lecoc, *Pages héroiques de la 5ᵉ Division d'Infanterie* (Paris: S.T.D.I.5., 1918), p. 117.

[75] 74ᵉ RI and 5ᵉ RI *JMO*s. The breakdown is as follows:

74ᵉ RI: 83 killed, 442 wounded, 2 missing;

5ᵉ RI: 63 killed, 374 wounded, 51 missing.

[76] Legentil, "Notes de campagne," pp. 50.

in 1903 or it would after 11 November 1918. As the *Pages héroiques* put it, "the energy of the French had to last one-quarter hour longer than the energy of the Germans."[77]

In a letter dated 25 August (three days before the attack), a soldier from the 224e RI provided a moving description of soldiers' willfully optimistic but volatile state of mind:

> It is impossible to describe to you the weariness, the discouragement (happily ephemeral) that was on the face of all these men, bowing under the same discipline, under a single will. There are moments when you are tempted to throw everything to the ground, but against yourself, in seeing all your comrades march, personal dignity rises up again, and self-respect once more takes hold of you. It is at this moment that the memory of those dear to you brings back the strength and the energy that had escaped. Nothing else could produce the same effects in getting you to hold on to the end. The prospect of new suffering does not frighten me. What's more, our present victories give greater encouragement to our weakening forces.[78]

The same soldier reported that this "single" will emerged under extraordinary circumstances. The 224e RI, he wrote, had become an "amalgam of the races," with soldiers from Cayenne, Réunion, Guadelupe, and Indochina mixed in with white French troops. Sociability, it turned out, could cross racial lines. He continued that he found "elements of solid comradery" among the non-European contingents, and "the necessary forces for our present and future existence."[79]

The staff officer writing the report in which this letter appeared tactfully observed that while soldiers' enthusiasm for the war never evaporated, they were aware that "certain attacks had not delivered what had been expected," and that "the combat to come was envisaged as becoming more and more difficult." Legentil certainly did not see the imminent end of the war that seemed so clear in retrospect.[80] He recalled that his section was assigned an advance of 3.5 kilometers on the first day of the attack, but that "once again, the staff proposed and the Boches disposed."[81] Concentrated

---

[77] *Pages héroiques*, p. 117.

[78] "Rapport de la sous-commission de contrôle de la correspondance metropolitaine (période du 30 août–5 septembre)," 16 N 1466.

[79] Although no reason exists to doubt the veracity of this statement, I have found no corroborating evidence of such an extraordinary racial integration of a regular metropolitan regiment.

[80] He confessed some momentary reservation about some new reinforcements, a combination of twenty-year-olds from the class of 1918 and men previously classified as unfit for active duty. But he affirmed that the new recruits quickly learned the art of soldiering from their more experienced comrades. Legentil concluded with satisfaction that "they performed their duty very well, even in the most critical moments." "Notes de campagne," p. 56.

[81] Ibid.

German machine-gun fire kept Legentil and the engineers pinned down on the left bank of the Aisne. The Germans issued countermanding orders the next day as well, orders that Legentil seemed to have taken more seriously than the French ones:

> On the 29th, at 10h, (by which time we were supposed to have advanced 6km!), the order arrived to try another crossing. In broad daylight, this was crazy! I was supposed to locate the enemy machine gun and make it possible for the bridge builders to complete their work. In the event, it was evident that even if I succeeded in neutralizing this piece, others placed elsewhere would resume their murderous fire.[82]

Legentil's most unambiguously successful episode according to conventional military wisdom involved the surrender of some one hundred German soldiers. The Germans had made their own calculation about proportionality and therein perhaps proved the empirical essence of Foch's "moral force" argument—convincing the enemy that further sacrifice was not proportional to the extent of the sacrifice demanded. Legentil suddenly heard Germans crying "*Kamarad!*" in the woods and surrendering in small groups. They reported that they had been given the suicide mission of slowing down the French attack by forming an island of resistance, and had been without food for four days. Like the surrendering French soldiers throughout this study, these Germans saw no point to heroic death as an end in itself when the enemy exerted a preponderance of force. Such a calculation encouraged Legentil to respond generously: "They were discouraged and famished, but smiling, happy to be safe and sound, and falling on the few pieces of bread we gave them."[83]

Legentil's account of his section's last days in the offensive emphasized that moral ascendancy could only accompany the French army's physical resources, not replace them. By 13 September, the progress of Legentil's section had come to a halt. The section was positioned on a plateau above the village of Sancy, which was still occupied by the Germans. They were thus exposed to fire both from the Germans to their rear and from French artillery overshooting the village. Renault light tanks sent to assist on 14 September were put out of action by German antitank shells before they even got as far as the plateau. Flamethrowers did not permit any further French advance on 15 September, and indeed a German counterattack obliged the French to retreat. Technological innovation and capital-intensive warfare had their limits.[84]

---

[82] Ibid.

[83] Ibid., p. 53.

[84] Legentil himself had left on leave on 16 September, two days before the division was withdrawn from the sector. The fact that leaves were granted at all under such circumstances showed that something had changed since the pitched battles of 1915 and 1916.

Epilogue: The Push in Belgium, 14 October–11 November

The last engagement of the 5ᵉ DI demonstrates both the grandeur and misery of proportionality, at least in a conventional military sense. The war for the 5ᵉ DI could be construed as ending in something of an anticlimax, much as it did elsewhere on the Western Front. The division entered Belgium against the background of an imploding German war effort. The surrender of Bulgaria on 29 September and the gradual disintegration of the Habsburg Monarchy in October opened Germany's southern flank to Gen. Franchet d'Esperey's Armée de l'Orient marching northwest from Greece. Prince Max of Baden's appeal to President Wilson on 4 October opened the floodgates of war weariness in Germany itself. In the field, the German army functioned more coherently than the German High Command or the German government. The German army retreated in clear and unbroken lines, but it retreated all the same—and faster than at any time since the first battle of the Marne.

Throughout the last month of fighting, the 5ᵉ DI was attached to the Armée française de Belgique, which together with some British units and the Belgian army pushed east of the former Ypres salient into Flanders. From either a win/lose or experiential perspective, the Belgian offensive was in some ways the 5ᵉ DI's least interesting major engagement during the entire war. Simply put, the Germans retreated and the French followed. German resistance consisted of rearguard actions by the artillery and especially machine-gun nests covering the retreat of the German infantry. As the division progressed, according to General de Roig, "the Belgians received our troops with cries of 'Vive la France!'"[85] An attack scheduled for 0700 on 17 October had to be called off because the Germans had already retreated from the objectives.[86]

But as shown in table IX-2, the advance of the 5ᵉ DI into Belgium remained surprisingly dangerous given its uninteresting military character. To the end, misery accompanied grandeur. The defense retained a certain advantage, as soldiers marching through the open Flanders countryside proved vulnerable to machine guns and artillery. The Germans returned home after the armistice not looking like a defeated army in no small measure because their rear guards had covered their retreat so effectively. As late as 10 November, General de Roig reported that "the enemy resists above all with numerous and active machine-guns that have an excellent firing field over our sector."[87] The number of French soldiers reported "missing" is suspiciously high, given that the division actually made very

---

[85] "Compte-rendu des événements du 15 au 16 octobre 1918, No. 13/F-3," in 5ᵉ DI, 3ᵉ Bureau, 24 N 96.

[86] "Compte-rendu des événements du 16 au 17 octobre 1918, No. 18/F-3," in ibid.

[87] "Compte-rendu des événements du 10 novembre 1918," in ibid.

TABLE IX-2
Infantry Casualties, 5ᵉ DI:
13 October–11 November 1918
(All Ranks Combined)

Unit	Killed	Wounded	Missing
5ᵉ RI	78	368	81
74ᵉ RI	66	327	89
224ᵉ RI	66	373	40
Total	210	1,068	210

Source: "Pertes du 13 octobre au 11 novembre 1918," 22 November 1918, in 5ᵉ DI, 3ᵉ Bureau, 24 N 96.

little contact with German infantry that could have taken them prisoner. Conceivably, a number actually deserted, though no wave of court-martial prosecutions occurred after the armistice.

In all, the division had advanced over forty kilometers in its last campaign, and captured over 1,350 prisoners, eleven artillery pieces, plus machine guns and trench mortars in "great quantities."[88] Still, French losses on the scale noted help explain why Foch granted an armistice when he did instead of waiting for a total military victory, and why the armistice required large amounts of materiel to be turned over immediately. The French interest in disarming the German war machine went beyond simple Gallic vindictiveness.

It is difficult to add much to a standard narrative of the outbreak of peace at 1100 on 11 November 1918—the descent of an eerie calm after the guns stopped firing and the general incredulity that the war was actually over. The significance of the outbreak of peace to this study lies in the simple human joy felt by the combatants, a joy perhaps based not least in the preservation of some human dignity rendered through combatants' contribution to shaping their own wartime experience.

The drama leading to the armistice is perhaps best conveyed through Legentil's memoir. As early as 10 October, he knew that Prince Max of Baden had exchanged telegrams with President Wilson, and that the war might soon be over. He recalled cheerfully that a few days later when the division went back into the front lines "the recent good news has not weakened our courage, and it was always with the same resignation that we all got ready to 'do it all again.'"[89]

Once in the sector, of course, Legentil's principal concern revolved around not getting killed in the last quarter hour of the war. On the first day

[88] "Prises faites du 14 octobre au 11 novembre 1918," 22 November 1918, in ibid.
[89] Legentil, "Notes de campagne," p. 57.

of the offensive, he accepted the surrender of a group of Germans. But as he was preparing the orders for his section to depart bullets from two snipers started whizzing by. Miraculously, no one was hurt. When the two snipers surrendered shortly thereafter, Legentil recalled, "I could feel my revolver acting on its own in my hand," though ultimately, "we were content to give them a well-placed smack."[90] The division was resting behind the lines from 24 October–8 November, raising soldiers' hopes anew that they would not have to go into the lines before peace broke out. The second disappointment was received with less equanimity than the first: "Everyone was depressed, because we knew that the Boches had asked for an armistice and we were hoping that news would come before our turn came to go back into line. Alas, there was none, and each of us, feeling the end near, was afraid of dying so close to the end."[91]

When the end came, it seemed at first like an anticlimax within an anticlimax. At 0930 on 11 November, Legentil's section entered the village of Dikkelvenne, which the Germans had left some time ago. Ten minutes later, the captain commanding the machine-gun company learned of a German line of resistance of unknown strength about one kilometer away. On his own authority, he suspended any attack until 1100, in case the widespread rumors of an armistice proved correct. Not long thereafter, a bicyclist arrived from the regimental colonel, and disappeared into the battalion headquarters nearby. A minute later, the battalion commander emerged, waving his helmet and crying, "*Ça y est, les gars! C'est fini!* [That's it boys, it's over!]" Legentil recalled that initially the news "produced a brutal shock in our brains, which were insufficiently prepared to believe it. It took several minutes for us to be convinced that it was the truth." Once the information was processed, all distinctions of rank among the soldiers of the 5e DI disappeared for a moment in common elation, as a new chapter opened in all their lives:

> Reactions were very different according to the individual. Characters always differ, and as we began to loosen up, some hugged each other, others jumped up and down and danced, others tried to sing, while some cried. As for me, five minutes later, I was still in a daze. My head hurt, and I wanted to laugh as much as I wanted to cry. Finally, my lucidity completely returned, and I felt the joy, the immense joy, rising up in my heart, as my thoughts turned to my loved ones.[92]

[90] Ibid., p.60. The French reads: "nous nous contentons de leur foutre une râclée bien soignée."
[91] Ibid., p. 71.
[92] Ibid., p. 75.

CHAPTER X

Conclusion

THE NARRATIVE presented here of the experience of the 5ᵉ DI might appear to end in something of an anticlimax, because it fails to define a causal relationship between the evolution of the power dynamic within the French army between soldiers and commanders and the outcome of the war. That we are tempted to seek such a relationship speaks to the abiding influence of the "win/lose" narrative conventions of military history. I have argued here that in some sense soldiers "won" their battle within the army because they proved able to play a meaningful role in shaping the parameters of command authority. But while the outcome of this struggle may have prevented France from losing the war, neither did that outcome in itself determine the French "victory." Indeed, to the extent that France "won" in 1918, the causes were to a good degree circumstantial, in that they lay outside France and its army. The Germans broke the stalemate by achieving the *percée* against the British in March 1918, and thereby restoring the war of movement. The American presence (or perhaps more accurately the promise of unlimited American resources in men and materiel) saw to it that the Western Front did not recongeal as it had in 1914.

The task remains, then, of locating other contexts besides those of conventional military history, and situating my conclusions in these contexts. World War I historiography has enjoyed something of a renaissance since the late 1970s, and offers a variety of analytical approaches. Two broad areas will be considered here. First, I will consider the relationship of this study to a debate between what might broadly be referred to as "cultural" versus "social" historians of World War I. Second, I will compare other national models of soldiers and society during World War I to the French citizen-soldier.

"Cultural" historians are identified here simply as historians of intellectual and artistic responses to the war.[1] These historians could be considered heirs to the literary tradition of World War I. For them, the war marked a watershed in Western history, in which the nineteenth-century belief in the certainty of progress alongside social stability became the most universal casualty. Samuel Hynes, to cite one example, argued that English culture generated a "Myth of the War" completely formulated by the

[1] That such a distinction is not in the end so simple is outlined in an elegant survey by Lynn Hunt, "Introduction: History, Culture, and Text," in idem, ed., *The New Cultural History* (Berkeley and Los Angeles: University of California Press, 1989), pp. 1–22.

1930s and not fundamentally altered since. This myth (meaning a set of cultural icons) revolved around innocent and idealistic young men being sent by their elders to death or physical and emotional mutilation that "separated their own generation from the past and from their cultural inheritance."[2]

Even historians such as Robert Wohl, who saw a "lost generation" in formation well before the guns of August 1914 began to fire, argued for the primacy of wartime experience: "The front taught an unforgettable lesson in generationalism to those who came to know it."[3] Likewise, Modris Eksteins emphasized the prewar origins of modernity, of what he called "the contemporary interpretation of Goethe's invocation *stirb und werde,* die and become."[4] Eksteins drew his title from Igor Stravinsky's 1913 ballet developing this theme, *The Rite of Spring.* But to Eksteins as well as Wohl, the war itself carried the cultural messages of modernity to European society at large.

Certainly, to historians of cultural dislocation, no intellectual or artistic premonitions could adequately have prepared the thoughtful people of Europe for the horrors of 1914–18 and the ensuing discontinuities with inherited Western beliefs in progress and in a rationally ordered universe. Paul Fussell observed that "every war is ironic because every war is worse than expected," in that "its means are so melodramatically disproportionate to its presumed ends."[5] But even so, World War I proved "more ironic than any before or since," because of the century of bourgeois certainty preceding it.[6] Eric Leed examined the ways these ironies were internalized by soldiers. Once the initial process of "liminality" stripped away combatants' prewar identities, they could relocate themselves only in the context of their shared experience at the front.[7] "The front" in an emotional sense remained the soldiers' only home even after the war ended, through a variety of veterans' communities, some of which served as direct conduits to fascism in the 1920s and 1930s. Eksteins likewise connected subsequent twentieth-century traumas to unhealed cultural wounds of World War I. Trench veteran Cpl. Adolf Hitler and his Nazi movement offered "spring without end," meaning the chance to "die and become" perpetually.[8]

In contrast, social historians, in the tradition of the Annales School, have

---

[2] Samuel Hynes, *A War Imagined: The First World War and English Culture* (New York: Atheneum, 1991), p. xii.

[3] Robert Wohl, *The Generation of 1914* (Cambridge: Harvard University Press, 1979).

[4] Modris Eksteins, *Rites of Spring: The Great War and the Birth of the Modern Age* (New York: Houghton Mifflin, 1989), p. xiii.

[5] Paul Fussell, *The Great War and Modern Memory* (New York: Oxford University Press, 1975), p. 7.

[6] Ibid., p. 8.

[7] Eric Leed, *No Man's Land: Combat and Identity in World War I* (New York: Cambridge University Press, 1979), especially "The Internalization of War," pp. 210–13.

[8] Eksteins, *Rites of Spring,* chapter 10, "Spring without End," pp. 300–331.

stressed the *longue durée* (long run) of resilience and social cohesion beneath the *événements* (particular events) of cultural fragmentation that so traumatized the elites.[9] Not surprisingly, such conclusions have been especially prominent among French historians. To some extent, this can be seen as part of a general revision of twentieth-century French history, in which "Eternal France" endures beneath the successive traumas of World War I, the Depression, the defeat of 1940, Vichy, and the Algerian War.[10] The Pedroncini thesis on the 1917 mutinies belongs to this historiographical school, through its focus on the abiding institutional soundness of the French army. Likewise, Antoine Prost argued forcefully that the link between trench experience and fascism through veterans' organizations had been much exaggerated. In a masterful three-volume study, he concluded that consistent loyalty to the Third Republic characterized these organizations as a whole.[11]

But the thesis of underlying French resilience in World War I is most directly connected to Jean-Jacques Becker, widely recognized as the doyen among living French historians of the war. In his definitive 1977 study of French public opinion in 1914, Becker described a general population motivated from the outset by grim resolution rather than by Eksteins's frantic, nihilistic nationalism.[12] In a survey of the whole war published in 1980, Becker concluded that the *Union sacrée* at the outbreak of the war weakened, but never broke.[13] For the French, "even the duration of the war incontestably contributed to their resolution or their submission to it. One could not admit defeat after having consented to so much effort, so many sacrifices, so many dead."[14] Becker reaffirmed this conclusion in 1988; "the great mutation" brought about by the war concerned principally material society, specifically postwar inflation and the demographic aftershock the devastating blow the war caused the active male population. As

[9] On the Annales School, see Traian Stoianovich, *French Historical Method: The Annales Paradigm* (Ithaca: Cornell University Press, 1976); and Lynn Hunt, "French History in the Last Twenty Years: The Rise and Fall of the *Annales* Paradigm," *Journal of Contemporary History* 21 (1986): 209–24.

[10] Recent Vichy historiography has figured especially prominently in this trend, as historians have sought to modify the conclusions of Robert O. Paxton, *Vichy France: Old Guard and New Order* (New York: Alfred A. Knopf, 1972). See, for example, Pierre Laborie, *L'Opinion française sous Vichy* (Paris: Éditions du Seuil, 1990).

[11] Antoine Prost, *Les Anciens Combattants et la société française, 1914–1939*, 3 vols. (Paris: Presses de la Fondation des Sciences Politiques, 1977).

[12] Jean-Jacques Becker, *1914: Comment les français sont entrés dans la guerre* (Paris: Presses de la Fondation nationale des Sciences politiques, 1977).

[13] The term "Union sacrée" refers specifically to a parliamentary truce, in which representatives of the Left, Right, and Center agreed to bury their hatchets of difference for the duration.

[14] Jean-Jacques Becker, *Les Français pendant la grande guerre* (Paris: Éditions Robert Laffont, 1980), p. 305.

for the French people, from 1914 on "they believed themselves deeply patriotic, but they did not want to know that they would no longer have the force to demonstrate their patriotism."[15]

Becker's thesis continued to gain ground over the course of the 1980s. His most prominent student, Stéphane Audoin-Rouzeau, argued in a 1986 study of trench newspapers that the mature and reflective patriotism of French soldiers survived four years of ubiquitous death, pain, and (not least) official and unofficial censorship.[16] In another study, Audoin-Rouzeau traced the construction of the World War I *Union sacrée* back to the Franco-Prussian War of 1870–71.[17] The French interest in the continuities maintained through World War I has spread to social historians from other countries. J. M. Winter, drawing as well from the demographic history tradition at Cambridge University, published a 1985 study pointing to surprisingly positive effects of the war on living standards and mortality rates for the British population as a whole.[18] A collection of essays edited by Winter and Richard Wall published in 1990 explored similar social continuities in Britain, France, Germany, and Belgium.[19] Gender historians of World War I have also stressed continuity, though in a much less positive light. *Behind the Lines*, an important collection of essays mostly by American scholars published in 1987, critiqued gender identities and inequalities that persisted through both world wars.[20]

To be sure, the conclusions of the present study identify more clearly with those of the "social" historians of World War I than those of "cultural" historians. Like Pedroncini, Prost, and Becker and his school, I find the axiom of a human spirit broken or maimed by World War I highly problematic outside intellectual or artistic circles. My conclusions certainly suggest that the human capacity to adapt and endure is stronger than an impulse toward spiritual entropy in the face of calamity. Moreover, I have narrated the evolution of soldierly resilience drawing from reflective, consensual patriotism based on popular sovereignty as the official ideology of the Republic of France. Indeed, France not losing the war remained the fixed point around which soldiers and commanders agreed, and around which the negotiation of proportionality and authority relations took place.

15 Jean-Jacques Becker, *La France en guerre, 1914–1918: la grande mutation* (Bruxelles: Éditions Complexe, 1988), p. 204.
16 Stéphane Audoin-Rouzeau, *À travers leur Journaux: 14–18, les combattants des tranchées* (Paris: Armand Colin, Éditeur, 1986).
17 Stéphane Audoin-Rouzeau, *1870: La France dans la guerre* (Paris: Armand Colin, Éditeur, 1989).
18 J. M. Winter, *The Great War and the British People* (London: Macmillan, 1985).
19 Richard Wall and Jay Winter, eds., *The Upheaval of War: Family, Work and Welfare in Europe, 1914–1918* (Cambridge: Cambridge University Press, 1990).
20 Margaret Randolph Higonnet, et al., eds., *Behind the Lines: Gender and the World Wars* (New Haven: Yale University Press, 1987).

But the conclusions of the historians of social resilience beg some significant questions. From the vantage point of the last decade of the twentieth century, the notion that French and indeed European society as a whole did not slide into oblivion because of World War I suggests itself intuitively, perhaps to the point of being obvious. Significant questions also remain to be answered about the character of power relations behind the broader narrative of social durability. How can power in World War I be explained historically in terms of what might loosely be called "national character"? What was unusual about the construction of the French citizen-soldier of World War I against the backdrop of other national models, and what could a comparison of some of these models reveal about war and European societies in the early twentieth century?[21]

As constructed historically, the British soldier went to war in 1914 against the cultural backdrop of Tommy Atkins, best known through Rudyard Kipling's 1893 poem of that name. Tommy (most often referred to by the first name alone, in the manner of a child or a domestic servant), epitomized the Edwardian soldier, a lower-class volunteer who probably did not fit well into civilian society before he joined up. Once in the army, he remained a used and abused outsider, systematically excluded from pub and cinema. A British historian writing in 1981 still described him as motivated by "beef, beer, and lust."[22] But civilian society depended completely on Tommy, and Tommy knew it: "For its 'Saviour of 'is Country' when the guns begin to shoot." In a way, he almost relished his marginalization, for it gave him a distinct identity and occasionally even status in an otherwise unreceptive social and political environment. But at the same time, Tommy knew and accepted his place on the Edwardian chain of being. His natural duty was to serve as a subject-soldier; he lived and died "a soldier 'hof the Queen."

With the coming of war in 1914, most historians of the British army would agree, the external signifiers of Tommy's exclusion fell away as Britain fielded its first mass army. As J. M. Brereton put it in 1986: "The soldier was recognized for what he was: an ordinary member of society who happened to be in uniform, his business to preserve freedom."[23] Tommy remained closely linked to civilian society even in the trenches. Indeed, J. G. Fuller, much influenced by social historians of World War I, argued persuasively in 1990 that transferal to the front of civilian popular

<hr/>

[21] I am limiting the comparison here to three other European protagonists—Britain, Germany, and Russia. I have declined to consider Italy, Austria-Hungary, and the Ottoman Empire because of the relatively limited literature from these countries on the social history of soldiers.

[22] Byron Farwell, *Mr. Kipling's Army: All the Queen's Men* (New York: W. W. Norton & Company, 1981), from the title of chap. 6.

[23] J. M. Brereton, *The British Soldier: A Social History from 1661 to the Present Day* (London: The Bodley Head, 1986), pp. 139–40.

culture, particularly soccer, rugby, and the music hall, played a vital role in sustaining British military morale.[24]

But the prewar British soldier's characteristic willingness stoically to accept adversity and self-sacrifice proved easily transferable to British manhood at large. As Tommy became recast, he acquired an additional sobriquet—the "poor bloody infantry." In a moving if largely anecdotal account, Denis Winter described a British soldier characterized by genial simplicity, good will, and amazing courage.[25] Tommy could withstand anything with minimal complaint—from the deadly and strategically useless Ypres salient to the calamitous first day of the Somme offensive.[26] British soldiers asked only to be led bravely and decisively. Such a view was largely accepted even by two historians of the Left, Gloden Dallas and Douglas Gill, who provided a rare study in 1985 of mutinies in the British army after the Armistice.[27] Soldiers' own consciousness, Dallas and Gill concluded, did not go beyond that of the urban working classes. To raise their consciousness to meet the requirements of the Marxist narrative, British soldiers simply would have required appropriate leadership from organized political socialism, leadership that in the event proved wanting.[28]

In short, then, historians of the British army during World War I have widely agreed that Tommies in the trenches well deserved the description of them attributed to Erich Ludendorff, that they were "lions led by donkeys." Of course, whether British military commanders actually *were* donkeys has proven a subject of lively historiographical dispute. Indeed, in the study of World War I military leadership, historians of the British army remain without rivals. One of the finest, Tim Travers, has drawn a useful distinction between "internal" and "external" schools of thought as to the quality of British military leadership.[29] The "internal" school accepts Ludendorff's assessment, and emphasizes the heartless and murderous myopia of the British senior command. The "external" school argues for a sadder-but-wiser narrative not of lost opportunities, but of no opportunities to lose. Military technology and deep-seated cultural impediments in Britain to the formation of a mass army on the continental model left senior commanders few options.

[24] J. G. Fuller, *Troop Morale and Popular Culture in the British and Dominion Armies* (Oxford: Clarendon Press, 1990).

[25] Denis Winter, *Death's Men: Soldiers of the Great War* (London: Allen Lane, 1978).

[26] On the Somme, see the moving narrative in John Keegan, *The Face of Battle: A Study of Agincourt, Waterloo, and the Somme* (New York: Penguin Books, 1976), pp. 207–89.

[27] Gloden Dallas and Douglas Gill, *The Unknown Army: Mutinies in the British Army in World War I* (London: Verso, 1985).

[28] See ibid., chap. 12.

[29] Tim Travers, *The Killing Ground: The British Army, The Western Front and the Emergence of Modern Warfare, 1900–1918* (London: Unwin Hyman, 1987), pp. xvii–xxi. Travers also provides numerous additional bibliographical references.

Over the course of the war, to be sure, some influence over the conduct of the war made itself felt from below. Shelford Bidwell and Dominick Graham have shown how British artillery tactics slowly and painfully improved in response to innovation in the field.[30] Likewise, lessons learned about infantry tactics by Capt. Basil Liddell Hart certainly influenced British thinking at the highest levels between the wars.[31] Robin Prior and Trevor Wilson have usefully highlighted the importance of intermediate command structures in the relearning of strategy and tactics that took place during the war.[32] But in all, and in a behavioral sense, depictions of the British soldier have remained close to the Clausewitzian ideal. His was not to question why, and historians of the British soldier have not as yet much pursued the question of whether he did so. The argument of the present study suggests that the history of power relations within the British army remains largely to be written.

If our historical understanding of the British soldier has been most informed by Tommy Atkins, our understanding of the German soldier has been informed by the single most important narrative tradition in the writing of modern German history, that of the German *Sonderweg*. The *Sonderweg* means a "unique path" of German political development that separated Germany from "normal" Western democracies such as Britain or France. The Prussian army played a key role in determining German separateness. The kings of Prussia, obsessed with security in a realm without defensible borders and surrounded by implacable enemies, made the army the center of Prussian state-building in the ancien régime. Indeed, as a contemporary of Frederick the Great once put it, Prussia was not a state with an army, but an army with a state.[33]

Following German unification in 1871, the Imperial German army did much to determine that Germany would not experience the same sort of "bourgeois revolution" that took place elsewhere in the West. Gordon Craig's conclusions of 1955 largely endure that the army remained "the state within the state."[34] The German bourgeoisie partly abdicated from public life and public responsibilities; in return, it was largely left alone by the army and the state to pursue industrial wealth. In addition, the army

[30] Shelford Bidwell and Dominick Graham, *Firepower: British Army Weapons and Theories of War, 1914–1945* (London: George Allen & Unwin, 1982), chaps. 4–8.

[31] John J. Mearsheimer, *Liddell Hart and the Weight of History* (Ithaca: Cornell University Press, 1988).

[32] Robin Prior and Trevor Wilson, *Command on the Western Front: The Military Career of Sir Henry Rawlinson, 1914–1918* (Oxford: Blackwell Publishers, 1992).

[33] Cited in Wolfgang Petter, " 'Enemies' and 'Reich Enemies': An Analysis of Threat Perceptions and Political Strategy in Imperial Germany, 1871–1914," in Wilhelm Deist, ed., *The German Military in the Age of Total War* (London: Berg, 1985), p. 22.

[34] Gordon Craig, *The Politics of the Prussian Army: 1640–1945* (New York: Oxford University Press, 1955), from the title of chap. 6.

not only served as the ultimate guarantor of internal security, but even partly opened its ranks to the bourgeoisie by giving its young men the chance to become reserve officers, who became essential to the development of a mass conscript army.[35]

The German army before 1914 had become exactly the sort of separate state and society that Clausewitz had warned against in ancien régime armies. But if Clausewitz had chided old dynastic armies for allowing the culture of violence to disappear (thereby undermining their military effectiveness), the reverse happened in the German case. The separateness of German military society meant that its geopolitical ambitions could grow unchecked, as could its willingness to embark upon or even provoke a war to realize these ambitions. The end result was the Schlieffen Plan, which made German encirclement and a two-front war a self-fulfilling prophecy. Despite decades of intense historiographical debate, Fritz Fischer's thesis has continued to find broad support—that the German general staff essentially provoked war in 1914 and that its ambitions of a German-dominated *Mitteleuropa* escalated as the war continued.[36]

To be sure, an important part of the Prussian-German military tradition stressed efficiency, a feature that has assumed the proportions of a national stereotype. During World War I, the military fixation on efficiency led to innovation, part of which percolated up from junior officers and NCOs in the field.[37] Indeed, the Germans revolutionized infantry tactics, based on infiltration of the enemy positions and highly devolved command authority. More than any other single factor, new German infantry tactics broke the stalemate on the Western Front in 1918. The incorporation of tanks into these tactics made possible the *Blitzkrieg* in World War II.[38]

One might have thought German innovation in infantry tactics to have led to the sort of obstreperous and partly self-empowered citizen-soldier described here in France. But the reverse is actually the case, at least as the

[35] See, among others: Petter, "'Enemies' and 'Reich Enemies'"; Karl Demeter, *The German Officer-Corps in Society and State* (New York: Praeger, 1968 [originally published in German in 1962]); and Martin Kitchen, *The German Officer Corps, 1890–1914* (Oxford: Clarendon Press, 1968).

[36] See *Germany's War Aims in the First World War*, no translator noted (New York: W. W. Norton & Company, 1967 [originally published in German in 1961]); *World Power or Decline?: The Controversy over Germany's Aims in the First World War*, Lancelot L. Farrar, Robert Kimber, and Rita Kimber, trans. (New York: W. W. Norton & Company, 1974 [originally published in German in 1965]); and *From Kaiserreich to Third Reich: Elements of Continuity in German History, 1871–1945*, Robert Fletcher, trans. (London: Allen & Unwin, 1986 [originally published in German in 1979]).

[37] See Bruce I. Gudmundsson, *Stormtroop Tactics: Innovation in the German Army, 1914–1918* (New York: Praeger Publishers, 1989).

[38] See Robert M. Citano, *The Evolution of Blitzkrieg Tactics: Germany Defends Itself Against Poland, 1918–1933* (New York: Greenwood Press, 1987); and S. J. Lewis, *Forgotten Legions: German Army Infantry Policy, 1918–1941* (New York: Praeger Publishers, 1985).

German soldier has been constructed historically. The World War I soldier who emerged from German military culture and the *Sonderweg* to which it both drew from and contributed to was, like Tommy Atkins, a subject-soldier rather than a citizen-soldier. He was expected to withstand anything and to make any sacrifice for kaiser and *Vaterland*, without questioning or complaint. But he was even more subservient than Tommy, and much more unambiguously and much more totally victimized by the war. It is perhaps no coincidence that the most enduring literary image of the soldier-victim of World War I came from Germany—the young Paul Bäumer from Erich Marie Remarque's 1928 novel *All Quiet on the Western Front*.[39] Paul became the archetype that so influenced cultural historians of World War I.

Indeed, so maimed was the German soldier by the war that he became unfit for the responsibilities of citizenship once the Weimar Republic was established in 1919. Robert Weldon Whalen argued in 1984 that Weimar continued the victimization of the soldier by its heartless approach to welfare and pension problems, and so did little to earn the veteran's loyalty.[40] This contributed to the chronic interwar weakness of democratic institutions in Germany, and helped speed Germany's path, supposedly inexorably, down the *Sonderweg* toward Adolf Hitler.

Perhaps surprisingly, the historiography of the Russian soldier in World War I provides the most suggestive example relative to the story of the French citizen-soldier as told here. In the war and the Revolution and civil war that followed, the Russian soldier made the transition from the tsar's subject-soldier to the Bolshevik citizen-soldier. In the tsar's army, an ancien régime system of authority persisted into the early twentieth century. This system was rooted in the countryside, whence the vast majority of the tsars' soldiers originated. The peasant soldier, according to Elise Wirtschafter and John Bushnell, had two related but strikingly different conceptions of authority.[41] Immediate authority emanated from the landowner or the officer. That authority generally proved capricious and irresistible. The peasant-soldier could only submit and hope for better in the imaginary future, most often the next life. But another conception of authority existed in the rural Russian imagination that drew from deep folk traditions—of the distant but benevolent and nearly all-powerful tsar, the "little father" of his people whose will was constantly thwarted by those who exercised immediate authority.

[39] Originally published as *Im Westen Nichts Neues* (Berlin: Ullstein A.G., 1928).

[40] See Robert Weldon Whalen, *Bitter Wounds: German Victims of the Great War, 1914–1939* (Ithaca: Cornell University Press, 1984).

[41] Elise Kimmerling Wirtschafter, *From Serf to Russian Soldier* (Princeton: Princeton University Press, 1990); John Bushnell, *Mutiny Amid Repression: Russian Soldiers in the Revolution of 1905–1906* (Bloomington: Indiana University Press, 1985).

As Wirtschafter has argued, the tsarist state endeavored to reconcile these two concepts of authority in the nineteenth century military reforms, through according veterans an otherwise unattainable civil status after a long (twenty to twenty-five year) period of service. In this way, military reformers hoped to render the army a more effective instrument of modern state power. But down to 1914, reformers' hopes continued to be largely unrealized. Conscription remained the most onerous form of peasant obligation, with the peasant-soldier fundamentally unincorporated into any sort of "nation" in a modern sense.

Bushnell argued that the persistence of the ancien régime in the Russian army was dramatically illustrated in the Revolution of 1905. Only the soldiers' ancient and dual conception of authority could explain how they could mutiny against their commanders one day and bloodily repress striking workers the next. Bushnell concluded that the variable proved how soldiers perceived the prospects of the tsar's regime at any given moment. When soldiers reckoned the center weak, they rebelled according to the folk traditions of peasant revolts. When the center seemed viable, "normal" peasant submission predominated, which made them suitable instruments of repression. Bushnell argued that the revolutionaries, as part of urban "European Russia," failed to understand the paradox of peasant-soldiers' conceptions of authority, and consequently never presented a viable alternative.

As Alan Wildman recounted in a masterful two-volume study, World War I finally broke down the ancien régime conception of authority in the army as it shattered the tsar's regime itself.[42] As in the West, politics gradually lost control over war between 1914 and 1917. Along the Eastern Front, a stalemate of space analogous to the stalemate of force along the Western front combined with a gradual deterioration of the tsar's authority at the center. When Nicholas II assumed personal command of his forces in 1916, he tied the fate of his regime to the fate of his army, just when his regime was at its weakest.

When soldiers began the reconquest of war by politics through the imperial army mutinies of March 1917, the points of similarity to the French army mutinies two months later are striking. Soldiers voiced the same anguish for their families at home, sympathies for strikers in the cities, and anger at the ever-broadening disproportionality between ends and means in the way the war was being carried out. At this stage in what became the Russian Revolution, soldiers also exhibited a general deference to their officers and a willingness to hold the lines, provided they were not

---

[42] Alan Wildman, *The End of The Russian Imperial Army: Volume I, The Old Army and the Soldiers' Revolt (March–April 1917); Volume II, The Road to Soviet Power and Peace* (Princeton: Princeton University Press, 1980, 1987).

ordered into a new offensive. Also as in France, soldiers were much more restive behind the lines than in them.[43]

But in the end, the differences between the Russian and French examples proved far more dramatic than the similarities. Nicholas II invoked the final disintegration of his authority in March 1917 when he unsuccessfully ordered soldiers to repress popular demonstrations in the major cities. Overnight, soldiers became free political agents, just as did the French soldiers who refused to advance into the trenches. But unlike the French, the former imperial soldiers had had no national political experience as citizens before or during the war. The Provisional Government, led by Alexander Kerensky and inspired by the successes of the armies of the French Revolution, tried to transform the subject-soldier of the tsar into the citizen-soldier in a matter of months.

But in the former imperial army a new source of authority had already emerged in the ranks—the soldiers' committees, more commonly known as the soldiers' soviets.[44] The soviets had made explicit and institutionalized the dialogical relationship between soldiers and commanders that lay hidden behind the mask of the "official transcript" of conventional command authority in the French army. They negotiated the parameters of authority on a daily basis, on matters ranging from food distribution to military justice to whether and how to take up particular positions in the lines. Whoever could gain control over the soviets could gain control over what remained of the former imperial forces.

Kerensky, the Provisional Government, and the remnants of the imperial general staff tried to circumvent and ignore the soldiers' soviets whenever possible, and to maintain the fiction of conventional command authority. Indeed, in the summer of 1917, they endeavored to carry out another "over the top" general offensive not militarily distinguishable from its predecessors—something Pétain and the French Third Republic would not have dared at the time. In other words, the Russian revolutionaries made far greater demands than the French on their newborn citizen-soldiers on a far more uncertain basis of support. By the fall of 1917, republicanism and moderate socialism had gone the way of autocracy in Russia.

Only the Bolsheviks really understood how soldiers' politics had transformed war on the Eastern Front. With the ancien régime system of authority swept away at the center, land and peace meant more to soldiers than whether Russia won or lost the war. The Bolsheviks understood the Russian soldier of 1917 in ways that Kerensky did not, in Wildman's words, "as scions of a peasant culture with its indigenous parochial concerns. The

[43] See Ibid, *The Old Army*, chap. 3.
[44] See Ibid., chaps. 7–8; and vol. 2, *The Road to Soviet Power*, chap. 2.

war was simply one more intrusion into this private world of the demands of the holders of political and social power, robbing them of their lives and substance."[45] The Bolsheviks gained ascendancy over the soviets through a keen sense of what was to be done today versus what had to be left to the future.

Bolshevik proportionality, to incorporate this point into the language of the present study, involved understanding that soldiers had ceased to judge aggression (or even defensive combat) against the Central Powers relevant to their most important concerns. The issue was not aggression per se; the Civil War of 1918–1920 showed that the Russian soldier (Red or White) had plenty of fight left in him. The Bolsheviks judged that sufficient numbers of soldiers could be mustered to take up arms against the restoration of the ancien régime. As Francesco Benvenuti has shown, the Red Army that won the civil war was an unusual amalgam of revolutionary organization and remnants of the imperial army.[46] But state building and the inculcation of national political loyalties in a modern sense would have to wait for another day.

Mark von Hagen has described this process as it took place between 1917 and 1930. He has argued persuasively that the Soviet state and the Red Army essentially constructed each other through what he called "militarized socialism."[47] The Bolsheviks and the emerging Soviet state offered soldiers a new civic identity, as the vanguard of the proletarian dictatorship. Military service, and its attending processes of political education, became the ticket to social mobility through the party and state bureaucracies. The state, in turn, looked more and more to the military as the institutional exemplar of socialist discipline and conformity. When Joseph Stalin turned to the Red Army to collectivize the countryside in the late 1920s, he found a nearly perfect Clausewitzian instrument. The "citizen"-soldiers of the Red Army by that time were ready to wage total war on the internal enemies of the regime.

These three examples obviously tell very different stories of the relationship between soldiers and society, and highlight very different points of the respective national histories. It remains to connect them to each other and to the corresponding analysis for France. In addition, some explanation is needed of how national histories of the relationship between soldiers and society enhance our understanding more broadly of power relations in Europe in the early twentieth century. Perhaps the best way to do this is to

[45] Idem, vol. 2, *The Road to Soviet Power*, p. 404.
[46] Francesco Benvenuti, *The Bolsheviks and the Red Army, 1918–1922*, Christopher Woodall, trans. (Cambridge: Cambridge University Press, 1988).
[47] Mark von Hagen, *Soldiers in the Proletarian Dictatorship: The Red Army and the Soviet Socialist State, 1917–1930* (Ithaca: Cornell University Press, 1990), p. 6.

return to the different conclusions of "cultural" and "social" historians of World War I—to ask whether the war represented a watershed in the development of power relations.

Though in very different ways, I would suggest that according to the present state of the historiographical literature, for Britain and Germany the answer is no. The individual "Tommy" and the collective "poor bloody infantry" both drew from and contributed to the amazing resilience of British institutions. However many thousands of individual lives may have been shattered, British institutions continued to modernize gradually and without continental revolutionary trauma, much as they had done in the eighteenth and nineteenth centuries. Likewise in Germany, the war simply reaffirmed a preexisting path, here the *Sonderweg* away from Western liberal "normalcy." The German soldier was an incomplete subject for democratic citizenship, and the war rendered him even more unsuitable. But at the same time, the analysis presented in this study also suggests that these two national stories fit just a bit *too* neatly into the respective national histories. Much work remains to be done to explore whether Tommy Atkins or his German counterparts were really as pliant as our present understanding suggests, and what the resulting implications might be.

In Russia, the war certainly marked a great watershed that led to a new understanding of power. The Bolsheviks prevailed in the Revolution to no small degree because they could correctly read the politics of discontented soldiers—specifically the fact that more than anything else, soldiers wanted land and peace. Because the Bolsheviks prevailed, they could set about the construction of a new civic identity. The tsar's peasant-soldiers, who could only submit and hope for a better life only in some dreamy future was transformed into the Bolshevik citizen-soldier, a key figure in the vanguard of the proletarian dictatorship. The Bolsheviks learned all too well how to manipulate this identity. Indeed, Hitler's initial success in the invasion of the Soviet Union in 1941 showed that the Red Army had become an entity far better suited to dealing with internal enemies of the regime than external ones. The construction of a new civic identity, this example indicates, did not need to take place within the framework of Western liberal democracy.

French historians never weary of highlighting the complexities and ambiguities of the history of France. In the end, my conclusions on whether World War I marked a watershed in the development of the power relations in France are very much a part of this tradition. The quote from Michel Foucault used as an epigraph to this study encapsulates the essential points made here. Throughout the war, soldiers provoked power relations amid "the recalcitrance of the will and the intransigence of freedom." I would suggest that this aspect of power relations fundamentally characterizes the

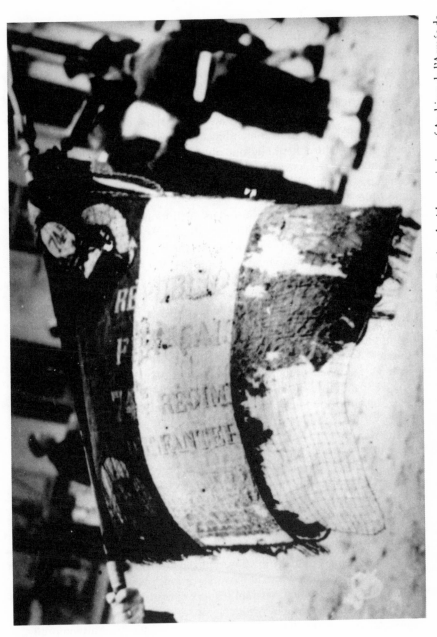

Fɪɢ. X-1. Regimental Flag, 74ᵉ RI (undated, sometime after 1918). Reprinted with permission of Archives de l'Armée de Terre, Vincennes.

history of soldiers and society in modern France, and in this respect also the resilience that has so drawn the attention of the social historians.

The *poilu* of the 5ᵉ DI was a very different political creature from, say, Tommy Atkins—at least as the latter is presently understood. Indeed, of the national varieties examined here, only the French soldier was a citizen of a republic before, during, and after the war. He served neither king, nor kaiser, nor tsar, rather himself and his compatriots. I depart from even a late-foucauldian analysis in contending that consent to the power relations implicit in the Third Republic not only existed, but had real historical significance. The recalcitrance of the will and the intransigence of freedom became meaningful through soldiers' consent to the resulting power relationship.

Consent to the Third Republic and its institutions set the outer limits of French soldiers' resistance to authority during World War I. They internalized this consent in ways that prevented the French army mutinies from going the way of the Russian army mutinies—at a time when no external use of power could have. When mutiny came in 1917, the dialogical nature of authority institutionalized by the soviets in Russia had long been tacitly recognized in the workings of the French army. French soldiers already had a civic identity analogous to but very different from the civic identity transmitted to the former imperial soldiers by the Bolsheviks.

But few would argue that, on balance, World War I proved a life-affirming experience for the Third Republic. The weakness of the Republic in the 1930s and defeat in 1940 haunt the history of twentieth-century France, much as the *Sonderweg* and Hitler haunt the history of modern Germany. I have alluded to some skepticism here concerning the notion that the war undermined the capacity of the German soldier to become a responsible civic creature. This skepticism is even stronger of the admittedly somewhat dated tendency particularly in English-language historiography to look in the trenches of 1914–1918 for causes of the alleged moral collapse of France in 1940.

The point, perhaps, is rather that nothing was fixed in the power relationship linking French soldiers and their society in either world war. Had Pétain chosen the kind of offensive pursued by Kerensky in the summer of 1917, it is extremely unlikely that internalized loyalty to the French Republic would have prevented a major conflagration. Likewise, when the Republic and its military and civilian leaders offered French soldiers a militarily hopeless situation in 1940, some seventy years of constructed republican citizenship shattered, to be put back together only painfully over many years. If there is a general principle joining power relations in 1914–1918 and in 1940, it is that consent exists and it matters, but that it remains profoundly conditional.

Bibliography

Primary Sources

Archives

Archives de l'Armée de Terre, Château de Vincennes, Vincennes, France: Série N (1872–1919); Série J (Justice Militaire); Personal Dossiers; Fonds Gallieni; Fonds Clemenceau; Fonds Joffre

Archives du Département de la Seine-Maritime, Rouen, France: Série J (Cabinet du Préfet); Sous-série 5 J (Fonds Lafond)

Archives Nationales, Paris, France: Fonds Mangin (149 AP 20)

Newspapers

France Militaire
Journal de Caen
Le Canard de Boyau
La Dépêche de Rouen et de Normandie
Le Journal de Rouen

Memoirs (5e DI)

Brunel de Pérard, Jacques (43e RA). *Carnet de route, 4 août–25 septembre 1914.* Paris: Georges Cres & Cie., Editeurs, 1915. .

Champin, Jules (39e RI). *Mes Souvenirs.* Unpublished memoir, Bibliothèque de Service Historique de l'Armée de Terre, Château de Vincennes, côte D.227.

Desaubliaux, Robert (129e RI). *La Ruée: étapes d'un combattant.* Paris: Bloude & Gay, 1919.

Descaves, Lucien (129e RI). *Sous-Offs: roman militaire.* Paris: Éditions Stock, 1889.

Dorgelès, Roland (39e RI). *Les Croix de bois.* Paris: Albin Michel, Editeur, 1919.

———. "Souvenirs et réflexions sur les 'Croix de bois,' " *Nouvelles Litteraires*, 24 November 1928.

———. *Souvenirs sur les croix de bois.* Paris: À la cité des livres, 1929.

Dutheil, Henri (E.M., 5e DI). *De Sauret la honte à Mangin le boucher: roman comique d'un état-major.* Paris: Nouvelle Librarie Nationale, 1923.

Hallé, Guy. (74e RI). *Là-bas avec ceux qui souffrent.* Paris: Garnier, 1917.

La Chausée, Capitaine, J. (39e RI). *De Charleroi à Verdun dans l'Infanterie.* Paris: Éditions Eugène Figuier, no date, depôt légal, 1934.

Lefebvre-Dibon, Chef de Bataillon de Réserve Paul. (74e RI) *Quatre Pages du 3e Bataillon du 74e RI: extraits d'un carnet de campagne.* 2d ed. Nancy: Imprimerie Berger-Levrault, 1920.

Legentil (no first name, 74e RI). "Notes de campagne du 12 avril 1915 au 11 novembre 1918: Au jour le jour, bons et mauvais souvenirs." Unpublished memoir, Archives de l'Armée de Terre, Fonds Privés, 1 KT 76.

Mangin, Charles (5ᵉ DI). *Lettres de guerre*, edited by Stanislaus Mangin and Louis-Eugène Mangin. Paris: Fayard, 1950.

Maurois, Andre (74ᵉ RI). *Mémoires*. Paris: Flammarion, 1970.

Rimbault, Captain Paul (74ᵉ RI). *Le Soldat dans la guerre de demain: causeries morales sur la guerre, fait à ses hommes libérables par un officier d'infanterie.* Paris: Berger Levrault, 1912.

――――. *Propos d'un marmité: 1915–1917.* Paris: L. Fournier, 1920.

Roquerol, General Gabriel (3ᵉ CA). *La Battaile de Guise, 29 août 1914.* Paris: Berger-Levrault, 1932.

――――. *1914: Le 3ᵉ Corps d'Armée de Charleroi à la Marne, essai de psychologie miltaire, les combattants et le commandement.* Paris: Éditions Berger-Levrault, 1934.

Toussaint, Charles (74ᵉ RI). *Petites Histories d'un glorieux régiment: vecus par Charles Toussaint, soldat de 1ᵉʳᵉ classe au 74ᵉ Régiment d'Infanterie en guerre.* Montvilliers (Seine-Maritime): Binesse, 1973.

Other Memoirs

Clemenceau, Georges. *Grandeur et miserès d'une victoire.* 4 vols. Paris: Plon, 1930.

Foch, Maréchal Ferdinand. *Mémoires pour servir à l'histoire de la guerre de 1914–1918.* 2 vols. Paris: Plon, 1931.

Gamelin, General Maurice. *Manoeuvre et victoire de la Marne.* Paris: B. Grasset, 1954.

Genevoix, Maurice. *Les Eparges.* Paris: Flammarion, 1923.

Joffre, Maréchal Joseph. *Mémoires: 1910–1917.* 2 vols. Paris: Plon, 1932.

Lloyd-George, David. *War Memories of David Lloyd-George.* Boston: Little, Brown & Company, 1934.

Ludendorff, General Erich. *My War Memories: 1914–1918.* 2 vols. No translator noted. London: Hutchinson & Company, 1919.

Painlévé, Paul. *Comment j'ai nommé Foch et Pétain.* Paris: Alcan, 1923.

Pétain, Philippe. "A Crisis of Morale in the French Nation at War." Translated by Rivers Scott. In Maj. Gen. Sir Edward Spears, *Two Men who Saved France: Petain and De Gaulle.* London: Eyre and Spottswoode, 1966.

Pichot-Duclos, General Réné Agis. *Au G.Q.G. de Joffre: réflexions sur ma vie militaire.* Paris: Arthaud, 1947.

Poincaré, Raymond. *Au Service de la France.* 10 vols. Paris: Plon, 1926–1933.

Tocaben, Jean. *Virilité (au front de la grande guerre).* Paris: Flammarion, 1931.

Secondary Sources

Agulhon, Maurice. *La République au village: les populations du Var de la révolution à la seconde république.* Paris: Plon, 1970.

Allard, Paul. "Les Mutineries de l'armée française." *L'Oeuvre,* 26 August–1 September 1932.

Amouroux, Henri. *Pétain avant Vichy: la guerre et l'amour.* Paris: Fayard, 1967.

Andréani, Roland. "Anti-militarisme en Languedoc avant 1914." *Revue d'histoire moderne et contemporaine* 20 (1973).

Anonymous. *Le Plan XVII: étude stratégique*. Paris: Payot et Cie., 1920.

Arnold, Joseph C. "French Tactical Doctrine: 1870–1914." *Military Affairs* 42 (1976): 60–67.

Ashworth, Tony. *Trench Warfare, 1914–1918: The Live and Let Live System*. New York: Holmes & Meier, 1980.

Aublet, M. "L'Artillerie française de 1914 à 1918." *Revue militaire française* 33 (1929).

Audoin-Rouzeau, Stéphane. *À travers leurs Journaux: 14–18, les combattants des tranchées*. Paris: Armand Colin, 1986.

———. *1870: La France en guerre*. Paris: Armand Colin, 1989.

Barge, Walter. "The Generals of the Republic: The Corporate Personality of High Military Rank in France, 1899–1914." Ph.D. diss., University of North Carolina-Chapel Hill, 1982.

Baynes, John. *Morale, A Study of Courage: The Second Scottish Rifles at the Battle of Neuve Chapelle, 1915*. London: Cassel, 1967.

Becker, Jean-Jacques. *Le Carnet B: les pouvoirs publics et l'anti-militarisme avant la guerre de 1914*. Paris: Éditions Klinksieck, 1973.

———. *1914: Comment les Français sont entrés à la guerre*. Paris: Presse de la Fondation National des Sciences Publiques, 1977.

———. *Les Français dans la grande guerre*. Paris: Éditions Robert Laffont, 1980.

———. *La France en guerre, 1914–1918: la grande mutation*. Bruxelles: Éditions Complexe, 1988.

Benvenuti, Francesco. *The Bolsheviks and the Red Army, 1918–1922*. Translated by Christopher Woodall. New York: Cambridge University Press, 1988 (originally published in Italian in 1982).

Berenson, Edward. *The Trial of Madame Caillaux*. Berkeley: University of California Press, 1992.

Bertaud, Jean-Paul. "Napoleon's Officers," *Past and Present* 112, August, 1986.

———. *The Army of the French Revolution* Translated by R. R. Palmer. Princeton: Princeton University Press, 1988 (originally published in French in 1979).

Best, Geoffrey. *Humanity in Warfare*. New York: Columbia University Press, 1980.

Bidwell, Shelford, and Dominick Graham. *Firepower: British Army Weapons and Theories of War, 1914–1945*. London: George Allen & Unwin, 1982.

Bozon, Michel. *Les Conscrits: arts et traditions populaires*. Paris: Bibliothèque Berger-Levrault, 1981.

Brécy, Robert. *Le Mouvement syndical en France, 1871–1921: essai bibliographique*. Paris: Mouton & Cie., 1963.

Bredin, Jean-Denis. *L'Affaire*. Paris: Julliard, 1985.

Brereton, J. M. *The British Soldier: A Social History from 1661 to the Present Day*. London: The Bodley Head, 1986.

Brouard, Michel de, ed. *Histoire de la Normandie*. Toulouse: Edouard Privat, 1970.

Brown, Malcolm, and Shirley Seaton. *Christmas Truce*. New York: Hippocrene Books, 1984.

Burchell, Graham, Colin Gordon, and Peter Miller, eds. *The Foucault Effect: Studies in Governmentality*. Chicago: University of Chicago Press, 1991.

Burns, Michael. *Dreyfus: A Family Affair, 1789–1945.* New York: Harper Collins, 1991.

Bushnell, John. *Mutiny amid Repression: Russian Soldiers in the Revolution of 1905–1906.* Bloomington: Indiana University Press, 1985.

Carles, Colonel Pierre. *Un Historique des sous-officiers français.* Vincennes: SIRPA-Terre, 1988.

Carrias, Eugène. *La Pensée militaire française.* Paris: Presses Universitaires de France, 1960.

Challener, Richard. *The French Theory of the Nation in Arms, 1866–1939.* New York: Columbia University Press, 1952.

Chevron, Capitaine Alcide. *De l'Abandon de Poste.* Strasbourg: Imprimerie Strasbourgeoise, 1919.

Citano, Robert M. *The Evolution of Blitzkrieg Tactics: Germany Defends Itself Against Poland, 1918–1933.* New York: Greenwood Press, 1987.

Clausewitz, Carl Von. *De la Révolution à la restauration: écrits et lettres.* Edited and translated by Marie-Louise Steinhauser. Paris: Gallimard, 1976.

———. *On War.* Edited and translated by Michael Howard and Peter Paret. Princeton: Princeton University Press, 1976.

———. *Historical and Political Writings.* Edited and translated by Peter Paret and Daniel Moran. Princeton: Princeton University Press, 1992.

Cochet, Annick. "L'Opinion et le moral des soldats en 1916 d'après les archives du contrôle postal." 2 vols. Thèse pour le doctorat, Paris X-Nanterre, 1986.

Cognet, Commandant. *La Problème des réserves.* Paris: Chapelot, 1914.

Contamine, Henri, "Réflexions sur les forces en présence à la bataille des frontières." *Revue d'histoire de la guerre mondial* 16 (1938).

———. *La Revanche, 1871–1914.* Paris: Berger Levrault, 1957.

———. "De quelques Problèmes militaires en 1917." *Revue d'histoire moderne et contemporaine* 1 (1968): 108–21.

Cousine, Colonel André. "Essai Historique de Terme 'Limoger': La 12ᵉ Région en 1914, cinq départements." Unpublished paper, Service Historique de l'Armée de Terre, 1984.

Cox, Richard H. *Locke on War and Peace.* Oxford: Clarendon Press, 1960.

Craig, Gordon. *The Politics of the Prussian Army: 1640–1945.* New York: Oxford University Press, 1955.

Cru, Jean-Norton. *Témoins: Essai d'analyse et de critique des souvenirs de combattants édités en français de 1915 à 1928.* Paris: Les Etincelles, 1929.

Dallas, Gloden, and Douglas Gill. *The Unknown Army: Mutinies in the British Army in World War I.* London: Verso, 1985.

Dauzat, Albert. *L'Argot de la guerre: d'après une enquête des officiers et soldats.* Paris: Librairie Armand Colin, 1918.

Deák, István. *Beyond Nationalism: A Social and Political History of the Habsburg Officer Corps, 1848–1918.* New York: Oxford University Press, 1990.

Demeter, Karl. *The German Officer Corps, 1890–1914.* Oxford: Clarendon Press, 1968 (originally published in German in 1962).

Desbrière, E. "La Genèse du Plan XVII." *Revue d'histoire de la guerre mondiale* 1 (1923).

Deist, Wilhelm, ed. *The German Military in the Age of Total War.* London: Berg, 1985.

Duroselle, Jean-Baptiste. *Clemenceau.* Paris: Fayard, 1988.

Eksteins, Modris. *Rites of Spring: The Great War and the Birth of the Modern Age.* New York: Houghton Mifflin, 1989.

Ellis, John. *Eye-Deep in Hell: Trench Warfare in World War I.* New York: Pantheon Books, 1976.

Elwitt, Sanford. *The Making of the Third Republic: Class and Politics in France.* Baton Rouge: Louisiana State University Press, 1975.

Englander, David. "The French Soldier: 1914–1918." *French History* 1 (March 1987): 49–67.

Farwell, Byron. *Mr. Kipling's Army: All the Queen's Men.* New York: W. W. Norton & Company, 1981.

Fischer, Fritz. *Germany's War Aims in the First World War.* No translator noted. New York: W. W. Norton & Company, 1967 (originally published in German in 1961).

——. *World Power or Decline?: The Controversy over Germany's Aims in the First World War.* Translated by Lancelot L. Farrar, Robert Kimber, and Rita Kimber. New York: W. W. Norton & Company, 1974 (originally published in German in 1965).

——. *From Kaiserreich to Third Reich: Elements of Continuity in German History, 1871–1945.* Translated by Robert Fletcher. London: Allen & Unwin, 1986 (originally published in German in 1979).

Foch, Marshal Ferdinand. *The Principals of War.* Translated by Hilaire Belloc. London: Chapman and Hall, 1918.

Forest, Alan. *The Soldiers of the French Revolution.* Durham: Duke University Press, 1990.

Foucault, Michel. *Folie et déraison: histoire de la folie à l'age classique.* Paris: Plon, 1961.

——. *Discipline and Punish: The Birth of the Prison.* Translated by Alan Sheridan. New York: Basic Books, 1979 (originally published in French in 1975).

——. "The Subject and Power." In *Michel Foucault: Beyond Structuralism and Hermeneutics,* 2d ed., edited by Herbert L. Dreyfus and Paul Rabinow, 208–26. Chicago: University of Chicago Press, 1983.

——. "Power, Polemics, and Problematizations." In *The Foucault Reader,* edited by Paul Rabinow. New York: Pantheon Books, 1984.

——. "The Ethic of Care for the Self as a Practice of Freedom: An Interview with Michel Foucault on January 20, 1984." In *The Final Foucault,* edited by James Bernauer and David Rasmussen, and translated by J. D. Gauthier S.J., 1–20. Cambridge: MIT Press, 1988.

Fuller, J. G. *Troop Morale and Popular Culture in the British and Dominion Armies.* Oxford: Clarendon Press, 1990.

Fussell, Paul. *The Great War and Modern Memory.* New York: Oxford University Press, 1975.

Gies, Joseph. *Crisis 1918: The Leading Actors, Strategies, and Events in the German Gamble for Total Victory on the Western Front.* New York: W. W. Norton & Company, 1974.

Girardet, Raoul. *La Société militaire dans la France contemporaine, 1815–1839.* Paris: Plon, 1953.

Gorce, Paul-Marie de la. *La République et son armée.* Paris: Fayard, 1963.

Gudmundsson, Bruce I. *Stormtroop Tactics: Innovation in the German Army, 1914–1918*. New York: Praeger Publishers, 1989.

Guinard, Golonel Pierre, Jean-Claude Devos, and Jean Nicot. *Inventaire sommaire des archives de la guerre: Série N, 1872–1919*, vol. 1. Troyes: Imprimerie La Renaissance, 1975.

Heidigger, Martin. "The Origin of the Work of Art." In *Poetry, Language, Thought*. Translated by Alfred Hofstadter. New York: Harper & Row, 1975.

Higonnet, Margaret Randolph, Jane Jenson, Sonya Michel, and Margaret Collins Weitz, eds. *Behind the Lines: Gender and the World Wars*. New Haven: Yale University Press, 1987.

Holmes, Richard. *Acts of War: The Behavior of Men in Battle*. New York: The Free Press, 1985.

Horne, Alistair. *The Price of Glory: Verdun 1916*. London: Macmillan, 1962.

Horne, John. "'*L'impôt du sang*': Republican rhetoric and Industrial warfare in France, 1914–1918." *Social History* 14 (1989): 201–23.

Howard, Michael. *Clausewitz*. Oxford: Oxford University Press, 1983.

———. "Men against Fire: The Doctrine of the Offensive in 1914." In *Makers of Modern Strategy: From Machiavelli to the Nuclear Age*, 2d ed., edited by Peter Paret, 510–26. Princeton: Princeton University Press, 1986.

Hunt, Lynn. "French History in the Last Twenty Years: The Rise and Fall of the *Annales* Paradigm," *Journal of Contemporary History* 21 (1986): 209–24.

———. ed. *The New Cultural History*. Berkeley and Los Angeles: University of California Press, 1989.

Hynes, Samuel. *A War Imagined: The First World War and English Culture*. New York: Atheneum, 1991.

Isaac, Jules. *Joffre et Lanrezac: Étude critique des témoignages sur le rôle de la Ve Armée (août 1914)*. Paris: Etienne Chiron, Editeur, 1922.

———. "L'Utilization des réserves dans l'armée française et dans l'armée allemande en 1914." *Revue d'histoire de la guerre mondiale* 2 (1924).

Janowitz, Morris. *The Professional Soldier: A Social and Political Portrait*. Glencoe, Il.: The Free Press, 1960.

Jauffret, Jean-Charles. "L'Organisation de la réserve à l'époque de la revanche, 1871–1914." *Revue Historique des Armées* 1 (1989): 27–37.

Jaurès, Jean. *L'Armée nouvelle: l'organisation socialiste de la France*. Paris: L. Rouff, 1911.

Jay, Martin. "Two Cheers for Paraphrase: The Confessions of a Synoptic Intellectual Historian." In *Fin de Siècle Socialism and Other Essays*. New York: Routledge, 1988.

Jeanneney, Jean-Noël. "Les Archives des commissions de contrôle postal aux armées (1916–1918): une source précieuse pour l'histoire contemporaine de l'opinion et des mentalités." *Revue d'histoire moderne et contemporaine* (Janvier–Mars 1968): 209–33.

Johnson, James Turner. *Ideology, Reason, and the Limitations of War: Religious and Secular Concepts, 1200–1740*. Princeton: Princeton University Press, 1975.

———. *Just War Tradition and the Restraint of War: A Moral and Historical Inquiry*. Princeton: Princeton University Press, 1981.

Jolinon, Joseph. "La Mutinerie des Coeuvres." *Mercure de France*, 15 August 1920.

Kaiser, David. *Politics and War: European Conflict from Phillip II to Hitler*. Cambridge: Harvard University Press, 1990.

Karsten, Peter. *Law, Soldiers, and Combat*. Westport, Conn.: Greenwood Press, 1978.

Keegan, John. *Opening Moves: August 1914*. New York: Ballentine Publishers, 1971.

———. *The Face of Battle: A Study of Agincourt, Waterloo and the Somme*. New York: Viking Press, 1976.

Keen, M. H. *The Laws of War in the Late Middle Ages*. London: Routledge and Keegan Paul, 1965.

Kitchen, Martin. *The German Officer Corps, 1890–1914*. Oxford: Clarendon Press, 1968.

LaCapra, Dominick. "Rethinking Intellectual History and Reading Texts." In *Rethinking Intellectual History: Texts, Contexts, Language*. Ithaca: Cornell University Press, 1983.

Laffargue, General André. *Foch et la Bataille de 1918*. Paris: Arthaud, 1967.

Lanrezac, General Charles. *Le Plan de campagne français et le premier mois de la guerre (2 août–3 septembre 1914)*. Paris: Payot & Cie., 1921.

Lecoc, Louis. *Pages héroiques de la 5ᵉ Division d'Infanterie*. Paris: S.T.D.I.5., 1918.

Leed, Eric. *No Man's Land: Combat and Identity in World War I*. New York: Cambridge University Press, 1979.

Lefranc, Commandant. "La Prise de Neuville–Saint Vaast (9 mai–9 juin 1915)." *Revue militaire française* 33 (1929): 331–49.

Lottman, Herbert. *Petain: Hero or Traitor? The Untold Story*. New York: Murrow, 1984.

Lynn, John. *The Bayonets of the Republic: Tactics and Motivation in the Army of Revolutionary France, 1791–94*. Urbana: The University of Illinois Press, 1984.

Madelin, Louis. *La Bataille de France (21 mars–11 novembre 1918*. Paris: Plon, 1920.

———. *La deuxième Bataille de la Marne*. Paris: Plon, 1920.

Mangin, Charles. *La Force Noire*. Paris: Hachette, 1911.

———. *Comment finit la guerre*. Paris: Plon, 1920.

Mangin, Louis-Eugène. *Le Général Mangin, 1866–1925*. Paris: Éditions Fernand Lanore, 1986.

Markus, R. A. "Saint Augustine's Views on the 'Just War.'" In *The Church and War: Papers Read at the Twenty-First Summer Meeting and Twenty-Second Winter Meeting of the Ecclesiastical History Society*, edited by W. J. Shiels. London: Basil Blackwell, 1983.

Marshall, General S.L.A. *Men Against Fire*. New York: William Morrow & Company, 1947.

Masse, J. "L'Antimilitarisme dans le Var avant 1914." *Cahiers d'histoire* 8 (1968).

Maurin, Jules. *Armée, guerre, société: soldats languedociens, 1889–1919*. Paris: Publications de la Sorbonne, 1982.

Mearsheimer, John J. *Liddell Hart and the Weight of History*. Ithaca: Cornell University Press, 1988.

Menu, Colonel Charles. "Les Journées du 29 et 30 août 1914." *Revue militaire française* 55 (1935): 145–92, 281–321.

Merlier, G. "L'Esprit de l'offensive dans l'armée française à la lecture de Grand-maison." *Bulletin de la société d'histoire moderne* 8 (1966).

Meyer, Jacques. *La Vie quotidienne des soldats pendant la grande guerre.* Paris: Hachette, 1966.

Miller, Steven, ed. *Military Strategy and the Origins of the First World War.* Princeton: Princeton University Press, 1985.

Ministère de la Guerre. *Réglement de Manoeuvre d'Infanterie du 20 avril 1914.* Paris: Henri Charles Lavauzelle, 1914.

———. G.Q.G., 3e Bureau. *Manuel du chef de section d'infanterie.* Paris: Imprimerie Nationale, 1916.

———. G.Q.G., des Armées du Nord et du Nord-Est. *Instruction sur le combat offensif des petits unités.* Paris: Imprimerie Nationale, 1918.

———. *Réglement général du 5 septembre 1917 rélatif aux permissions et congés, avec les rectifications du 20 septembre et suivi de la circulaire du 12 août rélative aux titres de permissions.* Paris: Berger Levrault, 1920.

———. *Les Armées françaises pendant la grande guerre.* 10 tomes. Paris: Imprimerie Nationale, 1922–1939.

Miquel, Pierre. *La Grande Guerre.* Paris: Fayard, 1983.

Mitchell, Allan. *Victors and Vanquished: The German Influence on Army and Church after 1870.* Chapel Hill: University of North Carolina Press, 1984.

Monteilhet, Joseph. *Les Institutions militaires de la France, 1914–1932: de la paix armée à la paix désarmée.* Paris: Librarie Felix Alcan, 1932.

Nobécourt, R. G. *Les Fantassins du Chemin des Dames.* Paris: Robert Laffont, 1965.

Paret, Peter. *Clausewitz and the State: The Man, His Theories, and His Times.* Princeton: Princeton University Press, 1976.

Pedroncini, Guy. *Les Mutineries de 1917.* Paris: Presses Universitaires de France, 1967.

———. "Les Cours martiales pendant la grand guerre." *Revue historique* 512 (1974): 393–408.

———. *Pétain, général en chef: 1917–1918.* Paris: Presses Universitaires de France, 1974.

———. "Le Moral de l'armée française in 1916" In *Verdun 1916: actes du colloque international sur la bataille de Verdun.* Verdun: Association National du Souvenir de la Bataille de Verdun, Université de Nancy II, 1975.

———. *Pétain: le soldat et la gloire, Tome I, 1856–1918.* Paris: Perrin, 1989.

———, ed. *1917: Les Mutineries de l'armée française.* Paris: Julliard, Collection "Archives," no. 35, 1968.

Porch, Douglas. *The March to the Marne: The French Army, 1871–1914.* Cambridge: Cambridge University Press, 1981.

———. *The Conquest of Morocco.* New York: Alfred A. Knopf, 1982.

———. "Clausewitz and the French: 1871–1914." In *Clausewitz and Modern Strategy,* edited by Michael I. Handel. London: Frank Cass, 1986.

———. *The French Foreign Legion: A Complete History of the Legendary Fighting Force.* New York: Harper Collins, 1991.

Prior, Robin, and Trevor Wilson. *Command on the Western Front: The Military Career of Sir Henry Rawlinson, 1914–1918*. Oxford: Blackwell Publishers, 1992.

Prost, Antoine. *Les Anciens Combattants et la société française*. 3 vols. Paris: Presses de la Fondation des Sciences Politiques, 1977.

Ralston, David. *The Army of the Republic: The Role of the Military in the Political Evolution of France*. Cambridge: Harvard University Press, 1967.

Ratinaud, Jean. *1917 ou la Révolte des poilus*. Paris: Fayard, 1960.

Rebérioux, Madeleine. *La République radicale: 1891–1914* (Nouvelle Histoire de la France Contemporaine, vol. 11). Paris: Éditions du Seuil, 1975.

Remarque, Erich Marie. *All Quiet on the Western Front*. Translated by A. W. Ween. New York: Fawcett Crest, 1958 (originally published in German in 1928).

Roquerol, General J. *Le Chemin des Dames*. Paris: Payot, 1934.

Russell, Frederick H. *The Just War in the Middle Ages*. Cambridge: Cambridge University Press, 1975.

Sanson, R. *Les 14 juillet, fêtes et consciences nationales: 1789–1975*. Paris: Flammarion, 1976.

Scott, James C. *Weapons of the Weak: Everyday Forms of Peasant Resistance*. New Haven: Yale University Press, 1985.

———. *Domination and the Arts of Resistance: Hidden Transcripts*. New Haven: Yale University Press, 1990.

Scott, Joan Wallach. *Gender and the Politics of History*. New York: Columbia University Press, 1988.

Serman, William. *Les Officiers français dans la nation: 1848–1914*. Paris: Aubier Montaigne, 1982.

Siegfried, André. *Tableau politique de la France de l'ouest sous la troisième république*. Paris: A. Colin, 1913.

Simkins, Peter. *Kitchener's Army: The Raising of the New Armies 1914–1916*. Manchester: Manchester University Press, 1988.

Smith, Leonard V. "Command Authority in the French Army, 1914–1918: The Case of the 5e Division d'Infanterie." Ph.D. diss., Columbia University, 1990.

———. "The 'Crisis of Masculinity' of World War I in the Fifth Infantry Division," *Proceedings of the Western Society for French History* 17 (1990): 447–54.

———. "The Disciplinary Dilemma of French Military Justice: The Case of the 5e Division d'Infanterie." *The Journal of Military History* 55 (1991): 47–68.

———. "Literary and Non-literary Accounts of Battle: Roland Dorgelès at Neuville–St. Vaast in 1915." Paper presented at the Annual Meeting of the Society for French Historical Studies, Vancouver, British Columbia, 21 March 1991.

Snyder, Jack. *The Ideology of the Offensive: Military Decision Making and the Disasters of 1914*. Ithaca: Cornell University Press, 1984.

Spears, General Sir Edward. *Liaison 1914: A Narrative of the Great Retreat*. London: William Heinemann, Ltd., 1930.

———. *Prelude to Victory*. London: Jonathan Cape, 1939.

Stoianovich, Traian. *French Historical Method: The Annales Paradigm*. Ithaca: Cornell University Press, 1976.

Strachan, Hew. *European Armies and the Conduct of War*. London: George Allen & Unwin, 1983.

Taylor, A.J.P. *The First World War: An Illustrated History*. London: Hamish Hamilton, 1963.

Terraine, John. *To Win a War: 1918, The Year of Victory*. New York: Doubleday & Company, 1981.

Theweleit, Klaus. *Male Fantasies, Volume 2: Psychoanalyzing the White Terror* Translated by Erica Carter, Chris Turner, and Stephan Conway. Minneapolis: University of Minnesota Press, 1989 (originally published in German in 1978).

Tooke, Joan D. *The Just War in Aquinas and Grotius*. London: S.P.C.K., 1965.

Travers, Tim. *The Killing Ground: The British Army, the Western Front and the Emergence of Modern Warfare, 1900–1918*. London: Allen & Unwin, 1987.

Von Hagen, Mark. *Soldiers in the Proletarian Dictatorship: The Red Army and the Soviet Socialist State, 1917–1930*. Ithaca: Cornell University Press, 1990.

Wall, Richard, and Jay Winter, eds. *The Upheavals of War: Family, Work and Welfare in Europe, 1914–1918*. Cambridge: Cambridge University Press, 1990.

Walzer, Michael. *Just and Unjust Wars: A Moral Argument with Historical Illustrations*. New York: Basic Books, 1977.

———. "The Lonely Politics of Michel Foucault." In *The Company of Critics: Social Criticism and Political Commitment in the Twentieth Century*. New York: Basic Books, 1988.

Watt, Richard M. *Dare Call it Treason*. New York: Simon and Schuster, 1963.

Weber, Eugen. *The Nationalist Revival in France, 1905–1914*. Berkeley: University of California Press, 1959.

Whalen, Robert Weldon. *Bitter Wounds: German Victims of the Great War, 1914–1939*. Ithaca: Cornell University Press, 1984.

White, Hayden. *The Content of the Form: Narrative Discourse and Historical Representation*. Baltimore: Johns Hopkins University Press, 1987.

———. *Metahistory: The Historical Imagination in Nineteenth-Century Europe*. Baltimore: Johns Hopkins University Press, 1973.

Wildman, Alan. *The End of the Russian Imperial Army: The Old Army and the Soldiers' Revolt*. Princeton: Princeton University Press, 1980.

———. *The End of the Russian Imperial Army: The Road to Soviet Power and Peace*. Princeton: Princeton University Press, 1987.

Wilentz, Sean, ed. *Rites of Power: Symbolism, Ritual, and Politics Since the Middle Ages*. Philadelphia: University of Pennsylvania Press, 1985.

Williams, John. *Mutiny 1917*. London: William Heinemann, Ltd., 1962.

Williamson, Samuel J., Jr. *The Politics of Grand Strategy: Britain and France Prepare for War, 1904–1914*. Cambridge: Harvard University Press, 1969.

Winter, Denis. *Death's Men: Soldiers of the Great War*. London: Allen Lane, 1978.

Winter, J. M. *The Great War and the British People*. London: Macmillan, 1985.

———. *The Experience of World War I*. New York: Oxford University Press, 1989.

Wirtschafter, Elise Kimmerling. *From Serf to Russian Soldier*. Princeton: Princeton University Press, 1990.

Wohl, Robert. *The Generation of 1914*. Cambridge: Harvard University Press, 1979.

Woloch, Isser. "Napoleonic Conscription: State Power and Civil Society." *Past and Present* 111 (May 1986).

Index

Agulhon, Maurice. *See* sociability

Alsace and Lorraine, 27–28, 35, 76, 101–2, 194–95, 212, 230

American army, 205, 215, 228–29, 244

Annales School. *See* "social" historians of World War I

Aquinas, Thomas, 5–6

artillery, 42–44, 49, 53–54, 56–57, 59, 61–62, 66, 92, 109–11, 116, 120–21, 139–42, 157–60, 162–63, 165, 217, 219, 222, 224, 232–36, 238n, 241, 250; and *barrage roulant* (rolling barrage), 156, 171–72, 179–80. *See also* live and let live system; particular engagements; particular sectors

Ashworth, Tony. *See* live and let live system

Atkins, Tommy. *See* British army

Audoin-Rouzeau, Stéphane, 85n, 190n, 247

Augustine of Hippo, 4–6n

Bastille Day, 25, 31, 38

battle narratives: conventional World War I, 11–13, 48–49, 99–100, 121; explanation of "win/lose" vs. "experiential," 39–42. *See also* military history, particular engagements

Baynes, Richard, 13n

Becker, Jean-Jacques, 23, 125n, 189n, 246–47. *See also* "social" historians of World War I

Bidwell, Shelford, 250

Bois de la Caillette. *See* Verdun

Brereton, J. M., 248

Brimont, 5ᵉ DI attack on (September 1914). *See* Marne, First Battle of

British army, 42, 58, 115, 117–18, 158, 228–30, 237; historiography of, 13, 248–50, 256; officers in, 13, 79n

Bushnell, John, 252–53

Cafard, le. See foucauldian despair

Caillaux, Henriette, 34

Canard de Boyau, Le (74ᵉ RI), 155, 230

casualties, 12–13, 75, 126, 231; changing meaning attached to, 108, 131, 161–62, 164; in pitched battle 14; in trench warfare, 90n, 161, 220. *See also* particular engagements; particular regiments; particular sectors

Challener, Richard, 21

Champagne region, 84, 115, 219n, 224

Champin, Jules (36ᵉ RI), 55–57

Charleroi, Battle of (August 1914), 73, 87; casualties in, 45, 49–50, 144; compared to Battle of Guise, 52, 54–55; and French strategy, 42–43; win/lose narrative of, 42–45; experiential narrative of, 45–52. *See also* Vᵉ Armée; Joffre, Joseph; Lanrezac, Charles; Sauret, Henry; Verrier, Elie; particular regiments

Chemin des Dames Offensive (April 1917), 18, 101, 156n, 175, 203; relationship to mutinies, 175–77, 179–82, 200; strategy of, 179–80; problems liquidating, 180–81. *See also* Chemin des Dames sector; Mangin, Charles; mutinies of 1917; Nivelle, Robert; Pétain, Philippe

Chemin des Dames sector (trench warfare in, Summer 1917), 187, 208, 219–29; and desertion convictions; 225–26; casualties, 220; unsuitability to defense in depth, 219–20. *See also* Hindenburg Line; particular regiments

citizen-soldier, French, 7–8, 11, 127, 175–76, 183, 189, 244, 258; compared to other national models, 248–58. *See also* mutinies of 1917; Third Republic

Clausewitz, Karl, 7–11, 79: and ancien régime armies, 8–9, 251; and components of war, *Zweck* (end), *Mittel* (means), *Ziele* (intermediary stages), 10, 79, 118–19, 125; and dictum on war and politics, 9–11, 13, 16, 20–21, 175, 255; and "friction," 10–11, 16, 38, 88; and proportionality, 9, 16–17

Clemenceau, Georges, 101, 175, 206n, 215

colonial troops, 104, 168, 187n, 188, 190, 211, 221